THE COLLECTED
WORKS OF
JEREMY BENTHAM

General Editor
Philip Schofield

PRINCIPLES OF LEGISLATION

Of the Limits of the Penal Branch of Jurisprudence, written in 1780–2, is the continuation of *An Introduction to the Principles of Morals and Legislation*, and thus part of the introduction to the projected penal code on which Bentham worked in the late 1770s and early 1780s. The work emerged from Bentham's attempt to distinguish between civil and penal law, which led him into an exposition of the nature and scope of an individual law and an analysis of such key legal terms as power, duty, right, property, contract, and conveyance. Bentham addresses the relationship between different 'aspects' of the legislator's will, such as command, prohibition, and permission, and in so doing develops a 'logic of the will' which anticipates modern deontic logic. He explains that the disposition of the people to obey constitutes the basis of political and legal power, and distinguishes between law addressed to the sovereign and law addressed to the people. Dealing with some of the most fundamental problems in jurisprudence and the theory of human action, *Of the Limits of the Penal Branch of Jurisprudence* is a work of outstanding originality and seminal importance in the field of legal philosophy.

The Collected Works of Jeremy Bentham

The new critical edition of the works and correspondence of Jeremy Bentham (1748–1832) is being prepared and published under the supervision of the Bentham Committee of University College London. In spite of his importance as jurist, philosopher, and social scientist, and leader of the utilitarian reformers, the only previous edition of his works was a poorly edited and incomplete one brought out within a decade or so of his death. The overall plan and principles of this edition are set out in the General Preface to *The Correspondence of Jeremy Bentham*, vol. 1 (Athlone Press), which was the first volume of the *Collected Works* to be published.

Volumes published by Oxford University Press

Constitutional Code
Volume 1
Edited by F. Rosen and J. H. Burns

Deontology, together with A Table of the Springs of Action and Article on Utilitarianism
Edited by Amnon Goldworth

Chrestomathia
Edited by M. J. Smith and W. H. Burston

First Principles preparatory to Constitutional Code
Edited by Philip Schofield

Securities against Misrule and other Constitutional Writings for Tripoli and Greece
Edited by Philip Schofield

Official Aptitude Maximized; Expense Minimized
Edited by Philip Schofield

Colonies, Commerce, and Constitutional Law: Rid Yourselves of Ultramaria and other writings on Spain and Spanish America
Edited by Philip Schofield

'Legislator of the World': Writings on Codification, Law, and Education
Edited by Philip Schofield and Jonathan Harris

Political Tactics
Edited by Michael James, Cyprian Blamires, and Catherine Pease-Watkin

Rights, Representation, and Reform: Nonsense upon Stilts and other writings on the French Revolution
Edited by Philip Schofield, Catherine Pease-Watkin, and Cyprian Blamires

Writings on the Poor Laws
Volumes 1 & 2
Edited by Michael Quinn

Correspondence, volume 6: January 1798 to December 1801
Edited by J. R. Dinwiddy

Correspondence, volume 7: January 1802 to December 1808
Edited by J. R. Dinwiddy

Correspondence, volume 8: January 1809 to December 1816
Edited by Stephen Conway

Correspondence, volume 9: January 1817 to June 1820
Edited by Stephen Conway

Correspondence, volume 10: July 1820 to December 1821
Edited by Stephen Conway

Correspondence, volume 11: January 1822 to June 1824
Edited by Catherine Fuller

Correspondence, volume 12: July 1824 to June 1828
Edited by Luke O'Sullivan and Catherine Fuller

OF THE LIMITS OF THE PENAL BRANCH OF JURISPRUDENCE

edited by

PHILIP SCHOFIELD

CLARENDON PRESS · OXFORD

OXFORD
UNIVERSITY PRESS

Great Clarendon Street, Oxford OX2 6DP

Oxford University Press is a department of the University of Oxford.
It furthers the University's objective of excellence in research, scholarship,
and education by publishing worldwide in

Oxford New York

Auckland Cape Town Dar es Salaam Hong Kong Karachi
Kuala Lumpur Madrid Melbourne Mexico City Nairobi
New Delhi Shanghai Taipei Toronto

With offices in

Argentina Austria Brazil Chile Czech Republic France Greece
Guatemala Hungary Italy Japan Poland Portugal Singapore
South Korea Switzerland Thailand Turkey Ukraine Vietnam

Published in the United States
by Oxford University Press Inc., New York

First published 2010

British Library Cataloguing in Publication Data
Data available

Library of Congress Cataloging in Publication Data
Data available

Typeset by Anne Joshua, Oxford
Printed in Great Britain
on acid-free paper by the
MPG Books Group, Bodmin and King's Lynn

ISBN 978-0-19-957073-7

3 5 7 9 10 8 6 4 2

PREFACE

The Bentham Committee wishes to thank the British Academy, the Arts and Humanities Research Council, the Economic and Social Research Council, and University College London for their continuing support of *The Collected Works of Jeremy Bentham*.

Thanks are due to University College London Library for permission to publish material from its collection of Bentham Papers.

For reasons explained in detail in the Editorial Introduction, the Bentham Committee has decided that the present edition should supersede *Of Laws in General*, edited by H. L. A. Hart and published by the Athlone Press in 1970, as a volume in *The Collected Works of Jeremy Bentham*. This should not obscure the fact that a massive debt is owed to Professor Hart's pioneering work on these difficult manuscripts. His version of the text and his editorial footnotes are the foundation on which the present edition is constructed. Over the years, the Bentham Project has gained a much greater understanding of Bentham's working methods and of the categories of manuscript material which he generated. The present edition, which reconstructs the text as Bentham envisaged it at the time of its composition, draws on that improved understanding, and presents a text that is more faithful to Bentham's intentions, and much more coherent, than that which appeared in *Of Laws in General*. The transcription has been meticulously rechecked and a great many cross-references restored to the text, while the information provided in the editorial footnotes has been expanded. While the ordering of the sections of the work has remained largely unchanged, a significant number of important revisions have been made to the internal ordering of a number of those sections. The text is presented as a Chapter in continuation of the work published in 1789 as *An Introduction to the Principles of Morals and Legislation*, rather than as a work in its own right. The advantage of the present arrangement is that it reproduces as the central text the most complete version of the work which Bentham drafted, but also allows the reader, by reference to the material which appears in the Appendices, easily to reconstruct the versions through which the work progressed in the course of its composition.

The present volume owes its emergence to the decision taken by Professor Frederick Rosen to produce a second edition of *Of*

Laws in General, incorporating the corrections to the text which had appeared in a 'Corrigenda' issued in 1976. When I offered to check the text against the manuscript in order to ensure that all the errors had been identified, I had no conception that a new volume would eventually result. In the course of editing the volume, I have drawn upon the talents and expertise of my colleagues at the Bentham Project—Mrs Katharine Barber, Ms Catherine Fuller, Dr Oliver Harris, Mrs Irena Nicoll, Mrs Catherine Pease-Watkin, and Mrs Anna Schüle—who have helped in a whole variety of ways, but most particularly in researching and checking the annotation, commenting on the Editorial Introduction, and proof-reading. As always, I am grateful to Ms Gillian Furlong, Ms Susan Stead, and their colleagues in the Special Collections department of UCL Library for their never-failing assistance and advice.

I gratefully acknowledge help from Dr Paola Rudan and Professor Richard Whatmore in elucidating certain allusions in the text, and from Dr George Letsas, who checked the Greek text.

P.S.

CONTENTS

SYMBOLS AND ABBREVIATIONS

Symbols

| |	Space left in manuscript.
[to]	Word(s) editorially supplied.
⟨. . .⟩	Word(s) torn away.
⟨so⟩	Conjectural restoration of mutilated word.
[?]	Reading doubtful
[. . .?]	Word(s) proved illegible.

Abbreviations

CW	This edition of *The Collected Works of Jeremy Bentham*.
UC	Bentham Papers in the Library of University College London. Roman numerals refer to boxes in which the papers are placed, Arabic to the folios within each box.
MS add.	Text added to the original manuscript reading.
MS alt.	Alternative manuscript reading, usually interlinear or marginal.
MS del.	Word(s) deleted in manuscript.
MS orig.	Original manuscript reading.

EDITORIAL INTRODUCTION

The present edition of *Of the Limits of the Penal Branch of Jurisprudence* supersedes *Of Laws in General*, edited by H. L. A. Hart and published by the Athlone Press in 1970,[1] as a volume in *The Collected Works of Jeremy Bentham*. Not long after the publication of *Of Laws in General*, it was brought to the attention of the Bentham Committee that the text was marred by errors in the transcription of the manuscripts. A 'Corrigenda for Of Laws in General', containing over one thousand emendations, of which 'the vast majority' were said to be 'minor ones', was subsequently issued in 1976. With the exhaustion of the Athlone edition, Oxford University Press, the current publishers of *The Collected Works*, agreed to publish a second edition incorporating the emendations. A new study of the manuscript sources revealed not only a number of transcription errors which had not been incorporated into the 'Corrigenda', but also, and more fundamentally, serious problems with the internal ordering of parts of the text. A thorough revision of the text has, therefore, been undertaken, with a view to reflecting as accurately as possible Bentham's intentions at the time of composition.

'Of the Limits of the Penal Branch of Jurisprudence' (usually referred to here by its short title 'Limits') is intimately related to the work which was printed, as Bentham himself tells us, by November 1780[2] and published in 1789 as *An Introduction to the Principles of Morals and Legislation*, and which formed the first part of an introduction to Bentham's projected penal code.[3] 'Limits' was originally conceived as the continuation of *An Introduction to the Principles of Morals and Legislation* and hence of the introduction to the penal code as a whole. The bulk of the text appears to have been written in 1780 before the completion of the printing of *An Introduction to the Principles of Morals and Legislation*,[4] though

[1] *Of Laws in General*, ed. H. L. A. Hart, London, 1970.

[2] See *An Introduction to the Principles of Morals and Legislation*, ed. J. H. Burns and H. L. A. Hart, London, 1970 (*CW*), p. 301.

[3] It was Bentham's intention that his 'Plan of a Penal Code' would be divided into two Books, the first dealing with the provisions of the code itself and the second with procedure: see 'Plan of a Penal Code—Prospectus', copied by Bentham's father Jeremiah Bentham (1712–92), at British Library Additional MS 33,556, fos. 139–42.

[4] Several cross-references to 'Limits' in *An Introduction to the Principles of Morals and Legislation*, Ch. XVI indicate that composition was well advanced by the time this material was being printed: see *An Introduction to the Principles of Morals and Legislation* (*CW*), pp. 206–7 n., 228 n., 237 n., 256 n., 263 n.

some further material was written in 1782.[1] As well as 'Limits', Bentham planned, and wrote material for, several more chapters in continuance of the introduction to the penal code: 'Indirect Legislation' would deal with strategies which did not involve direct prohibition but which the legislator might adopt to prevent actions detrimental to the happiness of the community; 'Place and Time' with the way in which legislation might vary according to different circumstances; and 'Corpus Juris' with the question of what constituted a complete code of law and the ways in which its content might be conveniently divided. As with 'Limits', and the projected penal code, none of this material was printed or published by Bentham himself,[2] with the exception of the first two sections of 'Limits', which appeared as Ch. XVII, §§1–2 of *An Introduction to the Principles of Morals and Legislation*.

The present text has been previously published in two versions. The work was 'discovered' amongst the Bentham Papers deposited in University College London Library by Charles Warren Everett, who recognized it as the continuation of *An Introduction to the Principles of Morals and Legislation*, and published it for the first time in 1945 with the title *The Limits of Jurisprudence Defined: Being Part Two of An Introduction to the Principles of Morals and Legislation*. The second version, as noted above, was edited by H. L. A. Hart, and published in 1970 as part of *The Collected Works of Jeremy Bentham* with the title *Of Laws in General*. While Hart acknowledged its provenance as a Chapter in continuance of *An Introduction to the Principles of Morals and Legislation*, he chose to present it as a separate work, reflecting a decision which Bentham seems to have made in 1782. Hart went on to link 'Limits' with the work which Bentham, at the time of the publication of *An Introduction to the Principles of Morals and Legislation* in 1789, announced would form 'Part the 10th' of an expanded introduction to the penal code.[3] The structure of the Everett and Hart versions is very similar in that, of the twenty-one Chapters of Everett's edition, all but the first two correspond to the nineteen Chapters of the Hart edition. The first two Chapters of Everett's edition appear

[1] See §17, p. 188 n. and Appendix C, p. 261 n. below, where Bentham states explicitly that he is writing in 1782.

[2] The material was, however, extensively drawn upon by Bentham's Genevan editor Pierre Étienne Louis Dumont (1759–1829) for his French recension *Traités de législation civile et pénale*, 3 vols., Paris, 1802. For English versions of 'Indirect Legislation' and 'Place and Time' see Bowring, i. 533–80, 169–94 respectively.

[3] See *Of Laws in General*, Editorial Introduction, p. xxxii. The question of the identity between 'Limits' and the work described in *An Introduction to the Principles of Morals and Legislation* as 'Part the 10th' is discussed at pp. xxxv–xxxvi below.

as Appendices in Hart's edition, which also contains several further Appendices. Both editors rely principally on a letter from Bentham to Baron Ashburton of 3 June 1782 in which Bentham lists and gives a brief description of the contents of the Chapters, and explains that the text is a continuation of *An Introduction to the Principles of Morals and Legislation*.[1] Neither Everett nor Hart published the two sections which Bentham himself printed and published in *An Introduction to the Principles of Morals and Legislation*.

In relation to the respective titles under which the two versions appear, there is, as Hart points out, no justification whatsoever for Everett's title, in that the phrase 'The Limits of Jurisprudence Defined' does not appear in Bentham's manuscripts. Hart justifies his choice of title from the fact that it appears at the head of a list of contents dating from the time when Bentham had 'determined that these chapters should form a separate work', and that the title itself was an entirely appropriate reflection of the substance of the work.[2] The title chosen by Hart is, however, equally open to objection. First, it may be doubted whether the title does adequately reflect the substance of the work, whose purpose was to distinguish between the civil and the penal law, and hence prepare the ground for a penal code. In order to achieve this object, Bentham realized that he needed to provide an exposition of the characteristics, or 'respects' as he termed them, of a single law, and this exposition is the focus of the bulk of the text. His concern, in other words, was with *a* law, rather than with *laws*. Second, when Bentham used the title 'Of Laws in general', he did so in relation to a wider body of material than that contained in 'Limits'. The list of contents to which Hart refers is headed 'Of Laws in general. Table of the Chapters', and was composed either in or before March 1782.[3] The ordering of the chapters corresponds exactly with that given in the letter to Ashburton of 3 June 1782. The crucial point, however, is that the list of Chapters for 'Of Laws in general' includes not only the material which had been written for 'Limits', but also the Chapters on 'Indirect Legislation', 'Place

[1] Bentham to Lord Ashburton, 3 June 1782 (the second letter of this date), *The Correspondence of Jeremy Bentham*, vol. iii, ed. I. R. Christie, London, 1971, pp. 123–6. John Dunning (1731–83), first Baron Ashburton, Solicitor General 1768–70, Chancellor of the Duchy of Lancaster 1782–3, was a political associate of Bentham's mentor William Petty (1737–1805), second Earl of Shelburne and first Marquis of Lansdowne, leader of the administration from July 1782 to April 1783.

[2] *Of Laws in General*, Editorial Introduction, pp. xxxiii–xxxiv. The list of contents is at UC xxix. 1, and is reproduced in *Of Laws in General*, Appendix F, pp. 312–13.

[3] For the dating of the 'Table of Chapters' see p. xv below.

and Time', and 'Corpus Juris', and a further Chapter entitled 'Plan of Book I [i.e. of the penal code]'. As a title for the whole of this material together, 'Of Laws in general' does seem entirely appropriate. When Bentham wrote to Ashburton on 3 June 1782, he made no mention of the overarching 'Of Laws in general', presumably because he had given up the idea of presenting the whole of the relevant material as a single work under that title.[1] Instead, he suggested that 'Indirect Legislation' and 'Place and Time' would be published as two separate works, as would another projected work entitled 'Essay on Reward'.[2] Since the first two sections of 'Limits' were destined to appear as Chs. 17–18 of *An Introduction to the Principles of Morals and Legislation* (simply a reflection of the fact that they had already been printed), this left the remaining nineteen chapters of 'Limits' and the single chapter 'Corpus Juris', forming together, as Bentham stated, 'a sort of anatomy of any entire body of the law whatsoever consider'd nakedly as a collection of expressions of will'.[3] While Bentham did not state explicitly that the remainder of 'Limits' and 'Corpus Juris' would appear as a separate work, that must be the implication, if the material was to appear at all.[4] In short, the title 'Of Laws in general' represents a particular combination of materials which Bentham on one occasion considered publishing together. 'Limits' would have formed one part of that larger work, but did not in itself constitute it.

In the Editorial Introduction to *Of Laws in General*, Hart argues that there was a transition in Bentham's conception of the text from a single Chapter (divided into sections) in continuation of *An Introduction to the Principles of Morals and Legislation*, to a series of separate Chapters (each section becoming a separate chapter) still in continuation of *An Introduction to the Principles of Morals and Legislation*, to a separate work entitled *Of Laws in General*.[5] With the exception of the claim that the separate work should be entitled *Of Laws in General*, this account is broadly correct. The 'Table of Chapters' gives two distinct enumerations of the chapters. The first and earlier, in Arabic numerals, presents them as a continuation of *An Introduction to the Principles of Morals and Legislation* (i.e. Chs. 17–37). The second and later, in Roman

[1] Comparing the 'Table of Chapters' with the letter to Ashburton, the latter shows that Bentham had decided that 'Corpus Juris' should precede, rather than follow, 'Indirect Legislation' and 'Place and Time', while in the latter 'Plan of Book I' is not mentioned.

[2] *Correspondence* (*CW*), iii. 127–9.

[3] Ibid. 126–7.

[4] In the event, Bentham appears to have incorporated the small amount of material he had written for 'Corpus Juris' into 'Limits': see pp. xxviii–xxix below.

[5] *Of Laws in General*, Editorial Introduction, pp. xxxi–xxxiii.

numerals, begins a new series (i.e. Chs. I–XXI), thus indicating that they represent chapters in a separate work. The dating of the 'Table of Chapters' is not straightforward in that the date of March 1782 which appears on the relevant folio relates to a separate 'Ordo' which reorders Chs. 23–8 (or VII–XII), and which, from its location, appears to have been added to the folio after the composition of the 'Table of Chapters'. This means that the 'Table of Chapters' could not have been compiled any later than March 1782. Bentham, then, at some point in or possibly before March 1782, had come to the view that the material might be presented as a separate work, and, as noted above, still seems to have regarded this as a possibility, albeit with the addition of 'Corpus Juris', at the time he wrote to Ashburton on 3 June 1782. However, he always adhered to the idea that 'Limits', whether or not it was presented as a separate work, was a continuation of the introduction to the penal code. When writing to Ashburton, where both the provenance of the text as a continuation of *An Introduction to the Principles of Morals and Legislation* and the possibility of its appearing as a separate work are discussed, there is, as stated above, no mention of the title 'Of Laws in general'. Given that the vast majority of the text sheets, as well as the related rudiments and marginal contents sheets,[1] carry the heading 'Limits', it seems appropriate, in terms of fidelity to the existing manuscripts, and to Bentham's intentions at the time he composed the bulk of the material, to retain the original Chapter title as the title of the text, and to retain the division into sections. This arrangement has the additional advantages of minimizing editorial intervention with the form of Bentham's numerous cross-references (many of which the Hart edition does not reproduce) and of allowing the reconstruction of both earlier and later versions of the text.

HISTORY OF THE WORK

The basis of the present edition is a version of the text that is referred to here as the 'principal draft'. This is not the first draft of the text, but rather appears to have constituted at one point a virtually complete and coherent draft, before Bentham began to rewrite parts of it. It seems likely that Bentham had completed the 'principal draft' by the end of 1780, and then composed the revisions to it in early 1782, but in the almost total absence of

[1] For Bentham's working practice, and the relationship between the various categories of manuscript, see pp. xxxvii–xxxix below.

any explicit dating of the manuscripts, it is difficult to offer any precise account of the order in which the material was written. The 'principal draft' was preceded by a draft which is referred to here as the 'primary draft', but which survives only partially.[1] This in turn was preceded by a first, much shorter draft.[2] The 'principal draft' has been reconstructed with the aid of Bentham's paragraph numbers[3] and, with more difficulty, from his pagination. Both paragraph numbers and pagination were revised, in many cases more than once, as the work developed. Many of the page numbers in particular have been struck through so firmly that they are illegible, making it impossible to recreate all the mutations through which the text progressed. Moreover, it appears that manuscripts written for the 'primary draft' were in places reused for the 'principal draft', and indeed for revisions of that draft, with some being cut up in the process, and some being discarded and presumably lost or destroyed. A very small proportion of the text sheets for the 'principal draft' itself have not been located. In these instances, the extent of the missing material is described in an editorial footnote. After the 'principal draft' had been completed, Bentham composed two further categories of material. The first consisted in additions to the 'principal draft', and these have been inserted in the text in their appropriate place. The second consisted in new versions of parts of the 'principal draft', and these generally appear in the text where the corresponding pages of the 'principal draft' are missing, or in Appendices where they are not.

As well as the page and paragraph numbers, other internal evidence taken from the text sheets, including headings, marginal subheadings, and cross-references, has helped in the reconstruction of the text. Further information has been gleaned from the marginal contents sheets, rudiments, and especially the surviving plans.[4] The earliest plan appears to be that contained in the final lines of Ch. XVII, §2 of *An Introduction to the Principles of Morals and Legislation*, and hence in §2 of the present edition, where Bentham states that the remainder of the Chapter will be divided into three sections. The third section will deal with the question of 'what *a law* is', the fourth with that of 'the parts into which a law, as such, is capable of being distinguished', and the fifth with that of

[1] The relevant material is described and presented in Appendix E. For further details see pp. xxxii–xxxiv below.

[2] The relevant material is described and presented in Appendix A. For further details see pp. xxix–xxx below.

[3] For the editorial policy respecting paragraph numbers see p. xxxix below.

[4] See UC xcix. 86–108, of which xcix. 101–4, 107 relate to the text as a whole. Those sheets associated with particular sections of the text are mentioned as appropriate below.

'the import of the word *criminal*'.[1] These three sections eventually grew into a total of sixteen sections (§§3–18 of the present edition). The process, then, was one of expansion of the text, and this is reflected in the plans, of which four survive. The third and fourth, chronologically speaking, are the 'Table of Chapters' of March 1782 and the letter to Ashburton of 3 June 1782, which both give the final and complete list of sections or chapters. The first and second plans appear to have been drawn up in 1780 as Bentham was composing the bulk of the text. The shorter of these two plans, which, given that Bentham expanded the text as he composed it, must be the earlier, and which represents the 'primary draft', lists the following six sections:

§1. Distinction between Private Ethics and Jurisprudence.[2]
§2. Jurisprudence—its branches.
§3. Of a law and its parts.
§4. Limits between civil and penal law shewn in detail.
§5. Distinction between civil law and criminal.
§6. Analysis of the matter of a body of laws.[3]

The longer, and later, plan, which represents the 'principal draft', lists the following eight sections:

§1. Limits between ethics and Jurisprudence.
§2. Jurisprudence, its branches.
§3. A law, its parts.
§4. Compleatness and unity of a law.
§5. Customary law, what it consists of.
§6. Separation of the civil branch from the penal.
§7. The criminal branch not distinguishable from the civil.
§8. Uses of this chapter.[4]

In this latter plan, Bentham has added sections on the completeness of a law and on customary law (this material, as we shall see, was initially drafted as part of §3, separated to form a new section, and then itself divided into two sections) and a final section on uses, while discarding the section dealing with the analysis of a body of laws. The expansion of the 'principal draft', however, did not in the main arise from the immediate addition of new sections to the text, but rather in the addition of 'respects' to the section dealing with the parts of a law, and then the transformation of these discussions into discrete sections. In the final version of the text, this section was divided into thirteen separate sections. When this is taken into account, the structure of the work as listed in the

[1] See pp. 22–3 below.
[2] MS orig. 'Legislation'.
[3] UC xcix. 99.
[4] UC xcix. 107.

plan for the 'principal draft' corresponds with the structure of the work as conceived in the 'Table of Chapters' and the letter to Ashburton, with the exception of the addition of the section dealing with the distinction between civil and criminal procedure (§20 of the present edition). There was no major rearrangement or re-ordering of sections or chapters once Bentham had settled the outline of the 'principal draft'.

As noted above, the first two sections of the present edition were originally printed in 1780 as the first two sections of Chapter XVII of *An Introduction to the Principles of Morals and Legislation.*[1] It seems likely that, by November 1780 when the printing had advanced to this point, Bentham was still drafting and reworking the rest of the Chapter, and so postponed any further printing. When he eventually published *An Introduction to the Principles of Morals and Legislation* in 1789, he did not print any of the additional material he had composed for 'Limits', but added a 'concluding note' in which he explained that 'Limits' had grown to such a length that it constituted a book in its own right.[2] Nevertheless, the fact remains that throughout the bulk of the time in which he was drafting it (and, as noted above, most of the text appears to have been written before the printing of *An Introduction to the Principles of Morals and Legislation* had been completed in November 1780), Bentham conceived of 'Limits' as a single chapter and as a continuation of the introduction to his projected penal code. The first two sections, as printed in *An Introduction to the Principles of Morals and Legislation*, are, therefore, integral to the text, and, indeed, explain the purpose and scope of it. To exclude these two sections, as both the Everett and Hart editions do, is to obscure Bentham's intentions and to contradict his instructions. Each and every plan for the text includes these two sections, the only possible exception being the letter to Ashburton of 3 June 1782, where Bentham states: 'The chapters then which contain the remaining part of the matter designed for the introduction stand at present as follows: Chap. 18 (dismembered from Chap. 17) Jurisprudence its branches.'[3] This may be taken to suggest that Chapter 17 no longer belonged with the remainder of 'Limits'. Bentham, however, was simply explaining that, now that he had come to regard the proposed sections of Chapter 17 as

[1] The text sheets no longer survive, though the corresponding marginal contents sheet for §1 is at UC xcix. 25. An early draft of the beginning of §1 is at UC c. 24.

[2] See *An Introduction to the Principles of Morals and Legislation* (*CW*), pp. 301–11. The title is taken from the marginal content for the first paragraph: 'Occasion and purpose of this concluding note.'

[3] *Correspondence* (*CW*), iii. 124.

chapters in their own right, Chapter 17 would be formed of what had been printed as Ch. XVII, §1, and that Ch. 18 would be formed of what had been printed as Ch. XVII, §2. In other words, his purpose was to outline how he intended to continue the introduction to the penal code in relation to the material already printed and sent to Ashburton, and not to divorce the proposed Chapter 17 (i.e. Ch. XVII, §1) from the remainder of 'Limits'. The first two sections of Chapter XVII, which would become Chapters 17 and 18 respectively, formed part of a continuous whole, preceded by what had been printed and would later be published as Chs. I–XVI of *An Introduction to the Principles of Morals and Legislation* and succeeded by the remainder of 'Limits'.[1]

Hence, the present text begins with the first two sections which Bentham inserted into *An Introduction to the Principles of Morals and Legislation*, and thereby restores them to the text which was written to answer the questions which are posed there.[2] The text of these two sections follows the version of *An Introduction to the Principles of Morals and Legislation* printed in 1780,[3] and so excludes the 'concluding note' which Bentham added for the first published edition of 1789, and some material added to the second published edition of 1823.[4] In the printed version of *An Introduction to the Principles of Morals and Legislation*, Bentham adopted a particular format for the chapter titles and corresponding running headings. Within each chapter title, a single word or short phrase was capitalized and placed within square brackets (Bentham's square brackets appear in the present text as braces): for instance 'Of the Principle of {UTILITY}' and 'Of the {PRINCIPLES ADVERSE} to that of Utility'. The style adopted for the present text was 'Of the {LIMITS} of the penal branch of

[1] That they might be presented in two separate works, possibly divided after Ch. 18 (see p. xiv above), does not mean that the material was not continuous.

[2] The omission of the first two chapters from *Of Laws in General* means that Chs. I–XIX of that edition correspond to §§ 3–21 of the present edition, with the exception of Chs. XII and XIII, which correspond to §§ 15 and 14 respectively.

[3] This statement may not be strictly accurate. When Bentham sent a copy of the printed text to Ashburton on 3 June 1782, he included what he described as the only copy of the proofs of pages 313 to 320 (i.e. pages cccxiii to cccxx as printed), which may have constituted the final proof sheet printed at this time (the work was printed as a quarto, and hence each sheet contained eight pages). (See Bentham to Lord Ashburton, 3 June 1782 (the first letter of this date), *Correspondence (CW)*, iii. 121–2.) Bentham later complained that the proof sheets had not been returned to him. (See Bowring, x. 124.) In other words, while the sheets printed in 1780 constituted the bulk of the published text of 1789, the final part of that text, namely from p. cccxiii (i.e. from part way through paragraph 12 of Ch. 17, §1) may have consisted of sheets printed in 1789.

[4] i.e. the footnote on the subject of constitutional law and the paragraph at the end of the footnote dealing with the term 'international': see *An Introduction to the Principles of Morals and Legislation (CW)*, pp. 281 n. and 297 n. respectively.

jurisprudence'. The capitalized word or phrase constituted Bentham's short title for the chapter, and, together with the surrounding square brackets, was the form in which he presented his cross-references (albeit not capitalized, with the exception of the first letter of the word or phrase).[1]

One part of §2, namely the footnote which appears in the final paragraph, is based on a manuscript source.[2] This footnote introduces the main themes to be addressed in the remainder of the chapter. It seems likely that Bentham decided to exclude it from the printed version of 1780 because it referred to discussions which, at that time, he had decided not to print, or rather because he had not decided on the final format in which they were to appear. By the time that *An Introduction to the Principles of Morals and Legislation* was published in 1789, the footnote had been superseded by the 'concluding note'. The footnote as reproduced here is based directly on the manuscript source, and shows a number of variations, most of which are minor, from that which was inserted in the *Collected Works* edition of *An Introduction to the Principles of Morals and Legislation*.[3]

The first two printed sections carry paragraph numbers 1–29. The third section of the work (Ch. I in the Hart edition), and the first based on manuscript sources, introducing the parts of a law, consists, in its original form, in paragraph numbers 30–1.[4] The paragraph numbers, therefore, confirm that Bentham intended this latter section to form a direct continuation from the two printed sections, and confirm that these two sections can be properly regarded as belonging to the 'principal draft' (all three sections may also have belonged to the 'primary draft').[5] From §3 onwards, the text is based exclusively on manuscript sources. The first of the two paragraphs which originally constituted the whole of this section (i.e. paragraph 30) contains Bentham's definition of a law, and the second (i.e. paragraph 31) a list of eight 'respects' in which a law might be considered. These eight 'respects' represent the scope of the discussion at a certain point in the development of the 'principal draft'. According to the plans for both the 'primary

[1] For the presentation of the printed text see pp. xxxvi–xxxvii below.

[2] UC lxxxviii. 344–6, reproduced at pp. 21–3 n. below. The sheets carry Bentham's instruction that the text is to form a 'Note to p. cccxxvii', that is the relevant page in the printed version of Ch. 17, §2.

[3] See *An Introduction to the Principles of Morals and Legislation* (*CW*), pp. 299–300 n.

[4] UC lxxxviii. 102–3. The page containing paragraph 30 carries the marginal subheading 'Definition', and those containing paragraph 31 'Particulars'. Related rudiments on the subject of 'parts in general' are at UC xcix. 93–6, 108. For the relationship between folios and pages see p. xxiii n. below.

[5] See pp. xxxii–xxxiv below.

draft' and the 'principal draft' reproduced above, Bentham originally intended the consideration of these 'respects' to form a continuation of, and thus be part of, the third section. In due course, he expanded the discussion to include a further four 'respects', which were inserted at various points into the 'principal draft'.[1] He then decided to detach the material containing the definition of a law and to dedicate a separate section to each of the twelve 'respects', and so what had been intended as one long section eventually became thirteen separate sections.[2]

Bentham composed an insertion for §3,[3] consisting of an extended discussion of the definition of the term 'law' given in paragraph 30. The first folio of this insertion contains paragraph numbers 2–3. Bentham may have regarded paragraph 30 of the 'principal draft' as paragraph 1 of the inserted sequence. Certainly, the insertion is best placed after paragraph 30, on which it forms a commentary, and before paragraph 31, which itself forms an introduction to the following twelve sections.[4] Bentham abandons his enumeration of the paragraphs after paragraph 3, with the exception of paragraph 11.[5] It is possible that Bentham would have eventually given a separate paragraph number to each of the discussions of the seven intervening terms for a law, and they would thereby have constituted paragraphs 4–10. However, given Bentham's failure to insert the bulk of the paragraph numbers, the existing paragraph numbers (i.e. 2, 3, and 11) have been suppressed.

This insertion contains an account of sovereignty which is superseded by a further account presented in material which was added to §8. In the account given in §3, Bentham argues that constitutional law is not properly understood as law, but rather

[1] The four additional 'respects' were Ends (§5), Parties affected (§8), Duration (§10), and Generality (§11).

[2] An alternative, but abandoned, draft of paragraph 31, which refers to the final total of twelve 'respects', at UC lxxxviii. 88, is reproduced at p. 40 n. below.

[3] UC lxxxviii. 90–1, 89, 92–100b. The sheets carry the marginal subheading 'Distinctions', with the exception of UC lxxxviii. 89 and 96 which carry the marginal sub-heading 'Definition'. The pagination indicates that UC lxxxviii. 89 may have been a later insertion into the sequence. A superseded draft, which represents the beginning of an alternative commentary on the definition of a law in paragraph 30, at UC lxxxviii. 101 is reproduced at p. 25 n. below. Related fragments are at UC lxxxviii. 237a, 237b^{v}.

[4] In the Hart edition, this insertion is placed at the conclusion of the corresponding Chapter, in other words after paragraph 31 (see *Of Laws in General*, pp. 3–17). The first problem with this arrangement is that it divorces the insertion from the definition of a law which appears in paragraph 30. The second problem is that it obscures the connection between paragraph 31 and the discussion of the 'respects' of a law contained in §§ 4–15, to which that paragraph forms an introduction.

[5] See UC lxxxviii. 94.

as a form of positive morality. In the account given in §8, he argues that constitutional law is properly understood as law since it emanates from the sovereign like all other law, but, distinguishing between law *in principem* and law *in populum*, states that it is enforced by the moral or religious sanction, rather than by the political sanction. As the text appears in Hart's edition, both passages have equal status in that both are presented as indicative of Bentham's thinking at the same point of time.[1] However, the account in §8 was written at a later date, and appears to represent, in Bentham's own mind, a new departure in his thought. This is shown by the fact that Bentham added two marginal comments to the manuscript containing the earlier passage. The first comment appertains to the following part of the earlier passage:

> In the definition that hath just been given of a legal mandate, it follows that the mandate of the sovereign, be it what it will, cannot be illegal: it may be cruel; it may be impolitic; it may even be unconstitutional: but it cannot be illegal. It may be unconstitutional, for instance, by being repugnant to any privileges that may have been conceded to the people whom it affects: but it would be perverting language and confounding ideas to call it *illegal*: for concessions of privileges are not mandates: they are neither commands nor countermands: in short they are not *laws*. They are only promises from the sovereign to the people that he will not issue any law, any mandate, any command or countermand but to such or such an effect, or perhaps with the concurrence of such or such persons.

Bentham's marginal comment is as follows: 'Alter. These are laws not *in populum* indeed, but *in principem*.'[2] The second comment appertains to the following part of the earlier passage:

> The principal contents of the Imperial capitulations are either concessions of privileges or treaties, according to the relation which the Emperor is consider'd as bearing at the several periods to the other states. I would not, without examining them in this particular view, be sure of their containing any matter of the mandative kind.

Bentham's marginal comment is as follows: 'They are *leges in principem* in which the party favoured is either a subject or co-imperant or an independent prince.'[3] As Bentham was working on the text, he discovered or invented the distinction between laws *in populum* and *in principem*, which he developed in the additional material written for §8, and thereby superseded the earlier exposition of constitutional law contained in §3. Both passages

[1] See *Of Laws in General*, pp. 16–17, 64–71 respectively.
[2] See p. 38 & n. below. [3] See pp. 39–40 n. below.

are retained in the present edition, with editorial footnotes drawing attention to their status.

A further addition to §3 is a footnote discussing William Blackstone's definition of a law.[1] Bentham did not indicate precisely where this footnote should be placed, but given that the title to the section contains a footnote marker,[2] that the content of the note seems entirely apposite, and that there is no other relevant material, it seems reasonable to assume that it is this material which belongs here.[3]

The next twelve sections, as noted above, each deal with one of the twelve 'respects' in which, according to Bentham, a law might be considered. Again as noted above, Bentham originally intended that the discussion of the 'respects' would be included in §3, but at a relatively late point in the drafting of the work, decided to devote a single section to each 'respect'. The discussion of each respect begins with a numerical adverb, such as 'Secondly' and 'Thirdly', and often with an alternative as well. The enumeration represents various stages in the organization of this material, and is in most instances inconsistent with the final order adopted. In the text, the appropriate enumeration has been editorially supplied where necessary, with the manuscript variants given in editorial footnotes.

In the 'principal draft', the fourth section, dealing with the source of law, constitutes paragraphs 32–6, but the corresponding text sheets have not been located. Given that the final page of paragraph 31 is numbered 50, and the first page of paragraph 37 (the opening paragraph of §5) is numbered 59, it appears that, in the 'principal draft', §4 ran to a maximum of eight pages.[4] The present text reproduces a later draft which consists of thirty-four pages,[5] and, therefore, represents a considerable extension of the discussion. The beginning of this sequence bears paragraph

[1] UC lxxxviii. 104–5, reproduced at pp. 24–5 n. below, commenting on a passage at *Commentaries on the Laws of England*, 4 vols., Oxford, 1765–9, i. 53–6. Sir William Blackstone (1723–80), first Vinerian Professor of English Law at the University of Oxford 1758–66, Justice of Common Pleas 1770, 1770–80, and Justice of King's Bench 1770.

[2] See UC lxxxviii. 102.

[3] It certainly seems to be misplaced at the end of paragraph 31, which is where it appears in the Hart edition: see *Of Laws in General*, pp. 2–3 n.

[4] Most of the text for 'Limits' is written on bifolia (for a more detailed description see pp. xxxvii–xxxviii below), hence eight pages represent two bifolia. However, not all four pages of both bifolia may have been used. In general, where reference is made below to the number of pages which constitute a particular section, the number represents the pages enumerated by Bentham, which does not necessarily correspond with the number of pages on which he actually wrote. Blank pages and blank parts of pages often appear part way through a sequence of text, as well as at the end.

[5] UC lxxxviii. 229–237b. The sheets carry the marginal subheading 'Source'.

numbers 1–3, but the remainder has not been numbered. In view of Bentham's failure to continue the paragraph enumeration, these three paragraph numbers have been suppressed.

The fifth section, dealing with the ends or objects of a law, is an addition to the 'principal draft'.[1] The text consists of eight pages, with a complete and consistent series of paragraph numbers 1–4, which have been retained. In the 'principal draft', the sixth section, dealing with the subjects of a law, originally constituted paragraphs 37–8.[2] The material was then revised by Bentham. He retained paragraph 37, but discarded paragraph 38, replacing it with a greatly extended discussion.[3] He renumbered paragraph 37 as paragraph 1, and supplied a complete and consistent series of paragraph numbers (i.e. 2–10) for the remainder of the sequence, and these have been retained. In the 'principal draft', the seventh section, dealing with the objects of a law, constitutes paragraphs 39–48, of which the complete text survives.[4] A later draft is reproduced in Appendix B.[5]

The eighth section, dealing with the parties affected by a law, is an addition to the 'principal draft'. Bentham's paragraph enumeration for this material is sparse and inconsistent, and has been suppressed. It appears that the section was written in two stages, with the discussion of sovereignty, which closes the section, constituting a later addition.[6] There is a difficulty in understanding Bentham's intentions in relation to the point at which the two passages meet. The passage on sovereignty is in itself unproblematic in that it is consistently paginated 29–52. However, the final two folios in the first part of the section, namely UC lxxxviii. 219

[1] UC lxxxviii. 238–9. The sheets carry the marginal subheading 'End'.

[2] See UC lxxxviii. 241, which contains, along with paragraph 37, the cancelled beginning of paragraph 38 (reproduced at pp. 58–9 n. below). The pagination of the 'principal draft' indicates that the remainder of the section consisted of six pages, which have not been located.

[3] UC lxxxviii. 242–6. The sheets carry the marginal subheading 'Subjects'. A related fragment, headed 'Subjects or Objects', is at UC lxxxviii. 240.

[4] UC lxxxviii. 256–64. The sheets carry the marginal subheading 'Objects. Circumstances'.

[5] For further details see p. xxx below. In the Hart edition, the two drafts are presented sequentially, with the later draft preceding the earlier draft: see *Of Laws in General*, pp. 41–52. It appears that Hart was misled by the enumeration of the folios in the Bentham Papers into thinking that he was dealing with a linear draft.

[6] The first part of the section is at UC lxxxviii. 212–19, 221 (see pp. 75–86 below), and the discussion of sovereignty at lxxxviii. 220, 222–6 (see pp. 86–93 below). For the significance of this discussion of sovereignty see pp. xxi–xxiii above. The sheets for the first part carry the marginal subheading 'Parties affected'. On the sheets dealing with sovereignty, the main heading is 'Parties affected', rather than the usual 'Limits', with the exception of the first sheet (UC lxxxviii. 220) which carries 'Limits' as the main heading, and 'Parties affected' as the marginal subheading.

and 221, are paginated 27–30 and 29–32 respectively. Moreover, each of these folios, as well as the first in the sequence on sovereignty, contains a paragraph numbered 13. In other words, three different paragraphs are numbered 13. This may simply be a mistake in enumeration on Bentham's part, or it may indicate that he intended to discard some or all of the material at UC lxxxviii. 219 and 221. The material at UC lxxxviii. 221, which bears the marginal heading 'Use and importance of the above distinctions',[1] forms a conclusion to the section, and Bentham may have thought it inappropriately located once he had decided to follow it with a discussion of sovereignty. However, in the absence of any clear indication, this material has been retained at the end of the first part of the section.

In the 'principal draft', the ninth section, dealing with the local extent of a law, constitutes paragraphs 49–50, but the corresponding text sheets have not been located. The present text is based on a later draft.[2] The tenth section, dealing with the duration of a law, is an addition to the 'principal draft'.[3] Neither of these sections carry paragraph numbers. The eleventh section, dealing with the generality of a law, is an addition to the 'principal draft'.[4] The section carries a consistent and complete set of paragraph numbers, which has been reproduced in the present text.

In the 'principal draft', the twelfth section, dealing with aspects of a law, constitutes paragraphs 51–86. The text sheets for paragraphs 51–2, and the first part of paragraph 53, which together consisted of six pages, have not been located. The present edition, therefore, commences part way through paragraph 53. Otherwise, the 'principal draft' is complete.[5] Bentham did rework the text,[6] and repaginated it, but the original order is restored in the present text. He seems to have abandoned this attempt to reorganize the 'principal draft', and decided instead to produce a new draft. Indeed, his failure to reorganize this material satisfactorily may be related to his decision to draw on the 'primary draft' when

[1] See p. 85 below.

[2] UC lxxxviii. 265. This sheet carries the marginal subheading 'Local extent'.

[3] UC lxxxviii. 267. This sheet carries the marginal subheadings 'Duration' and 'Time'. At the head of the sheet, Bentham has added: 'Postpone to Generality.' This indicates that at some point Bentham considered incorporating this 'respect' into the discussion of 'Generality', though both plans of 1782 list it as a discrete section.

[4] UC lxxxviii. 266, 268–79. The sheets carry the marginal subheading 'Generality'.

[5] UC lxxxviii. 181, 201, 182–4, 188–200b, 202–11. The sheets carry the marginal subheading 'Aspect'. The marginal subheading 'Conditional' has been added to UC lxxxviii. 194. A related rudiments sheet is at UC xcix. 91.

[6] UC lxxxviii. 201, for instance, has been moved from near the beginning of the sequence, to two-thirds of the way through, and several insertions appear on clipped sheets.

composing this new draft, which is reproduced in Appendix C, but which itself remained incomplete.[1] The presentation of the discussion of 'aspects' in the Hart edition is particularly problematic, in that an attempt has been made to combine the 'principal draft' and the later draft, resulting in a confused and incoherent text.[2]

In the 'principal draft', the thirteenth section, dealing with the force of a law, which constitutes paragraphs 87–113, and the fourteenth section, dealing with the signs of a law, which constitutes paragraphs 114–17, are both complete.[3] In the 'principal draft', the fifteenth section, dealing with the appendages of a law, constitutes paragraphs 118–122, but the final two paragraphs are missing.[4] The pagination indicates that four pages of text are missing. In both the 'Table of Chapters' of March 1782 and the letter to Ashburton of 3 June 1782, Bentham reverses the order of the fourteenth and fifteenth sections, but the original order as written for the 'principal draft' has been retained in the present edition.[5]

In the 'principal draft', the fifteenth section, dealing with the appendages of a law, concludes the discussion of the various 'respects', and, therefore, of the material that Bentham envisaged in the original plan of the 'principal draft' would constitute the third section of Chapter XVII. As stated above, Bentham later divided this material into thirteen sections, the first containing the definition of a law, and the remainder each dealing with one of the twelve 'respects', of which eight were identified in paragraph 31 of the 'principal draft', and four subsequently added. The 'principal draft' continues with the discussion of a complete law, which Bentham in the first instance envisaged as a continuation of Ch. XVII, §3,[6] but which, as evidenced by the plan for the 'principal draft', he soon came to regard as a discrete section. Bentham then divided this section into two, with the latter part becoming a new section dealing with customary law. In the final ordering of the text,

[1] For further details see p. xxxi below. A fragment discussing 'repugnancy' between laws at UC lxxxviii. 179–80 seems to be related to the 'principal draft' of this section, rather than to the later draft, in that it uses terminology which is expounded in the 'principal draft', but not in the later draft.

[2] For further details see pp. xxxi–xxxii below.

[3] See UC lxxxviii. 280–97 and 298–301 respectively. The former sequence carries the marginal subheading 'Force', and the latter 'Expression', with the exception of UC lxxxviii. 301, which carries 'Signs. Forms'.

[4] UC lxxxviii. 302–3. The sheets carry the marginal subheading 'Appendages'.

[5] In the Hart edition, the corresponding Chapters are presented in the revised order.

[6] The title for the section has been inserted into the first text sheet at UC lxxxviii. 304, which confirms that, when first drafted, the material was intended simply as a continuation of §3.

these topics constitute the sixteenth and seventeenth sections respectively. The first part of the 'principal draft' of § 16 consists of paragraphs 123–32.[1] The next paragraph is numbered 133, but also carries the deleted number 109,[2] which represents an earlier enumeration of the paragraphs of the 'principal draft'. The second part of the 'principal draft' of § 16 continues with paragraphs 110–16.[3] For the sake of consistency, and to avoid confusion, these paragraph numbers have been editorially amended to 134–40. The discrepancy perhaps arose when Bentham revised the paragraph numbering of the 'principal draft' due to an insertion placed in a preceding part of the text. It may have been at that point that he composed an alternative draft of the second part of § 16, to which he gave paragraph numbers 133–40 in continuation of the revised paragraph numbers of the 'principal draft', and superseding the original version from paragraph 109/133 onwards. The alternative draft is reproduced in Appendix D.[4]

The seventeenth section dealing with customary law, as noted above, was originally written as the final part of the section dealing with a complete law.[5] The paragraph numbers for this material, namely 117–26, continue in sequence from the paragraph numbers of the first draft of the second part of § 16. A later addition to the text, apparently intended as a 'Conclusion' to the section, carries paragraph numbers 126–8.[6] This addition, however, is abandoned, with the final paragraph consisting merely in the paragraph number and a marginal heading, with an associated marginal note by Bentham.[7] It is not clear whether Bentham intended paragraph 126 of the 'Conclusion' to supersede paragraph 126 of the first sequence, or whether he simply made a mistake in his enumeration. Both paragraphs have been retained in the present text. As in the previous section, the paragraphs have been editorially renumbered, so that paragraphs 117–26 and 126–8 appear in the present text as paragraphs 141–53 respectively.[8]

[1] UC lxxxviii. 304–15. The sheets carry the marginal subheading 'Compleat'.

[2] See UC lxxxviii. 315–16.

[3] UC lxxxviii. 316–19, 331–2. The sheets carry the marginal subheading 'Compleat', with the exception of UC lxxxviii. 331, where 'Compleat' is crossed through, and the alternative 'Uses' has been added.

[4] For further details see p. xxxii below.

[5] UC lxxxviii. 333–9. The sheets carry the marginal subheading 'Compleat. Cust. Law' or 'Common Law'.

[6] UC lxxxviii. 340a, 340b. The sheets carry the marginal subheading 'Customary. Conclusion'.

[7] See p. 197 below.

[8] A note which Bentham composed for this section, but failed to indicate where it should be inserted, at UC lxxxviii. 341, is reproduced at p. 185 n. below.

The eighteenth section deals with the separation of the penal and civil branches of the law.[1] Though the paragraphs are not numbered, and from this perspective are not integrated into the 'principal draft', the range of page numbers (273–80) indicate a relationship with a lengthy preceding text, which can only be the 'principal draft'. Moreover, the section is introduced as 'an answer to the question we set out with', with a cross-reference to paragraph 29,[2] which appears at the end of §2,[3] thereby indicating that this material forms a conclusion, or the beginning of a conclusion, to the intervening discussion. The title on the first text sheet is marked §5.[4] It is possible that, at the time he wrote it, Bentham had separated the material on a 'Compleat' law from the discussion of 'respects', but had not separated 'Customary' from 'Compleat'. By the time he composed the plan of the 'principal draft' at UC lxxxviii. 107, 'Customary' had been detached from 'Compleat', and it appears as §6.

The nineteenth and twentieth sections were written at a very early stage in the drafting of 'Limits'. The former section, dealing with the distinction between the civil and criminal law,[5] originally formed the continuation of the material presented here in Appendix A, and hence the third section in the very earliest draft of Ch. XVII.[6] It also appears as §5 in the 'primary draft'.[7] The sequence carries a consistent set of paragraph numbers, which have been retained. The manuscripts for the twentieth section, which discusses the distinction between penal and civil procedure, are headed 'Corpus Juris', rather than 'Limits' (although the heading 'Limits' has been added to the first and final pages).[8] The material does not appear to have been revised after its insertion into 'Limits', as evidenced by the fact that a cross-reference to 'Limits' has not been amended.[9] The paragraphs have not been numbered. 'Corpus Juris', as stated above,[10] was one of the projected Chapters in continuation of the introduction to the penal code. However, apart from this sequence, no other material

[1] UC lxxxviii. 342–3. The sheets carry the marginal subheading 'Separation'.

[2] See p. 198 & n. below.

[3] See pp. 21–3 below.

[4] See UC lxxxviii. 342.

[5] UC lxxxviii. 84–7. The marginal contents sheet is at UC xcix. 98, which adds four marginal contents to the end of the section for which no corresponding text has been located: see p. 206 n. below.

[6] See pp. xxix–xxx below.

[7] See p. xxxiii below.

[8] UC lxxxviii. 351, 353–60. The sheets carry the marginal subheading 'Proced. Pen. x Civil' or 'Penal x Civil'. Six pages at UC lxxxviii. 351–2, which Bentham excised from the text, are reproduced at pp. 207–8 n. below. A related marginal contents sheet is at UC xcix. 106.

[9] See UC lxxxviii. 356 and p. 212 n. below.

[10] See p. xii above.

headed 'Corpus Juris' appears to survive in the Bentham Papers. Given the provenance of the nineteenth and twentieth sections—the former being written before the work had been expanded into its final form, and the latter being written for a different Chapter—it is not unreasonable to suggest that Bentham would have undertaken a thorough revision of their content had he put the work through the press.

The twenty-first and final section, dealing with the 'Uses' of the Chapter,[1] consists of a sequence of forty-four pages which carries paragraph numbers [1]–9 (Bentham failed to enumerate the first paragraph, so this number has been editorially supplied). At the head of the section, Bentham noted that the text had been 'Settled as far as p. 19 inclusive' (i.e. the third page of UC lxxxviii. 365),[2] indicating that he had revised less than half of the section. When drawing up the complete plans for the work, namely the 'Table of Chapters' of March 1782 and the letter to Ashburton of 3 June 1782, Bentham gives the title as 'Uses of the eighteen preceding chapters', that is §§3–20 of the present edition. This might be interpreted as indicating that Bentham had decided to exclude the first two sections (or chapters) from the work. However, it should first be recalled that both these sections (or chapters) appear on both plans, and that there is no indication that they should be divorced from the text which follows. Second, it was in the first two sections (or chapters) that Bentham outlined the problems he wished to address, and it was in the following eighteen sections (or chapters) that he provided his answers. The allusion to the preceding eighteen chapters, then, refers to the text in which the answers are provided, rather than to the whole text. It does not imply that the first two chapters (or sections) do not belong with that text.

Appendix A reproduces the very earliest draft of the second section of Chapter XVII, entitled 'Distinction between penal law and civil'.[3] The material has a consistent series of paragraph numbers, which have been retained. The section was originally preceded by Ch. XVII, §1 as printed in *An Introduction to the Principles of Morals and Legislation*, and followed by the material which was eventually used for §19 of the final text. Indeed, the two

[1] UC lxxxviii. 361–71. The sheets carry the marginal subheading 'Uses', with the following supplementary subheadings on the appropriate sheets: 'Plan', 'Digest', 'Alterability', 'Matter', 'Interpretation', 'Comparison', and 'Parsing'. The corresponding marginal summary sheet is at UC xcix. 107. A related fragment at UC lxxxviii. 374–5, which carries the marginal subheading 'Plan', is reproduced at p. 219 n. below, and a related fragment at lxxxviii. 372, which carries the marginal subheading 'Parsing', at p. 233 n. below.

[2] See p. 224 n. below.

[3] UC lxxxviii. 82–4.

sections which form Appendix A and §19 were written consecutively, as evidenced by the fact that the final two pages of the former section share the same bifolium with the first two pages of the latter section,[1] and the two sections share the same marginal contents sheet.[2] When composing this material, Bentham presumably envisaged that the task he had set himself, namely to distinguish penal law from civil law, would be relatively straightforward, and hence the comparatively cursory way in which he initially dealt with it.[3]

Appendix B reproduces a later draft of §7, dealing with the objects of a law,[4] intended to replace the corresponding material in the 'principal draft'. This later draft, which consists of thirty-two pages divided into eight numbered paragraphs, is complete and coherent. The first ten pages supersede an earlier beginning of three-and-a-half pages.[5] While the earlier beginning consists of two numbered paragraphs, the later alternative consists of three, although Bentham failed to number the first. Bentham also failed to amend the subsequent paragraph numbers, hence the paragraph enumeration runs [1], 2–3, 3–7. For the sake of clarity and consistency, the paragraph numbers have been editorially amended to run from 1 to 8 respectively.

Appendix C reproduces a later draft of §12, dealing with the aspects of a law, intended to replace the corresponding material in the 'principal draft'. When composing this new draft, Bentham decided to divide this lengthy section into subsections. In the first subsection, entitled 'Plan of this Chapter',[6] he announces his intention to present the material in four further subsections,

[1] i.e. UC lxxxviii. 84.

[2] UC xcix. 98. A related rudiments sheet is at UC xcix. 100, 99 (the bifolium has torn down the middle, with the result that each sheet has been given a separate folio number).

[3] See Bentham to Ashburton, 3 June 1782, *Correspondence* (*CW*), iii. 123: 'As the distinction between the penal branch of the law and the civil is so familiar, I had all along taken for granted that the line of separation between those objects might be traced within the compass of a page or two.'

[4] UC lxxxviii. 248–249b, 251–5. The sheets carry the marginal subheading 'Objects'. A related fragment, on the relationship between circumstance and property, is at UC lxxxviii. 250.

[5] UC lxxxviii. 251. The final half-page of this bifolium contains paragraph 3, which Bentham retained, though it appears in the present edition as paragraph 4.

[6] UC lxxxviii. 163, consisting of four pages, divided into two numbered paragraphs. This sheet carries the main heading 'Aspect', and the marginal subheading 'Plan'. There are two alternative drafts of 'Plan' at UC lxxxviii. 164. This sheet carries the main heading 'Limits', and the marginal subheading 'Plan. Aspect'. The second and later of these drafts is reproduced at p. 250 n. below. In the Hart edition, the later alternative draft is added to the end of the first subsection (see *Of Laws in General*, Ch. X, para. 2, p. 94). As it announces a different method of organizing the section, the result is, needless to say, extremely confusing.

each dealing with one of the 'modifications of which a law' considered from the point of view of its aspect 'is susceptible': 1. 'the case where there is only one mandate applying itself to one act'; 2. 'where there is a mandate applying itself to an act to which another mandate of the same aspect has applied already'; 3. 'where there is a mandate applying itself to an act to which another mandate of a different aspect has applied already'; and 4. 'where there is a mandate applying to one act an aspect which is spoken of as having been applied already to another'.[1] The short titles for these four modifications were 'primordial', 'reiterative', 'alterative', and 'extensive' respectively. In the event, Bentham completed the second subsection dealing with primordial mandates,[2] and composed a lengthy but unfinished sequence for the third dealing with reiterative mandates.[3] No new material was written for the proposed fourth and fifth subsections. An earlier draft of part of the third subsection on reiterative mandates,[4] on which Bentham drew when composing the later,[5] seems to have belonged to the 'primary draft'. Indeed, the pagination suggests that this material may have at one time been intended to follow the second subsection dealing with primordial mandates.[6] This seems to indicate that Bentham overlooked the 'principal draft' in favour of the 'primary draft' when redrafting this section. As noted above, the Hart edition combines the 'principal draft' and the later draft. The first three sections are taken from the later draft, and the fourth and fifth sections from the corresponding discussion in the 'principal draft'. Hart includes a further fragment which deals with 'repugnancy' between laws as a sixth and final section, though this material is related to the 'principal draft' rather than to the incomplete second draft.[7] Finally, Hart presents the initial pages of the 'principal draft', which he did not include in the Chapter itself, together with the fragment on

[1] See p. 251 below.

[2] UC lxxxviii. 165–8, consisting of sixteen pages, divided into ten numbered paragraphs. The sheets carry the main heading 'Aspect', and the marginal subheading 'Primordial'.

[3] UC lxxxviii. 169–77, consisting of thirty-six pages. The sheets carry the main heading 'Aspect', and the marginal subheading 'Reiterative'. The pagination runs 1–16, 9–28, indicating that the first sequence of pages 9–16 (i.e. UC lxxxviii. 171–2) were a later insertion. The first four paragraphs, which appear on UC lxxxviii. 169, are the only paragraphs which have been numbered.

[4] UC lxxxviii. 185–7, 178. The sheets carry the marginal subheading 'Aspect', except for UC lxxxviii. 178 which carries the main heading 'Aspect' and the marginal subheading 'Reiterative'.

[5] Material at UC lxxxviii. 185–6, for instance, is redrafted at lxxxviii. 170 and 174.

[6] The material on primordial mandates is paginated 1–16, and the fragment on reiterative mandates 17–30.

[7] See p. xxvi n. above.

reiterative mandates from the 'primary draft',[1] as a single linear sequence in his Appendix D.[2]

Appendix D in the present edition reproduces the alternative version of the latter part of the sixteenth section of the 'principal draft', dealing with the idea of a complete law.[3] The first of four 'patterns' to which a law might correspond, announced at the beginning of the section,[4] is developed in greater detail in this alternative version than in the 'principal draft' proper, but it then concludes with a very cursory discussion of the remaining three 'patterns'. In contrast, the four 'patterns' are each discussed in some detail in the 'principal draft' proper. It is possible that Bentham abandoned this alternative version. In the Hart edition, the corresponding Chapter reproduces both the 'principal draft' proper and the alternative version, together with a related fragment on the law of property (reproduced in Appendix F in the present volume), as a single linear sequence. Hart begins the Chapter with all but the final two folios of the original version of the 'principal draft', continues with the alternative version, then inserts the fragment on the law of property, and concludes with the final two folios (consisting of six pages) of the 'principal draft' proper.[5]

Appendix E reproduces part of an early version of the text which, as explained above, is referred to here as the 'primary draft', and which corresponds with the earliest plan of the work at UC xcix. 99, and which represents the second version of the text that it is possible to reconstruct. According to the plan, §3 is entitled 'Of a law and its parts' and §4 is entitled 'Limits between civil and penal law shewn in detail'. These two sections were preceded by Ch. XVII, §§1–2 as printed in *An Introduction to the Principles of Morals and Legislation*. A considerable amount of material belonging to §3 is missing, though several fragments have been identified.[6] Appendix E begins with the final part of §3, from part way through paragraph 76 to paragraph 82.[7] If paragraphs 30–1 of the

[1] i.e. UC lxxxviii. 181, 201, 183, 182, 183–4 and lxxxviii. 185–7, 178 respectively.

[2] See *Of Laws in General*, pp. 298–303.

[3] UC lxxxviii. 320–5. The sheets carry the marginal subheading 'Compleat. Unity'.

[4] See p. 168 below.

[5] See *Of Laws in General*, pp. 156–83. The order in the Hart edition simply follows the order in which the folios appear in the Bentham Papers, i.e. UC lxxxviii. 304–32.

[6] See, for instance, UC xxvii. 50, 51^{v}, lxxxviii. 178, 185–7, 259^{v}. It is possible that various clipped sheets which have been incorporated at various points into the 'principal draft' belonged to the 'primary draft'. The renumbering of pages and paragraphs of the 'primary draft' indicates that, like the 'principal draft', it went through several stages of expansion and was possibly reordered.

[7] UC lxxxviii. 117, 106–8. The sheets carry the marginal subheading 'Matter circumstantiative'. The marginal contents for paragraphs 81–2 are at UC xcix. 108.

'principal draft' at one time formed the equivalent paragraphs in the 'primary draft', then around fifty paragraphs of intervening material appertaining to §3 of the 'primary draft' have generally either not survived or have been reused elsewhere. On the other hand, if Bentham began §3 of the 'primary draft' with a fresh sequence of paragraph numbers, a proportionately larger amount of material has not survived. The Appendix continues with the whole of the fourth section, which consists of paragraphs 83–99.[1] Bentham runs through the various classes of offences he identifies in Ch. XVI of *An Introduction to the Principles of Morals and Legislation*, and discusses whether the relevant law is of a penal or of a civil nature. This topic is not pursued in any subsequent version of 'Limits'. In the Hart edition, the material constituting the third and fourth sections of the 'primary draft' is tacked on to the end of Ch. XVI (corresponding to §18 of the present edition).[2]

The plan for the 'primary draft' lists 'Distinction between civil law and criminal' as §5. This is the material which formed §2 of the earliest version of the work, and which, after appearing as §7 on the plan for the 'principal draft', eventually became §19 of the present edition.[3] This material is not repeated in this Appendix. The sixth and final section on the plan is entitled 'Analysis of the matter of a body of laws'. The corresponding sequence, consisting of seventy-two pages, was originally headed 'Analysis', though later amended to 'Exposition'.[4] The Appendix is completed by a seventh section which has been editorially supplied

[1] UC lxxxviii. 109a–116. The title 'Limits between civil and penal law particularized' appears at the very end of UC lxxxviii. 108. The corresponding marginal contents sheet is at UC xcix. 97.

[2] See *Of Laws in General*, pp. 198–208 (i.e. from paragraph 6), where the text begins part way through paragraph 78 of the 'primary draft'.

[3] See p. xxviii above.

[4] UC lxxxviii. 119, 118, 120–37. The first sheet was originally headed 'Analysis', but this has been crossed through and replaced by '{Limits.} Exposition'. The paragraphs of the sequence are numbered 1, 1 continued or inserendum, 2–31, 31*, 32–55, 59–72. This enumeration has been retained. Bentham seems to have been unsure about the relationship between the paragraph numbered '1 continued or inserendum' and the preceding one. Paragraph 31* was an insertion into the text (the use of an asterisk was Bentham's normal method of indicating an insertion). The corresponding marginal contents sheet at UC xcix. 88 contains three marginal contents corresponding to paragraphs 56–8 (reproduced at p. 307 n. below), for which no text has been located, though the text may not have been written since the pagination does not indicate any missing pages.

Related rudiments sheets are at UC xcix. 89–90.

Fragments of an earlier draft survive at UC lxxxviii. 145–6 (pp. 5–10, paragraphs 2–10), lxxxviii. 149 (pp. 15–18, paragraphs 16–17 and 17 again), lxxxviii. 152 (pages 33–4, paragraphs 34–7), and lxxxviii. 153–4 (pp. 39–46, paragraphs 46–7). The corresponding marginal contents sheet for this earlier draft at UC xcix. 86 shows that lxxxviii. 119 preceded lxxxviii. 145, which indicates that some of the material written for the earlier draft was used by Bentham in the later draft.

with the title 'Conclusion'.[1] The addition of this material, while conjectural, seems appropriate given that it carries the heading '{Limits.} Analysis' and is clearly related in content to the preceding section. In the Hart edition, §6 of the 'primary draft' is reproduced as Part I of Appendix B, with the addition of two related fragments.[2]

Appendix F reproduces a sequence of twenty pages on the law of property,[3] which is possibly the material referred to in a passage of a letter written by Bentham to his brother Samuel on 29 October 1780. Bentham explains that, when working on what would become Ch. XVI of *An Introduction to the Principles of Morals and Legislation*, he found himself 'obliged to lay the foundation of another work by drawing up (without inserting) an analysis of the possible modifications of *property*'.[4] The text sheets carry the marginal subheadings 'Law of Property' and 'Compleat'. There is no conclusive evidence regarding the exact relationship between these headings, but it is possible that 'Law of Property' was the original heading, and that at some point Bentham decided that the material might be used in §16 of 'Limits' on the idea of a complete law. The material was not, however, incorporated by Bentham into the text of 'Limits'. In the Hart edition, this material is inserted in the Chapter on the idea of a complete law (i.e. Ch. XIV), together with both the first and partial second versions of the 'principal draft'.[5]

When Bentham published *An Introduction to the Principles of Morals and Legislation* in 1789, he explained in the 'Preface' that the work formed part of what had been intended as an introduction to a penal code, and that he had published it despite his concerns that 'the performance fails of coming up to the author's own ideas of what should have been exhibited' in a work with that title.[6] He also explained that he had abandoned the introduction as a whole because he had found himself 'unexpectedly

[1] UC lxxxviii. 143–4, 147–8, 150–1.

[2] i.e. UC lxxxviii. 138 and 139. See *Of Laws in General*, pp. 251–79. Part II of Hart's Appendix B (ibid., pp. 279–88) reproduces material at UC lxxxviii. 156–62, which was written for *An Introduction to the Principles of Morals and Legislation*, Ch. XVI, and does not, therefore, properly belong with 'Limits'.

[3] UC lxxxviii. 326–30. The corresponding marginal contents sheet is at UC xcix. 105.

[4] See Bentham to Samuel Bentham, 25 August–30 October 1780, *The Correspondence of Jeremy Bentham*, vol. ii, ed. T. L. S. Sprigge, London, 1968 (*CW*), p. 488. Samuel Bentham (1757–1831), naval architect and engineer, was at this time based in St Petersburg.

[5] See *Of Laws in General*, where the material on property is at pp. 176–82, the original 'principal draft' of the idea of a complete law is at pp. 152–70, 182–3, and the alternative 'principal draft' at pp. 170–6, respectively.

[6] *An Introduction to the Principles of Morals and Legislation* (*CW*), p. 4.

entangled in an unsuspected corner of the metaphysical maze'.[1] He went on to state that his 'defeat' had been the result of the 'difficulties' he had discovered when he had attempted 'to solve the questions' which he had posed at the end of Ch. XVII, §2, namely: '*Wherein consisted the identity and* completeness *of a law? What the distinction, and where the separation, between* a penal *and a* civil *law? What the distinction, and where the separation, between the* penal *and* other branches *of* the law?'[2] It appears, then, that Bentham himself was, in the end, dissatisfied with the answers he had provided in 'Limits', and that this not only led him to abandon 'Limits' itself, but the whole of the introduction to the projected penal code, including the material on 'Indirect Legislation' and on 'Place and Time'. It was, perhaps, fortuitous that he had already printed the first sixteen Chapters, and the first two sections of the seventeenth Chapter, of the introduction before he had become aware of the 'unsuspected corner of the metaphysical maze' which 'Limits' represents, otherwise the work which eventually appeared under the title of *An Introduction to the Principles of Morals and Legislation* might itself have remained unpublished.

At the end of Ch. XVII, §2 of *An Introduction to the Principles of Morals and Legislation* printed in 1780, as noted above, Bentham announced that the Chapter would contain a further three sections, the third and fourth of which would 'ascertain what *a law* is' and 'what are the parts into which a law, as such, is capable of being distinguished', while the fifth would deal with 'the import of the word *criminal*, as applied to law.'[3] When *An Introduction to the Principles of Morals and Legislation* was eventually published in 1789, the second section was followed not by the three proposed sections, but by a 'concluding note' which explained that the remaining sections of the Chapter would 'not here, nor now be given; because to give them in a manner tolerably complete and satisfactory might require a considerable volume. This work will form a work of itself, closing the series of works mentioned in the preface.'[4] In the 'Preface', Bentham outlined ten proposed 'Parts' which would form an introduction to a complete code of law. He described the tenth and final Part as follows:

> Plan of a body of law, complete in all its branches, considered in respect of its *form*; in other words, in respect of its method and terminology; including a view of the origination and connexion of the ideas expressed

[1] Ibid., p. 1.

[2] Ibid., p. 8.

[3] See ibid., pp. 299–300, and pp. 22–3 below.

[4] *An Introduction to the Principles of Morals and Legislation* (*CW*), p. 301.

by the short list of terms, the exposition of which contains all that can be said with propriety to belong to the head of *universal jurisprudence*.

Bentham thereupon added the following footnote: 'Such as obligation, right, power, possession, title, exemption, immunity, franchise, privilege, nullity, validity, and the like.'[1] It seems highly unlikely, however, that Bentham would have simply used the text written for 'Limits' to form 'Part the 10th' of the new introduction. First, despite expanding during its composition into twenty-one sections or chapters, 'Limits' remained unfinished and was, in fact, abandoned by Bentham. Second, even if he had drawn upon this material, he would surely have reworked and rewritten it, if only because he would have had the benefit of nearly a decade's further reflection on the subject. Third, 'Part the 10th' seems to be more concerned with approaching directly and explicitly the question of the 'form' of a body of law, whereas 'Limits' was written with a view to explaining the distinction between penal and civil law. While the two questions were intimately linked in Bentham's mind, the way in which he described 'Part the 10th' does seem to involve a shift of focus. In short, Bentham's continued interest in the subject-matter of the work does not mean that the work he would have published as 'Part the 10th' sometime after 1789 would have been that which he had abandoned in 1782.

PRESENTATION OF THE TEXT

The Printed Text

The first two sections of the present edition of *Of the Limits of the Penal Branch of Jurisprudence* correspond as closely as possible with the style and conventions, including spelling, capitalization, punctuation, the use of italics and other devices, of the version of *An Introduction to the Principles of Morals and Legislation* printed in 1780, and published in 1789, with the following variations. First, in the printed version, the subsections (or paragraph numbers, as they may be more conveniently called, even though each subsection often contains more than one paragraph) within the text have been enumerated by means of Roman numerals, centred above the beginning of the first paragraph of the corresponding text. The numbers have here been rendered in bold Arabic numerals, and placed at the beginning of the relevant paragraph or sequence of paragraphs. This renders the presentation of the two sections

[1] *An Introduction to the Principles of Morals and Legislation* (*CW*), p. 6 & n.

which are based on printed text consistent with the presentation of the remaining nineteen sections which are based on manuscript sources.[1] Second, the footnote markers in the printed text consist in two separate series. The first series, formed by superscript letters in one alphabetical sequence throughout the two sections, represent markers for textual notes. The second series, formed by symbols (for instance * and †) in separate sequences on each page, represent markers for cross-references. This distinction reflects Bentham's practice on his manuscripts. In the present text, the two sequences have been combined into a single sequence, formed by superscript letters, with a separate series for each page of text. Third, the symbols and superscript letters placed inside the appropriate punctuation are placed outside the punctuation. Fourth, double inverted commas indicating quotations are replaced with single inverted commas. Fifth, the heading 'CHAP. XVII' which appears above the title of §1, and the text 'INTROD. CH. XVII.' which appears at the top of the margin of each page, have been suppressed. Sixth, Bentham's square brackets are replaced with braces. Seventh, the original running headings, which consisted in the title of the Chapter on both recto and verso pages, have been replaced with the appropriate Section title on the recto page. Otherwise, editorial apparatus has been confined to the use of square brackets to indicate editorially inserted words or numerals: in these cases, where text has been excluded, the original reading is indicated in an editorial footnote.

The Manuscripts

The remainder of the work, namely §§3–21 and Appendices A–F, have been reconstructed from Bentham's manuscripts. The bulk of the text is written on double sheets of foolscap (bifolia), although a significant amount is written on single sheets of foolscap and some appears on clipped sheets. The sheets are ruled with a wide margin and with a double line at the top, where Bentham inserted the main heading. At the top of the margin he added a subheading, and occasionally more than one. At this time,

[1] Bentham himself authorized this change for the second edition of *An Introduction to the Principles of Morals and Legislation* published in 1823, though his instructions were not followed: see 'Dicenda to Bowring', 9 July 1822, UC clxxiii. 81^{v}, and *An Introduction to the Principles of Morals and Legislation* (*CW*), Editorial Introduction, p. xliii & n. John Bowring (1792–1872), merchant, later radical MP, diplomat, and Bentham's literary executor, appears to have had some involvement in putting the second edition through the press: see ibid., p. xl. n.

Bentham was not in the habit of dating his text sheets. He wrote on both the rectos and versos of the text sheets, which he paginated consecutively with Arabic numerals. Many of the sheets bear more than one series of pagination. As he expanded the text, the previous series was often crossed through, and a new series added. He often divided his text with paragraph numbers using Arabic numerals, which he inserted above the relevant paragraph (to refer to these as paragraph numbers is convenient, if slightly misleading, in that one such number might represent a sequence of several paragraphs). He also often added marginal contents, that is short summaries of the subject-matter of the text, in the margin at the head of the relevant paragraph in the text. These marginal contents are reproduced in the margin of the present text. Once he had drafted a body of material corresponding to an intended section or other division of the text, it was Bentham's practice to transfer the marginal contents, with the appropriate page numbers of the text sheets, to other sheets of foolscap known as marginal contents sheets. These sheets are ruled into four columns with a double line at the top for headings. Very few such sheets survive, however, for this particular text. There survive a handful of sheets containing 'rudiments', often referred to by Bentham as 'brouillons'. These sheets, which contain general statements or positions, notes of ideas and themes for possible development, examples for illustration, and plans, are normally written on double sheets of foolscap, each sheet being ruled into four columns with a double line at the top for headings.

It has been editorial policy to reflect as far as possible the manuscript sources on which the texts in this volume are based, but without sacrifice thereby of clarity and sense. Bentham's spelling and capitalization have been retained in most instances, although editorial discretion has been exercised with regard to his punctuation, which is often inconsistent and sparse. Punctuation marks have been adjusted and supplied where clearly indicated by the sense, or required for the sake of clarity, but not in cases where this might involve a dubious interpretation of the meaning. The words and phrases underlined by Bentham for emphasis have been rendered in italics, as have all foreign words and phrases, some of which Bentham underlined and some of which he did not.

The manuscripts contain many additions (either interlinear or marginal), deletions, and emendations which represent Bentham's later corrections to the text. The latest variant has usually been preferred, while original readings have not usually been indicated. Where there is no text corresponding to some part of a marginal contents sheet, the appropriate marginal content is reproduced in an editorial footnote. Square brackets in the text are reserved for editorially inserted words, while Bentham's original is, where appropriate, given in an editorial footnote. Thus, for instance, where Bentham has erred in identifying the location of a cross-reference, the correct reference has been supplied in square brackets, and the original indicated in an editorial footnote. Bentham's square brackets are replaced by braces. Round brackets are those supplied by Bentham. Vertical strokes indicate a gap or blank space in the manuscript. Bentham's own footnotes are indicated by superscript letters, and editorial footnotes by superscript numerals, with a separate sequence for each page of text.

The manuscripts have been left in a confused state. The work went through several stages of drafting, with each successive draft representing an expansion of the text, either through the addition of new sections, or the breaking up of a single section into two or more new sections. There is no particular difficulty in relation to the ordering of the sections at each of these stages, since the surviving plans appear to be an accurate guide to Bentham's intentions. However, there are significant difficulties in establishing the relevant text appertaining to each successive draft, and in determining the internal structure of several of the sections. The organization of the text has been ascertained by paying regard, where applicable, to the pagination of the text sheets, the numbering of the various sections, the numbering of the paragraphs, and of course the sense. The location of any related fragments has been indicated above.

In relation to paragraph numbers, the text is in large part based on what is referred to here as the 'principal draft'. The 'principal draft' carries a relatively coherent and continuous set of paragraph numbers, and these have been retained, albeit with some editorial intervention towards the end of the sequence. Other parts of the text, however, carry either discrete sequences of paragraph numbers, sometimes complete and sometimes incomplete, or no such numbers at all. Where these discrete sequences of paragraph numbers are complete, they have been retained, but otherwise they have been suppressed. Hence, the paragraph numbers of the 'principal draft' do not appear as a continuous sequence, but are often interrupted by discrete sequences beginning again at number 1, or by sequences which do not carry any paragraph numbers.

For the manuscripts used in this edition, reference should be made to the Table of Manuscripts below.

Table of Manuscripts

	MSS (UC lxxxviii)
§3	102, (104–5),[1] 90–1, 89, 92–100b, 102–3
§4	229–37b
§5	238–9
§6	241–6
§7	256–64
§8	212–19, 221, 220, 222–6
§9	265
§10	267
§11	266, 268–79
§12	181, 201, 183, 182,[2] 183–4, 188–200b, 202–11, 210
§13	280–97
§14	298–301
§15	302–3
§16	304–19, 331–2
§17	333–6, 337a, 338, 337a, (337c),[3] 339–40a
§18	342–3
§19	84–7
§20	351, 353–60
§21	361–71
Appendix A. §2	82–4
Appendix B. §7	248–9b, 251–5
Appendix C. Ch. 12,	
§1	163
§2	165–8
§3	169–77
Appendix D. §16	320–5
Appendix E. §3	117, 106–8
§4	109a–13, 112, 114, 113, 114–15, 114, 116
§5	——
§6	119, 118, 120–9, 128, 130–6
§7	143–4, 147–8, 150–1
Appendix F	326–30

[1] i.e. footnote [a] at pp. 24–5 below.
[2] i.e. footnote [b] at pp. 116–17 below.
[3] i.e. footnote [a] at pp. 194–5 below.

OF THE
LIMITS
OF THE
PENAL BRANCH
OF
JURISPRUDENCE

§1. *Limits between private ethics and the art of legislation.*

1. So much for the division of offences in general.[1] Now an offence is an act prohibited, or (what comes to the same thing) an act of which the contrary is commanded, by the law: and what is it that the law can be employed in doing, besides prohibiting and commanding? It should seem then, according to this view of the matter, that were we to have settled what may be proper to be done with relation to offences, we should thereby have settled every thing that may be proper to be done in the way of law. Yet that branch which concerns the method of dealing with offences, and which is termed sometimes the *criminal*, sometimes the *penal*, branch, is universally understood to be but one out of two branches which compose the whole subject of the art of legislation; that which is termed the *civil* being the other. Between these two branches then, it is evident enough, there cannot but be a very intimate connection; so intimate is it indeed, that the limits between them are by no means easy to mark out. The case is the same in some degree between the whole business of legislation (civil and penal branches taken together) and that of private ethics. Of these several limits however it will be in a manner necessary to exhibit some idea: lest, on the one hand, we should seem to leave any part of the subject that *does* belong to us untouched, or, on the other hand, to deviate on any side into a track which does *not* belong to us. Use of this chapter.

In the course of this enquiry, that part of it I mean which concerns the limits between the civil and the penal branch of law, it will be necessary to settle a number of points, of which the connection with the main question might not at first sight be suspected. To ascertain what sort of a thing *a* law is; what the *parts* are that are to be found in it; what it must contain in order to be *compleat*; what the connection is between that part of a body of laws which belongs to the subject of *procedure* and the rest of the law at large:—All these, it will be seen, are so many problems, which must be solved before any satisfactory answer can be given to the main question above mentioned.

Nor is this their only use: for it is evident enough, that the notion of a compleat law must first be fixed, before the legislator can in any case know what it is he has to do, or when his work is done.

[1] See *An Introduction to the Principles of Morals and Legislation*, ed. J. H. Burns and H. L. A. Hart, London, 1970 (*CW*), Ch. XVI, pp. 187–280. For the provenance of the present edition as Ch. XVII of this work see the Editorial Introduction, pp. 000 above.

Ethics in general, what.

2. Ethics at large may be defined, the art of directing men's actions to the production of the greatest possible quantity of happiness, on the part of those whose interest is in view.

Private ethics.

3. What then are the actions which it can be in a man's power to direct? They must be either his own actions, or those of other agents. Ethics, in as far as it is the art of directing a man's own actions, may be stiled the *art of self-government*, or *private ethics*.

The art of government: that is, of legislation and administration.

4. What other agents then are there, which, at the same time that they are under the influence of man's direction, are susceptible of happiness? They are of two sorts: 1. Other human beings who are stiled persons. 2. Other animals, which, on account of their interests having been neglected by the insensibility of the ancient jurists, stand degraded into the class of *things*.[a] As to other

Interests of the inferior animals improperly neglected in legislation.

[a] Under the Gentoo and Mahometan religions, the interests of the rest of the animal creation seem to have met with some attention. Why have they not, universally, with as much as those of human creatures, allowance made for the difference in point of sensibility? Because the laws that are have been the work of mutual fear; a sentiment which the less rational animals have not had the same means as man has of turning to account. Why *ought* they not? No reason can be given. If the being eaten were all, there is very good reason why we should be suffered to eat such of them as we like to eat: we are the better for it, and they are never the worse. They have none of those long-protracted anticipations of future misery which we have. The death they suffer in our hands commonly is, and always may be, a speedier, and by that means a less painful one, than that which would await them in the inevitable course of nature. If the being killed were all, there is very good reason why we should be suffered to kill such as molest us: we should be the worse for their living, and they are never the worse for being dead. But is there any reason why we should be suffered to torment them? Not any that I can see. Are there any why we should *not* be suffered to torment them? Yes, several. See B. I. tit. {Cruelty to animals.}[1] The day has been, I grieve to say in many places it is not yet past, in which the greater part of the species, under the denomination of slaves, have been treated by the law exactly upon the same footing as, in England for example, the inferior races of animals are still. The day *may* come, when the rest of the animal creation may acquire those rights which never could have been withholden from them but by the hand of tyranny. The French have already discovered that the blackness of the skin is no reason why a human being should be abandoned without redress to the caprice of a tormentor.[a] It may come one day to be recognized, that the number of the legs, the

[a] See Lewis XIVth's Code Noir.[2]

---

[1] The cross-reference is to Bentham's projected penal code, to which the present text was intended to form part of the introduction: see the Editorial Introduction, pp. xi–xii above.

[2] Louis XIV (1638–1715), King of France from 1643. See 'Edit du Roi, Touchant la Police des Isles de l'Amérique Françoise. Du mois de Mars 1685. Régistré au Conseil souverain de S. Domingue, le 6 Mai 1687', pp. 28–58, in *Le Code Noir, ou recueil des reglemens rendus jusqu'à présent. Concernant le Gouvernement, l'Administration de la Justice, la Police, la Discipline & le Commerce des Negres dans les Colonies Françoises. Et les Conseils & Compagnies établis à ce sujet*, Paris, 1767. The code regulated the status of slaves in the French West Indies. It forbade the torture and killing of slaves by their masters, and gave

human beings, the art of directing their actions to the above end is what we mean, or at least the only thing which, upon the principle of utility, we *ought* to mean, by the art of government: which, in as far as the measures it displays itself in are of a permanent nature, is generally distinguished by the name of *legislation:* as it is by that of *administration*, when they are of a temporary nature, determined by the occurrences of the day.

Art of education.

5. Now human creatures, considered with respect to the maturity of their faculties, are either in an *adult*, or in a *non-adult* state. The art of government, in as far as it concerns the direction of the actions of persons in a non-adult state, may be termed the art of *education*. In as far as this business is entrusted with those who, in virtue of some private relationship, are in the main the best disposed to take upon them, and the best able to discharge, this office, it may be termed the art of *private education:* in as far as it is exercised by those whose province it is to superintend the conduct of the whole community, it may be termed the art of *public education*.

Ethics exhibits the rules of, 1. Prudence. 2. Probity. 3. Beneficence.

6. As to ethics in general, a man's happiness will depend, in the first place, upon such parts of his behaviour as none but himself are interested in; in the next place, upon such parts of it as may affect the happiness of those about him. In as far as his happiness depends upon the first-mentioned part of his behaviour, it is said to depend upon his *duty to himself.* Ethics then, in as far as it is the art of directing a man's actions in this respect, may be termed the art of discharging one's duty to one's self: and the quality which a man manifests by the discharge of this branch of duty (if duty it is to be called) is that of *prudence*. In as far as his happiness, and that of any other person or persons whose interests are considered, depends upon such parts of his behaviour as may affect the interests of those about him, it may be said to depend upon his *duty to others*; or, to use a phrase now somewhat antiquated, his *duty to his neighbour*. Ethics then, in as far as it is the art of directing a man's actions in this respect, may be termed the art of

villosity of the skin, or the termination of the *os sacrum*, are reasons equally insufficient for abandoning a sensitive being to the same fate? What else is it that should trace the insuperable line? Is it the faculty of reason, or, perhaps, the faculty of discourse? But a full-grown horse, or dog, is beyond comparison a more rational, as well as a more conversible animal, than an infant of a day, or a week, or even a month, old. But suppose the case were otherwise, what would it avail? the question is not, Can they *reason?* nor, Can they *talk?* but, Can they *suffer?*

---

the royal authorities the power to protect slaves from maltreatment. It also provided that a slave freed in the West Indies should become a French citizen without naturalization.

discharging one's duty to one's neighbour. Now the happiness of one's neighbour may be consulted in two ways: 1. In a negative way, by forbearing to diminish it. 2. In a positive way, by studying to encrease it. A man's duty to his neighbour is accordingly partly negative and partly positive: to discharge the negative branch of it, is *probity:* to discharge the positive branch, *beneficence.*

Probity and beneficence how they connect with prudence.

7. It may here be asked, How it is that upon the principle of private ethics, legislation and religion out of the question, a man's happiness depends upon such parts of his conduct as affect, immediately at least, the happiness of no one but himself: this is as much as to ask, What motives (independent of such as legislation and religion may chance to furnish) can one man have to consult the happiness of another? by what motives, or, which comes to the same thing, by what obligations, can he be bound to obey the dictates of *probity* and *beneficence?* In answer to this, it cannot but be admitted, that the only interests which a man at all times and upon all occasions is sure to find *adequate* motives for consulting, are his own. Notwithstanding this, there are no occasions in which a man has not some motives for consulting the happiness of other men. In the first place, he has, on all occasions, the purely social motive of sympathy or benevolence: in the next place, he has, on most occasions, the semi-social motives of love of amity and love of reputation. The motive of sympathy will act upon him with more or less effect, according to the *bias* of his sensibility:[a] the two other motives, according to a variety of circumstances, principally according to the strength of his intellectual powers, the firmness and steadiness of his mind, the quantum of his moral sensibility, and the characters of the people he has to deal with.

Every act which is a proper object of ethics is not of legislation.

8. Now private ethics has happiness for its end: and legislation can have no other. Private ethics concerns every member, that is, the happiness and the actions of every member, of any community that can be proposed; and legislation can concern no more. Thus far, then, private ethics and the art of legislation go hand in hand. The end they have, or ought to have, in view, is of the same nature. The persons whose happiness they ought to have in view, as also the persons whose conduct they ought to be occupied in directing, are precisely the same. The very acts they ought to be conversant about, are even in a *great measure* the same. Where then lies the

[a] Ch. vi. {Sensibility} iii.[1]

[1] See *An Introduction to the Principles of Morals and Legislation* (*CW*), Ch. VI, para. 3, p. 51.

difference? In that the acts which they ought to be conversant about, though in a great measure, are not *perfectly and throughout* the same. There is no case in which a private man ought not to direct his own conduct to the production of his own happiness, and of that of his fellow-creatures: but there are cases in which the legislator ought not (in a direct way at least, and by means of punishment applied immediately to particular *individual* acts) to attempt to direct the conduct of the several other members of the community. Every act which promises to be beneficial upon the whole to the community (himself included) each individual ought to perform of himself: but it is not every such act that the legislator ought to compel him to perform. Every act which promises to be pernicious upon the whole to the community (himself included) each individual ought to abstain from of himself: but it is not every such act that the legislator ought to compel him to abstain from.

The limits between the provinces of private ethics and legislation, marked out by the cases unmeet for punishment.

9. Where then is the line to be drawn?—We shall not have far to seek for it. The business is to give an idea of the cases in which ethics ought, and in which legislation ought not (in a direct manner at least) to interfere. If legislation interferes in a direct manner, it must be by punishment.[a] Now the cases in which punishment, meaning the punishment of the political sanction, ought not to be inflicted, have been already stated.[b] If then there be any of these cases in which, although legislation ought not, private ethics does or ought to interfere, these cases will serve to point out the limits between the two arts or branches of science. These cases, it may be remembered, are of four sorts: 1. Where punishment would be groundless. 2. Where it would be inefficacious. 3. Where it would be unprofitable. 4. Where it would be needless. Let us look over all these cases, and see whether in any of them there is a room for the interference of private ethics, at the same time that there is none for the direct interference of legislation.

[a] I say nothing in this place of reward: because it is only in a few extraordinary cases that it can be applied, and because even where it is applied, it may be doubted, perhaps, whether the application of it can, properly speaking, be termed an act of legislation. See infra, §3.[1]

[b] Ch. xiii. {Cases unmeet.}[2]

---

[1] See §13, pp. 142–6, and especially p. 145 & n., below. When he composed this passage, Bentham envisaged that the Chapter would contain five sections (see pp. 21–3 below), of which the third would discuss the parts of a law (i.e. the material that constitutes §§ 3–15 in the present edition).

[2] See *An Introduction to the Principles of Morals and Legislation* (*CW*), Ch. XIII, pp. 158–64.

1. Neither ought to apply where punishment is *groundless.*

10. 1. First then, as to the cases where punishment would be *groundless.* In these cases it is evident, that the restrictive interference of ethics would be groundless too. It is because, upon the whole, there is no evil in the act, that legislation ought not to endeavour to prevent it. No more, for the same reason, ought private ethics.

2. How far private ethics can apply in the cases where punishment would be *inefficacious.*

11. 2. As to the cases in which punishment would be *inefficacious.* These, we may observe, may be divided into two sets or classes. The first do not depend at all upon the nature of the act: they turn only upon a defect in the timing of the punishment. The punishment in question is no more than what, for any thing that appears, ought to have been applied to the act in question. It ought, however, to have been applied at a different time; viz. not till after it had been properly denounced. These are the cases of an *ex-post-facto* law; of a judicial sentence beyond the law; and of a law not sufficiently promulgated. The acts here in question then might, for any thing that appears, come properly under the department even of coercive legislation: of course do they under that of private ethics. As to the other set of cases, in which punishment would be inefficacious; neither do these depend upon the nature of the act, that is, of the *sort* of act: they turn only upon some extraneous *circumstances,* with which an act of *any* sort may chance to be accompanied. These, however, are of such a nature as not only to exclude the application of legal punishment, but in general to leave little room for the influence of private ethics. These are the cases where the will could not be deterred from any act, even by the extraordinary force of artificial punishment: as in the cases of extreme infancy, insanity, and perfect intoxication: of course, therefore, it could not by such slender and precarious force as could be applied by private ethics. The case is in this respect the same, under the circumstances of unintentionality with respect to the event of the action, unconsciousness with regard to the circumstances, and mis-supposal with regard to the existence of circumstances which have not existed; as also where the force, even of extraordinary punishment, is rendered inoperative by the superior force of a physical danger or threatened mischief. It is evident, that in these cases, if the thunders of the law prove impotent, the whispers of simple morality can have but little influence.

How far, where it would be unprofitable.

12. 3. As to the cases where punishment would be *unprofitable.* These are the cases which constitute the great field for the exclusive interference of private ethics. When a punishment is unprofitable, or in other words too expensive, it is because the evil of the punishment exceeds that of the offence. Now the evil of the punishment, we may remember,[a] is distinguishable into four branches: 1. The evil of coercion, including constraint or restraint, according as the act commanded is of the positive kind or the negative. 2. The evil of apprehension. 3. The evil of sufferance. 4. The derivative evils resulting to persons in *connection* with those by whom the three above-mentioned original evils are sustained. Now with respect to those original evils, the persons who lie exposed to them may be two very different sets of persons. In the first place, persons who may have actually committed, or been prompted to commit, the acts really meant to be prohibited. In the next place, persons who may have performed, or been prompted to perform, such other acts as they fear may be in danger of being involved in the punishment designed only for the former. But of these two sets of acts, it is the former only that are pernicious: it is, therefore, the former only that it can be the business of private ethics to endeavour to prevent. The latter being by the supposition not mischievous, to prevent them is what it can no more be the business of ethics to endeavour at, than of legislation. It remains to shew how it may happen, that there should be acts really pernicious, which, although they may very properly come under the censure of private ethics, may yet be no fit objects for the legislator to controul.

Which it may be, 1. Although confined to the guilty.

13. Punishment then, as applied to delinquency, may be unprofitable in both or either of two ways: 1. By the expence it would amount to, even supposing the application of it to be confined altogether to delinquency: 2. By the danger there may be of its involving the innocent in the fate designed only for the guilty. First then, with regard to the cases in which the expence of the punishment, as applied to the guilty, would outweigh the profit to be made by it. These cases, it is evident, depend upon a certain proportion between the evil of the punishment and the evil of the offence. Now were the offence of such a nature, that a punishment which, in point of *magnitude*, should but just exceed the profit of it, would be sufficient to prevent it, it might be rather difficult perhaps to find an instance in which such punishment would clearly appear to be unprofitable. But the fact is, there are many cases in which a punishment, in order to have any chance of being efficacious, must, in point of magnitude, be raised a great deal above that level. Thus it is, wherever the danger of detection is, or, what comes to

[a] See ch. xiii. {Cases unmeet.} §iv.[1]

[1] See ibid., Ch. XIII, §iv, para. 14, p. 163.

the same thing, is likely to appear to be, so small, as to make the punishment appear in a high degree uncertain. In this case it is necessary, as has been shewn,[a] if punishment be at all applied, to raise it in point of magnitude as much as it falls short in point of certainty. It is evident, however, that all this can be but guess-work: and that the effect of such a proportion will be rendered precarious, by a variety of circumstances: by the want of sufficient promulgation on the part of the law:[b] by the particular circumstances of the temptation:[c] and by the circumstances influencing the sensibility of the several individuals who are exposed to it.[d] Let the *seducing* motives be strong, the offence then will at any rate be frequently committed. Now and then indeed, owing to a coincidence of circumstances more or less extraordinary, it will be detected, and by that means punished. But for the purpose of example, which is the principal one, an act of punishment, considered in itself, is of no use: what use it can be of, depends altogether upon the expectation it raises of similar punishment, in future cases of similar delinquency. But this future punishment, it is evident, must always depend upon detection. If then the want of detection is such as must in general (especially to eyes fascinated by the force of the seducing motives) appear too improbable to be reckoned upon, the punishment, though it should be inflicted, may come to be of no use. Here then will be two opposite evils running on at the same time, yet neither of them reducing the quantum of the other: the evil of the disease, and the evil of the painful and inefficacious remedy. It seems to be partly owing to some such considerations, that fornication, for example, or the illicit commerce between the sexes, has commonly either gone altogether unpunished, or been punished in a degree inferior to that in which, on other accounts, legislators might have been disposed to punish it.

2. By enveloping the innocent.

14. Secondly, with regard to the cases in which political punishment, as applied to delinquency, may be unprofitable, in virtue of the danger there may be of its involving the innocent in the fate designed only for the guilty. Whence should this danger then arise? From the difficulty there may be of fixing the idea of the guilty

[a] Ch. xiv. {Proportion} xviii. Rule 7.[1]
[b] Ch. xiii. {Cases unmeet} §iii.[2] Append. tit. {Promulgation.}[3]
[c] Ch. xi. {Disposition} xxxv. &c.[4]
[d] Ch. vi. {Sensibility.}[5]

[1] See ibid., Ch. XIV, para. 18, p. 170.
[2] See ibid., Ch. XIII, §iii, para. 8, p. 160.
[3] This was one of several Appendices intended for Bentham's projected penal code: see the Editorial Introduction, pp. xi–xii above.
[4] See *An Introduction to the Principles of Morals and Legislation* (*CW*), Ch. XI, paras. 35–8, pp. 137–8.
[5] See ibid., Ch. VI, pp. 51–73.

action: that is, of subjecting it to such a definition as shall be clear and precise enough to guard effectually against misapplication. This difficulty may arise from either of two sources: the one permanent, to wit, the nature of the *actions* themselves: the other occasional, I mean the qualities of the *men* who may have to deal with those actions in the way of government. In as far as it arises from the latter of these sources, it may depend partly upon the use which the *legislator* may be *able* to make of language; partly upon the use which, according to the apprehension of the legislator, the *judge* may be *disposed* to make of it. As far as legislation is concerned, it will depend upon the degree of perfection to which the arts of language may have been carried, in the first place, in the nation in general; in the next place, by the *legislator* in particular. It is to a sense of this difficulty, as it should seem, that we may attribute the caution with which most legislators have abstained from subjecting to censure, on the part of the law, such actions as come under the notion of rudeness, for example, or treachery, or ingratitude. The attempt to bring acts of so vague and questionable a nature under the controul of law, will argue either a very immature age, in which the difficulties, which give birth to that danger are not descried; or a very enlightened age, in which they are overcome.[a]

Legislation how far necessary for the enforcement of the dictates of *prudence*.

15. For the sake of obtaining the clearer idea of the limits between the art of legislation and private ethics, it may now be time to call to mind the distinctions above established with regard to ethics in general. The degree in which private ethics stands in need of the assistance of legislation, is different in the three branches of duty above distinguished. Of the rules of moral duty, those which seem to stand least in need of the assistance of legislation, are the rules of *prudence*. It can only be through some defect on the part of the understanding, if a man be ever deficient in point of duty to himself. If he does wrong, there is nothing else that it can be owing to but either some *inadvertence*[b] or some *mis-supposal*,[b] with regard to the circumstances on which his happiness depends. It is a

[a] In certain countries, in which the voice of the people has a more especial controul over the hand of the legislator, nothing can exceed the dread which they are under of seeing any effectual provision made against the offences which come under the head of *defamation*, particularly that branch of it which may be stiled the *political*. This dread seems to depend partly upon the apprehension they may think it prudent to entertain of a defect in point of ability or integrity on the part of the legislator, partly upon a similar apprehension of a defect in point of integrity on the part of the judge.

[b] See ch. ix. {Consciousness.}[1]

[1] See ibid., Ch. IX, paras. 6–13, pp. 90–3.

standing topic of complaint, that a man knows too little of himself. Be it so: but is it so certain that the legislator must know more?[a] [b] It is plain, that of individuals the legislator can know nothing: concerning those points of conduct which depend upon the particular circumstances of each individual, it is plain, therefore, that he can determine nothing to advantage. It is only with respect to those broad lines of conduct in which all persons, or very large and permanent descriptions of persons, may be in a way to engage, that he can have any pretence for interfering; and even here the propriety of his interference will, in most instances, lie very open to dispute. At any rate, he must never expect to produce a perfect compliance by the mere force of the sanction of which he is himself the author. All he can hope to do, is to encrease the efficacy of private ethics, by giving strength and direction to the influence of the moral sanction. With what chance of success, for example, would a legislator go about to extirpate drunkenness and fornication, by dint of legal punishment? Not all the tortures which ingenuity could invent would compass it: and, before he had made any progress worth regarding, such a mass of evil would be produced by the punishment, as would exceed, a thousand-fold, the utmost possible mischief of the offence. The great difficulty would be in the procuring evidence; an object which could not be attempted, with any probability of success, without spreading dismay through every family,[c] tearing the bonds of sympathy asunder,[d] and rooting out the influence of all the social motives. All that he can do then, against offences of this nature, with any prospect of advantage, in the way of direct legislation, is to subject them, in cases of notoriety, to a slight censure, so as thereby to cover them with a slight shade of artificial disrepute.

—Apt to go too far in this respect.

16. It may be observed, that with regard to this branch of duty, legislators have, in general, been disposed to carry their inter-

[a] On occasions like this, the legislator should never lose sight of the well-known story of the oculist and the sot. A countryman who had hurt his eyes by drinking, went to a celebrated oculist for advice. He found him at table, with a glass of wine before him. 'You must leave off drinking,' said the oculist. 'How so,' says the countryman? '*You* don't, and yet methinks your own eyes are none of the best.'—'That's very true, friend,' replied the oculist: 'but you are to know, I love my bottle better than my eyes.'

[b] Ch. xvi. {Division} lii.[1]

[c] Evil of apprehension: third branch of the evil of a punishment. Ch. xiii. §iv.[2]

[d] Derivative evils: fourth branch of the evil of a punishment. Ib.

---

[1] Bentham's cross-reference to ibid., Ch. XVI, para. 52, pp. 255–7, appears to be a slip, since that paragraph deals with 'Offences touching the condition of a husband'.

[2] See ibid., Ch. XIII, §iv, para. 14, p. 163.

ference full as far as is expedient. The great difficulty here is, to persuade them to confine themselves within bounds. A thousand little passions and prejudices have led them to narrow the liberty of the subject in this line, in cases in which the punishment is either attended with no profit at all, or with none that will make up for the expence.

17. The mischief of this sort of interference is more particularly conspicuous in the article of religion. The reasoning, in this case, is of the following stamp. There are certain errors, in matters of belief, to which all mankind are prone: and for these errors in judgment, it is the determination of a Being of infinite benevolence, to punish them with an infinity of torments. But from these errors the legislator himself is necessarily free: for the men, who happen to be at hand for him to consult with, being men perfectly enlightened, unfettered, and unbiassed, have such advantages over all the rest of the world, that when they sit down to enquire out the truth relative to points so plain and so familiar as those in question, they cannot fail to find it. This being the case, when the sovereign sees his people ready to plunge headlong into an abyss of fire, shall he not stretch out a hand to save them? Such, for example, seems to have been the train of reasoning, and such the motives, which led Lewis the XIVth into those coercive measures which he took for the conversion of heretics, and the confirmation of true believers.[1] The ground-work, pure sympathy and loving-kindness: the superstructure, all the miseries which the most determined malevolence could have devised.[a] But of this more fully in another place.[b]

—Particularly in matters of religion.

[a] I do not mean but that other motives of a less social nature might have introduced themselves, and probably, in point of fact, did introduce themselves, in the progress of the enterprize. But in point of possibility, the motive above-mentioned, when accompanied with such a thread of reasoning, is sufficient, without any other, to account for all the effects above alluded to. If any others interfere, their interference, how natural soever, may be looked upon as an accidental and inessential circumstance, not necessary to the production of the effect. Sympathy, a concern for the danger they appear to be exposed to, gives birth to the wish of freeing them from it: that wish shews itself in the shape of a command: this command produces disobedience: disobedience on the one part, produces disappointment on the other: the pain of disappointment produces ill-will towards those who are the authors of it. The affections will often make this progress in less time than it would take to describe it. The sentiment of wounded pride, and other modifications of the love of reputation and the love of power, add fewel to the flame. A kind of revenge exasperates the severities of coercive policy.

[b] See B. I. tit. {Self-regarding offences.}[2]

[1] The Revocation of the Edict of Nantes by Louis XIV in October 1685 deprived the Huguenots, or French Protestants, of all civil and religious rights.

[2] A cross-reference to Bentham's projected penal code.

—How far necessary for the enforcement of the dictates of probity.

18. The rules of *probity* are those, which in point of expediency stand most in need of assistance on the part of the legislator, and in which, in point of fact, his interference has been most extensive. There are few cases in which it *would* be expedient to punish a man for hurting *himself*: but there are few cases, if any, in which it would *not* be expedient to punish a man for injuring his neighbour. With regard to that branch of probity which is opposed to offences against property, private ethics depends in a manner for its very existence upon legislation. Legislation must first determine what things are to be regarded as each man's property, before the general rules of ethics, on this head, can have any particular application. The case is the same with regard to offences against the state. Without legislation there would be no such thing as a *state:* no particular persons invested with powers to be exercised for the benefit of the rest. It is plain, therefore, that in this branch the interference of the legislator cannot any where be dispensed with. We must first know what are the dictates of legislation, before we can know what are the dictates of private ethics.[a]

—of the dictates of beneficence.

19. As to the rules of beneficence, these, as far as concerns matters of detail, must necessarily be abandoned in great measure to the jurisdiction of private ethics. In many cases the beneficial quality of the act depends essentially upon the disposition of the agent; that is, upon the motives by which he appears to have been prompted to perform it: upon their belonging to the head of sympathy, love of amity, or love of reputation; and not to any head of self-regarding motives, brought into play by the force of political constraint: in a word, upon their being such as denominate his conduct *free* and *voluntary*, according to one of the many senses given to those ambiguous expressions.[b] The limits of the

[a] But suppose the dictates of legislation *are* not what they *ought to be:* what are then, or (what in this case comes to the same thing) what ought to be, the dictates of private ethics? Do they coincide with the dictates of legislation, or do they oppose them, or do they remain neuter? a very interesting question this, but one that belongs not to the present subject. It belongs exclusively to that of private ethics. Principles which may lead to the solution of it may be seen in A Fragment on Government, p. 150. Lond. 1776.[1]

[b] If we may believe M. Voltaire,[*a*] there was a time when the French ladies who

[*a*] Quest. sur l'Encyclop. Tom. 7. art. Impuissance.[2]

[1] See *A Comment on the Commentaries and A Fragment on Government*, ed. J.H. Burns and H.L.A. Hart, London, 1977 (*CW*), 'A Fragment on Government', Ch. IV, paras. 21–41, pp. 483–92. Bentham's reference is to the first edition published in 1776.

[2] See *Questions sur l'encyclopédie, distribuées en forme de dictionnaire. Par des amateurs. Seconde edition,* 9 vols., [n.p.], 1771–2, vii. 167: 'Les femmes eurent la liberté de présenter requête pour être *embesognées*, c'était le mot dont elles se servaient dans notre gaulois; car d'ailleurs on instruisait les causes en latin.'

law on this head seem, however, to be capable of being extended a good deal farther than they seem ever to have been extended hitherto. In particular, in cases where the person is in danger, why should it not be made the duty of every man to save another from mischief, when it can be done without prejudicing himself, as well as to abstain from bringing it on him? This accordingly is the idea pursued in the body of the work.[a]

Difference between private ethics and the art of legislation recapitulated.

20. To conclude this section, let us recapitulate and bring to a point the difference between private ethics, considered as an art or science, on the one hand, and that branch of jurisprudence which contains the art or science of legislation, on the other. Private ethics teaches how each man may dispose himself to pursue the course most conducive to his own happiness, by means of such motives as offer of themselves: the art of legislation (which may be considered as one branch of the science of jurisprudence) teaches how a multitude of men, composing a community, may be disposed to pursue that course which upon the whole is the most conducive to the happiness of the whole community, by means of motives to be applied by the legislator.

We come now to exhibit the limits between penal and civil jurisprudence. For this purpose it may be of use to give a distinct though summary view of the principal branches into which jurisprudence, considered in its utmost extent, is wont to be divided.[1]

thought themselves neglected by their husbands, used to petition *pour être [embesognées]:*[2] the technical word, which, he says, was appropriated to this purpose. These sort of law-proceedings seem not very well calculated to answer the design: accordingly we hear nothing of them now-a-days. The French ladies of the present age seem to be under no such difficulties.

[a] A woman's head-dress catches fire: water is at hand: a man, instead of assisting to quench the fire, looks on, and laughs at it. A drunken man, falling with his face downwards into a puddle, is in danger of suffocation: lifting his head a little on one side would save him: another man sees this and lets him lie. A quantity of gunpowder lies scattered about a room: a man is going into it with a lighted candle: another, knowing this, lets him go in without warning. Who is there that in any of these cases would think punishment misapplied?

[1] For the original continuation of the text see Appendix A, pp. 237–41 below, and §19, pp. 201–6 below. For further details see the Editorial Introduction, p. xxix above.

[2] *An Introduction to the Principles of Morals and Legislation 'embesoignces'.*

§2. *Jurisprudence, its branches.*

Jurisprudence, expository—censorial.

21. Jurisprudence is a fictitious entity: nor can any meaning be found for the word, but by placing it in company with some word that shall be significative of a real entity. To know what is meant by jurisprudence, we must know, for example, what is meant by a book of jurisprudence. A book of jurisprudence can have but one or the other of two objects: 1. To ascertain what the *law*[a] is: 2. To ascertain what it ought to be. In the former case it may be stiled a book of *expository* jurisprudence; in the latter, a book of *censorial* jurisprudence; or, in other words, a book on the *art of legislation*.

Expository jurisprudence, authoritative—unauthoritative.

22. A book of expository jurisprudence is either *authoritative* or *unauthoritative*. It is stiled authoritative, when it is composed by him who, by representing the state of the law to be so and so, causeth it so to be; that is, of the legislator himself: unauthoritative, when it is the work of any other person at large.

Sources of the distinctions yet remaining.

23. Now *law*, or *the law*, taken indefinitely, is an abstract and collective term; which, when it means any thing, can mean neither more nor less than the sum total of a number of individual laws taken together.[b] It follows, that of whatever other modifications the subject of a book of jurisprudence is susceptible, they must all of them be taken from some circumstance or other of which such individual laws, or the assemblages into which they may be sorted, are susceptible. The circumstances that have given rise to the principal branches of jurisprudence we are wont to hear of, seem to be as follow: 1. The *extent* of the laws in question in point of dominion. 2. The *political quality* of the persons whose conduct they undertake to regulate. 3. The *time* of their being in force.

[a] The word *law* itself, which stands so much in need of a definition, must wait for it awhile, (see §3):[1] for there is no doing every thing at once. In the mean time every reader will understand it according to the notion he has been accustomed to annex to it.

[b] In most of the European languages there are two different words for distinguishing the abstract and the concrete senses of the word *law:* which words are so wide asunder as not even to have any etymological affinity. In Latin, for example, there is *lex* for the concrete sense, *jus* for the abstract: in Italian, *legge* and *diritto:* in French, *loi* and *droit:* in Spanish, *ley* and *derecho:* in German, *gesetz* and *recht*. The English is at present destitute of this advantage.

In the Anglo-Saxon, besides *lage*, and several other words, for the concrete sense, there was the word *right*, answering to the German *recht*, for the abstract; as may be seen in the compound *folc-right*, and in other instances. But the word *right* having long ago lost this sense, the modern English no longer possesses this advantage.

---

[1] See pp. 24–5 below.

4. The manner in which they are *expressed.* 5. The concern which they have with the article of *punishment.*

24. In the first place, in point of extent, what is delivered concerning the laws in question, may have reference either to the laws of such or such a nation or nations in particular, or to the laws of all nations whatsoever: in the first case, the book may be said to relate to *local*, in the other, to *universal, jurisprudence* Jurisprudence, local—universal.

Now of the infinite variety of nations there are upon the earth, there are no two which agree exactly in their laws: certainly not in the whole; perhaps not even in any single article: and let them agree to-day, they would disagree to-morrow. This is evident enough with regard to the *substance* of the laws: and it would be still more extraordinary if they agreed in point of *form*; that is, if they were conceived in precisely the same strings of words. What is more, as the languages of nations are commonly different, as well as their laws, it is seldom that, strictly speaking, they have so much as a single *word* in common. However, among the words that are appropriated to the subject of law, there are some that in all languages are pretty exactly correspondent to one another: which comes to the same thing nearly as if they were the same. Of this stamp, for example, are those which correspond to the words *power, right, obligation, liberty,* and many others.

It follows, that if there are any books which can, properly speaking, be stiled books of universal jurisprudence, they must be looked for within very narrow limits. Among such as are expository, there can be none that are authoritative: nor even, as far as the *substance* of the laws is concerned, any that are unauthoritative. To be susceptible of an universal application, all that a book of the expository kind can have to treat of, is the import of words: to be, strictly speaking, universal, it must confine itself to terminology. Accordingly the definitions which there has been occasion here and there to intersperse in the course of the present work, and particularly the definition hereafter given of the word *law,* may be considered as matter belonging to the head of universal jurisprudence. Thus far in strictness of speech: though in point of usage, where a man, in laying down what he apprehends to be the law, extends his views to a few of the nations with which his own is most connected, it is common enough to consider what he writes as relating to universal jurisprudence.

It is in the censorial line that there is the greatest room for disquisitions that apply to the circumstances of all nations alike: and in this line what regards the substance of the laws in question is as susceptible of an universal application, as what regards the words. That the laws of all nations, or even of any two nations, should coincide in all points, would be as ineligible as it is impossible: some leading points, however, there seem to be, in respect of which the laws of all civilized nations might, without inconvenience, be the same. To mark out some of these points will, as far as it goes, be the business of the body of this work.[1]

—internal and international.

25. In the second place, with regard to the *political quality* of the persons whose conduct is the object of the law. These may, on any given occasion, be considered either as members of the same state, or as members of different states: in the first case, the law may be referred to the head of *internal*, in the second case to that of *international*[a] jurisprudence.

Now as to any transactions which may take place between individuals who are subjects of different states, these are regulated by the internal laws, and decided upon by the internal tribunals, of the one or the other of those states: the case is the same where the sovereign of the one has any immediate transactions with a private member of the other: the sovereign reducing himself, *pro re natâ*, to the condition of a private person, as often as he submits his cause to either tribunal; whether by claiming a benefit, or defending himself against a burthen. There remain then the mutual transactions between sovereigns, as such, for the subject of that branch of jurisprudence which may be properly and exclusively termed *international*.[b]

With what degree of propriety rules for the conduct of persons of this description can come under the appellation of *laws*, is a

[a] The word *international*, it must be acknowledged, is a new one; though, it is hoped, sufficiently analogous and intelligible. It is calculated to express, in a more significant way, the branch of law which goes commonly under the name of the *law of nations:* an appellation so uncharacteristic, that, were it nor for the force of custom, it would seem rather to refer to internal jurisprudence. The chancellor D'Aguesseau has already made, I find, a similar remark: he says, that what is commonly called *droit* des *gens*, ought rather to be termed *droit* entre *les gens.*[a]

[b] In the times of James I. of England,[2] and Philip III. of Spain,[3] certain merchants at London happened to have a claim upon Philip, which his

[a] Oeuvres, Tom. II. p. 337, Edit. 1773, 12mo.[4]

[1] i.e. of the projected penal code.

[2] James VI (1566–1625), King of Scotland from 1567, and as James I, King of England and Ireland from 1603.

[3] Philip III (1578–1621), King of Spain from 1598.

[4] Henri-François d'Aguesseau (1668–1751) was Chancellor of France 1717–18, 1720–2, 1727–50. See *Discours et œuvres mêlées de M. Le Chancelier d'Aguesseau*, 2 vols., Paris, 1771 (not 1773 as Bentham states), ii. 337: 'ce que l'on doit nommer proprement *le Droit de Gens* (*Jus Gentium*), le Droit des Nations, qu'il seroit peut-être encore mieux d'appeller *le Droit entre les Nations* (*Jus inter Gentes*)'.

question that must rest till the nature of the thing called *a law* shall have been more particularly unfolded.

It is evident enough, that international jurisprudence may, as well as internal, be censorial as well as expository, unauthoritative as well as authoritative.

26. Internal jurisprudence, again, may either concern all the members of a state indiscriminately, or such of them only as are connected in the way of residence, or otherwise, with a particular district. Jurisprudence is accordingly sometimes distinguished into *national* and *provincial*. But as the epithet *provincial* is hardly applicable to districts so small as many of those which have laws of their own are wont to be, such as towns, parishes, and manors; the term *local* (where universal jurisprudence is plainly out of the question) or the term *particular*, though this latter is not very characteristic, might either of them be more commodious.[a]

Internal jurisprudence, national and provincial, local or particular.

27. Thirdly, with respect to *time*. In a work of the expository kind, the laws that are in question may either be such as are still in force at the time when the book is writing, or such as have ceased to be in force. In the latter case the subject of it might be termed *antient*; in the former, *present* or *living* jurisprudence: that is, if the

Jurisprudence, ancient—living.

ambassador Gondemar[1] did not think fit to satisfy. They applied for counsel to Selden,[2] who advised them to sue the Spanish monarch in the court of King's Bench, and prosecute him to an outlawry. They did so: and the sheriffs of London were accordingly commanded, in the usual form, to take the body of the defendant Philip, wherever it was to be found within their bailywick. As to the sheriffs, Philip, we may believe, was in no great fear of them: but, what answered the same purpose, he happened on his part to have demands upon some other merchants, whom, so long as the outlawry remained in force, there was no proceeding against. Gondemar paid the money.[a] This was internal jurisprudence: if the dispute had been betwixt Philip and James himself, it would have been international.

[a] The term *municipal* seemed to answer the purpose very well, till it was taken by an English author of the first eminence, to signify internal law in general, in contradistinction to international law, and the imaginary law of nature.[3] It might still be used in this sense, without scruple, in any other language.

[a] Selden's Table-Talk, tit. LAW.[4]

[1] Diego Sarmiento de Acuña (1567–1626), conde de Gondomor, Spanish Ambassador to England 1613–18, 1619–22.

[2] John Selden (1584–1654), lawyer and scholar.

[3] Bentham presumably has in mind Sir William Blackstone (1723–80), first Vinerian Professor of English Law at the University of Oxford 1758–66, Justice of Common Pleas 1770, 1770–80, and Justice of King's Bench 1770. For Blackstone's definition and description of municipal law see *Commentaries on the Laws of England*, 4 vols., Oxford, 1765–9, i. 44–58.

[4] See *Table-Talk: being the Discourses of John Selden, Esq. Being His Sense of various Matters of Weight and high Consequence; relating especially to Religion and State*, London, 1689, no. LXXVII, p. 72.

substantive *jurisprudence*, and no other, must at any rate be employed, and that with an epithet in both cases. But the truth is, that a book of the former kind is rather a book of history than a book of jurisprudence; and, if the word *jurisprudence* be expressive of the subject, it is only with some such words as *history* or *antiquities* prefixed. And as the laws which are any where in question are supposed, if nothing appears to the contrary, to be those which are in force, no such epithet as that of *present* or *living* commonly appears.

Where a book is so circumstanced, that the laws which form the subject of it, though in force at the time of its being written, are in force no longer, that book is neither a book of living jurisprudence, nor a book on the history of jurisprudence: it is no longer the former, and it never was the latter. It is evident that, owing to the changes which from time to time must take place, in a greater or less degree, in every body of laws, every book of jurisprudence, which is of an expository nature, must, in the course of a few years, come to partake more or less of this condition.

The most common and most useful object of a history of jurisprudence, is to exhibit the circumstances that have attended the establishment of laws actually in force. But the exposition of the dead laws which have been superseded, is inseparably interwoven with that of the living ones which have superseded them. The great use of both these branches of *science*, is to furnish examples for the *art* of legislation.[a]

[a] Of what stamp are the works of Grotius, Puffendorf, and Burlamaqui?[1] Are they political or ethical, historical or juridical, expository or censorial?—Sometimes one thing, sometimes another: they seem hardly to have settled the matter with themselves. A defect this to which all books must almost unavoidably be liable, which take for their subject the pretended *law of nature:* an obscure phantom, which, in the imaginations of those who go in chace of it, points sometimes to *manners*, sometimes to *laws*; sometimes to what law *is*, sometimes to what it *ought* to be.[a] Montesquieu sets out upon the censorial plan: but long before the conclusion, as if he had forgot his first design, he throws off the censor, and puts on the antiquarian.[2] The Marquis Beccaria's book, the first of any account that is uniformly censorial, concludes, as it sets out, with penal jurisprudence.[3]

[a] See Ch. II. {Principles adverse} xiv.[4]

---

[1] Hugo Grotius (1583–1645), Samuel Pufendorf (1632–94), and Jean-Jacques Burlamaqui (1694–1748) were renowned writers in the natural law tradition.

[2] Charles Louis de Secondat, baron de la Brède et de Montesquieu (1689–1755) was author of *De l'esprit des loix*, 2 vols., Geneva, 1748, translated into English by Thomas Nugent (*c.* 1700–72) as *The Spirit of the Laws*, 2 vols., London, 1750.

[3] Cesare Beccaria (1738–94), marchese de Beccaria-Bonesana, was author of *Dei delitti e delle pene*, Geneva, 1764, translated into French by André Morellet (1727–1819), and

 [*See opposite page for n. 3 cont. and n. 4*]

28. Fourthly, in point of *expression*, the laws in question may subsist either in the form of *statute* or in that of *customary* law. As to the difference between these two branches (which respects only the article of form or expression) it cannot properly be made appear till some progress has been made in the definition of *a* law.

Jurisprudence, statutory—customary.

29. Lastly, The most intricate distinction of all, and that which comes most frequently on the carpet, is that which is made between the *civil* branch of jurisprudence and the *penal*, which latter is wont, in certain circumstances, to receive the name of *criminal*.

Jurisprudence, civil—penal—criminal.

What is a penal code of laws? What a civil code? Of what nature are their contents? Is it that there are two sorts of laws, the one penal the other civil; so that the laws in a penal code are all penal laws, while the laws in a civil code are all civil laws? Or is it, that in every law there is some matter which is of a penal nature, and which therefore belongs to the penal code; and at the same time other matter which is of a civil nature, and which therefore belongs to the civil code? Or is it, that some laws belong to one code or the other exclusively, while others are divided between the two?[a] To

Question, concerning the distinction between the civil branch and the penal, stated.

[a] To any one who should come new to the subject, the questions mentioned in the text will naturally appear to be the very ABC of Jurisprudence: they must long ago, he would think, have met with a full and satisfactory solution: to say any thing at all about them here would, therefore, appear idle: to say any thing new, impossible. So many ages as have been spent in the study of the laws, so many libraries-full as have been written on them, not know yet what a law is? So many laws as have been made, not know the ingredients they are made of? Incredible.—And yet nothing is more true. To write to any purpose a man must begin *ab ovo*: I see no fund open that he can draw upon: what he makes use of, he must make.

Necessity of the following section.

The wonder will cease when it comes to be perceived[a] that the idea of a law, meaning one simple but entire law, is in a manner inseparably connected with that of a compleat body of laws: so that what is a law and what are the contents of a compleat body of the laws are questions of which neither can well be answer'd without the other. A body of laws is a vast and complicated piece of mechanism of which no part can be fully explained without the rest. To understand the functions of a ballance-wheel, you must take to pieces the whole watch: to understand the nature of a law, you must take to pieces the whole code.

The subject we are now entering upon belongs to a particular branch of logic,

[a] See infra | |.[1]

published as *Traité des délits et des peines, traduit de l'italien, d'après la troisième édition, revue, corrigée & augmentée par l'auteur. Avec des additions de l'auteur, qui n'ont pas encore paru en italien*, [Paris], 1766, and into English as *An Essay on Crimes and Punishments, Translated from the Italian; with a Commentary, Attributed to Mons. Voltaire, Translated from the French*, London, 1767.

[4] See *An Introduction to the Principles of Morals and Legislation* (*CW*), Ch. II, para. 14, pp. 25–6 & 26–9 n.

[1] See §16, pp. 168–84 below.

answer these questions in any manner that shall be tolerably satisfactory, it will be necessary to ascertain what *a law* is: meaning one entire but single law: and what are the parts into which a law,

untouched by Aristotle.[1] The main and ultimate business of the school-logic, of which that philosopher was the father, is to exhibit the several forms of *argumentation*: the business of the branch now before us is to exhibit the several forms of *imperation*: or (to take the subject in its utmost extent) of sentences expressive of volition: a leaf which seems to be yet wanting in the book of science.

All language whatsoever, every sentence whatsoever, in as much as it *expresses* something, must *assert* something: something expressive of the state and condition, real or pretended, of the mind of him whose language it is: that is either of his understanding or his will: for at bottom, whatever is said even of external events resolves itself into this. In the first case, the sentence expressive of it has been stiled exclusively a *sentence of assertion*: in the other case, a *sentence of volition*:[a] of which latter, a *sentence of interrogation* is a particular species.[b] 'The robber is killed:'—'Kill the robber:'—'Is the robber killed?'—This is as much as to say, 'I *understand* or I believe that the robber is killed.'—'My *will* is that you kill the robber:'—'My *will* is that you tell me whether the robber be killed or no:' that is, that if the robber is killed, you tell me he is killed: if not, that he is not killed. Now, it is to sentences of the assertive kind that the logic of the Schools has confined itself: those which concern volition it has left untouched. The demesnes of the logical branch of science appear, then, to be more extensive than has commonly been suspected: the language of the will being a new and unexplored province which, neglected as it has been hitherto, might be cultivated, it is probable, to at least as good a purpose as the old. It is the branch here in question that is more particularly applicable to the business of government: that subdivision which concerns the forms of imperation at large having a more particular regard to legislation; that which concerns the forms of interrogation, to the less dignified but not less necessary business of collecting verbal information: a process subservient to the business as well of the legislative as of the executive departments.

Had Aristotle happened to turn his views this way, as many pens might perhaps have been employ'd on this branch of logic as on the other: like that it might have had its algebraical method of notation, its graphical schemes, and its *memoriter* verses: the *'Asserit A negat B'* . . . : the *'Barbara, celarent, darii, ferioque'* of the schoolmen[2] might here have found their parodies: and every piece of intellectual machinery which the ingenuity of those subtle speculatists has ever invented for the accommodation or affrightment of beginners might here have been imitated and improved.

Had this happen'd to be the case, the subject we are entering upon would, it is to be presumed, by this time have stood in a much clearer light than that in

[a] Harris's Hermes B. I. Ch. 2. p. 17.[3]

[b] Ibid.

[1] Aristotle (384–322 BC), the celebrated Greek philosopher.

[2] These were mnemonic terms designating the various moods of the syllogism according to Aristotelian logic.

[3] See James Harris, *Hermes, or a philosophical inquiry concerning universal grammar*, 2nd edn., London, 1765, pp. 15–17, and especially p. 17: 'EVERY SENTENCE WILL BE EITHER A SENTENCE OF ASSERTION, OR A SENTENCE OF VOLITION'.

as such, is capable of being distinguished: or, in other words, to ascertain what the properties are that are to be found in every object which can with propriety receive the appellation of *a* law. This then will be the business of the third and fourth sections: what concerns the import of the word *criminal*, as applied to law, will be discussed separately in the fifth.[1]

which, in the course of a cursory review, I have been able to place it: the business of a great part of the following pages might in that case have been dispatched by a few references. As it is, I mean not to descend any deeper into the subject than is absolutely necessary in order to find the requisite materials for the task actually in hand: content with opening the mine, I leave the working of it out to others.

[1] In the event, the 'business' of the third and fourth sections was expanded into §§3–18, pp. 24–200 below, and that of the fifth section became §19, pp. 201–6 below. For Bentham's expansion of the text, and revision of the number of sections, see the Editorial Introduction, pp. xvi–xviii above.

§3. *Of a law*[a] *and its parts.*

A law defined. **30.** A law may be defined an assemblage of signs *declarative* of a *volition* conceived or adopted by the *sovereign* in a state, concerning the conduct to be observed in a certain *case* by a certain person or class of persons, who in the case in question are, or are supposed to be, subject to his power: such volition trusting for its accomplishment to the expectation of certain events which it is

Parts contained in a Law. Blackstone. [a] According to the great oracle of English jurisprudence, 'every' law consists of four parts:[a] a declaratory, a directory, a remedial, and a vindicatory, which he calls also the sanction. By the declaratory (to judge from such faint lights as can be extracted out of the thickest obscurity), he seems to mean that which contains the description of the act: by the vindicatory, that which contains the description of the punishment. The directory, as he describes it, is a vague repetition of the substance of the declaratory and the vindicatory taken together. By the remedial, he means one or other, or both together, of two very different things: 1. that part of the law in question which appoints compensation: 2[ly], so much of the system of Procedure as is subservient to the execution of that law. Now, the former of these articles may be consider'd as a branch of what he calls the vindicatory: being a direction concerning the disposal of the whole or a part of the produce of the punishment: that is in the case where the punishment is, any part of it, of that sort the peculiar nature of which it is to be capable of yielding a beneficial transferrable produce. As to this part of the law, it is plain there are but two cases in which it can have existence: 1. where the offence is of a private nature: 2. where, being of a semi-public or of a public nature, and being levelled against property, the fund to the prejudice of which it operates is assignable. As to what belongs to the head of Procedure, this, so far from being a part of the law in question, or indeed a part of any law, is a complex mass consisting of a multitude of laws put together. It contains a multitude of separate regulations or commands: commands which are not so much as addressed to the same person as that is which constitutes the law in question; but to a prodigious variety of other persons.

If the author had made a point with himself to find one example for all these parts as he has done for some of them, he would have given no account of this matter at all, or he would have given a different one. 'Stealing is a crime:' that, says he, is the declaratory part of a law: 'Thou shalt not steal:' this, he says, is the directory part of the same law. What is the remedial part of it? what the vindicatory? This he has not told us: for he could go no farther. To illustrate the remedial he takes up another specimen: and here again he gives us the declaratory part and the directory, as before *in terminis. The field or inheritance which belonged to Titius's father is vested by his death in Titius.* This, says he, is the declaratory part. *It is forbidden that any one enter on another's property without leave of the owner.* This he gives for the directory. What then is the remedial? Here for the second time he is at a stand—*bis patriæ cecidere manus.*[b] There being no

[a] Blackst. Comm. Introd. §. 2. p. 53–56.[1]

[b] Espr. des Loix. Pref.[4]

[1] See Blackstone, *Commentaries on the Laws of England*, i. 53–6.

[2] See Montesquieu, *Spirit of the Laws*, i. pp. vii–viii, citing (without acknowledgment) Vergil, *Aeneid*, VI. 33, which Nugent translates as '*I every day felt my paternal hands fall*'.

intended such declaration should upon occasion be a means of bringing to pass, and the prospect of which it is intended should act as a motive upon those whose conduct is in question.[1]

The idea exhibited by this definition more extensive than

The[2] latitude here given to the import of the word *law* is, it must be confessed, rather greater than what seems to be given to it in common: the definition being such as is applicable to various

such thing, there was no producing it: instead, then, of giving the thing itself, he gives this general account of it, which let any one make a meaning of that can. 'If Gaius after this will presume to take possession of the land, the remedial part of the law will then interpose it's office; will make Gaius restore the possession to Titius and also pay him damages for the invasion.' *Voces inopes rerum, nugæque canoræ.*[3] There remains still his vindicatory part, which no attempt is made to exemplify, not even as the remedial is exemplified: not even by description. All this for want of the light of genuine metaphysics: wandering in a labyrinth of rights and wrongs, and duties, and obligations, and laws of nature, and other fictitious entities.[4]

Of this nature is the analysis, given by that admired writer, of the parts to be found in every law: and his analysis of the contents of a whole body of laws is of a piece with it.

---

[1] Bentham at one time intended to insert the following passage at UC lxxxviii. 101, with the marginal heading 'Law how distinguished from a piece of advice or exhortation', at this point, but later deleted it. The beginning of the passage quotes an MS orig., which Bentham subsequently amended.

'The concluding part of the definition which runs in these words, "the party of whose will it is the expression trusting for its accomplishment to the expectation of certain events the prospect of which he intends should act as a motive and which he intends the declaration in question should upon occasion be a means of bringing to pass", this part, I say, was inserted for the sake of distinguishing *law* from exhortation and advice or counsel, or to speak more precisely, of distinguishing a law from a piece of exhortation or advice. Advice and exhortation administer neither of them any new motives. Advice, the only sort of advice from which any instruction is to be gained, is the language of the understanding: [In the margin, Bentham has noted at this point: 'Advice is either motived or unmotived.'] exhortation is the language of will adding a motive | | to advice. He who advises applies no new motives: all he does is to suggest and bring to view the probability of such interesting events as seem likely to come to pass from other sources: he who exhorts expresses a wish that the party exhorted would be determined to pursue the conduct in question, but without furnishing any fresh motives, except in as far as the desire of gratifying the party exhorting may chance to operate in that character.[a]

'[a] Between advice and exhortation it is difficult to draw the line. Many people, when they pretend to give advice, give nothing but exhortation; what they call advice, instead of bringing latent facts or probabilities under review, is nothing more than the unmotived expression of their own wishes.'

[2] The following passage, through to the beginning of paragraph 31 (see p. 40 below), is a later insertion into the 'principal draft'. For further details of the 'principal draft' see the Editorial Introduction, pp. xv–xvi above.

[3] i.e. 'Sounds devoid of substance and melodious nonsense.' Adapted from Horace, *Ars poetica*, 322.

[4] MS del. continues: 'instead of gathering up that clue that might have been afforded by an attentive consideration of such particulars as the acts which are made offences, the circumstances with which they are accompanied, the persons whose acts they are, the persons who are sufferers by them, the pain experienced by those persons, the pain to be inflicted on the offenders, and so on throughout the region of real entities.'

what is commonly annexed to the word *law*

objects which are not commonly characterized by that name. Taking this definition for the standard, it matters not whether the expression of will in question, so as it have but the authority of the sovereign to back it, were his by immediate conception or only by adoption: whether it be of the most public or of the most private or even domestic nature: whether the sovereign from whom it derives its force be an individual or a body: whether it be issued *propter quid*, as the phrase may be, that is on account of some particular act or event which is understood to warrant it (as is the case with an order of the judicial kind made *litis causâ*, in the course of a cause), or *mero motu*, without the assignment of any such special ground: or whether it be susceptible of an indefinite duration or whether it be *suâ naturâ* temporary and undurable: as is most commonly the case with such expressions of will the uttering of which is looked upon as *a measure of administration*: whether it be a command or a countermand: whether it be expressed in the way of statute, or of customary law.[a] Under the term 'law', then, if this definition be admitted of, we must include a judicial order, a military or any other kind of executive order, or even the most trivial and momentary order of the domestic kind, so it be not illegal: that is, so as the issuing of it be not forbidden by some other law.

—more extensive than it ought to be to correspond to the phrases legislation and legislative power

Judging, however, from analogy, it would naturally be expected that the signification given to the word *law* should be correspondent to that of its conjugates *legislation* and *legislative power*: for what, it will be said, is legislation but the act of making laws? or legislative power but the power of making them? that, consequently, the term *law* should be applied to every expression of will, the uttering of which was an act of legislation, an exertion of legislative power; and that, on the other hand, it should not be applied to any expression of will of which those two propositions could not be predicated. Accordingly, in the former of these points it does indeed quadrate with these two expressions: but it can not be said to do so in the latter. It has all the amplitude which they have: but the import of it is not every where confined within the bounds which limit their's. This will be seen in a variety of examples.

viz: by including domestic orders.

In the first place, according to the definition, the word *law* should be applicable to any the most trivial order, supposing it to be not illegal, which a man may have occasion to give for any of the most inconsiderable purposes of life: to any order which a master may

[a] These distinctions will all of them be explained at large, as we proceed.

have occasion to give to his servant, a parent to his child, or (where the request of a husband assumes the harsh form of a command) of a husband to his wife. Yet it would seem a strange catachresis to speak of the issuing of any such order as an act of legislation, or as an exercise of legislative power. Not but that in cases like these the word *law* is frequently enough employ'd: but then it is in the way of figure. Even where there is no such legal superiority, a man may say to another out of compliment, 'your commands are laws to me:' but on occasions like these, the impropriety of the expression is the very reason of its being chosen.

Temporary orders of administration.

2. With equal propriety (according to the definition) would the word *law* be applicable to a temporary order issued by any magistrate who is spoken of as exercising thereby a branch of *executive* power, or as exercising the functions belonging to any department of *administration*. But the executive power is continually mentioned as distinct from the legislative: and the business of administration is as constantly opposed to that of legislation.[a] Let the Board of Treasury order a sum of money to be paid or issued to such or such a person, let the Commander-in-chief order such or such a body of troops to march to such a place, let the Navy Board order such or such a ship to be fitted out, let the Board of Ordnance order such or such a train of artillery to be dispatched to such a destination.—Who would ever speak of any of these orders as acts of legislative power, as acts of legislation?

Judicial orders.

3. With equal propriety again would the word law, according to the definition, be applicable to any *judicial* order, to any order which, in the course of a cause of any kind, a man might have occasion to issue in the capacity of a Judge. Yet the business of judicature is constantly looked upon as essentially distinct from the business of legislation and as constantly opposed to it: and the case is the same between the judicial and the legislative powers. Even suppose the order to have been ever so general, suppose the persons to whom it is addressed to be ever so numerous and indeterminate, and the duration of it ever so indefinite, still, if issued in the course of a forensic contestation, the act of issuing it would not be looked upon in general as coming under the notion of an act of legislation, or as an exercise of legislative power. The fate of a province may be determined by a judicial decree: but the pronouncing of the decree will not on that account be looked upon

[a] v. supra | |.[1]

[1] For Bentham's distinction between legislative and executive power see *An Introduction to the Principles of Morals and Legislation* (*CW*), pp. 263–4 n., and between legislation and administration see §1, para. 4, pp. 4–5 above.

as being capable, with any sort of propriety, of being termed an act of legislation.

Monarchical orders if particular and *suâ naturâ* temporary.

4. Of course the term *law* would, according to the definition, be applicable to any order whatsoever emaning directly from the sovereign. But it is not in all cases that the issuing of any such order is looked upon as an act of legislation. Where the sovereign is a body corporate, there indeed, if the matter be consider'd with reference to the English language, there seem to be no exceptions. In Great Britain, for example, the sovereignty is in the King, Lords and Commons in Parliament assembled. It would be hardly possible for that complex body to issue any order the issuing of which would not be looked upon as an act of legislation. What power was it that it exercised when it made the act by which the Earl of Strafford suffered death,[1] or that by which the Earl of Clarendon was driven into banishment?[2] The answer would, I suppose, be in both cases, the legislative: and in this case the command which was the result of such act of legislation would accordingly be termed a law.[a] How would it be with a command of the like nature issued by the Diet of Poland or that of Sweden, by the sovereign councils of Berne, Venice, Genoa or Amsterdam? This would depend partly upon the political notions prevalent in the respective states, partly upon the terminology of the respective languages. As to Rome in the time of the Commonwealth, we know from Cicero[b] what the language was there: such a command was termed a *privilegium*; which, being a conjugate of the word *lex*, shewed that the power, of which such command was deemed the exercise, was the legislative.[3]

[a] I choose here for examples such orders as have their physical termination in a man's body, and are capable in their own nature of being fulfilled by a single person. Those which regard property will generally be very complex, according to the different articles which a man's property may consist of. In these examples, the acts in question would in fact be found resolvable into a variety of orders, issued to different persons: but the effect of the most material articles might by possibility have been obtained by one.

[b] | |.[4]

[1] Thomas Wentworth (1593–1641), first Earl of Strafford, was executed on 12 May 1641 in accordance with a Bill of Attainder which had received the Royal Assent two days previously.

[2] Edward Hyde (1609–74), first Earl of Clarendon, Lord Chancellor 1658–67, having been dismissed from office by Charles II (1630–85), King of England, Scotland, and Ireland from 1660, went into exile in November 1667, amidst demands for his impeachment.

[3] The following paragraph is a later insertion.

[4] See Cicero, *De legibus*, III. xix. 44: *in privatos homines leges ferri noluerunt: id est enim privilegium*, i.e. 'They desired that no laws should be proposed which penalized particular individuals, for that is what a law of personal exception is.'

But where the sovereignty is in a single person and the party who is looked upon as being principally affected by it is an individual, neither the word *law*, nor any conjugate of it, seems, in common speech at least, to be employ'd. When the King of France orders a man to quit the metropolis, or sends him to the Bastile, the power he exercises is not spoken of as legislative power, nor the act he performs as an act of legislation. *Lettres de cachet* are not ordinarily termed laws. They are termed *ordres souverains*, sovereign orders, or by some such name. Will it be said that the orders in question are seldom issued but on account of some offence committed or apprehended, and that, therefore, the power exercised by them is either of the judicial or the *phthano-paranomic*[1] kind? Be it so. But even let the exercise of it be as far as possible from all dependence upon any particular event, as much so as any the widest-extending law can be, in short let the *sic volo* even have no other reason than the *non amo te*,[2] still the power exercised upon the occasion would hardly be looked upon as at all the better entitled to the name of legislative.

Thus much for the *privilegia odiosa*: and the case is the same where the *privilegium* is of the favourable kind; the most striking part of it's effects consisting in the *benefit* of which it is productive to an individual. If the Parliament of England order money to be paid to any body, it is by an act of legislation, and the command is called a law: but nobody, I suppose, thinks of giving that name to a command of the like nature issued by the King of France.

—laws made by a magistrate the most conspicuous part of whose power is of the judicial kind.

5. There are even cases in which, although the command were in every point a general one, although it were issued *mero motu*, and although the party from whom it emaned were a complex body, it might be a matter of dispute whether the command itself were, according to common notions, entitled to the appellation of a law, or the act of issuing it to that of an act of legislation: and, perhaps, with not only equal, but still stronger appearance of reason, whether the power in virtue of which such command was issued would admitt of the appellation of the legislative power. These are the cases where either the power from whence the magistrates by whom the commands in question are issued take their official name, or that of the magistrate from whose appointment they derive their office, comes under the denomination of either of those powers which are wont to be put in contradistinction to the legislative. In England, the same sets of magistrates

[1] i.e. 'crime-preventing': see *An Introduction to the Principles of Morals and Legislation* (*CW*), p. 198 n.

[2] i.e. 'such is my will' because 'I do not love you'.

who exercise the judicial power are allow'd, many of them, to establish *ex mero motu* regulations of a durable nature, regulations that are general in all points concerning the conduct of such parties as shall chance thereafter to be any how concerned in litigation. These regulations, though in every other circumstance except that of their not emaning directly from the sovereign power they agree with those which are universally and without scruple termed by the name of laws, are not usually characterized by that name: they are called sometimes *orders*, sometimes by a compound sort of name *rules and orders*, of the court from which they emane: and sometimes, for distinction's sake, *standing orders*: nor would the magistrates who are allow'd to issue them be spoken of as exercising acts of legislation, or as possessing any share of legislative power.

—or of the executive kind

6. In the same country, the magistrate whose powers taken collectively are commonly termed by the appellation of the executive power, I mean the King, is also allow'd to establish of himself and *ex mero motu* a multitude of regulations; regulations which are to such a degree general that the conduct and the fate of large and numerous classes of individuals are regulated and determined by them, and which, accordingly, in point of duration, though limited by positive institution, are in their own nature susceptible of perpetuity. The articles of war for the government of the army, and the instructions given to privateers, may serve for examples. I say nothing here of the power of making treaties nor of the power of making war and peace: powers of which the nature is too complicated, and the relation which they bear to legislative too faintly characterized, to be adduced for the purpose of illustration in the present stage of our enquiry.

These, then, are so many other sets of articles which the definition would comprise under the name of laws. At the same time, the issuing of the commands referable to these heads would hardly without some reluctance be acknowledged as acts of legislation; and the power in virtue of which they were issued would probably not without a still greater degree of reluctance be admitted to the title of legislative power.

—or by one whose legislative power is derived from a magistrate the most conspicuous part of whose power is of the executive kind.

7. Some difficulty there may also be, though perhaps not so much, with regard to various orders (general in point of extension or perpetual in point of duration or both) which are wont to be issued by various sets of magistrates, all of whom derive their authority originally, and many of them immediately, from the King. I am speaking of those, for instance, which are issued by the governing part in corporate towns and other corporations for the

government of the members of the corporation; as also of those which are issued by Justices of the Peace for the levying of rates in the counties for which they are commissioned. The unwillingness to employ in these cases the terms *law, act of legislation* and *legislative power* will probably encrease as the field of dominion becomes less extensive. No man ever made a difficulty about employing them in the case of Ireland, of the American provinces or other distant members of the empire; yet to many it might seem odd to apply the same high-sounding appellatives to the powers, acts and operations of a fraternity of weavers or tallow chandlers in a little town or parish. At the same time, it would be impossible, perhaps, for the most scrupulous to draw any line of separation. The parish of Halifax in Yorkshire is in point of territory not many times less, and in point of population probably even more, considerable than the Kingdom of Man.

Necessity of these verbal discussions.

These discussions, local as they are, could scarcely be avoided on account of the influence which local establishments and local notions have on the idiom of the language. Such words as the language a man writes in furnishes, such must he make use of: and whatever word he makes use of on any occasion, he will, of course, be understood to annex the same idea to as every body else annexes to it, unless he gives warning to the contrary: such warning, therefore, he must give if he means to be understood, wherever the language is inconsistent with itself. In the present instance, from the confused ideas which men are wont to annex to the terms legislative power and executive power, little can be collected but that the former, it is thought, is something superior to the latter; and where legislature and legislative power are mentioned without any epithet of addition, supreme legislature and supreme legislative power are commonly intended. In constitutional topics like these, and under popular governments more especially, the judgments of men are in continual danger of being disturbed by the influence of their passions: nor is it to be wonder'd at if a consciousness of the inferences that may be drawn from the significations assigned to particular words should on such occasions dispose them to regard the most phlegmatic and impartial discussions with an eye of jealousy.

In some cases, the very proximity which there is in point of importance between two branches of power is the very cause of the repugnance which is felt at the thoughts of extending to the one the appellation which is currently given to the other. The two Houses of Parliament are each allow'd to issue their standing orders, as well as the King his proclamations: which orders have every quality (that of sovereignty excepted) which is to be found in those of which the title to the name of *laws* stands clearest from dispute: at the same time, it has been a practise of such frequency and a point of such importance to refuse to these orders and proclamations the name of laws in the sense in which the word *law* is put for an object of equal authority with an act of parliament, that it would not be to be wonder'd at if more aversion should be manifested to the applying of the name in question to these objects than to any other: insomuch that, in the eyes of those who are upon the watch for political heresies, it might seem a more dangerous solecism to attribute the legislative power in severalty to these high authorities, than to attribute it to an inconsiderable fraternity of petty tradesmen.

Reason of extending the import of the word law so as to make it include the articles above mentioned.

Such, then, are the various sorts of expressions of will to which men would be apt, for one reason or other, to deny the appellation of *a law*: such, therefore, are the points in which the definition here given of that important word outstretches the idea which common usage has annexed to it. And these excluded objects have, in every point except that of the manner of their appertaining to the sovereign, in every point, in short, except their immediate *source*, the same nature with those whose title to the appellation stands clearest of dispute. They are all referable *ultimately* to one common source: they have all of them alike their subjects and their objects, their local extent and their duration: in point of logical extent, as it may be called, they must all of them be either general or particular; and they may in most instances be indifferently either the one or the other: they are all of them susceptible of the same diversities with respect to the *parties* whom they may affect, and the *aspects* which they may present to the acts which are their objects: they require all of them the same *force* to give them effect, and the same *signs* to give them utterance.

No other word would answer the purpose so well: viz:

To characterize at once a set of objects so intimately allied, and to which there would be such continual occasion to apply the same propositions, it was necessary to find a common appellative: that which seemed least exceptionable upon the whole was the term *law*. The only words that could come into competition with it in this view seem to be those which follow: command, commandment, order, injunction, precept, decree, statute, ordinance, edict, constitution, regulation, establishment, institution, mandate. Of the reasons for adopting it in preference to all these several appellatives, it may be proper to give a general idea.

1. Command.

1. The word command seemed inadequate in three respects. 1. It gives no intimation that the will in question is in any manner

referable to the sovereign. 2. It does not include a countermand. 3. It is not applicable without some degree of harshness to any material instrument, such as a written or printed paper, whereby the will in question is expressed. When applied to any thing written, it seems to denote the will which is expressed, in exclusion of the writing by which it is expressed.[a]

2. The same objections seem to apply to the word *commandment*: add to which that usage hath in a manner confined the application of it to a few particular commands which are consider'd as emaning immediately from the Deity:[1] nor is there any word that corresponds to it in the manner that *countermand* does to *command*; unless we were to coin a word and say *countermandment*. 2. Commandment.

3. The word *order* may, perhaps, without impropriety be looked upon as free from the second of the above objections: for example in the instance of military orders: and it is indisputably clear from the third. But 1. It is open to the first of the objections which apply to the word *command*. 2. Another objection to it is that it seems confined to such commands as are looked upon either as not being very *general* in respect of the multitude of the persons they extend to, or as not emaning directly from the sovereign authority, or as not of a nature to be *perpetual*. To speak of the orders of Justinian, meaning those contained in the *Corpus Juris*,[2] or of the Emperor Charles the 5th, meaning those contained in the Carolinian Code,[3] would seem little less improper on the one hand, than on the other hand it would seem to be were we to apply the name of *laws* to the directions a mistress of a family gives to her cook about the dressing of a dinner. 3. Order.

4. The word *injunction* is open to the objections which apply to the word *command* as well as to those which apply to the word *order*: add to which that, in English, it has, besides it's ordinary and general sense, a technical and confined sense, in which it is put for a particular kind of order issuable by a particular set of judges in a particular kind of cause. 4. Injunction.

[a] We do not call a written paper a command: but where it is called an *order*, or in a complimental way of speaking put upon the footing of an order, we speak of the commands contained in it, that is expressed by it.

---

[1] i.e. the Ten Commandments, found in Exodus 20: 1–17.

[2] The *Corpus Juris Civilis* was compiled between 527 and 534 on the order of Justinian (*c.* 482–565), Byzantine Emperor from 527, as an attempt to state the whole Roman law in a relatively concise and consistent form.

[3] The *Constitutio Criminalis Carolina* was an ordinance dealing with penal procedure promulgated on 27 June 1532 by Charles V (1500–58), King of Spain from 1516, Holy Roman Emperor from 1519 until his abdication in 1556.

5. Decree. [5.] The word *decree* in its larger sense means rather a resolution to issue a command than a command itself: and it lies open to the second of the objections that lie against the word *command*: besides that in this enlarged sense it is seldom applied but to such resolutions as are attributed to the deity, or in a figurative way to some fictitious personage such as Fate or Providence. Moreover, in English, it is embarassed with a narrow technical sense somewhat analogous to that which adheres to the word *injunction*.

6. Precept. [6.] The word *precept* in its larger sense is applied rather to advices than commands: to such expressions of will as seek their accomplishment rather by motives represented as accruing of themselves from other sources, than by motives which the party represents himself as about to be instrumental in bringing into play. The only sense in which it is unequivocally significative of a command is a narrow technical sense which it has of its own, after the manner of the two words preceding.

7. Statute. [7.] The word *statute* stands clear of the first of the objections which apply to the words *command, order,* and the like. But it lies open to several objections: 1. It is not applicable to domestic commands: 2. nor to commands issued *litis causâ*. 3. By reason of certain circumstances peculiar to the British constitution, it would seem to exclude (after a few exceptions which could not be reduced to any rule) all other laws but what emaned immediately from the sovereign. 4. It denotes a particular expression of will no otherwise than through the medium of a particular instrument or assemblage of signs: denoting the ideas signified, not howsoever signified, but only as signified by those signs: being in this respect the reverse of the word *command*. 5. It, accordingly, means not any determinate portion of the matter of which laws are made; but such a quantity of that matter, be it ever so great or ever so little, as happens to be issued at one enactment, or, as we may say, *uno flatu*.

This objection to the word statute regards rather a meaning which I wish to see annexed to the term *law* than one which it has any settled and exclusive possession of already: and as the distinction between this new idea and the idea already annexed to the word *statute* is nice, as well as the use that I propose to make of it an important one, it will demand some attention. The idea for which I want to find an expression is that of so much of the matter of which laws and statutes are made as constitutes one entire command or countermand and nothing more. To this purpose the word *law*, after proper notice given, is capable of being applied. In this very sense, indeed, it hath no doubt been frequently employ'd already: all that remains to be done is to appropriate it: for the idea having never yet been distinctly pointed out, the word *law* has hitherto been indiscriminately applied to this and to the more variable idea which belongs to the word *statute*. This being premised, I will, for shortness sake, suppose the word *law* to be already fixed in the possession of the particular sense to which I purpose to confine it: which done, the distinction between this and the word *statute* may be farther illustrated as follows. The idea of a law is the idea of an object which may be purely intellectual, existing no where but in the mind of him who speaks of it: the idea of a statute is constantly the idea of a material object, copies of which may be had any where at the bookseller's. If a coarse allusion may be allow'd, a law in comparison with a statute, is what a single but entire muscle as dissected off by an anatomist is to a steak or a joint as cut off by a butcher. The idea of a law as thus determined is what must previously be formed in order to serve as a pattern to which the contents of a statute or any number of statutes may be reduced, and the several parts they consist of referred to the several stations they belong to in the system. Laws, in short, are the elements of which statutes are composed, and into which, in order to be understood, they must be resolved.

[8.] The words *ordinance* and *edict* lie open to all the objections, except the third, of those which lie against the word *statute*. 8. Ordinance and edict.

[9.] The word *constitution* lies open to all the objections which lie against the words *ordinance* and *edict*: besides which, the more confined sense in which it is put for the aggregate of those laws in a state which are stiled collectively the public law, or rather for a kind of fictitious entity, the supposed product of those laws, renders it in many cases inconvenient for use. 9. Constitution.

[10.] The word *regulation* lies open to the second of the objections which lie against the word *statute*: it being scarcely applicable to commands issued *litis causâ*. With regard to the 4th of those objections, this word is not confined to denote neither more nor less than one entire command or countermand: it may indeed mean exactly one such expression of will: but it may also include more as well as less; but more naturally less, than, to any considerable degree, more. 10. Regulation.

[11.] The word *establishment* lies open to the objections following: 1. Although it may in certain cases be employ'd instead of the word *law*, it can no more be made to take the place of it in all cases than a genus can in all cases be put in the place of a species that is contained under it: for establishment is no otherwise significative of a law than in as far as it denotes a work of any kind considerable 11. Establishment.

in point of relative importance, and promising a certain degree of stability: or rather, perhaps, a kind of fictitious entity, looked upon as being the result of the labour employ'd in such a work; just as the constitution (as above mentioned) is consider'd as the result of what is done by the laws of which *jus publicum* is composed. 2. It lies open to the second of the objections which lie against the word [*statute*],[1] not extending to commands issued *litis causâ*. 3. With regard to the fourth of those objections, it stands much upon a footing with the word *regulation*. It seems likewise to lie open, in a slight degree at least, to another objection or two not worth insisting on. In short, it is only in a very vague and uncharacteristic as well as imperfect manner that it can serve for representing the word *law*: since it can signify no laws that are not permanent, and it signifies any thing else almost that is so.[a]

12. Institution. [12.] The word *institution* lies open to the objections following: 1. It lies open to an objection similar to the first of those which lie against the word *establishment*. It is put for the cause of a practise or habit of any kind prevailing among a considerable assemblage of persons, whether that cause were the act of making a positive law or only the act of using persuasion or setting an example, and thence, by metonymy, for the practise or habit itself so caused.[b] In short, it signifies what we mean by law no otherwise than in as far as it signifies any work that has had a beginning, consider'd in respect to its having had such a beginning. 2. It lies open to the second of the objections which apply to the word *statute*.

13. Mandate. [13.] Of all the words that have been mentioned, that which seems the best adapted to express in all its amplitude and under all its modifications the large and comprehensive idea to which, from necessity, I have ventured to appropriate the term *law*, is the word *mandate*. It is not confined by any of those peculiarities which limit the extent of the word *order*, any more than by those which limit that of the word *law* consider'd as the emanation of legislative power: it is equally applicable to the laws of the sovereign as to the orders of the judge, of the general, or of the master of a private

[a] In French, indeed, there is a collection of laws known by the name of the *Establishments of S[t] Louis*:[2] but this is a particular case.

[b] Games, festivals, orders of knighthood are spoken of as institutions: and though laws may have been made on the occasion of these institutions, yet the institutions were possible and intelligible without the laws.

---

[1] MS '*law*' appears to be a slip.

[2] Compiled by 1273, and consisting of ordinances issued during the reign of Louis IX (1214–70), King of France from 1226, *Les Établissements de Saint Louis* dealt with procedure in the Châtelet, the principal law court in Paris, and with the customs of Touraine-Anjou and Orléans.

family: it may even be applicable without distinction to the will which is expressed, and to the material instrument made use of to express it; perhaps, too, it might even without much violence be extended to signify a countermand as well as a command itself.

In short, it might with great advantage have been made use of as the *genus generalissimum* in the room of the word *law* had it not been for two objections, the latter of which arises out of the former. In the first place, it is upon no better a footing than the words *command, order*, and *injunction* in respect to its not conveying any intimation that the expression of will to which it is applied has the sovereign for its source: it is as natural to speak of an illegal, as of a legal, mandate. In the next place, it does not, upon the face of it, appear to mean that sort of thing which forms the contents of the sort of book which is called a book of law: so that had I taken for the subject of the definition the word *mandate* instead of the word *law*, the reader would have been apt to have asked himself what the former had to do here, and how it came that no mention was made of the latter. Indeed, who could have endured that, in a book professing to treat of laws, the leading term should be other than the word law?[a]

Although not qualified to stand as the leading term, the word *mandate* is, however, so much more extensive and unrestricted in its import than the word *law*, that it may be substituted in the room of it with advantage in an occasional analytical sketch, the object of which is to give an analytical view of the principal distinctions which obtain between the objects to which the definition has given the name of *laws* consider'd in respect of their *source*;[1] by which means the conformities and disconformities that subsist between the expressions of the will to which men are wont in common to refuse the name of laws and those which they are accustomed to characterize by that name may be exhibited. This, however, must in course be deferred to the next section.[2]

Thus much, however, it will be convenient to observe before a period is put to the present section. In such an analysis, the first partition would be into *legal* and *illegal*. By a legal mandate is to be

[a] For the difference between a law or mandate and a piece of advice see supra 1. n.[3] For the import of the words *invitation, requisition,* see infra §12. 3. n.[4]

[1] In the margin, in relation to the preceding part of this sentence, Bentham has noted: 'Cut down.'

[2] See pp. 42–54, and especially p. 54, below.

[3] See the passage headed 'Law how distinguished from a piece of advice or exhortation' at p. 25 n. above.

[4] See p. 116 n. below.

understood such an one, and such only, as, in a manner more or less immediate (a distinction which will be explained at large in the next section),[1] emaneth from the sovereign; by an illegal mandate, every other mandate whatsoever. These are distinctions which bear reference to the *source*: in that point a legal and an illegal mandate differ. But in all other points, they will be found to agree: so that, under every other head, what is predicated of the one may with equal truth be predicated of the other.[a] In future, then, it will be sufficient to make use of the word *mandate* simply, without prefixing to it the epithet *legal*; more especially as the mandates with which our business is at present, are such, and such only, as come under this description. The word *mandate*, then, if the sense of it be strained so as to make it include the import of the word *countermandate*, may be taken for the *genus generalissimum* of that class of things of which the most material species are known by the name of laws, and from whence, by abstraction, is drawn the fictitious entity called *law*.

Concessions of sovereigns are not laws.[2]

In the definition that hath just been given of a legal mandate, it follows that the mandate of the sovereign, be it what it will, can not be illegal: it may be cruel; it may be impolitic; it may even be unconstitutional: but it can not be illegal. It may be unconstitutional, for instance, by being repugnant to any privileges that may have been conceded to the people whom it affects: but it would be perverting language and confounding ideas to call it *illegal*: for concessions of privileges are not mandates: they are neither commands nor countermands: in short they are not *laws*.[b] They are only promises from the sovereign to the people that he will not issue any law, any mandate, any command or countermand but to such or such an effect, or perhaps with the concurrence of such or such persons.[3] In this respect they are upon the footing of treaties

[a] In as far as the source of the mandate comes in question, what is predicated of it belongs exclusively to jurisprudence: but every thing else that is said of it belongs equally to the hitherto undenominated branch of logic above spoken of, which may be called the *logic of imperation*, or more generally and exactly, the *logic of the will*: in contradistinction to the logic which may be termed the *logic of the judgement*. v. supra | |.[4]

[b] See Ch. | | {Corpus Juris}.[5]

---

[1] See pp. 42–54 below.

[2] The following account of sovereignty, as indicated by Bentham's marginal comments reproduced in editorial footnotes, is superseded by his account at pp. 86–93 below. For further details see the Editorial Introduction, pp. xxi–xxiii above.

[3] In the margin, in relation to the preceding part of the paragraph, Bentham has noted at this point: 'Alter. These are laws not *in populum* indeed, but *in principem*.'

[4] See pp. 21–3 n. above.

[5] Bentham at one time intended that 'Corpus Juris' would form a further Chapter in the

with foreign powers. They are a sort of treaties with the people. It is not the people who are bound by it, it is not the people whose conduct is concerned in it, but the sovereign himself; in as far as a party can be bound who has the whole force of the political sanction at his disposal. The force, then, which these treaties have to depend upon for their efficacy is what other treaties have to depend upon, the force of the moral and religious sanctions. The effect of such a concession is to weaken, on the part of the people, in the event of its being violated, that disposition to submission and obedience, by which the power of the sovereign, in point of fact, is constituted: as the effect of a treaty is to weaken, in the event of its being violated, that disposition on the part of the other sovereign by which a state of amity on his part is constituted; I mean the disposition to restrain his subjects from hostility.

No more are treaties between sovereigns.

It may be observed here for the sake of regularity, though after what has been said in the last article it is but repetition, that a treaty made by one sovereign with another is not itself a law; from which indeed it is plainly distinguished by the definition we set out with giving of the word *law*. It has an intimate connection, however, with the body of the laws, in virtue of its being apt to be converted by construction into an actual law or set of laws, and at any rate from the expectation it affords of the establishment of express laws conformable to the stipulations of which it is composed.[a]

Local names of statutes dismissed.

The above seem to be the principal terms whose import it can be of any use to compare in the present stage of our enquiries with that of the word *law*: I mean in a book of which, though the language is local, yet the plan, as far as is consistent with the locality of the language, is universal. I omitt, therefore, all those expressions which, whatever footing they may happen to have got in the English language, are in their respective originals neither more nor less than so many synonyms to the word *statute*. Of this stamp are *act* (meaning act of Parliament) in Great Britain, *declaration* (meaning a declaration of the King) in France, *Bull* in the German empire and the ecclesiastical state, *Recess* (meaning a statute made at the recess of the Diet) and *Capitulation*[b] in the

[a] v. Ch. xx. {Corpus Juris}.

[b] The principal contents of the Imperial capitulations are either concessions of privileges or treaties, according to the relation which the Emperor is consider'd as bearing at the several periods to the other states. I would not, without

introduction to the projected penal code. For further details see the Editorial Introduction, p. xii above.

German Empire, *pragmatic sanction* in the Byzantine and German Empire, *placard* in the Low Countries, and the like.

It may be consider'd with relation to 1. its source: 2. its subjects: 3. its objects: 4. its extent: 5. its aspects: 6. its force: 7. its expression: 8. its occasional appendages.

31.[1] According to this definition, a law may be consider'd in eight[2] different respects.[3]

1. In respect to its *source*: that is in respect to the person or persons of whose will it is the expression.[a]

2. In respect to the quality of its *subjects*: by which I mean the persons and things to which it may apply.[b]

3. In respect to its *objects*: by which I mean the *acts*, as characterised by the *circumstances*, to which it may apply.[c]

4. In respect to its *extent*, the generality of its application or *amplitude*: that is in respect to the determinateness of the persons whose conduct it may seek to regulate.[d]

5. In respect to its *aspects*: that is in respect to the various manners in which the will whereof it is the expression may apply itself to the acts and circumstances which are its objects.[e]

examining them in this particular view, be sure of their containing any matter of the mandative kind.[4]

[a] infra 32.[5]

[b] infra 37.[6]

[c] infra [39].[7]

[d] infra 49.[8]

[e] infra 51.[9]

---

[1] The beginning of an alternative draft of this paragraph is at UC lxxxviii. 88: 'These obscurities being cleared up, these difficulties being removed, we may now proceed to develop more at length the several varieties of which the sort of thing described under the name of *a law* is susceptible. A law, then, according to the above definition may be consider'd in twelve different respects:

'1. In respect of its *source:* that is in respect of the person or persons of whose will it is the expression.

'2. In respect of the *end* it has in view.'

[2] The eight 'respects' listed below represent the scope of the discussion as it appeared at one point of time in the 'principal draft'. In due course, Bentham expanded the discussion to include twelve 'respects'. The four additional 'respects', not listed below, but inserted at some later date into the 'principal draft', deal with Ends (§5, pp. 55–7 below), Parties affected (§8, pp. 75–93 below), Duration (§10, pp. 96–7 below), and Generality (§11, pp. 98–114 below). In the 'principal draft', the discussion of 'respects' originally formed a continuation of §3. Bentham eventually decided to dedicate a separate section to each 'respect', and that arrangement has been adopted in the present edition. For further details see the Editorial Introduction, pp. xv–xviii above.

[3] i.e. the definition of a law, pp. 24–5 above.

[4] In the margin, Bentham has noted at this point: 'They are *leges in principem* in which the party favoured is either a subject or co-imperant or an independent prince.'

[5] i.e. §4, pp. 42–54 below. The text sheets for the 'principal draft' of this 'respect' have not been located. A later draft is reproduced below.

[6] i.e. §6, pp. 58–65 below.

[7] MS '38' is a slip. See §7, pp. 66–74 below.

[8] i.e. §9, pp. 94–5 below. The text sheets for the 'principal draft' of this 'respect' have not been located. A later draft is reproduced below.

[9] i.e. §12, pp. 115–41 below.

6. In respect to its *force*: that is in respect to the *motives* it relies on for enabling it to produce the effect it aims at, and the laws or other means which it relies on for bringing those motives into play: such laws may be stiled its *corroborative appendages*.[a]

7. In respect to its *expression*: that is in respect to the nature of the *signs* by which the will whereof it is the expression may be made known.[b]

8. In respect to its *remedial appendages*, where it has any: by which I mean certain other laws which may occasionally come to be subjoined to the principal law in question; and of which the design is to obviate the mischief that stands connected with any individual act of the number of those which are made offences by it, in a more perfect manner [than][1] can be done by the sole efficacy of the subsidiary appendages to which it stands indebted for its force.[c]

[a] infra 87.[2]
[b] infra 114.[3]
[c] infra 118.[4]

[1] i.e. §13, pp. 142–60 below.
[2] i.e. §14, pp. 161–4 below.
[3] MS 'that'.
[4] i.e. §15, pp. 165–7 below.

§4. *Source of a law.*[1]

A law must come from a sovereign

First, then, with respect to its *source*. Consider'd in this point of view, the will of which it is the expression must, as the definition intimates, be the will of the sovereign in *a* state. Now, by a sovereign I mean any person or assemblage of persons to whose will a whole political community are (no matter on what account) supposed to be in a disposition to pay obedience:[a] and that in preference to the will of any other person.[b] Suppose the will in

[a] I do not say in all cases: cases in which the sovereign shall not make any law, acts which he shall neither command nor prohibit, laws already subsisting which he shall not alter, *may* be settled in a variety of ways: by the original compact where any such thing has taken place:[*a*] by subsequent compacts and engagements such as we see enter'd into by sovereigns every day: as in the cases of conquest, capitulation, cession, exchange, succession, union. I speak all along as to what is practicable: as to the matter of expediency, that is not in question here.[*b*]

[b] It may happen that one person or set of persons shall be sovereign in some cases, while another is as compleatly so in other cases.[*c*] On this supposition, they may be consider'd as composing all together but one sovereign. The truth of these propositions, which, perhaps, may be found not very conformable to the most current notions, may presently be made appear. Power over persons, is either power over their passive faculties merely, or power over their active faculties: which latter may be termed *power of imperation*. Now, in point of fact, not to meddle at present with the point of right (or, to speak more intelligibly, with the point of utility or expediency, since right independently of law and of utility is unintelligible)—in point of fact, I say, the ultimate efficient cause of all power of imperation over persons is a disposition on the part of those persons to obey: the efficient cause, then, of the power of the sovereign is neither more nor less than the disposition to obedience on the part of the people. Now, this disposition, it is obvious, may admitt of innumerable modifications: and that even while it is constant; besides that it may change from day to day. The people may be disposed to obey the commands of one man against all the world in relation to one sort of act, those of another man in relation to another sort of act: else what are we to think of the constitutional laws of the Germanic body? those of one man in one place, those of another man in another place; as we see all the world over: those of one man (for instance the Dictator at Rome) at one time, those of another man or set of men (for instance the assembly of the governing part of the Roman

[*a*] See Fragm. on Gov:[t] Ch. IV. par. 34.[2]

[*b*] ib. 37.[3]

[*c*] See Ch. 16 {Division} 17 n. (n).[4]

---

[1] The following passage, through to the beginning of paragraph 37 (p. 58 below), is a later draft of this 'respect'. The original discussion constituted paragraphs 32–6 of the 'principal draft', but the corresponding text sheets have not been located. For further details see the Editorial Introduction, pp. xxiii–xxiv above.

[2] See *A Fragment on Government* (*CW*), Ch. IV, paras. 34–6, pp. 488–90.

[3] See ibid., para. 37, p. 490.

[4] See *An Introduction to the Principles of Morals and Legislation* (*CW*), p. 200 n. The note appears as note [x] in *CW*, but as note [n] in the edition published in 1789.

question not to be the will of *a* sovereign, that is of some sovereign or other, in such case, if it come backed with motives of a coercive nature, it is not a law, but an illegal mandate: and the act of issuing it is an offence.[a]

people) at another: they may be disposed to obey a man if he *commands* a given sort of act: they may be disposed not to obey him if he *forbids* it: and *vice versâ*. In some of these cases, sharp, one should think, must be the eye that can detect encroachments, and resolute the hand that can bear up against them, and that can say to the torrent of sovereign power, thus far shalt thou go and no farther. But there is nothing of this sort which religion can not do at any time: in the purest monarchies as well as in the freest commonwealths. The Jews would have done every thing else for Antiochus, but they would not eat his pork.[1] The exiled Protestants would have done any thing else for Lewis,[2] but they would not go to mass: the Catholics of Great Britain would obey any other law of the Parliament of Great Britain, but they will not stay away from mass. In all other points they will obey the temporal sovereign for the time being: in this point alone they choose to obey the commands of departed sovereigns, or of the Pope, or what comes to the same thing, what to them appear to be the dictates of the religious sanction. Why might not this (in point of practicability I mean) be settled by law, as well as by an inward determination which bids defiance to the law? Does not the Briton, when in France, obey the sovereign of France? does not the Frenchman, when in Great Britain, obey the sovereign of Great Britain? and do not the Briton and the Frenchman both, when at Rome, do as they do at Rome? Let it be observed once more; I consider here not what is most eligible, but only what is possible.

One great difficulty is to draw the boundary line betwixt act and act, betwixt such classes of acts as the sovereign may, and such as he may not, take for the objects of his law, and to distinguish it by marks so clear as not to be in danger of being mistaken: especially where religion and the *acumen* and pertinacity which that principle inspires are out of the question. The plainest marks are those which are made by *place* and *time*. By place: for this is all that there is to distinguish the power of any one sovereign from that of another. By time: accordingly at Rome, even in a rude age, a man could be absolute for six months without any hope or chance of protracting his power a day longer:[3] so in regencies, as we see every day, though the minority be ever so long. As to *place*, where that circumstance is the mark, the line is the stronger, in as much as the physical power terminates in great measure with the political.

But to examine these matters in detail belongs to the particular head of constitutional law.

[a] If the mandate (being a command) comes to be obey'd, the act of issuing it is an act of *simple injurious restrainment*, or *simple injurious compulsion*, according as the command is [negative or positive]:[4] (see infra, §. 12)[5] if not obey'd, it is an attempt to committ the one or the other of those offences: at any rate, as also if it be a countermand, it is a *disturbance*, or, if on pretence of title, an *usurpation*, of

[1] The attempt by soldiers sent to Jerusalem by Antiochus IV (Epiphanes) (*c.* 215–164 BC), ruler of the Seleucid Empire from 175 BC, to force Jewish men to eat pork led to the Maccabean Revolt of 168/7 BC.

[2] i.e. the Huguenots and Louis XIV respectively.

[3] An allusion to the office of Dictator.

[4] MS 'positive or negative' appears to be a slip.

[5] See pp. 115–41 below.

—to whose power the party in question is subject.

If the person of whose will it is the expression be a sovereign, but a sovereign to whose power, in the case in question, a person of the description in question happens not to be subject, it is a law, which as to that person indeed has no force, yet still it is a law.[a] The law having no force, the not obeying it is either no offence or an offence which can not be punished. Yet, still, it can not here be said that the issuing it is an offence: because the person from whom it issues is one whose act, as such, can not be invested with the character of an offence. Were the Lord High Treasurer of Great Britain to issue of his own authority an order for levying a tax on all the inhabitants of Great Britain, the issuing of that order would indeed be an offence: since the Lord High Treasurer of Great Britain is no more a sovereign in Great Britain than he is any where else. But were the King of France to issue an order to the same effect addressed to the same persons, such law would indeed be of no force, but yet it would hardly be looked upon as coming under the name of an offence: why?—because the King of France,

some branch of power beneficial or fiduciary, private or public. See Ch. 16 {Division} liv n. p. cclxxxvii.[1]

[a] It is evident that, in point of fact (for to that point I still exclusively adhere), sovereignty over any given individual is a matter which is liable to much diversity and continual fluctuation. Subjection depends for it's commencement upon birth: but for it's continuance it depends upon a thousand accidents. In point of fact, a man is subject to any and to every sovereign who can make him suffer: whether it be in person (that is in body or in mind), in reputation, in property or in condition.[a] In body, he can be subject to but one at a time: but in mind, in reputation and in property, he may be subject to multitudes at once. Every Catholic, for example, or, if there be any difference, every Papist who is so at heart, whatever nation he belong to, is in a certain sense subject to the Pope, in virtue of those pains of the religious sanction[b] which the head of the Catholic church has it in his power to inflict upon minds whose religious biases[c] prepare them for such impressions: pains the infliction of which, were it an offence, would come under the head of simple mental injuries.[d]

[a] See Ch. 16. {Division} 11[2] and B. I. tit. {Persons subject}.[3]
[b] See Ch. 5. {Pleasures and Pains} 9.[4]
[c] Ch. 6. {Sensibility} 19.[5]
[d] Ch. 16. {Division} 33.[6]

[1] See *An Introduction to the Principles of Morals and Legislation* (*CW*), Ch. XVI, para. 54, IX. OFFENCES against the SOVEREIGNTY, p. 263 n. Bentham's page-reference is to the printed version of the work which appeared in 1780: for further details see the Editorial Introduction, pp. xix–xx above.

[2] See ibid., Ch. XVI, para. 11, pp. 191–4.

[3] A cross-reference to Bentham's projected penal code.

[4] See *An Introduction to the Principles of Morals and Legislation* (*CW*), Ch. V, para. 9, p. 44.

[5] See ibid., Ch. VI, para. 19, p. 57.

[6] See ibid., Ch. XVI, para. 33, pp. 222–4.

though not sovereign in Great Britain, is sovereign elsewhere; to wit in France: on his part, then, it would be an act not of delinquency, but of hostility.

Now, a given will or mandate may be the will or mandate of a given person in either of two ways: in the way of *conception*, as it may be called (that is of original conception), or 2. in the way of *adoption*. A will or mandate may be said to belong to a sovereign in the way of conception when it was he himself who issued it, and who first issued it, in the words or other signs in which it stands expressed: it may be said to belong to him by adoption when the person from whom it immediately emanes is not the sovereign himself (meaning the sovereign for the time being), but some other person: insomuch that all the concern which he to whom it belongs by adoption has in the matter is the being known to entertain a will that, in case such or such another person should have expressed or should come to have expressed a will concerning the act or sort of act in question, such will should be observed and looked upon as his.[a]

This it may do 1. in the way of conception: or 2. of adoption.

Where a mandate appertains to the sovereign only by adoption, such adoption may be distinguished in several respects; 1. in respect of the *time* in which the mandate adopted appears with reference to that of the adopting mandate: 2. in respect of the persons whose mandates are thus adopted: 3. in respect of the *degree* in which the adoption is performed: 4[thly] in respect of the *form* of expression by which it may be performed.

Adoption is either 1. susception: or 2. pre-adoption.

First, then, with regard to *time*, the mandate which the sovereign in question is supposed to adopt may be either already issued, or not: in the former case, it may be said to be his by *susception*; in the latter, by *pre-adoption*.[1] Where the sovereign holds himself thus in readiness to adopt the mandates of another person whensoever they shall happen to have been issued, he may thereby be said to invest that person with a certain species of power, which may be termed a *power of imperation*. Examples of this distinction we shall see immediately.

[a] In this there is no mystery: the names perhaps are new, but the distinction itself is continually exemplified, and that in the most ordinary concerns of life. You are giving orders to your servant: this, it is plain, you may do in either of two ways: by saying to him, 'Go and do so and so,' mentioning what: or by saying to him, 'Go and do what M[r] such-an-one bids you.' One of these ways is just as familiar as the other: the order you yourself give in the former case is your's by conception: the order M[r] such-an-one gives in the latter case is your's by adoption.

[1] In the margin, Bentham has noted in relation to the remainder of the paragraph: 'Qu. whether in a Note?'

Persons whose mandates he adopts—1. Former Sovereigns.

2. As to the *persons* whose mandates the sovereign may have occasion to adopt, it would be to little purpose here, and indeed it would be premature, to attempt reducing the enumeration of them to an analytic method. In the way of susception, the sovereign for the time being adopts as well the mandates of former sovereigns as those of subordinate *power-holders*:[a] in the way of pre-adoption, he can adopt the last mentioned mandates only: for to pre-adopt the mandates of subsequent sovereigns would be nugatory, since whatever actual force there is in sovereignty rests in the sovereign for the time being: in the living, not in the dead. As the propensity to obedience may admit of every imaginable modification, it is just conceivable indeed that the people should in certain points obey the mandates of a deceased sovereign in preference to those of his living successor. Lycurgus, if the story be a true one, found means by a trick, thus to reign after his death:[1] but it is a trick that would hardly succeed a second time: and the necessity he found himself under of having recourse to that expedient would be a sufficient proof, if there required any, how little need the sovereign who is recognized as such for the time being has to be beholden for his power to his departed predecessors.

2. Subordinate power-holders.

As to the subordinate power-holders, whose mandates the sovereign pre-adopts, these are, of course, as many and as various as the classes of persons to whom the law gives either *powers of imperation* or the contrary *powers of de-imperation*, if such is the name that may be given to the power of undoing what by imperation has been done. These powers it may give to the power-holder on his own account, in which case the power is beneficial, or on that of another; in which case it is fiduciary: and in this latter case, on account of an individual, or on account of the public at large; in which latter case, again, the power is of the public or constitutional kind. It is thus that every mandate that is issued within the limits of the sovereignty, and that is not illegal, is in one sense or the other the mandate of the sovereign. Take any mandate whatsoever, either it is of the number of those which he allows or it is not: there is no medium: if it is, it is his; by adoption at least, if not by original conception: if not, it is illegal, and the

[a] {*Power-holders.*} So I will take leave to term those who stand invested with a power: the term is analogous in it's formation to the words *landholder, freeholder, housholder.*

[1] Lycurgus, the legendary Spartan lawgiver, made the Spartans promise that they would not change the laws until he had returned with the judgment of the Delphic oracle on their wisdom. Having consulted the oracle, Lycurgus starved himself to death without returning to Sparta, in order to make the laws immutable. See Plutarch, *Life of Lycurgus*, xxix. 1–6.

issuing it an offence. Trivial or important makes no difference: if the former are not his, then neither are the latter. The mandates of the master, the father, the husband, the guardian, are all of them the mandates of the sovereign: if not, then neither are those of the general nor of the judge. Not a cook is bid to dress a dinner, a nurse to feed a child, an usher to whip a school boy, an executioner to hang a thief, an officer to drive the enemy from a post, but it is by his orders. If any one should find a difficulty in conceiving this, he has only to suppose the several mandates in question to meet with resistance: in one case as well as in another, the business of enforcing them must rest ultimately with the sovereign. Nor is there any thing of fiction in all this: if there were, this is the last place in which it should be found.

To continue the laws of preceding sovereigns, and the powers of the various classes of magistrates, domestic as well as civil, is (in every tolerably well settled commonwealth at least) a matter of course. To suffer either of those systems of institutions to perish, and not to establish any thing in their stead, would be to suffer the whole machine of government to drop to pieces. The one course no man was ever yet mad enough, the other none was ever yet industrious enough, to pursue. If the adoption be not declared in words, it is because the fact is so notorious, that any express form of words to signify it would be unnecessary. It is manifested by means not less significant than words, by every act of government, by which the enforcement of the mandates in question is provided for. If it be alledged that the trivial transactions that pass in the interior of a family are not specifically in the contemplation of the sovereign (trivial as they may be termed when individually consider'd, though in their totality they are the stuff that human life is made of), the same may be said of the transactions of fleets and armies: of those which become the objects of the mandates issued by the general or the judge. The same may even be said of those laws which emane directly from the very presence of the sovereign. It is only by the general tenor of their effects, and not by any direct specification, that individual acts of any kind can be comprised under extensive and general descriptions.

It is in this very way that conveyances and covenants[a] acquire all the validity they can possess, all the connection they have with the system of the laws: adopted by the sovereign, they are converted into mandates.[b] If you give your coat to a man, and the gift is valid, Concern which the sovereign has in giving legality to conveyances and covenants.

[a] This is another of the many occasions that occur in a work of general jurisprudence in which it is difficult to find a proper term to make use of. The word *promise* would have been too extensive: since, even of such promises as it is

 [*See p. 48 for n. a cont. and p. 50 for note b*]

and nobody else has a right to meddle with your coat, it is because a mandate subsists on the part of the sovereign, commanding all persons whatever to refrain from meddling with it, he to whom you

lawful to make, it is not every one that the law will oblige a man to observe: and the same thing may be said of the words *agreement* and *engagement*. The word *stipulation* is liable to objections which it would take up too much room to discuss here. The word *pact* is not in common use, and it has no conjugates belonging to it. The word *compact* might seem to exclude the case of a *nudum pactum*, where there is but one pact, one promise, between the parties: without any promise or any thing else to which English lawyers give the name of a *consideration* given on the other side. The word *contract* (though at first sight it might seem more apposite than any that have been mentioned) is too extensive. In the Roman law, it is applied to various sorts of mixed transactions: to transactions consisting of a conveyance on each side, as in *emptio-venditio*: to transactions consisting of a perpetual conveyance on one side and a covenant or covenants on the other, as in *mutuum*: to transactions consisting of a temporary conveyance on one side, and a covenant or covenants on the other, as in *depositum* and *commodatum*: of a conveyance which might be temporary or perpetual according to contingencies, and a covenant or covenants on the other, as in *pignus*: not to mention cases in which there was neither conveyance nor covenant between the parties, but only certain obligations imposed upon them in consequence of some community of interest by the law itself: as might be the case in *societas* where, for instance, the thing had accrued to the *soccii*, the partners, by the gift of a third person. In the English law there is a similar confusion, though not the same. The name of *contract* is given to some transactions in which there is nothing but pure conveyance, as in *sale* and *exchange*: to others in which there is conveyance and covenant both, as in *Bailment,* and in *Hiring* and *Borrowing*: to other cases in which there is neither conveyance nor covenant, but an obligation to convey arising from some other source; as in several cases of *debt*. It is not a place here to enter into any further discussions concerning the Roman *contractûs* or the English *contracts*, or to draw any parallel between them. The ideas respectively annexed to these terms are compound ideas, consisting of conveyances, covenants and other sources of obligation made up in various mixtures. To understand these mixtures, a man must understand the elements of which they are composed; that is he must know in what respects those elements are distinct not only from other things, but from one another. Among those elements are conveyances and covenants. But of the difference between a conveyance and a covenant, no lawyer that has ever written seems yet to have entertained a clear idea. This, at least, must be said of all those who have acquiesced in this part of the nomenclature either of the Roman or of the English Law. The Roman jurisprudence on this subject is a perfect chaos: the English jurisprudence is as perfect an one in another way: and one may venture to affirm that there is no other system of jurisprudence any where that is in any better case. To infuse order into this chaos, to throw light upon this darkness, is impossible to a man who has not some such analysis as the following before his eyes.

Let any obligation, to which one man can be subjected in favour of another, be conceived. Such obligation either is incumbent upon you or is not: if not, and the case is that once it was imposed upon you, it must have been taken off. Whether it remains incumbent on you or has been taken off, the imposition or removal must have been performed either directly by the law itself, without the intervention of

give it alone excepted, upon the event of your declaring such to be your pleasure. If a man engages or covenants to mend your coat for you, and such an engagement is valid, it is because a mandate

any other will either on your own part or on that of any other person, or else by an individual or individuals in virtue of powers conferred on them by the law. In the first case, there is neither covenant nor conveyance. In the other case, if the obligation is imposed upon yourself alone by yourself alone (I mean in the first instance), the expression of will which it is imposed by is a covenant: in all other cases, whether it be that an obligation is taken off in the first instance or imposed, the expression of will whereby such effect is produced is a conveyance: a conveyance of a right to him from whom an obligation is taken off, or in whose favour an obligation is imposed on some one else. (I say in the first instance: for whatever further operations may be necessary either to *corroborate* a right and give it that degree of force which in most systems of law it possesses, or to turn the possession of it to the account of a third person, these of themselves may be looked upon as sufficient to create it. Concerning the corroborative provisions alluded to, see the next paragraph in the text.) It appears, then, that on a large view of the subject, a covenant may be regarded as a species of conveyance: it is a conveyance of a right to certain services: but it can never be a conveyance of any thing but a right to services; nor of any other services than those of the conveyor or covenantor himself. Saving this exception, as on the one hand a man may always covenant without conveying; so on the other hand may he always convey without covenanting: and though it often happens that the operations of covenanting and conveying are performed together, yet this does not render them in themselves the less distinguishable. The case in which the effect of a covenant comes nearest to that of a conveyance, is that of a covenant to convey: but even in this the difference is manifestly discernible. Every one knows that a person in whose favour a covenant to convey a piece of land, for instance, has been made, which covenant has not been performed, is not yet in the case of one in whose favour that covenant has been performed, and a conveyance has been made accordingly. In the first case, occupation of the land on his part would as yet be wrongful, whatever wrong there may be in the behaviour of the other who *withholds* from him the sort of *service* which consists in the making such conveyance as would render the occupation lawful: in the other case, such service having been render'd, the occupation is not wrongful any longer.

It perhaps may be thought superfluous to observe, that by *covenant* I mean all along what people at large are in use to mean by it: viz: a promise, any promise whatsoever, which is render'd binding by the law: and not such promises only, for the breach of which the remedy given by the English law is call'd, in the technical language of that law, *an action of covenant.*[1]

As the word *contract* is applied to transactions where there is conveyance and to transactions where there is covenant, one might be tempted at first sight to look upon it as a term that might be made use of as a common name for conveyances and covenants in all cases. But this would not by any means agree

[1] The following passage, which belongs here, has been marked by Bentham for deletion: 'Superfluous it would indeed be were it certain that no lawyer would ever look into this book, or none but what was superior to the prejudices of his profession. But it must often have been observed, that when a man gets the habit of using words in the technical sense to which the use of them is confined by lawyers, he is apt to lose the memory of the more extensive sense which is given to them by other men.'

on the part of the sovereign hath been issued, commanding any person, upon the event of his entering into any engagement (exceptions excepted), and thereby that particular person in consequence of his having enter'd into that particular engagement (it not being within the exceptions), to perform it: in other words, to render you that particular service which is render'd to you by performance of the act which he has engaged for.

Thus, then, in all cases stands the distinction between the laws which belong to the legislator in the way of conception, and those which belong to him in the way of pre-adoption. The former are the work of the legislator solely: the latter, that of the legislator and the subordinate power-holder conjunctively, the legislator sketching out a sort of imperfect mandate which he leaves it to the subordinate power-holder to fill up.[a] In the first case, there are no other mandates in the case than those which emane from the legislator *immediate*: in the latter case, whatever mandates there are emane from the subordinate power-holder *immediate*, and whenever they happen to be issued can only be said to emane *potestative* from the legislator. In the former case, there are mandates from the first that exist *in actu*: in the latter, untill issued by the subordinate power-holder, whatever mandates there may be conceived to be exist only *in potentiâ*. In the former case, the law will more readily than in the other be perceived to be occupied in issuing or repealing commands: in the other case, it will be apt to appear as if it were employ'd solely in giving descriptions: for example of the *persons* by whom powers shall be possessed; of the *things* over which, or persons over whom, such powers shall be possessed: of the *acts* to which such power shall extend, that is of which the performance shall

with the nomenclature either of the English or of the Roman Jurisprudence. To covenants, the word contract might perhaps be applied in every case without any great apparent harshness; although there are some cases in which it is not usually thus applied. But in regard to conveyances, it could not without great violence be applied to any others than those to which it has usually been applied: because the particular usage of lawyers, which seems in this instance to have grown up in repugnancy to common usage, will not bear a man out in such repugnancy any farther.

[b] See Ch. 16. Division. 35 n. (n).[1]

[a] This is one way among innumerable others in which, as will be seen hereafter, the compleat power of imperation or de-imperation may be broken into shares. See §. 11. {Generality}.[2]

---

[1] See *An Introduction to the Principles of Morals and Legislation* (*CW*), Ch. XVI, para. 35, p. 228 n. The note appears as note [g3] in *CW*, but as note [n] in the edition published in 1789.

[2] See pp. 98–114 below.

be deemed an exercise of such power: of the *place* in which, and the *time* during which, such powers shall be exercised, and so on. Yet, still, such descriptions have so much in them of the nature of a command or what stands opposed to it, that whenever the power which they confer or limit comes to be exercised, the expression of will whereby it is exercised may, without any alteration made in the import of it, be translated into the form and language of a mandate: of a mandate issuing from the mouth of the lawgiver himself.[a]

Degrees of adoption.

Next, as to the degree in which the mandate of a subordinate power-holder may be adopted by the sovereign: or in other words, the degree of force which such mandate acquires by the adoption. Take any single manifestation of the sovereign's will, and all the assistance that the mandate of a subordinate power-holder can receive from it consists in a bare permission: this is the first step that the sovereign takes towards the giving validity to subordinate mandates: the first and least degree of assistance, or rather countenance, that the inferior can receive from the superior: the not being made the subject of a law commanding him not to issue the subordinate mandate which is in question. The part thus far taken by the sovereign is, we see, merely a negative one. Nor wou'd it be worth while, or indeed proper, to notice him as taking any part at all, since it is no more than what is taken by every the merest stranger, were it not for its lying so much in his way to take the contrary part; a part which he actually does take in relation to the greater number of the other members of the community. If any farther degree of countenance is shewn, it must be by another law or set of laws: a law permitting the subordinate power-holder to punish with his own hand the party who is made subject to the mandate in case of disobedience, by a law permitting others to assist in the administering such punishment, by a law commanding others to assist; and so on. Such ulterior corroborative laws, however, are not to be reckoned as exclusively [necessary][1] to the particular business of adoption: for a set of subsidiary laws like them are equally necessary, as will be seen hereafter, to the giving

[a] The fundamental law of those by which conveyances of property in things corporeal are adopted is that which corresponds to and prohibits the offence of wrongful occupation of property: that by which covenants are adopted, is that which corresponds to and prohibits the offence of wrongful withholding of services. See Ch. 16 {Division}.[2]

[1] MS 'necessarily'.

[2] See *An Introduction to the Principles of Morals and Legislation* (*CW*), Ch. XVI, para. 35, note [g3], p. 228 n.

force and efficacy to such laws as emane from the sovereign himself in the most immediate manner.[a]

Forms of adoption. Next, as to the form or manner in which the adoption may be performed. We have already intimated that it may be done by permission: that is by a legislative permission: but it may also be done by mandate, by a legislative mandate: by a permission addressed in the first instance to the power-holder; a permission to issue the mandates which it is proposed to adopt; or by a mandate addressed immediately to those whom it is meant to subject to his power; a mandate commanding them to obey such and such mandates whensoever, if at all, he shall have thought fit to issue them. In the former case, the mandate of the subordinate power-holder, whenever it comes to be issued, is a *primordial* one: in the latter case, it is *superventitious*, the mandate of the sovereign being the primordial one of which this which is superventitious is *re-iterative*. These terms, should they appear obscure, will hereafter be explained.[b] Whichever be the form, it comes exactly to the same thing: and the difference lies rather in the manner in which we may conceive the inclination of the sovereign to be expressed, than in the inclination itself. In both cases, the mandate depends for its force upon a farther set of mandates, as hath been already intimated and will be shewn more particularly farther on. Whether these subsidiary mandates be annexed to a mandate on the part of the sovereign *ab initio*, or to the mandates of the subordinate power-holder when they arise, is a matter of indifference.

By-laws, what. The mandate of a subordinate power-holder, when it has the requisite degree of permanency and generality to constitute it, according to common speech, *a law*, is, in the language of the English jurisprudence, in many cases termed a *by-law*. It was first applied to the laws made by the governing body in corporate towns, being so much as to say a *town-law*.[c] In process of time it has been extended to laws made by any other bodies corporate; although they had nothing to do with the government of particular towns: such as trading, banking and insurance companies. It might with equal propriety and convenience be extended to any subordinate laws whatever. In Great Britain, King's proclamations,

[a] v. infra §.13 {Force}.[1]
[b] Infra §. 12 {Aspect}.[2]
[c] Spelm: Gloss. tit. *Bellagines*.[3]

[1] See §13, paras. 97–106, pp. 146–56 below.
[2] See, in particular, §12, para. 86, pp. 139–41 below.
[3] See Henry Spelman, *Archæologus. In modum Glossarii ad rem antiquam posteriorem*, London, 1626, pp. [94]–5.

wherever they are any thing more than admonitions to observe the already established laws, are by-laws: King's Charters, in as much as they confer new powers of legislation, are by-laws: the articles of war, which it is the custom for the King to establish for the government of the army, are by-laws: treaties enter'd into by the King, in as far as they contain any thing that binds the subject *ipso facto*, are by-laws: the ordinances established by James when Duke of York and Lord High Admiral for the government of the Dock-Yards[1] are by-laws: Standing Regulations which the Justices of the Peace are allow'd in certain cases to make in their judicial capacity or otherwise for the government of their respective counties are by-laws: standing rules of Court made *mero motu* by judges of all sorts are by-laws: so in France many of the *arrêts* of their parliaments, though ranked without distinction under the same name with their judicial mandates, will be found upon examination to be by-laws; as, in short, are all other permanent mandates whatsoever which bear not the signature of the King. General ordinances established by the several states of the German Empire within their respective dominions are, in as far as they hold themselves subject to the dominion of the Diet, no more than by-laws. Ordinances issued by the assembly of the States General of the Dutch United Provinces for the government of the provinces of the generality (*pays de la généralité*) are no more than by-laws, the sovereignty over the States General being consider'd as residing in the collective or aggregate body composed of the several sovereignties of the seven provinces, or perhaps of the several independent townships, who for this purpose must be understood as constituting all together but one sovereign. This aggregate sovereign, if the ordinances of their delegates, the States General, require to be ratified by the several component sovereignties before they receive their binding force, imperates so far in the way of original conception; if no such ratification is necessary, in the way of adoption: being the same way, and the only way, in which the [Members][2] of the British House of Commons and their electors imperate, in virtue of the share which is exercised by the House of Commons in the sovereignty of the British Empire.

[1] James, Duke of York (1633–1701), later James II, King of England, Scotland, and Ireland 1685–8, was officially appointed as Lord High Admiral of England in 1661, and retained the office until 1673. Bentham may have had in mind 'Instructions to the Navy Board for the government of the Navy' which James issued on 28 January 1662, and which appeared in print as *The Oeconomy of His Majesty's Navy-Office. Containing The several Duties of the Commissioners and Principal Officers thereof*, London, 1717.

[2] MS 'Electors'.

Analytical sketch of the different sorts of mandates distinguished according to their source.

I shall conclude this section with the analytical recapitulation promised in the last.[1] A mandate is either referable to the sovereign or it is not: in the latter case it is illegal, and what we have nothing to do with here.

A legal mandate, then, is either private or domestic, or else public or civil: a domestic mandate is one that emanes from a person having power in virtue of his being invested with a condition of the domestic kind, and is addressed to the person who stands invested with the correlative condition: a civil or public mandate is either sovereign or subordinate. If sovereign, either it is *suâ naturâ* permanent, or it is not: in the former case, it is a sovereign law at any rate: in the latter, if it proceeds from a number of persons possessing the sovereignty in conjunction, it is still a sovereign law as before; if from a single person possessing the sovereignty in severalty, it is a sovereign order. If the authority from which it immediately emanes be subordinate, it is issued either on the occasion of a suit, or independently of any such occasion: in the former case, it is a judicial order or mandate, and may be stiled an order *litis causâ* or *propter quid*: in the latter case, it may be stiled a subordinate legislative mandate *ex mero motu*. In this latter case again, if it is susceptible of perpetuity, it may be stiled a *subordinate law* or *by-law*: if not, it may be stiled an *executive order*.

In this analysis, conveyances and covenants are not included. This is owing to the multitude of different species there are of them, which could not here be brought all of them under the same head, nor yet distinguished without engaging in discussions for which we are not as yet prepared. Of the general nature of a suit at law and of the distinction of suits into civil and penal, more will be said hereafter.[a] [2]

[a] See infra §§. 13, and 14, and 20.[3]

---

[1] See p. 37 above.

[2] Bentham has noted at this point: 'Divide private into domestic and non-domestic. In non-domestic, a man imposes an obligation either on others or on himself alone: if on others, it is a conveyance; if on himself, a covenant.'

[3] See pp. 142–60, 161–4, 207–18 below respectively.

§5. *Ends which a law may have in view.*[1]

1. Secondly, with regard to the *end* which the law may have in view.[2] Now, by *end* is here meant not the eventual end, which is a matter of chance, but the intended end, which is a matter of design. But the intended end of any act in general, and, therefore, of the particular sort of act or measure which consists in the issuing of a law, is one of those objects which we have already had occasion to speak of under the appellation of a *motive*: to wit, the external motive in prospect.[a]

2. The end of a law is the external motive which he whose law it is had in prospect.

2. It is to be remember'd that a law may belong to the sovereign either in the way of conception or in the way of adoption: in the latter case, there are necessarily two persons whose law in these two different senses it may be said to be. These two persons, it may happen, may, in regard to the parts they have respectively taken in the establishment of the law, have been actuated by two different motives: they may have had in view two different ends. As to the sovereign, the end or external motive[b] he can have had in view in adopting the law can, upon the principle of utility, have been no other than the greatest good of the community:[c] which end we suppose his measures to be directed to of course: since it is only in as far as that is the case that these enquiries are calculated or designed to be of any use to him. But with regard to the party to

This end may in certain cases be the private interest of him from whom the law immediately emanes.

[a] See Ch. 10. {Motives} 5.[3]

[b] As to the internal motive, whether it be the purely social motive of benevolence, or, as in this case it is called, public spirit, or the semi-social motive of love of reputation, or the self-regarding motives of love of power, love of wealth and so forth, or, what is commonly the case, a mixture of all these together, these are points which as in most cases they are undiscoverable, so in all cases they are immaterial.

[c] v. Ch. 1. {Utility}.[4]

---

[1] This section constitutes a later addition to the 'principal draft'.

[2] The following passage which belongs here has been crossed through by Bentham: 'As to the general and ultimate end, this, upon the principle of utility, can be no other than the greatest good of the whole community. But the good of the community is the sum of the several particular *goods* (if the term may be employ'd) of the several individuals of which it is composed: [v. Ch. 1. {Utility}.] so that to augment the good of any such individual is *pro tanto* to augment the good of the whole community. A law, therefore, of which the immediate end is no other than the good or benefit of the person whose law it is, does not, on that account, cease to be such a law as is capable of being warranted by the principle of utility: much less does it cease to be entitled to the appellation of a law.'

Bentham's cross-reference is presumably to *An Introduction to the Principles of Morals and Legislation* (*CW*), Ch. I, paras. 3–7, pp. 12–13.

[3] See ibid., Ch. X, paras. 5–6, pp. 97–8.

[4] See ibid., Ch. I, paras. 3–7, pp. 12–13.

whom the law appertains in the way of conception, and from whom it immediately emanes, the case is different. In many instances it may happen, and that properly enough, that the end which he has in view is no other than his own particular benefit or satisfaction: which is the case with all those mandates which are issued in virtue of a power of the beneficiary kind: in this case are all the mandates, for instance, of the master acting as such, as also those of the parent and of the husband, in as far as the parent and the husband are allowed to act in the capacity of a master.[1] To the same head may also be referred even such mandates as persons possessed of fiduciary power are allowed to issue, in as far as that allowance is given them in the way of salary: though, indeed, wherever that is the case, the power may be and, to consider it in an accurate point of view, must be looked upon as being *pro tanto* of the beneficial kind, and the *power-holder* as being invested *pro tanto* with the authority of a master. To the same head, indeed, may also be referred even such mandates as are issued in the exercise of such power of the beneficial kind as the sovereign himself is allow'd, and upon the principle of utility may be allow'd, to exercise: either in the way of salary like any other trustee of the public, or as a member of the community whose interest there is just as much reason for consulting as any other's, and no more. In this as in so many other particulars he stands exactly upon a footing with a parent, in whose hands the beneficial power is blended with the fiduciary, and who is allow'd to exercise over his children the authority of a master, partly for their sakes, and partly for his own.

But the most conspicuous cases are those in which it ought to be the public good at large.

3. But the more conspicuous case and the more common with such mandates as, in consideration of their generality and their permanency, are usually distinguished by the name of *laws* is that in which the proper end of the sovereign who adopts, and that of the subordinate magistrate who issues, the mandate, coincide: being each of them not the particular good of the author of the mandate, but the general good of the community at large. This good may be consider'd either in respect of the parties it more immediately affects, or in respect of what it is in its own nature. In the former point of view, it will be particularly consider'd by and by.[a] In the latter point of view, it hath already in some measure

[a] See infra §7.[2]

[1] In the margin, Bentham has noted at this point: 'Power of conveyancing and covenanting, whether to be omitted?'

[2] See pp. 66–74 below.

been consider'd in a preceding chapter, though not in any great detail.[a] The sketch, then, which has been already given for the purpose of that chapter will likewise be made to answer the present purpose, by changing only the position in which it presents itself.

Analysis of this common or general end into the specific ends that are subordinate to it.

4. The common end of all laws as prescribed by the principle of utility is the promotion of the public good. But since good and evil are opposites, the promoting of good, where the good is negative, is but another name for the averting of mischief, where the mischief is positive:[b] as the averting of negative good is for the promoting of positive mischief. Now, in the chapter alluded to, offences (that is acts which appear to be of such a nature as to require their being made offences) are classed according to the nature of the mischiefs, negative as well as positive, which it is their tendency to produce. But to create an offence is to make a law: and the offence being given, the law is thereby given. Moreover, the mischief of the offence exhibits the end of the law, not in its natural situation indeed, but, as it were, in an inverted posture, by the rule of contraries: the end of the law being, not the mischief itself, but the good which consists in the prevention of that mischief. By classing offences, then, according to their mischiefs, laws have already been classed according to their ends: so that in giving an analysis of offences, we have given, as far as it has gone, an analysis of legal *ends*.

[a] See Ch. 16. {Division}.[1]

[b] For the offences that stand opposed to the promotion of positive good see Ch. 16. {Division} liv. n. (m).[2]

---

[1] Bentham perhaps has in mind the discussion of the 'Characters of the five classes' of offences at *An Introduction to the Principles of Morals and Legislation* (*CW*), Ch. XVI, §v, pp. 274–80.

[2] See ibid., OFFENCES against the POSITIVE INCREASE of the NATIONAL FELICITY, para. 54, p. 262 n. The note appears as note [r4] in *CW*, but as note [m] in the edition published in 1789.

§6. *Subjects of a law.*

—3. Subjects of a law, persons—things—as agents—or as patients.

37. 1. Thirdly, with regard to the *subjects*, that is the persons and things to which the law may have relation.[a] Either may come under the notice of the law in each of two capacities: as *agents* or as *patients*: as beings in which the act or motion which is the *object* of the law in question may have its commencement, or as those through which it makes its progress or in which it has its termination.[b] In the former case they may be termed the *agible*, in the latter the *passible*, subjects of the law.[c] A person, for example, may be the striker, or the party struck: a thing may be the thing destroy'd, or the instrument of destruction.[1]

[a] The distinction between the *subject* of a thing and the *object* is, it must be confessed, by no means an explicit one: nor does it seem possible to settle it by any general rule: since there are few cases perhaps in which, if the one of those appellations be proper, the other may not also be employ'd. Even in the present case the articles to which I have appropriated the former might perhaps with equal propriety have been characterized by the latter. A person or thing may as well be consider'd in the light of one which has been *thrown* and *stands* in the way of the law (*ob, jactum*), as in the light of one that has been thrown and *lies underneath* it (*sub, jactum*): and so *vice versâ* with regard to acts. What determined me to apply the substantive *subjects* to persons and things rather than to acts is that its conjugate, the adjective *subject*, seems to be more frequently applied to persons and things, but more particularly to persons, than to acts. To speak of persons as subject to the law, of countries as subject to the law, are expressions perfectly familiar. When all is done, the distinction can scarcely be kept up with any degree of perseverance beyond the particular occasion on which it is noticed: since on other occasions it will be scarcely possible to avoid applying the terms *subject* and *object* both to persons and things, as well as to acts.

If the appellation of *objects* is applied to persons and things as well as to acts, the two former may, for distinctions sake, be termed the *material*, or rather, to save ambiguity, the *substantial*, objects of the law, while the latter are termed its *modal* objects.

[b] v. Ch. 7. {Actions} 14.[2]

[c] The word *passible*, though not familiar, is already in the language. (See

---

[1] The remainder of the section is a later insertion. The 'principal draft' continues with the following passage, which carries the marginal heading 'Persons addressed by it in the first, second, &c. instance':

'**38.** Moreover, the persons who are conspicuous in the relation of subjects to the law may be mentioned under the appellation of the persons to whom it is addressed; or who are addressed by it: since it not only must be addressed to them, but must actually be present to their conceptions, before it can have any influence on their conduct: and of these, such as are consider'd by it in the capacity of agents may be said to be addressed by it in the first instance: while to those who are consider'd by it in the capacity of patients, as being liable to be affected by the conduct of the persons firstmentioned, it may be said to be addressed in the second instance.

Thus far the language held concerning persons is precisely the same as that concerning things. But the ideas annexed to this language is in the two cases very different, owing to the

 [*See opposite page for n. 1 cont. and note 2*]

2. The words *passible subject*, we may observe, as well as the correspondent word *termination*, apply as naturally to a person as to a thing: and there will be at least as much occasion for applying them to the former as to the latter. The parallelism may be carried on still farther. Of the persons and the things that are the passible subjects of the act which is the object of the law, and thence also of the law itself, it may be equally said that they are the persons *in* whom, and the things *in* which, that act hath its termination, and that they are the persons *upon* whom, and the things *upon* which, the act is exercised and the effects of it become conspicuous. From this identity in point of expression, one would naturally be apt to conclude that the ideas signified were also the same: that the meaning of the word *termination* were the same when applied to persons as when applied to things; and so with regard to the word *upon*. But this is far from being the case: so that if the idea raised in a man's mind by either of those words when applied to things, were to be transferred without alteration or addition to persons, it would be found very defective. This depends upon the different properties of the classes of beings which are respectively indicated by those terms: in virtue of which properties, an act may have various effects upon persons which it cannot have upon things. Things consider'd as such have none but physical properties: persons have mental as well as physical:[a] that is they have the faculty of sensation (I mean that of experiencing pain and pleasure), that of perception (I mean perception as distinct from pain and pleasure), and volition: the two former of which come under the head of merely passive, the last under that of active, faculties. In a thing, then, in which an act is consider'd as having its

Persons may be subjects of a law in a physical or in a pathological way.

Johnson's Dict.)[1] The word *agible*, for aught I can find, is new to it, though exactly correspondent to the other.

[a] Of the inferior animals I omitt, for shortness sake, to make any particular mention: in as far as their mental faculties are taken into the account, they stand upon a footing with persons: in as far as they are not taken into the account, they stand on a footing with inanimate things.

---

difference between the nature of the one class of beings and that of the other. To apprehend this, we must make a'

Bentham's pagination indicates that there are six missing pages in the 'principal draft' at this point, prior to the commencement of paragraph 39 (p. 66 below).

[2] See *An Introduction to the Principles of Morals and Legislation* (*CW*), Ch. VII, para. 14, p. 77.

[1] Samuel Johnson, *A Dictionary of the English Language: in which The Words are deduced from their Originals, and Illustrated in their Different Significations by Examples from the best Writers. To which are prefixed, A History of the Language, and An English Grammar*, 2nd edn., 2 vols., 1755–6, defines the word 'passible' as follows: 'Susceptive of impressions from external agents.'

termination, it can only have produced physical effects, viz: motions or quiescent situations: but in a person it may have produced volitions, perceptions or sensations. With regard to such of the effects of an act as consist of volitions or indifferent perceptions, we have not at present any concern: but those which consist of sensations may be termed its *pathological effects*. On a thing, then, an act can have only physical effects: on a person, it may have not only physical effects but (amongst others) pathological.

Pathological termination of an act—its various modifications.

3. As to the pathological effects or consequences of an act, they may either be of the pleasurable or of the painful kind; and each again may be consider'd either as certain or as contingent.[a] Be they of which of these kinds they may, the act by which they are produced will have been either according to law or not according to law: in which latter case, it is called an offence. For an analysis of the possible modifications of which the pathological termination of an act which is *not* according to law are susceptible, we have, therefore, only to turn to the division of offences: or if that be not particular enough, to the catalogue of pains and pleasures.[b] The same analysis will serve equally well for the case where the act *is* according to law; for instance, where it is an act of punishment.[c]

4. It will appear, then, that an act may have a physical termination and no pathological: or a pathological termination and no physical one: and that where it has both, the *locus* of its physical termination may be in one subject, and that of its pathological termination in another.

An act may have a physical termination and not a pathological

1. An act may have a physical and no pathological termination. This is the case with every act that is not in some way or other a *material* one. This appears sufficiently from the definitions of the two words.[d] In this case, indeed, it is not of the number of those which, upon the principle of utility, it can be proper to take for the object of a law. Still, however, it must be taken notice of as a case which at any rate is possible, and which in fact is every where but too frequent.

[a] See Ch. 12. {Consequences}.[1]
[b] Ch. 5.[2]
[c] See infra §8. p. 9.[3]
[d] See Ch. 7. {Actions} 3.[4]

[1] See *An Introduction to the Principles of Morals and Legislation* (*CW*), Ch. XII, para. 15, pp. 147–9.
[2] See ibid., pp. 42–50.
[3] i.e. the ninth page of the MS draft of the eighth section: see p. 77 below.
[4] See *An Introduction to the Principles of Morals and Legislation* (*CW*), Ch. VII, para. 3, p. 74 & n.

5. 2. An act may have a pathological termination and no physical one. This is the case where the act is merely of the negative kind:[a] for example that of a mother who should suffer her infant to starve for want of being suckled.

—or a pathological and no physical

6. 3. Where an act has a physical termination as well as a pathological one, the *locus* of the physical termination may be in one subject, while that of the pathological termination is in another. Indeed, there is but one case in which these two *loci* coincide: this is where the pleasure or pain which constitutes the material part of the effects of the act is of the corporeal kind. In all other cases, if the act be of the physical kind, the physical effects of it stop short before they reach the person whose mind is the *locus* of the pathological termination. A thief steals your houshold-goods: or the judge causes them to be seized in satisfaction of a fine. The physical termination of the act is in both cases in the goods themselves; and takes place, perhaps, as soon as the goods are set down out of your reach or knowledge: it reaches not to your person, which, perhaps, is at a hundred miles from the scene of action. At this period, the act, consider'd with respect to its pathological effects, must be consider'd as suspended or (as lawyers say) resting in *abeyance*: nor in respect of such of them as concern you does it come to its termination, till it produces in your mind the pain of privation resulting from the consciousness of having lost the goods; or at least deprives you of some satisfaction you might otherwise have had in using them.

—or a physical and a pathological in distinct subjects.

7. The necessity of this distinction will be still more apparent where the influence of the act is consider'd as extending itself to the community at large: insomuch that the community at large is consider'd (that is, strictly speaking, some individually unassignable members of it are consider'd) as constituting the passible subjects of the act: as where the act, being an offence, and that a private one, is consider'd with respect to its semi-public and public mischief: or, being an offence, is purely of a public or of a semi-public nature.[b] In these cases, after the physical termination of the act has taken place, the pathological termination of it may be consider'd as resting not only in abeyance but in contingency: that is, to speak strictly, as being more particularly uncertain, since in strictness every event is contingent while it is future.[c]

In as far as the consequences are of a public or semi-public nature, the pathological termination of the act is contingent.

[a] ib. 8 &c.[1]

[b] See Ch. 16. {Division} §1 and 5.[2]

[c] It may be said that, as no act any more than any other event which takes place

[1] See ibid., Ch. II, paras. 8–10, pp. 75–6.

[2] See ibid., Ch. XVI, §§ i and v, pp. 187–91 and 274–80 respectively.

Different senses of the word *upon* as applied to a person who is a passible subject of the law.

8. Without calling to mind these distinctions, it will hardly be possible (at least in my own case I found it was not possible) to find any clear ideas, any distinct images, to annex to the phrases in which a man is mentioned as one *upon* whom an act of punishment is exercised: one *upon* whom a punishment is inflicted. To this one expression correspond, in the three different cases that have been stated, three perfectly different ideas or pictures in the mind: in one case, the idea is that of an act of the positive kind terminating physically in the body of the person punished: in another, it is an act still of the positive kind, but never by it's ordinary physical effects extending to his body: in a third case, it is not so much as any positive act at all: it is nothing more than a mere negative act which has neither a termination nor a commencement any where. This negative act may indeed be preceded by judicial opinions, judicial orders, and the like: but these are acts of the positive kind;

without the limits of a man's person can reach his mind but by means of sensible signs, these signs must be looked upon as continuations of the physical act: that, therefore, as the physical act is not at an end till these signs have had their effect, and as thereupon the pathological effects immediately take place, the *locus* as well as the period of these two terminations are still in effect the same: that, for example, in the instance above produced, the pain you suffer by the loss of your goods, you yourself being at a distance, does not take place till you come to be informed of it, for example by the verbal relation of somebody, or by a letter. Thus far the objection. It may be answer'd, that every termination that is assigned to an act must at any rate be an arbitrary one; since it seems impossible for us to say where the chain of causes and effects ends any more than where it begun in any part of it. That, therefore, the best period which can be assigned for the physical termination of an act is that which can be easiest described: and that there can be no period so easily and certainly described, described in a manner so little liable to mistake, as that in which the progress or course it takes changes from a purely physical act to an act of so disparate a nature as an intelligible sign, or act of discourse. While the thief or the minister of justice is carrying away your goods to the place where they are to rest, the act or course of events is uniform and homogeneous: it changes into one of a quite different nature when a letter is written to you informing you of the misfortune, or when, upon sending a person for some of the goods, word is brought back to you that they are not to be found. The course of events that intervene between the misfortune and the suffering undergoes at such a period as great a change as a road does when, having taken its course for miles through a narrow lane, it opens into a common, where, instead of continuing in one track, it is in a manner lost by being broken into a thousand obscure paths of which the appearance is very different and whose commencements and terminations are oftentimes scarce discernible. The stand which takes place in point of time is another remarkable ground of distinction. A man may be years before a misfortune which has taken place has reached his ear: during which time the action may be not going on slowly and continually, as where the mischief is produced by the application of poison or of a cause of corrosion or putrefaction, but absolutely at a stand.

and as distinct from that in question as the province of the judge is from that of the executioner.

9. But farther, for perspicuity's sake, the articles which a given law takes for its subjects, whether agible or passible and whether things or persons, must, in consideration of the different ways in which they may be regarded by it, be distinguished into such as are its subjects in a *direct* manner, and such as are so in an *indirect* manner only: or, to speak more concisely, into the *direct* subjects of the law and the *indirect*. To the former head belong the examples above given. But the persons and the things whereof the names may happen to occur in the tenor of the law will naturally be looked upon all of them without distinction as being comprised under the appellation of its subjects: and why should they not? Nor can it well be otherwise: for that to all of them the law bears a certain relation cannot be denied: and by what other name can they be called in respect of that relation, if not by this? At the same time, in comparison of this great multitude of subjects as it may often prove, those which can be included under any of the descriptions above given will commonly be but a very few: these, then, may be distinguished by the appellation of its *direct* subjects; while the others may be indiscriminately stiled the *collateral* or *indirect* subjects of the law. And thus it is that the whole infinitude of material things or persons, whereof the names can for any purpose be introduced into any such discourse as is susceptible of the appellation of a law, is circumscribed. The indirect subjects of the law can be stiled so only with reference to the law: the direct subjects of it are also subjects of the act, and it is by being subjects of the act which is the object of a law that they become subjects of the law itself. It will be seen hereafter[1] that the persons and things here spoken of in the character of the indirect subjects of the law, are the same whose natures, conditions and changes of conditions form those *circumstances*, or collateral objects, by means of which the description of the acts which are taken for the direct objects of the law is diversified according to the exigency of the occasion.

Direct and indirect subjects of the law.

10. In separating in our minds the direct subjects of the law from the indirect, we must be careful not to be deceived by the irregularities of language. A law lays a tax, suppose, *upon* corn: from this expression we might naturally enough be led to think that corn was among the direct subjects of the law. Upon examination, however, we shall find the contrary to be the case. The object of such a law is not any act which either in its

Example of such as are indirect.

[1] See §7, pp. 66–74 below.

termination or in any part of its progress has any thing to do with *corn*: the only use which there is in mentioning the word *corn*, is to mark the occasion on which a certain act, an act that has nothing, physically speaking, to do with corn, shall be performed, viz: the act of paying, no matter to whom nor how, a certain sum of money. Let it be a tax on the exportation of corn: the word *corn*, then, is one of those which serve to mark the event upon the happening of which you are to pay a sum of money: you are to pay it upon the happening of the event which consists in your exporting a certain quantity of that commodity: such is the act you are commanded to perform whenever the *time* occurrs, if ever it should occurr, which is characterized by the circumstance just mentioned. On this occasion it happens that the only subjects which there is any occasion to mention by name in the tenor of the law (the person whom it takes for its agible subject, that is the party whom it is addressed to, or in other words the party who is bound by it, being excepted) are its indirect subjects: viz: the corn and what other things or persons there may be occasion to make mention of in the details: the act itself, which is the object of the law, viz: the act of payment, being in respect of its physical character and appearance so various, indeterminate and discretionary, that it would be endless to characterize it in general discourse any otherwise than by a name which has a view to the material part of its effects: viz: the causing him who has been paid to have a right[a] to the disposal of the money or whatever it is in

[a] To any one who is in this train of thinking, it may be easy to perceive that the words commonly exhibited by grammarians to serve as examples of active verbs are many of them but ill calculated to answer that intention. According to their account, the verb should signify the act together with the agible subject, while the substantive which the verb is said to govern should signify the passible subject in which the act hath its termination. This is verified perfectly well by the verb τυπτω, I beat, in the phrase τυπτω σε, I beat you: but *moneo te*, I advise you, does it but obscurely: φιλεω σε, *amo te*, I love you, still more obscurely, if at all: and in *audio te*, I hear you, the course taken by the act is the reverse of that which is attributed to it by the grammarian. If I *beat* you, the act proceeds from me and the impression, which is a physical one, terminates in you: if I *advise* you, the act proceeds from me, and the impression, which is a mental one, if any, terminates again in you: but if I *hear* you, the act which is a physical one proceeds from you, and the impression terminates in me: if I *love* you, the act (if any act be necessary in the case) has proceeded from you and the impression which is a mental one terminates again in me. The example to have begun with is that which stands first in order here: in this there is neither fiction nor obscurity. The others might then, if it were necessary, be explained by means of the analogy which they bear, or by fiction of language are supposed to bear, to this.

This note is thrown in, not for its own sake, but in hopes that a subject which is familiar may be a means of reflecting light upon remarks which are abstruse.

which he has been paid.[a] This is what may be done by any one of an indefinite number of different sets of signs: such as laying down money to such an amount upon a table, giving an order upon a third person to pay so much money, giving credit for so much money in an account, and so on: but as these sets of signs have nothing in them that is material over and above this common circumstance of their aptitude to produce the effects in question, it would be idle to go about to describe them in any other manner than by reference to those effects.

[a] See Ch. 16 {Division} 35 n.[1]

[1] See *An Introduction to the Principles of Morals and Legislation* (*CW*), Ch. XVI, para. 35 n., pp. 227–8 n., on the subject of 'Payment, what.'

§7. *Objects of a law.*[1]

Collateral—viz. Circumstances.

39. Next, with regard to the circumstances to which the will of a legislator may apply.[2] Now it has already been observed that there is no object whatever but may be spoken of under the appellation of a circumstance.[a b] The distinction, then, between acts and circumstances turns not so much upon the nature of the objects themselves as upon the manner in which they are respectively regarded by the law, or what comes to the same thing, the purpose for which the mention of them is introduced by it. Circumstances, as mentioned in a law, are not acts which the legislator wills should be performed or not performed, motions or situations which he wills should take place or not take place in consequence, but objects the names of which are made use of for the purpose of specifying and characterizing those acts, motions and situations. The manner, then, in which they are regarded by the law may be thus made out.[3]

Circumstances specificant, what.

40. When once a set of words are put together sufficient to characterize and point out an act of any sort as one which is the object of a law, if any other words be added, the objects signified by such other words may with relation to the act so expressed be termed *circumstances*:[4] and the effect of their being mentioned, if they have any, and if nothing is intimated to the contrary, is, (as we shall see more particularly farther on)[c] that of narrowing the description of the act: that is reducing the class (or *genus*) of

[a] Ch. VII. {Acts} XXII.[5]

'Circumstances' not applied to real entities.

[b] It is to be observed, however, that, according to the usage of language, the word *circumstance* is not commonly applied in a direct way to real entities: to apply it to a real entity, we first extract out of that real entity a kind of fictitious entity on purpose; and it is to that fictitious entity that the word *circumstance* is applied. Speaking of an act, we apply the word *circumstance*, not to the act itself, but to the *nature* of it, for example, or to the *happening* of it: speaking of a person or a thing, we apply the word circumstance not to the person himself, nor to the thing itself, but to the *nature* or *existence* of such person or such thing. Of this particularity in the use of the word *circumstance*, it seemed necessary that the reader should be apprized.

[c] infra 43, 65.[6]

---

[1] For a later draft of this 'respect' see Appendix B, pp. 242–9 below.

[2] In the margin, Bentham has noted at this point: 'These are *modes of being* of the indirect subjects of the law.'

[3] When revising this passage, Bentham ran together paragraphs 39 and 40.

[4] In the margin, Bentham has noted at this point: 'Circumstances are the modes of being incident to the indirect subjects of the law.'

[5] See *An Introduction to the Principles of Morals and Legislation* (*CW*), Ch. VII, para. 22, p. 79 & n.

[6] See pp. 71, 123 below respectively.

acts in contemplation from the extent and amplitude of that characterized by the words first made use of, to another class (or *species* as it is now called) coinciding as far as it extends with the former, but of less extent and amplitude, and consequently included under it. Circumstances of which the mention is thus introduced are stiled the circumstances *in* which it is the legislator's will that the act should, or should not, be performed. For distinction's sake, in order to mark the purpose for which they are introduced, they may be termed *specificant* circumstances with relation to the act: circumstances specificative or characteristic of the act. If there are no particular circumstances mentioned on the occasion, then, for any thing that appears on the face of the law, it is the lawgiver's will that the act should be performed, or not performed, or that a man should have the choice of performing it or not, *in* or *under* any circumstances whatever: that is in any *case*,[a] or, what comes to the same thing, in all cases whatsoever. The *circumstances*, then, or *cases* or *case* in which it is the intention of the legislator that the act as characterized by a given name should be performed are as material to consider as the act itself.

41.[1] It must be remember'd that the circumstances here in question under the name of the indirect or collateral objects of a law are called in for no other purpose than merely to mark out and characterize the sort of act which is the direct object of that law: so that, if the sort of act be sufficiently characterized without the

Whether the law has circumstances or no for its objects depends upon the wording.

[a] The word *case* denotes a sort of fictitious entity, an aggregate body extracted from, or composed of, the assemblage of any number of circumstances of any sort whatsoever. A case is an assemblage of circumstances. What may be called the *Archetypation* of the word is as follows. In the word *circumstance*, the image is that of an assemblage of objects standing round a given object. In the word case, it is that of an assemblage of objects falling, as it were, around the given object, and, by virtue of their common relation to that object, cemented, as it were, into one and forming a ring in which the object is said to *stand* or be. *Case*, in Latin *Casus*; in French *cas*; in Italian and Spanish *caso*; in German *falle*. The image is, in all these languages, the same. So in Greek πτωσις, though here the use of it is more confined. In the word *circumstance*, the analogy runs in the same manner through all those languages.

A case, what.

The connection between the idea belonging to the word *case* as here applied, and the idea belonging to the words *genus, species* or any other significative of a class, is this. Any individual act being of a certain *genus* or larger class, every such act, by having been attended with certain circumstances, by having been performed *in* certain circumstances, or in a certain case, may be said to be of a certain *species*, or smaller class. A circumstance or set of circumstances constitute the case which an individual act has been or may be performed in: a species or class which it is of.

[1] The following two paragraphs have been crossed through by Bentham.

mention of any such circumstances, the law can not be said to have any circumstances at all for its objects. The question, then, whether it has or has not, is a matter that depends solely upon the wording. Take any act, be it what it will, so it be such an one as is capable of being the object of a law, the idea of it necessarily includes a certain number of ideas that are distinguishable from one another, and which shall be mentioned presently. These ideas, then, must be expressed before any act of any sort can have been expressed. So long, then, as the words that are employ'd are no more than what are necessary to express these indispensable ingredients in the idea of an act, there are no specificant circumstances in the case: but let the words necessary to express these elementary ideas have been set down, then, if any other words are added, the objects signified by such additional words may be consider'd as circumstances: which circumstances, provided the effect of the mention that is made of them be to narrow the class of acts already denoted by the other words, but not otherwise, are what may be termed specificant circumstances.

Acts, we may remember, are either positive or negative.[1] Positive acts, again, are either acts of the body or acts of the mind: negative acts are nothing but the negations of the several sorts of positive acts: so that the description of the one follows in every respect that of the other. But among acts of the mind, such only can to any purpose be made the objects of a law as are related to and take their description from certain acts of the body; under which head come acts of intention: which, when explained, will appear to consist in the intention of performing certain acts of the body or their respective negatives.[2][a] When, therefore, we have stated the more simple ideas which are the elements of the complex idea belonging to an act of the body, an analysis will

[a] It might seem that acts of belief are capable, like any other acts, of being [made the][10] objects of the law: but this is not the case. Acts declarative of belief may indeed, and that with some effect: but these are always external acts: acts of the body. Whether a fact appears true to me or no, I may be hired or forced to tell an untruth and say, I believe it: but if it does not appear true to me, all the force in the universe will not make me believe it in reality. I am speaking of the direct and immediate efficacy of any such force: as to the indirect and gradual influence which the affections may exercise on the judgment, that is not to the present purpose.

[1] See *An Introduction to the Principles of Morals and Legislation* (*CW*), Ch. VII, paras. 8–10, pp. 75–6.

[2] In the margin, Bentham has noted at this point: 'Qu? what is to be said of acts of apprehension, memory, &c. ex. g. getting a task by heart &c?'

[3] MS 'the made'.

thereby have been given that will apply equally to every act which can become the object of a law.

In every act of the body there must be three particulars at least concerned: a body or portion of matter in which the motion in question is consider'd as commencing: this is what we called its *agible* subject: 2. a portion of matter in which it is consider'd as having its termination, i: e: a *passible* subject: 3. the abstract act or motion itself which is consider'd as having it's commencement in one of those portions of matter and its termination in the other. Without these particulars [being][1] all of them brought to view in every case, no individual act, nor consequently any *genus* of acts, can be brought to view: there is no basis formed to which any specificant circumstances can apply: no larger class out of which, by the application of such circumstances, a smaller specific class can be extracted. Not that it is always necessary that these three particulars should be each of them mentioned by name: all that it is absolutely necessary to mention is the name of the abstract act or motion, provided that name be such an one as serves to characterize the material part of its effects. By means of this single name it will then appear that the agible subject intended could be none other than a being which, at the same time that it is capable of being influenced by the will of the legislator, is capable of contributing to the production of the effects in question: as also with respect to the passible subject, that it could be none other than a being of such a class as to be susceptible of effects such as those by which the abstract act or motion as expressed by the above mentioned name is characterized. However, it is only in virtue of a mere grammatical ellipsis that the mention of either the one subject or the other can be dispensed with. The ideas that respectively belong to them must, at any rate, be present to the mind, or no image of any act whatsoever can be formed by it.

Example—a law against killing expressed without the help of any specificant circumstances:

42. By means of a few examples these positions, abstruse as they are, may perhaps be render'd tolerably clear. Conceive a law to be exhibited in these terms: 'Let no one kill.' Here, no subject at all is mentioned by any distinctive name: neither an agible subject nor a passible: all that is mentioned (in conjunction with the will of the legislator) is the act (I mean the class of acts) which that will has taken for its object: to wit the act of killing: that is any physical act or motion, in short any act whatever, the effect of which is to reduce a being to that condition which, when it is in it, is said to be *dead*. By the nature, then, of the act as characterized by its effects,

[1] MS 'be'.

the agible as well as the passible subject is in some sort limited and determined: the latter must be such a sort of being as is susceptible of being killed, viz: a being endued with life: the agible subject such a sort of being as is capable of contributing to the effect of another's being killed, and at the same time such an one on whose acts it is possible that the legislator can expect the expression of his will to have an influence. By virtue, then, of the word 'to kill', the intention of the legislator is thus far limited and determined, that the passible subject can not be a class of beings more extensive than that which includes all living creatures, nor the agible subject of a class more extensive than that which includes all human creatures.[a] It appears, then, that the words in question, 'let no *one* kill,' as coming out of the mouth of a legislator are exactly equivalent to these, 'Let no *person* kill any *animal*:' and supposing the idea of the animal to stand limited by any other consideration to that of a human creature, they will then be equivalent to these, 'Let no person kill any *person*.'

Now, let the law stand in either of these forms, what specificant circumstances can there be said to be in the case? None, it is plain, while it stood in the narrowest form—'let no one kill.' Nor yet when the words of it are, 'let no person kill any animal.' For a passible as well as an agible subject of some class or other the act must have, and there are no words introduced to limit either subject to a narrower class than it could otherwise have been of. Nor even supposing that, instead of saying 'let no person kill any animal,' it were to say 'let no person kill any person.' For a passible subject of some class or other the law must have had in view: and the class it

[a] What farther limitations the apparent intention of the legislator may receive from the consideration of any other circumstances that may present themselves to view is not to the present purpose. From the practise of most nations and the disposition of most legislators, it would indeed be a very natural conclusion to make, that the protection afforded by this law was not meant to extend to any more ample class of beings than that which is composed of human creatures. But such a conclusion, though a natural, would not, like the former, be a necessary one. Take, for instance, for your legislator a Pythagoras, and, to make him a little more consistent, let him be as studious to preserve his friends of the brute creation from being killed as from being eaten:[1] and if this be not enough, tincture him with a spice of Quakerism, and let him be as averse to the destroying of the lives of his fellow-animals as that inoffensive sect are to the shedding of the blood of their fellow-men. Even now, absurd as the opposite conclusion might appear in Europe, it would hardly appear equally so in Hindostan.

[1] Transmigration of souls and vegetarianism were doctrines associated with Pythagoreanism, the religious movement allegedly inspired by the sixth-century BC philosopher Pythagoras.

actually has in view, it [names][1] by the proper *univocal*[a] name of that class, without introducing any words importing that class to be a species of any other. A person is indeed a species of animal: viz: a rational animal: but persons are here mentioned under the name of *persons*, and not under the name of *rational animals*.

43. On the other hand let the law, instead of saying 'let no person kill any person,' say 'let no person kill any rational animal,' or, as it would be more natural to say, 'any human creature,' here there is a specificant circumstance taken for the object of the law. For without the word *rational*, there would have been a word to express a class of entities as being the passible subjects of the law: viz: the word *animal*: and the class of beings intended is here denoted by two words, the one expressive of one larger than that intended, and the other serving to express that the class intended is but a species or part of such larger class.

—with specificant circumstances:

44. Suppose, again, that the law were to stand thus: 'Let no person kill any animal having life.' Here, also, a circumstance would indeed be introduced: but this circumstance would not be a specificant one. Applied to another word, it might indeed be specificant: it is not so, however, as applied to the word here in question. It would have been specificant if applied to such a word as the word *being*: because there are other classes of beings than those which are endued with life. But as applied to the word *animal*, it is not: because of animals, there are not any other classes than those which are endued with life.

—with circumstances that are not specificant.

45. Let the law, again, instead of saying, 'let no one kill any person,' say 'let no one kill a judge.' The act is again reduced to a narrower class than it was of before. Still, however, no specificant circumstance is introduced: the passible subject is characterized, as before in the case of the word *person*, by it's own univocal name without the mention of any circumstance. But let it say, 'let no one kill *his* father,' here there is a specificant circumstance introduced: father, a father (viz: any person who bears the relation of paternity to any other person), is a genus, whereof the word *his*, which, being applied to the word *father*, determines it to mean the father of the person in question (a person who bears the relation of paternity to that particular person), indicates a species.

The law narrow'd with or without adding circumstances—ex. g. where the person killed is a judge

—or a man's father.

46. Let the law again stand thus: 'Let no one kill any person by poison.' Here, again, another circumstance is introduced, which

So, where the act is performed by poison

[a] By an *univocal* name, I mean a name consisting of no more than a single word.

[1] MS 'means' appears to be a slip.

also is specificant, as before. A subject in which the act has its commencement, viz: an agible subject, and a subject in which it has its termination, viz: a passible subject, being the only circumstances that are indispensably necessary to constitute an external act, stand already expressed without the words 'by poison:' the effect of these is to express a circumstance relative to the *progress* of the act:[a] viz: the circumstance of its having been performed by poison: that is of poison's having been of the number of the bodies concerned in the progress of the act from the agible subject to the passible subject in which the pathological effects[b] of the act were manifested, and in which the act is consider'd as having its termination.

—or with premeditation.

47. But let the law stand thus, 'Let no one poison any person;' here there are no specificant circumstances introduced: the specificant circumstances, which before were annexed to the name of the act in such manner as to stand detached from it, are now merged in the new name which is substituted in the room of the former. And yet the species or class of act designed in the two cases is just the same.

Suppose the law, again, to say: 'Let no one kill another with a premeditated design to kill.' Here, again, is another specificant circumstance introduced. But let it stand thus, 'let no man murder any person;' here, again, there is none. And yet the word 'murder' may include, amongst other circumstances, that of a premeditated design to kill considered as having subsisted on the part of the person killing.

Why in some cases it may appear to have a necessary respect to circumstances.

48. Notwithstanding what has been said, the distinction between acts that are not attended with circumstances and acts that are will be very apt to appear to be something more than nominal. Take, for example, once more the act of killing and the act of poisoning. To come under the notion of an act of the former sort, it may be thought that an act need not be attended with any circumstances: but that to come under the notion of an act of the latter sort, it must. The act of killing, it may be thought, is one that need not be attended with any circumstances: but that as to the act of poisoning, there is a circumstance with which it must necessarily be attended: the circumstance of poison's having been

[a] See Ch. 7. {Actions} 14.[1]
[b] v. supra 37 n.[2]

[1] See *An Introduction to the Principles of Morals and Legislation* (*CW*), Ch. VII, para. 14, p. 77.
[2] See pp. 58–9 n. above.

employ'd in the production of the effect. The reason, however, of such an appearance seems to be neither more nor less than this. A class of acts, like a class of any other objects, in order to represent itself to the mind with any degree of precision, must represent itself under some name: and the name under which, upon any given occasion, it will be most apt to represent itself, will be the name which is most in use. According to this position, it can scarcely happen that the word *poisoning* should ever present itself to the mind, without presenting some such word as *killing* or *murdering*, at the same time. The act, therefore, is recognized to be an act of killing as soon at least as it is recognized to be an act of poisoning: and as poisoning is distinguished from other acts of killing by certain circumstances, the act in question will be recognized to be an act of killing attended with certain circumstances. In point of fact, every act is attended with circumstances innumerable: from every being that exists, it derives a groupe of circumstances. It is not this, then, that can make any distinction between one class of act and another. The distinction, then, between acts which are and acts which are not attended with circumstances lies not in the things themselves: if, then, it lies any where, it must lie in the words. Accordingly, it seems to have no other ground than the manner in which we speak of the matter of fact. Where the act presents itself under no other name than one which, for the purpose of distinguishing the act in question from all others from which it is meant to distinguish it, may be made use of without the mention of any circumstances, there it is apt to appear as if the act were not necessarily attended with any circumstances. But there are two cases where it will appear as if an act, in order to bring it within a certain class, must necessarily be attended with certain circumstances: 1. where there is no name at all in use by which the act can be characterised without the mention of certain circumstances, that is where the class in question has no univocal name belonging to it at all: 2. where, although it has an univocal name, yet that name, whenever it presents itself, is apt to bring to view at the same time another name which, though it includes the class characterised by the former, can not be made to quadrate with it exactly till it has been narrow'd down by the application of certain circumstances. In short, when a definition of a thing, that is a definition of a class of objects (for classes of objects are the only things that can be defined), is given, the genus of which it is a species is narrow'd down to the extent of that species by the application of certain circumstances which constitute the specific properties of that species. If, then, the word to be defined, the name of the act in question, is such as is scarcely to be understood without being defined, the act which it stands for, the act of which it is the name, will be apt to appear as one which, whenever performed, is attended with certain particular circumstances, and to the notion of which the notion of certain circumstances is essential.

§8. *Of the parties which may be affected by a law.*[1]

[Fifthly],[2] with regard to the parties who may be concerned in or affected by a law: and the different ways in which they may be concerned in or affected by it. There are three sorts of ways in which a party may be concerned in or affected by a law: 1. by being *bound* or coerced by it: 2. by being exposed at least to *suffer* by it: 3. by being *favoured* or intended to be favoured by it. Upon examination, it will be found that, on the one hand there must necessarily be one or more persons concerned in all these three ways; on the other hand, that there are no other ways in which any person can be concerned in it.

Different ways in which persons may be affected by the law: viz: by being 1. bound or coerced: 2. made to suffer: or 3. favoured by it.

Upon a hasty glance it might seem that this source of division had been exhausted, that this topic had been discussed already: for that the parties concerned in or affected by the law could be no other than the persons who are its agible subjects, added to those who are its passible subjects. But upon a closer examination it will be perceived, that it is only part of their respective grounds that the two topics extend over in common. In the first place, under the head of the *subjects* (that is the passible subjects) of the law were included *things*.[3] But the consideration of the *things* that are concerned does not here come in question: it is only the consideration of the persons concerned that belongs to the present head. In this respect, therefore, the extent of the present topic falls short of that of the preceding one above-mentioned.[4] On the other hand, the parties favoured by the law could not, without doing a kind of violence to language, be comprised under the denomination of the persons who are its subjects. In this respect, then, the extent of the present topic stretches beyond that of the preceding one.[5]

This source of distinction different from that concerning the *subjects* of a law.

We may now proceed to shew, that in every law there must be one or more persons concerned in all these ways. First, then, that there must be some person or persons who are bound, or in other words coerced, by it is undeniable. These are the same persons who in other words have been termed the agible subjects of the law: without these, a law can not so much as be conceived. A law by which nobody is bound, a law by which nobody is coerced, a law by

That there must be 1. a party bound or coerced:

[1] This section constitutes a later addition to the 'principal draft'.

[2] MS '| |ly'.

[3] See pp. 58–60 above.

[4] i.e. the topic of 'Subjects'.

[5] In the margin, Bentham has noted at this point: 'N.B. Even these are, strictly speaking, among the number of the persons in whom the act has its pathological termination: though where they are only exempted from a chance of pain, this may seem strained.'

which nobody's liberty is curtailed, all these phrases, which come to the same thing, would be so many contradictions in terms.

2. a party made to suffer: In the second place, a condition equally necessary to the existence of a law is, that there should be some person or persons who are exposed at least to suffer by it. This condition is in truth a necessary consequence of the other. It may be laid down as an axiom in pathology, that there is no sort of act assignable which it is at all times a pleasure to a man to perform:[a] and this may even be extended to negative acts. Take even any given time, and at that time let the act itself be pleasant to perform, the idea of coercion intervening may of itself be sufficient to give it an opposite effect. Even were the truth of the position disputable in the latitude here given to it, still it must be admitted with regard to all such acts as it could answer any purpose to take for the objects of a command. Either, then, the law has no effect, or there is a party who is exposed at least to suffer by it: if no one else, yet at any rate the party whom it binds. It follows that a law, whatever good it may do at the long run, is sure in the first instance to produce mischief. The good it does may compensate the mischief it does a million of times over: but still it begins with doing harm. No law can ever be made but what trenches upon liberty: if it stops there, it is so much *pure*[b] evil: if it is good upon the whole, it must be in virtue of something that comes after. It may be a necessary evil: but still at any rate it is an evil. To make a law is to do evil that good may come.

True it is that the inconvenience a man is exposed to from this cause is in many cases in itself very uncertain and inconsiderable: that there are some obligations of which the burthen is in general very light: and that, of obligations which are even burthensome in themselves, the pressure may for the most part be taken off by the operation of other concomitant laws made in favour of the party who before was bound. Still, however, all the industry of man can not prevent but that, upon the intervention of particular circumstances, the pressure of coercion will get the better of its counterpoise, and make itself sensible in its original and essential form of inconvenience. A man takes upon him the office of a Receiver of

[a] v. supra | |. v. infra | |.[1]
[b] v. Ch. [4.][2] {Value}.[3]

[1] Sentiments similar to this are expressed in *An Introduction to the Principles of Morals and Legislation* (*CW*), Ch. VI, para. 3, p. 51, and at §12, para. 64 n., p. 122 n. below.
[2] MS '3' is a slip.
[3] See *An Introduction to the Principles of Morals and Legislation* (*CW*), Ch. IV, pp. 38–41, for Bentham's discussion of 'purity' as one of the elements of value in a pleasure or a pain.

public money: receiving money with one hand, he is obliged to pay it with the other. It follows not indeed from hence that he experiences a separate pang for every penny that he parts with: it is his business to part with money in that manner: he takes it in order to part with it, he has no hope of being able to keep it with impunity, and he is paid for parting with it. Still, however, there is not a penny of the money that he would not rather, were he at liberty, dispose of to purposes of his own. Particular circumstances may also render the obligation particularly irksome: he may wish he had the money to repair a casual deficiency in his own private funds: indolence, ill health, or the importunity of other avocations, necessary or pleasurable, may at a particular conjunction render it particularly unpleasant to him to give his time to the fulfilling of the requisite formalities.

That there should be a party who is exposed to suffer by a law any otherwise than in virtue of the coercion which it imposes on him, is not essentially necessary: whether there is or no depends upon the particular nature of the law. Where there is, he may be exposed to it either through necessity (that is not purposely) or purposely: if purposely, he is exposed to it for the purpose either of punishment or of vindictive compensation.[a] [1] In all three cases the suffering he is exposed to may be, as in the two latter it must be, intentional on the part of the legislator: but in the first case, it can only be obliquely intentional; in the second case, it is directly intentional, but still not ultimately: it is in the third case only that it is ultimately intentional.[b] In these two last cases, the law is of one or other of those species of adjective laws to which we have assigned a particular name: in the second case, of the punitory kind; in the third case, of the compensative. Of these, as well as of the case where the suffering is but obliquely intentional, more will be said a little farther on.

In the third place, in every law there must also be some person or persons who are favoured by it: meaning a person on whom it is the *intention* at least of the legislator to confer a benefit. To suppose the contrary is to suppose the legislator to act without a motive. Possibly, indeed, the party favoured may be one who 3. a party favoured.

[a] See Ch. 13. {Cases unmeet}.[2]

[b] See Ch. | |. {Intentionality}.[3]

[1] In relation to the remainder of this paragraph, Bentham has noted: 'Alter this. It is never ultimately intentional but where the legislator proceeds upon the principle of antipathy.'

[2] See *An Introduction to the Principles of Morals and Legislation* (*CW*), Ch. XIII, para. 2 n., pp. 158–9 n.

[3] See ibid., Ch. VIII, paras. 6–7, p. 86.

ought not thus to have been favoured: possibly no other than the legislator himself: still at any rate somebody who is favoured by it there must be. No effect without a cause: no act, no law, without a motive. Had the necks of the whole Roman people, according to the wish of Caligula, been consolidated into one;[1] and had his wish been follow'd up by a law, even to that law there would not have been wanting a party favoured: the law of Caligula would have been made in favour of Caligula.

Whether a party on whom it is the intention of the law to confer a benefit, shall really enjoy that or any other benefit, may depend indeed upon the event. It may design to benefit a man without benefiting him: it may benefit him without designing it: it may design to benefit one man and eventually benefit another. But since in the ordinary train of things the efficacy of laws, as far as it goes, is conformable to the intention, it will be proper to suppose that such is the case in each particular instance: if, then, the intention of the law appear to be that such a party be benefited, the presumption is that he is benefited: as on the other hand, if it appears that he is benefited, the presumption is that he was intended so to be.

There are no other ways in which a party can be affected than the above.

It now comes to be shewn that there are no other ways in which a party can be affected by a law than what are comprehended as above. Take any given person for example: the influence of the law either is material to him, or it is not: if not, he is not affected by it in any way: if it is, the tendency of it is either prejudicial with regard to him or beneficial: in as far as it is prejudicial, he is exposed to suffer by it: in as far as it is beneficial, he is favoured by it.

It is equally evident that either he is bound by the law or he is not: in which last case he is left at liberty. If he is bound, it has been shewn already, that he is at any rate in the first instance exposed to suffer: and besides that, he may be favoured or not, as the case may be: so may he likewise if he be left free.[2]

In what sense a party may be said to be favoured in point of agency.

As a party who is laid under coercion by a law is thereby exposed to suffer, so a party who is not laid under coercion by it may be said, in a negative sort of way, to be favoured by it: a party who is favoured in this particular sort of way may, for distinction's sake, be said to be *favoured in point of agency*. I say in a negative sort of

[1] When the audience at the Circensian games favoured a party in opposition to him, Gaius, better known as Caligula (12–41), Roman Emperor from 37, threatened them with the words *utinam populus Romanus unam cervicem haberet*, i.e. 'I wish the Roman people had but one neck': see Suetonius, *De vita Caesarum*, IV. xxx; and Cassius Dio, *Roman History*, LIX. xiii. 6.

[2] In the text, Bentham has noted at this point: 'N.B. In laws creative of self-regarding offences the same person is coerced, made to suffer, and favoured at the same time.'

way: for it is only in consideration of the aspect which the law *might* have borne towards him and of that which it does actually bear to other parties, in short it is only in a negative way and by comparison, that a man can be said to experience any favour from a law of such a nature. The aspect which the law turns to *him*, being negative, is inefficient: of itself, therefore, such aspect can do him neither good nor harm: his condition, as far as depends upon this part of the law, is just the same after the making the law as it was before; and as it would have been if there had been no law made about the matter.[a]

It is only in as far as it is a source of obligation, it is only by means of its coercive influence, that a primordial law can be of any benefit to a man: since, in fact, it is only by these means that it can produce any effect whatever. Suppose him, indeed, to be already laid under coercion by a primordial law, then, indeed, a superventitious law, a counter-mandate, may have an efficient influence in his favour. It is upon this principle that, where a mandate is issued by which others in respect of a given act are laid under coercion, an exception made to it in his favour may as such be consider'd as conferring on him a positive advantage: for every mandate which has an exception to it may be consider'd as consisting of two laws, the one primordial, the other superventitious, and *pro tanto* revocative of the former.[1]

By favouring one party in point of interest, the law gives another a right to *services*.

With regard to primordial laws, then, it is only by some obligation which they impose, that they can either shew a man any favour or indeed produce any other effect whatever.

Now, as to the party bound, he may either be the same party who, in point of interest, is favoured or it may be another. In the former case, the offence which the law, by imposing the obligation, creates, the duty which it enjoins, is of the self-regarding kind: in the latter case, of the extra-regarding kind.

Moreover, it hath already been observed, that the law, when it imposes on one party a duty of the extra-regarding kind, does thereby confer upon some other party a right to services: a right

Autocheiristic power not originally the work of law.

[a] It follows that an *autocheiristic* power over a person or a thing (that is the power of exercising any physical act which shall have its physical termination in the body of the person or the substance of the thing) is not properly speaking, any more than the right of performing acts of an intransitive nature, the work of law. To the law, indeed, a man must be indebted for any measures that are taken to secure him in the possession of the power in question, but that requires other laws addressed to other persons.

[1] For the distinction between primordial and superventitious laws see, for instance, Appendix C, §2, para. 1, p. 252 below.

to services to be render'd by the party on whom the duty is imposed: the doctrine of services, therefore, extends itself (as there hath already been occasion to observe)[1] over little less than the whole body of the law. Every primordial law that is efficient is a command: every legal command imposes a duty: every legal command, by imposing a duty on one party, if the duty be not merely of the self-regarding kind, conferrs a right to services upon another. So in laws of the revocative kind: every law that is revocative of an efficient law is a countermand: every legal countermand takes off a duty: every legal countermand, by taking off a duty from one party, if the duty be not merely of the self-regarding kind, takes away a right to services from another. As to the particular nature of such duty and such services, it is to be sought for in the nature of the act which is the object of the command, or, which comes to the same thing, in the nature of the opposite act which, by prohibiting it, the law turns into an offence.

Services are either affirmative or negative: they are of the affirmative stamp, where the duty is affirmative, the mandate which creates it a command, the act which is the object of the law a positive or, in other words, an affirmative act, consequently the offence which it creates, a negative offence: they are of the negative stamp, where the duty is negative, the mandate a prohibition, the act which is the object of the law a negative act, consequently the offence which it creates, a positive offence.

A party so favoured may be an individual, a subordinate class, or the community.

Who the party is that is favoured by the law may be seen by observing the nature of the offence. An offence which is extra-regarding may be either a private, a semi-public, or a public one: the party favoured may accordingly be either an individual, a subordinate class of persons, or the whole community at once. It is to be observed, however, that as semi-public offences are generally attended with a public mischief, and private offences with a semi-public mischief as well as a public, the public is favoured by every law in virtue of it's being injured in one way or other by every offence: the distinction is that in certain cases there is, besides the public at large, a particular individual who is a party favoured, in others none.

This distinction inapplicable to the party bound.

This distinction, I mean that which turns upon the question concerning the description of the party, whether an individual, a subordinate class or the whole community, it would be of no use to

[1] See *An Introduction to the Principles of Morals and Legislation* (*CW*), p. 228 n.: 'Were the word *services* to be taken in its utmost latitude (negative included as well as positive) this one head would cover the whole law.'

carry any farther. Important as it is[a] when applied to the party favoured, it is of no importance at all, or we may say, perhaps, is not so much as discernible, when applied to the party bound: coercion, if it attaches at all, can attach only upon individuals.[1] Benefit men may receive from the law in their collective capacity: but it is in their individual capacities that it is addressed to them: if proved to have been transgressed, it is by individuals that it must be proved to have been transgressed: if punished, it is upon individuals that it must be punished.

A party may in point of agency be favoured for his own sake or another's.

It is not in every case that the party favoured in point of agency is favoured in point of interest, any otherwise than in the negative way above mentioned. When a man is favoured by a law in point of agency, it may be either for his own sake or for that of another party. In the first case, the power or the right of which he is left in possession is of the beneficial kind;[b] in the latter case, of the fiduciary[c] kind. In this former case, there is but one party favoured, who may be said to be favoured on his account, *causâ propriâ* or *suâ*; in the latter case, there are two parties favoured: the one *causâ propriâ*, the beneficiary; the other *causâ alienâ*, the trustee. And reciprocally a party who, by means of a favour shewn to some one in point of agency, is favoured in point of interest may be thus favoured either by being himself favoured in point of agency, or by another's being so favoured on his account.

But to compleat the favour designed for such beneficiary requires another law.

By one and the same law, then, may one party be favoured in point of agency, and another in point of interest: the first left free to act in such or such a manner *in order that*, through his acting, the other may reap a benefit. But it is not this same law that is sufficient of itself to confer that benefit. It is sufficient to empower the trustee to render the services in question to the beneficiary: but it requires another law to make it his duty so to do.

To illustrate the observations we have been making concerning the different ways in which different parties may be affected by the same law, it may be of use to cast a slight glance over the several

[a] v. Ch. 16. {Division} §5.[2]
[b] v. Ch. 16. {Division}.[3]
[c] ibid.[4]

---

[1] In the margin, Bentham has noted at this point: 'This is not true in regard to offences against laws that are [. . .?] *ex parte subjecti agibilis* [i.e. 'on the part of the agible subject']. Coercion here attaches as much as favour in the other case.'

[2] See *An Introduction to the Principles of Morals and Legislation* (*CW*), Ch. XVI, §v, pp. 274–80.

[3] For the definition of a beneficial trust see ibid., Ch. XVI, para. 25, pp. 205–8.

[4] For the distinction between a beneficial and a fiduciary trust see ibid., para. 40, pp. 238–9.

classes of laws which there is need of in a state as determined by the several classes of offences to which they apply.

Parties affected in laws concerning offences against person and reputation:

First, as to the laws concerning offences against person. Here the parties bound are either all persons whatsoever: or, in particular cases, particular classes of persons from whom offences of the nature in question are particularly apprehended: the parties purposely exposed to suffer, none: the parties favoured in the first instance, each person in particular to whom protection for his person against the mischief in question is thus given. As to the parties favoured in the second and third instances, in respect of the mischief of the second and third orders against which they are protected, these have been already noticed, nor will it be necessary to make any farther mention of them.[1]

Secondly, the same observations may be applied to the laws respecting offences against reputation.

—property:

Thirdly, as to the laws concerning offences against property. Property is either in things or in the services of persons. Let us begin with property in things; taking for examples those subjects and those rights of which the description is most simple. To understand who are the parties affected by the laws of property, we must conceive as many laws as there are different things that are the subjects of property within the dominion of the state. The statement of the parties who are affected will be different in every such law. In a baker's shop, let there be two loaves, one of which you have just bought of him, and an other which, being as yet unsold, remains the baker's. In a law which gives or secures to you the property of that loaf which is your's, the parties bound are all mankind, the baker himself included, you excepted: the parties intentionally exposed to suffer, none as before: the party favoured, you and you alone. In a law which gives or secures to the baker the property of the loaf which remains his, the parties bound are all mankind, you included, the baker excepted: the parties intentionally exposed to suffer, none as before: the party favoured, the baker and he alone.

So in immoveables, which will afford a more convenient example for illustrating the manner in which the interests of the several parties are affected by the pair of laws which are necessary to constitute an article of fiduciary property. In a given district, let there be two acres of land contiguous; the one, which shall be called *y*, in your possession, the other, which shall be called *f*, in

[1] Bentham may have had in mind the distinction between the primary and secondary mischief of an act, with the latter being distinguished into alarm or danger, which appears at ibid., Ch. XII, paras. 3–5, pp. 143–4.

the possession of another person who shall be named *F*. In a law which gives or secures to you the exclusive possession of the acre which is your's, the parties bound are all mankind, except you: the party favoured, you and you alone. In a law which gives or secures to *F* the exclusive possession of the acre *f*, the parties bound are all mankind, except *F*: the party favoured, *F* and *F* alone.

But let the design of the law be that *F*, indeed, have the exclusive possession of the field *f*, but that another person, who shall be called *B*, have all the benefit: *F* alone gathering the produce of the field, but disposing of it entirely according to the orders, or in any other way for the benefit, of *B*: then is *F*, while this arrangement lasts, the fiduciary: *B*, the beneficiary, proprietor. For this purpose, a new law is requisite in addition to the former. By the former law, *F* was permitted to gather the produce of the field, by this latter he is commanded. In the former law, mankind in general were the parties bound; and the obligation was of the negative stamp; and *F* alone was the party favoured: by the latter law, *F* alone is the party bound; the obligation is an affirmative one, and *B* alone is the party favoured.[1] It is evident that the operation of gathering in the produce of the field and disposing of it for *B*'s benefit is a complex business not to be atchieved, perhaps, but by a variety of different sorts of acts: to these different acts correspond so many different services: which, if the description given of them requires to be different, may furnish matter for so many different laws.

So in regard to services. But of the manner in which the several parties are affected by the laws by which this species of property is created or secured, an exemplification has just been given. By the same law which renders *B* the beneficial possessor of the land cultivated by *F*, a right to certain services to be performed by *F* is created, as we have seen, and conferred on *B*.

Fourthly, as to the laws which concern offences relative to the several conditions in life. A man's condition is made up by clusters of duties, powers, rights, or the negations of these respective objects, variously compounded: to exhibit the ways in which the several parties may be affected by the laws relative to this topic, the condition in question must, therefore, be resolved into such of the constituent articles just mentioned of which it is compounded. —condition.

Fifthly, as to the laws relative to semi-public and public offences. Here the party favoured in the first instance is a whole class of persons: in those relative to offences of a public nature, the whole community.[2] Semi-public and public offences.

[1] Bentham has marked the remainder of the paragraph for possible deletion.

[2] In the margin, Bentham has noted at this point: 'Insert here self-regarding offences.'

Punitory laws.

Thus far with regard to laws of the substantive stamp.

In punitory laws, the parties bound are the ministers of justice: the party purposely exposed to suffer, the delinquent: the party favoured, the community at large.[1] In such laws of the compensative kind as have the same object or end in view as those of the punitory kind have, the parties are the same; except that in this case the favourable part of the influence of the law, before it reaches the community, extends itself in the first instance to a particular individual.

In a remote way many sets of parties may be exposed to suffer or favoured by the same law.

In considering the different ways in which a party may be affected by a law we have hitherto consider'd it with regard only to its immediate and obvious effects. But in two of those three ways[2] a party may be affected by a various and remote concatenation of causes and effects. As to the parties that are bound by it, so as the import of the law be clear, they are seen at once: but what other parties, if any, are exposed to suffer, and the parties who either intentionally or eventually are favoured, are not alike discernible or determinable. As to the parties who are exposed to suffer, a law, how beneficial soever it may be upon the whole, may, over and above the mischief it does by the restraint it lays on liberty, do a deal of mischief which is seen but can not be helped, as well as a good deal which perhaps can be neither helped nor seen. Every body knows, for example, into what a multitude of remote and sometimes imperceptible branches the mischief produced by a tax will oftentimes divide itself. Nor is the benefit which in some cases may result from it much less various and diffusive. Let a tax payable to the public be laid upon a manufacture: the law, then, upon the happening of the event from whence the obligation to pay the tax is made to take its rise, commands the manufacturer, suppose, to perform that sort of service which consists in the payment of a certain sum of money, to the person who, for the benefit of the public, is to receive it: the public, then, is by this means favoured in a way which is direct and obvious: but in another way which is less obvious, though perhaps, when pointed out, not less indisputable, so may another party, viz: the proprietor of a rival manufacture: the public is a gainer by what the manufacturer who is taxed works up in spite of the tax: the rival manufacturer by so much as the other is prevented from working up by reason of the tax.

But of the different ways in which, by the influence of remote

[1] In the margin, Bentham has noted at this point: 'i.e. 1st the individual, if any, prejudiced by the primary mischief, and so on.'

[2] i.e. the three ways mentioned at the opening of the present section, p. 75 above.

causes, a party may reap a benefit from a law, a pretty ample account will be given in a succeeding chapter.[a]

Use and importance of the above distinctions.

These various relations which may be born[e] to various parties by the same law must all of them be present to a man's mind before the true nature and influence of it can be understood by him. On the circumstance of there being a party whom it binds, a law depends for its essence: on the circumstance of there being a party whom it is designed at least to favour, it depends for its cause: on both together it depends for the sum total of its efficacy: without the last it never exists; without the first, it could not so much as be conceived. To trace out the mischievous part of its tendency, we must observe whom it lays under coercion, whom on any other account it exposes to suffer: and thence in what respects and to what amount it exposes them to suffer: to trace out the beneficial part of its tendency, we must observe whom it favours, and in what respects and to what amount it favours them.

All these several parties have need to be acquainted with it: and the benefit which any body can derive from it will be in proportion to the acquaintance which they have with it, as on the other hand the need they have to be acquainted with it will be in proportion to the amount of the detriment which they may individually incurr by it, or the benefit which they may individually derive from it. Both parties have need to be informed of it in order to determine them with respect to the different lines of conduct they have need to observe according to the different aspects which it bears to them: the party bound, that by timely obedience he may save himself from the lash of those laws of which the express business is to make men suffer: and that by timely consideration he may obliterate, or palliate at least, the inconveniences of obedience: the party who, in the event of his disobedience, it is designed should suffer, in order that he may consider and take warning from the sufferings that are prepared [for][1] him: the party who from necessity is exposed to suffer in order that he, as well as the party bound, may learn to accommodate himself to his situation: the party favoured in order that he may see what the law has done for him, to what favours it has given him a right, whom he is to resort to for the performance of them, and in case of failure on the part of those from whom they are due, what means are given him of making himself amends and bringing the wrongdoers to repen-

[a] Ch. | |. {Indirect Legislation}.[2]

[1] MS 'from'.

[2] For the projected Chapter entitled 'Indirect Legislation' see the Editorial Introduction, p. xii above.

tance. The party bound, and the party, where there is one, who is purposely exposed to suffer, will be sure enough to appear upon the face of the law, by description at least, if not by name: on the other hand, the parties who are favoured, whether on their own account or that of another, will be very apt to be out of sight: and insomuch that it may very well happen that, in a long string of laws by which a man is favoured, there shall not be a syllable which can serve to give him notice or to point him out to view. It is the business of the legislator for his own instruction to discover these latent interests, and for the information of the parties to announce them.[1]

Constitutional laws *in principem*.[2]

There yet remain a class of laws which stand upon a very different footing from any of those that have hitherto been brought to view. The laws of which we have hitherto been speaking have for their passible subjects not the sovereign himself, but those who are consider'd as being in subjection to his power. But there are laws to which no other persons in quality of passible subjects can be assigned than the sovereign himself. The business of the ordinary sort of laws is to prescribe to the people what *they* shall do: the business of this transcendent class of laws is to prescribe to the sovereign what *he* shall do: what mandates *he* may or may not address to *them*; and, in general, how he shall or may conduct himself towards them. Laws of this latter description may be termed, in consideration of the party who is their passible subject, laws *in principem*:[3] in contradistinction to the ordinary mass of

[1] The following continuation has been crossed through by Bentham: 'Take any law at pleasure, we may be sure it is made for the sake of somebody: for whose sake, it will always be material to enquire. This point being settled, in what manner does it affect him? if it be an individual, from what mischiefs, what pains, does it tend to preserve him? what benefits, what pleasures, does it tend to procure to him? If the party whom it is designed to favour be the same who at all events is coerced by [it], what advantages does it pay him for the encroachment it makes upon his liberty? If the interest and at all events the liberty of one set of men is made a sacrifice of for the benefit of another, what assurance is there that the detriment suffer'd by the community in the person of the one, is overbalanced by the advantage gained in the person of the other? Upon the answers that can be given depends the expediency or inexpediency of the law, the vindication or condemnation of the legislator: upon these principles, a tribunal may be set up in the bosom of the public: if well-informed as well as well-intentioned, he will be vindicated: if mistaken, he will be set right: if dishonest, brought to shame.'

In the margin, moreover, Bentham has noted: 'One great use of this topic of distinction is to serve as a criterion of the unity of a law. It can not be one law if it binds two different parties in two opposite ways. See infra §| |; also Ch. | |. {Corpus}.'

For the 'unity' of a law see §16, pp. 168–84 below. For the projected Chapter entitled 'Corpus Juris' see the Editorial Introduction, pp. xxviii–xxix above.

[2] The remainder of the section appears to have been a later addition. For the problems associated with the transition between the two parts of this section see the Editorial Introduction, pp. xxiv–xxv n. above.

[3] In the margin, Bentham has noted at this point: 'Distinguish here between *Le Souverain* and *Le Prince*.'

laws which, in this view, may be termed laws *in subditos* or *in populum*.

These laws *in principem* may be of either of two sorts, according to the party whose conduct they are designed to influence. This party may be the individual sovereign himself from whom they emane, or any future sovereign or sovereigns, his successor or successors: in the former case they are what are strictly and properly termed *pacts* or *covenants*: and to distinguish them from the ordinary covenants enter'd into by subjects, they may be stiled *pacta regalia* or *royal covenants*: in the latter case, they have not as yet acquired any separate denomination. In the common way of speaking, these, indeed, are likewise termed pacts or covenants: one man being consider'd as having covenanted in virtue of a covenant actually enter'd into by another: the succeeding sovereign in virtue of the covenant actually enter'd into by his predecessor. But this way of speaking, familiar as it is, is improper: it is inaccurate, inconsistent and productive of confusion:[a] to obviate which, acts of this sort may be stiled *recommendatory mandates*. When a reigning sovereign, then, in the tenor of his laws, engages for himself and for his successors, he does two distinguishable things. By an expression of will which has his own conduct for its object, he enters *himself* into a covenant: by an expression of will which has the conduct of his successors for its object, he addresses to *them* a recommendatory mandate. This mandate the successor, whenever the sovereignty devolves to him, will probably adopt: and then, and not till then, it is his covenant.[1]

They may be addressed to the law-giver, his successors or both together.

[a] I call it inaccurate: for a covenant is an expression of will on the part of the person whose covenant it is said to be: but the successor, who perhaps at the time of the entering into the covenant does not so much as exist, probably has not so much as entertained, certainly has not expressed, any will about the matter. I call it inconsistent: for inconsistent it is to make use of the same expression, where an object of any kind does exist, to announce the existence of that object, and, where no such object exists, to announce the existence of such an object notwithstanding: productive of confusion it must be, when a proposition which at one time is strictly true, and in order to a right understanding of the subject must be understood to be so, must for the same purpose at another time be understood not to be true, at the same time that there is nothing to give warning when it is to be regarded in the one of those lights and when in the other.

[1] The following continuation has been crossed through by Bentham: 'But this covenant, being but a covenant, how, it will be asked, does it become a law? whence does it acquire its binding force? The answer is, certainly not from the political sanction: for the whole force of this sanction is, by the supposition, already in the hands of him against whom, in case of transgression, it should be directed. There remain the two auxiliary sanctions, the moral and religious: on these sanctions it must depend for all the force it can possess: of these sanctions, and these only, it becomes a dictate.'

How recommendatory mandates *in successores* come to be looked upon in the light of covenants.Or thus: How *leges in principem* come to be adopted by successors.

The causes which originally produced the original covenant and the considerations of expediency which justified the engaging in it on the part of the predecessor will, in general, subsist to produce and justify the adoption of it on the part of the successor. In most instances, therefore, it will have happened that, upon any change taking place in the sovereignty, such adoption shall have taken place: it will have become customary for it so to do: the people, influenced partly by the force of habit and partly by the consideration of the expediency of such adoption, will be expecting it as a thing of course: and this expectation will add again to the motives which tend to produce such effect in any given instance. So great, in short, is the influence of all these causes when taken together, that in any tolerably well settled government the successor is as much expected to abide by the covenants of his predecessor as by any covenants of his own;[a] unless where any

[a] An uniform and universal expectation of this sort is not of such longstanding in society as at first sight might be imagined. Even history will carry us back to times at which the notion of the unity of the sovereign in different reigns was far from being perfectly established. An act of power is exercised, a declaration of will is issued on the part of the sovereign authority: is it, or is it not, to be understood to have continuance, to possess a binding force, after the decease of the individual sovereign whose pleasure it declared? This is a question which, in every state, must for a time have remained unsettled. Applied to acts of legislation, it would be settled first with regard to laws *in populum*, not till latterly with regard to laws *in principem*. Under the English constitution, instances are yet extant of its being subject to doubt with regard to this latter kind of laws: see Barrington's Observations on the antient Statutes.[1] Who can wonder at this, when, with regard to such acts of power as consist in the appointing men to offices,[a] the general rule is to this hour in the negative? By the original rule of the common law, upon the demise of the crown, most of the offices in the appointment of the crown become vacant. All military, all judicial, power is at an end. The laws themselves, though not expressly, are virtually repealed, by the extinction of every power that can give them force. The bonds of society are broken for ever, unless it should please this or that man to make them whole. Whose interests, by the bye, were most consider'd in this maxim, and for whose sake society was proposed to be maintained, the prince's or the people's, is easy to perceive.

[a] These there will hereafter be occasion to distinguish by a particular name, viz: acts of endynamistic power.[2]

---

[1] In the margin, Bentham has noted at this point: 'N.B. Coronation Oath.'
Daines Barrington (1727–1800), lawyer, antiquary, and naturalist, in *Observations on the Statutes, chiefly the more ancient, from Magna Carta to The Twenty-first of James the First, Ch. xxvii. With An Appendix; being A Proposal for new-modelling the Statutes*, London, 1766, p. 98, referring to the *Statuta Civitatis London* of 1285, writes: 'There seems . . . to have been a doubt at this time, whether an act of parliament, passed by the predecessor, bound the succeeding king . . . .'

[2] See p. 107 & n. below.

change of circumstances has made a manifest and indisputable change in the utility of such adherence. This expectation may even become so strong, as to equal the expectation which is entertained of the prevalence of that disposition to obedience on the part of the people by which the sovereignty *de facto* is constituted: insomuch that the observance of the covenant on the one part shall be looked upon as a condition *sine quâ non* to the obedience that is to be paid on the other. Things are most apt to be upon this footing in those governments in which the sovereignty is ascribed nominally to a single person who in reality possesses only a part, though perhaps the most conspicuous part, in it. But in all governments where either the whole or a principal part of the sovereignty is in the hands of a single person, the exercise of the sovereignty and the observance of the covenants enter'd into by preceding sovereigns are looked upon as being in such a degree connected that, upon taking upon him the former, a man is universally understood to have taken upon him the latter: understood, not only by the people, but by [the] sovereign himself. This notion is so universal and deep-rooted that if, by accident, a sovereign should in fact come to the throne with a determination not to adopt the covenants of his predecessors, he would be told that he had adopted them notwithstanding: adopting them tacitly by taking upon him those powers to the exercise of which the obligation of adopting those covenants stood annexed. Nor would this way of speaking, how untrue soever it may be by the very supposition, seem mis-applied: since it has become a habit among men of law to speak of the matter of right in the same terms in which they would speak of the matter of fact: that which, according to the general opinion, *ought* to be done being spoken of as if it *were* done.[a]

It appears, then, that there are two distinct sorts of laws, very different from each other in their nature and effect: both originating indeed from the sovereign, (from whom mediately or immediately all ordinances in order to be legal must issue) but addressed to parties of different descriptions: the one addressed to the sovereign, imposing an obligation on the sovereign: the other addressed to the people, imposing an obligation on the people. Those of the first sort may again be addressed either to the In what sense the sovereign may be said to bind himself:

[a] It is thus that, upon a thousand occasions, the question of right and the question of fact get confounded: insomuch that men pass backwards and forwards from the one to the other without perceiving it. See Fragm. on Gov:[t] Ch. | |.[1]

[1] See *A Fragment on Government* (*CW*), Ch. V, para. 10, pp. 498–9, where Blackstone is criticized for this confusion.

sovereign himself who issues them, (the sovereign for the time being) or to his successors, or (what is most common) to the one as well as to the other. It is evident, then, that, in the distinction between these two classes of laws, it is the quality of the parties who are respectively bound by them that is the essential and characteristic feature.

Here it may naturally enough be asked, what sense there is in a man's addressing a law to himself? and how it is a man can impose an obligation upon himself? such an obligation, to wit, as can to any purpose be effectual.—Admitt, indeed, we must, that for a man to address a law to himself, is what, indeed, there would be little sense in, were there no other *force* in the world but his: nor can a man, by his own single unassisted force, impose upon himself any effectual obligation: for granting him to have bound himself, what should hinder him on any occasion from setting himself free? On the other hand, take into the account an exterior force, and by the help of such force it is as easy for a sovereign to bind himself as to bind another. It is thus, as was seen in a former chapter,[1] that in transactions between subject and subject a man binds himself by the assistance of that force which is at the disposal of the sovereign. Nor is the assertion we make in speaking of a man's binding himself so wide from the literal truth as at first sight might appear. The force which binds depends, indeed, upon the will of a third person: but that will itself waits to receive its determination from the person who is said to bind, from the person who is the promulgator of the law. Without the covenantor, there would be no law at all: without the *guarantee*, as he is called, none that can be effectual. The law, then, may in strictness be consider'd as the work of both: and, therefore, in part, of either: but the share which the covenantor takes in it is by much the more conspicuous. It is this at all events that is taken first: it is seen to be taken while the other, perhaps, is expected only: it is certain; while the other, perhaps, is but contingent. In short, the part which the sovereign for the time being has in the establishment of a *pactum regium*, whereby he binds himself and his successors, may be as considerable [as] and as independent of the part which may come to be taken by those to whom belongs the enforcement of such covenant, as the part which is taken by the legislator in the case of a law of the ordinary stamp *in populum* is of the part which may come to be taken by the judge.

—by what means.

By what means, then, can a law *in principem* be enforced and render'd efficacious: what force is there in the nature of things that

[1] See §4, pp. 46–50 above.

is applicable to this purpose? To answer this question, we have nothing to do but to resort to the enumeration, that has been already given on a former occasion,[1] of the several sorts of forces by which the human will is liable to be influenced. The forces, and the only forces, by which the human will is influenced are *motives*: these, when consider'd in the mass, may be distinguished according to the sources from whence they issue: to these sources we set out with giving the name of *sanctions*. Of these sanctions, that which we termed the *physical* is out of the question: for the force in the case in question is supposed to be directed by *design*. There remain the political, the religious and the moral. The force of the political sanction is inapplicable to this purpose by the supposition: within the dominion of the sovereign, there is no one who, while the sovereignty subsists, can judge so as to coerce the sovereign: to maintain the affirmative would be to maintain a contradiction.[a] [b]

[a] v. supra | |.[2]

[b] This proposition stands in need of explanation: the truth of it depends upon the idea annexed to the word *sovereign*. The case is, that supposing the powers in the state to be thus distributed, there is no one person or body of persons in whose hands the sovereignty is reposed. Suppose two bodies of men, or for shortness sake two men, the one possessing every power of the state, except that the other in case of a public accusation, preferred in such or such forms, has the power of judging him: including such power as may be necessary to carry the judgment into execution. It is plain the sovereignty would not be exclusively in either: it would be conjunctively in both. Yet in common speech it is probable that the first man would be stiled *the* sovereign, or at least *a* sovereign: because his power would be constantly in exercise: the other's only occasionally, or perhaps never. Now then, if this narrow sense were to be given to the word *sovereign*, it is plain that the proposition above mentioned, concerning the impossiblity of the sovereign's being judged by any one, would not be true. A logician of the ordinary stamp (for nothing is more common than to be versed in the forms of dialectics without any clear notions of terminology) would find no difficulty in maintaining the contrary, and proving it by what to him might seem a demonstration. Taking advantage of the inexplicit notions annexed to the words *superior* and *inferior*, he would perhaps assume for his medium this proposition, that it is impossible for a man to be superior and inferior to another at the same time: or perhaps in different propositions he would use the same word *sovereign* in two different senses: at one time in its strict and proper sense; at another time in its popular and improper sense, according to the distinction above taken. Till men are sufficiently aware of the ambiguity of words, political discussions may be carried on continually, without profit and without end. It may occur, that the distribution of power above supposed is not an expedient one, or that it cannot be a lasting one. This may or may not be the case: but the expediency or the durability of such an

Whether the sovereign can to particular purposes have a superior.

[1] See the discussion of sanctions in *An Introduction to the Principles of Morals and Legislation* (*CW*), Ch. III, pp. 34–7.

[2] For a discussion of this point see *A Fragment on Government* (*CW*), Ch. IV, paras. 30–3, pp. 487–8.

But the force of the religious sanction is as applicable to this purpose as to any other: and this is one of the great and beneficial purposes to which the religious sanction, where it happens to have an influence, is wont to be applied. The same may be said of the force of the moral sanction. Now, the force of the moral sanction as applied to the purpose in question may be distinguished into two great branches: that which may be exerted by the subjects of the state in question acting without, perhaps even against, the sanction of political obligations, acting, in short, as in a state of nature; and that which may be exerted by foreign states. When a foreign state stands engaged by express covenant to take such a part in the enforcement of such a law as that in question, this is one of the cases in which such foreign state is said to stand with reference to such law in the capacity of a *guarantee*.[a] Of a covenant of this sort,

arrangement are points with which we have nothing to do here. I consider here only what is possible: now, it is possible: for every distribution, as well as every limitation, of power is possible that is conceivable. The power of the governor is constituted by the obedience of the governed: but the obedience of the governed is susceptible of every modification of which human conduct is susceptible: and the rules which mark it out, of every diversity which can be clearly described by words. Wheresoever one case can be distinguished from another, the same distinction may obtain in the disposition to obedience which may have established itself among the people. In the former case, they may be disposed to pay it to one magistrate, in the latter to another: or in the former case, they may be disposed to obey one of those magistrates, and in the latter, nobody. Many are the common-place phrases in use which would seem to assert the contrary: that an *imperium in imperio* is a monster in politics: that no man can serve two masters: that a house divided against itself cannot stand:[1] and these phrases are made to pass for arguments. There is, indeed, something specious in them at first sight: and without due examination a man may be easily misled by them. Thus much is indeed true, that the same individual branch of power cannot be possessed, and that exclusively, by two persons at the same time. But any two branches of power may that are distinguishable: and any one branch of power may be shared amongst ever so many. What gives rise to the internal contests by which states are agitated or destroy'd, is that two different men or bodies of men claim exclusively the same individual branch: which in governments that are not purely monarchical may ever be the case, and that on all sides with the best faith imaginable, while laws are wanting to decide the matter, or those which there are, are ambiguous or obscure.[2] The minuteness and refinement of which the distribution of powers in a state is susceptible depends upon the proficiency that is made in the anatomy of language, and the use that is made of that proficiency in the body of the laws.

[a] Berne and France guarantees to Geneva. France to Westphalia and all the German Powers. Gelon to the Carthaginians.[3]

[1] Matthew 12: 25; Mark 3: 25; Luke 11: 17.

[2] In the margin, Bentham has noted at this point: 'Draw the conclusion a little closer.'

[3] The Genevan constitution had been guaranteed by France, Berne, and Zurich under the *Médiation* of 1738, while the territorial sovereignty of the states of the Holy Roman Empire had been guaranteed by France and Sweden under the Peace of Westphalia of 1648. There

many examples are to be met with in the history of international jurisprudence. Of all these forces, even when put together, the efficacy, it must be confessed, is seldom so great as that of the political. How should it? when it is in the nature of the political sanction to draw with it in most instances a great part, if not the whole, of the force of the other two? But to deny them all efficacy would be to go too far on the other side. It would be as much as to say that no privileges were ever respected, no capitulation ever observed. It would be as much as to say, that there is no such system in Europe as the Germanic body: that the inhabitants of Austrian Flanders are upon no other footing than the inhabitants of Prussia: those of the *pays d'états* in France than those of the *pays d'élection*: that no regard was ever paid to the American charters by the British Parliament: and that the act of union[1] has never been any thing but a dead letter.[a]

[a] It is a trite and idle observation that the engagements of sovereigns are kept no longer than suits their convenience. This is in no other sense true, than in that in which it is also true of the engagements of private men. If it means that the engagements of sovereigns have never any effect, and that, after an engagement of that sort enter'd into, things are in precisely the same situation as if no such event had taken place, it is notoriously false: if it means any thing else than this, it is nugatory. No man acts without a motive: no man acts against a preponderant mass of motives: but, to the sum of motives which may tend to withhold a sovereign from pursuing a certain line of conduct, does a solemn engagement not to pursue it make no addition? Let experience decide.

This observation is of a piece with another observation equally trite concerning man in general, that he is never governed by any thing but his own interest. This observation in a large and extensive sense of the word interest (as comprehending all sorts of motives) is indubitably true: but as indubitably false in any of those confined senses in which, upon such an occasion, the word *interest* is wont to be made use of. These levelling notions are, in point of tendency, as pernicious as, in point of fact, they are ill-grounded: the tendency of them being constantly, and the design frequently, to cover and to cherish the very immorality the existence of which they maintain and pretend, perhaps, to deplore.

---

do not, however, appear to have been any guarantors of the treaty of 480 BC between Gelon (d. 478/7 BC), Tyrant of Gela from *c.* 491 BC, and the Carthaginians.

[1] i.e. the Act of Parliament (6 Ann., c. 11) uniting the crowns of England and Scotland, which came into force on 1 May 1707.

§9. *Of the local extent which a law may have.*[1]

Local extent of a law may be direct or indirect.

The field of dominion directly or indirectly subjacent.

[Sixthly],[2] with respect to the *local* extent or extension of a law: the extent of which it is susceptible in point of place.

The local extent of a law may be distinguished into direct and indirect. The former may be understood to depend upon the situation and magnitude of the territory or tract of land, with the space above and below it,[a] which is of the number of the *things* that are the passible subjects of the law: that is of the acts which are its objects. A law, then, in point of direct local extent extends or applies itself to such portion of land on which the acts which it takes for its objects come to have their termination: the fields which, among the persons who are the agible subjects of the law, some are permitted, others forbidden, to cultivate: the roads on which some are permitted, others perhaps forbidden, to travel: the waters (that is the grounds cover'd with waters) on which some are permitted, others perhaps forbidden, to travel, or to fish.

As to what may be termed the indirect local extent of a law, it is determined by some relation or other which the persons who are the agible subjects of the law are looked upon as bearing to the land: such as the being on it at the time of performing the acts in question, although those acts have no material influence on the condition of the land: the having been born upon it: the being of the number of those who are looked upon as being in the habit of paying obedience to persons who are in the habit of issuing laws, of which the land in question is a passible subject.[3] Accordingly, a law may, in point of indirect local extension, be said to apply to any tract of land which is so situated, that the relation of any kind which a person bears thereto is a circumstance which aggregates him to the agible subjects,[b] and his acts to the objects, of the law.

Thus the law which forbids the planting of tobacco any where in England is a law which extends in a direct manner to the country called England, and a law of which the local extent is determined in a direct manner by the situation and extent of the country so denominated. Thus, on the other hand, the English laws against treason, in as far as they include within the punishment appointed for that crime an attempt made upon the life of the King of England

[a] Each man's estate a quasi-pyramid.

[b] i: e: the parties who are looked upon as bound by it.

---

[1] In the 'principal draft', the topic of 'Extent' was discussed in paragraphs 49–50, but the corresponding text sheets have not been located. The present text is a later draft.

[2] MS del. 'Fourthly'.

[3] In the margin, Bentham has noted at this point: 'Territorial jurisdiction.'

by the subject of any other country so as the attempt be made in England, or an attempt made abroad so as the offender were a native or adopted subject of the British crown, may be said to apply in point of indirect local extent to England.[1]

This head reducible to the preceding.

This head, it may be observed, can scarcely be said to be a distinct one of itself: it being always reducible to one or other of the topics already noticed. The idea of the tract of land over which a law extends in a direct manner is included under the idea of the *things* that are its passible subjects: that over which it extends in an indirect way in the manner above mentioned is only a specificant circumstance made use of to characterise the *persons* who are its agible or its passible subjects. Deference, however, to usage and to the general common bent of men's notions on the subject seemed to dictate the propriety of mentioning it apart. The questions concerning the dominion of the sovereign and the jurisdiction of the judge are questions that seem to point to the local extent of the law without reference to any other circumstance.

[1] In the margin, Bentham has noted in relation to this sentence: 'Break into two.'

§10. *Of the duration of a law.*[1]

Extent in point of time—is also reducible to the preceding heads.

[Seventhly],[2] with regard to the extent which a law may have in point of *time*. This topic seems also to be reducible within the bounds of those already mentioned. To determine the time during which a given individual is commanded or forbidden to perform acts of a certain class, is to determine the multitude of those acts, and, thereby, the amplitude or logical extent, as it might be called, of the class which they compose. To determine the time during which the individuals of a given class are commanded or forbidden to perform acts of a certain class is to determine the multitude of the individuals which, by entering into that class, may have become the agible subjects of the law. Time, then, is but one out of an indefinite multitude of specificant circumstances which may be made use of to mark out the assemblage of individuals whom it is proposed to take for the subjects of the law.

Why mentioned separately.

For mentioning this as a separate topic there is the same reason, and seems to be the same necessity, as for mentioning the former[3] in the same light. Space and time, though nothing of themselves, are the inseparable and yet distinguishable accompaniments of every thing that is. The wider the space, and the greater the length of time, over which a law extends, the greater the number of acts of persons and of things, of objects, therefore, and of agible as well as passible subjects, it will be apt upon an average to extend to.

A law temporary by nature—by institution.

A law to the duration of which no express limits are set, such a law, provided it be general throughout, general in respect as well of its objects as of all its subjects, will, of course, if nothing appears to the contrary, be looked upon as perpetual: such, at least, is the mode of interpretation in every settled government. In such case, however, the duration of it may be contracted to any length by the express will of the legislator. On the other hand, where the law is in any respect particular, a necessary period is thereby put to its duration: it expires the instant that the article in respect of which it is particular is no more. If it be particular in respect of more articles than one, it then expires along with that article which first goes off the stage. In this latter case, it may be said to be *temporary in its own nature*: in the former, if it be temporary at all, it may be stiled temporary *by institution*.

This line of distinction, however, is not so clear an one as at first

[1] This section, at the head of which Bentham has noted 'Postpone to Generality', constitutes a later addition to the 'principal draft'.

[2] MS del. 'Fifthly'.

[3] i.e. 'extent': see §9, pp. 94–5 above.

sight it might be thought to be. It is, indeed, in general true that classes are longer lived than individuals: and in particular with regard to persons, individuals must die, though classes may be, and some of them, so long as any of the human race are left upon the globe, must be, immortal. But even classes die, or sleep at least, when the individuals which used to fill them are no more: and of individuals, when we come to speak of things, there are some to the existence of which it would not be easy to set a term. The laws concerning the killing of wolves in England expired along with the last wolf many centuries ago. The laws made in England against Jesuits have in our days been laid asleep, by the dissolution of that formidable order.[1] But should a fresh colony of Wolves be ever imported, and should the order of Jesuits be ever re-established, the laws against wolves and Jesuits would revive. The laws concerning Regents sleep every where during the majority of the prince, but awake upon the succession of a minor. The laws concerning enemies are dead in time of peace, but revive upon declaration of a war. The great bridge at Westminster[a] is an individual object: but should the zeal for constitutional reformation which from time to time hath been observed to break forth in the neighbourhood of that magnificent structure gather strength, perishable as it is, it may chance to outlive many a class of useless or supposed useless placemen.

In short, wherever the continuance or plenarty of a class of entities of any kind depends in any manner upon human will, that class, it is evident, can never have any other than a precarious existence.[2]

[a] There are particular laws made for the preservation of this Bridge by stat. 9. Geo. 2. ch. 29.[3]

There are, likewise, in different parts of the statute-book, other sets of laws relative to so many other bridges.

---

[1] The Society of Jesus had been suppressed in 1773 by order of Clement XIV (1705–74), Pope from 1769.

[2] In the text, Bentham has noted at this point: 'Laws which are temporary by institution must be revived by institution: Laws temporary by nature expire and revive again with their subjects without the aid of institution.'

[3] i.e. the Westminster Bridge Act of 1735.

§11. *Generality of a law.*[1]

A law may be particular, general, or both in one.

1. [Eighthly],[2] with regard to the *generality* or *particularity* of a law. This results from the generality or particularity of the persons, things and acts, of the subjects of all kinds and of the objects,[3] to which it relates. Consider'd in this point of view, a law is either particular throughout, or general throughout, or partly particular and partly general: and it is evident enough that, in one or other of those predicaments, every law must be. A law may be said to be particular throughout when its subjects of every class [and] its objects[4] are all of them individuals: partly particular and partly general if any one or more of those articles are individual: general throughout, if they are none of them individual, but are each of them a class.[a]

A law, I say, may be particular in any one point, and at the same

Imperfection of the language with relation to this topic.

[a] For expressing the distinctions relative to this head, the current language is very indifferently provided.

In the first place, there is no neutral term which can be applied in common to the ideas denoted by the words general and particular, so as to bring to view the one without putting an exclusion upon the other. To profess to consider laws in respect to their generality, and then to distinguish them into such as are general and such as are not so, is a sort of verbal contradiction which, however, it seemed impossible to avoid. Instead of *generality*, I might perhaps have said *logical extent*: but who would have conjectured what I meant by *logical extent* before the expression had been explained? Words which are made use of in expressing the heads of an arrangement should, if possible, be to such a degree familiar that, of the import of them, some idea, however loose, might be caught up at the first glance.

In the next place, the terms particular and general are both of them extremely vague and uncharacteristic. Had I the liberty of coining words without control, I would distinguish the former by some such name as *atomoprosectic*; the latter by some such name as *eidoprosectic*: ατομος an individual object, ειδος a species or class, προσεκτικος from προσεχομαι to concern or reach to: upon this plan, a law which was *atomoprosectic* in all points might be farther termed a law *atomoprosectic simpliciter*; one that was *eidoprosectic* in all points, *eidoprosectic simpliciter*: one that was atomoprosectic in some points and eidoprosectic in others might be termed indifferently *atomoprosectic secundum quid* or *eidoprosectic secundum quid*, according to the exigency of the case. Or, if it should seem less uncouth, instead of *atomoprosectic*, we might say *atomoscopous*; instead of *eidoprosectic, eidoscopous*: σκοπεω to regard, or relate to. Thus much may, perhaps, be pardoned in a note: but my heart failed me at the thoughts of introducing into the text words so uncouth and formidable as these, although fashioned out of the most pleasing

---

[1] This section constitutes a later addition to the 'principal draft'.

[2] MS del. 'Seventhly'.

[3] MS add. 'and of the parties' has been bracketed for deletion by Bentham, who has then added the following note: 'N.B. these are postponed.'

[4] MS orig. 'class, its objects, and the parties who are interested in it'.

time general in any other: the truth of this, when once announced, will be immediately perceived. Hitherto, however, the common way of dividing laws in relation to this head has been into general and particular only, as if nothing more were ever worth considering in a law than merely the *persons* it related to, and as if it could relate to but one set of persons at a time. Thus inaccurate must every speculation be that relates to law, so long as any part of the field belonging to this branch of science remains unsurvey'd.

Privilegia, what.

2. Upon the same inaccurate idea, such laws as appeared to come under the notion of particular laws have been termed in Latin *privilegia*: and these have been distinguished into unfavourable (*odiosa*) and favourable (*favorabilia*). By an unfavourable *privilegium* has been meant a law in which the party made to suffer in the first instance is an individual: by a favourable *privilegium*, one in which the party favoured in the first instance was an individual:[a] it is in the latter only of the two senses that the word *privilege*, or what corresponds to it, is used in the languages of modern Europe.

Domestic mandates the only ones that are particular throughout.

3. If we look for examples, we shall find none of any mandates that are particular in every point except those transient ones which emane from private power-holders, and of which the influence is confined within the circle of a private family. Even the *lettres de cachet*, those *privilegia odiosa* which are so much felt and so much heard of in one country in Europe, and whatever may answer to them in any other countries, can not be deemed particular in all points, upon the supposition of their emaning from a sovereign acting as such and for the benefit of his people; since, upon this supposition, the whole community is the party whom they are meant to *favour*. To look upon them as being particular in respect of the party favoured (except in the very few cases mentioned in a former section)[b] is to look upon them as emaning from a despot, the master of an immense family of slaves, acting for the gratification of his own particular passions or those of some individual favourite.

of all languages, must appear to any one to whom they are altogether new. The word *ατομος*, an atom or individual, being better known by its physical than its logical sense, may here seem misapplied: but it is the very word which is made use of to signify an individual by Aristotle and his commentator Porphyry. Arist. Topic. IV. 1. Porph. Eisag. cap. 2.[1]

[a] In this sense, the application of it is frequently enough extended to the case where a class of persons are the objects of the favour.

[b] §5.[2]

---

[1] The term *ατομος* is found in Aristotle, *Topics*, IV. i. 121a, and in several passages in Porphyry, *Isagoge*.

[2] See §5, para. 2, pp. 55–6 above.

Examples of laws which are particular *ex parte*: Domestic mandates.

4. Of laws which are particular *ex parte*, examples, as may well be imagined, are not difficult to meet with. Such mandates will hardly, however, be found in great abundance in the number of those laws which emane immediately from the sovereign. The mandates which are of this stamp are most commonly the work of some subordinate class of power-holders: mandates domestic; and among those of a public nature, mandates judicial and military; such, in short, as in contradistinction to *legislative mandates* or *laws*, are termed *executive mandates* or *orders*. Domestic mandates are commonly particular in all points. In respect of the persons who are concerned, they will seldom be otherwise than particular, unless where the family is very large: and the frequency of such as may be deemed general in this point, in comparison of such as are evidently but particular, will encrease in proportion to the largeness of the family. The boundary-line between the number of persons that composes a private family and the number that composes a public body is by no means fixed. Sometimes we see families so large, and at other times commonwealths so small, that the former shall be more numerous than the latter.[1]

Military, judicial and other public orders.

5. Judicial, military, and other public mandates are in the very essence of them general in respect of the persons who are favoured in the last instance: in other points they are sometimes general, sometimes particular, as it may happen. Among military mandates, the frequency of such as are general is apt to bear a greater ratio to the frequency of such as are particular than among judicial mandates: although as an army is but a part of the community to which it belongs, the circle out of which the agible subjects of judicial mandates are taken is less limited than that out of which the agible subjects of military mandates are taken.[2]

Covenants.

6. Among such mandates of subordinate power-holders as are issued *mero motu*, and may have in view the benefit of individuals or the public as it may happen, it may be proper to take a more particular notice of covenants and conveyances. Of covenants, it is an essential characteristic that the party covenanting, and consequently the party bound *ipso facto* by the very covenant itself, is always an individual or determinate assemblage of individuals.[a]

[a] It may be said, no: for that covenant enter'd into, for example, by the governing body in a corporation, an assemblage of determinate individuals, is oftentimes made to bind the community at large, an assemblage of persons

[1] In the margin, Bentham has noted at this point: 'Note. Give an instance.'

[2] In the margin, Bentham has noted at this point: 'They are directed to a whole regiment at once, to a whole company at once.'

7. In conveyances on the contrary, the parties bound, such of the agible subjects of the law as are bound by it, are almost always numerous and indeterminate. This, at least, is the case of those conveyances of which the passible subjects, the ***proprietary subjects*** as they may be called, are *things*. To give a man a property, if it be an exclusive property, in a thing, there must be two provisions: 1. a mandate prohibiting persons at large from meddling with it: 2. a countermandate operating as an exception to the mandate, and permitting such meddling on the part of him who is made proprietor. The former may be consider'd as the work of the sovereign alone: as to so much he imperates *immediate[ly]*: it is the latter that is the joint work of the sovereign and the individual: the individual issuing a countermandate repealing, as far as it goes, the mandate, to which countermandate the sovereign, by his adoption, gives the force of law. If, then, the imperative part of

Conveyances—in what respect general, and in what particular.

indeterminate. And in the same manner, the covenant of a single person is made to bind his Heirs, Executors, Administrators and Assigns for evermore: an assemblage of persons altogether unascertainable and indeterminate. But the plain truth of the matter is, that these, though bound by the covenant, or rather in consequence of the covenant, are not parties to the covenant: it is not they who enter into it, they are not contracting parties. Persons may be *spoken to* collectively, but if they speak, it is individually. To lawyers, who make no scruple of feigning a covenant wherever they want to justify an obligation, the plain truth of the matter may seem a paradox. But to understand a subject we must take for true that which *is* true and not that which is false. Now, whether a promise is made or no is always a matter of fact: and when it is known to be made by any one, he by whom it is made is always individually known and ascertainable. Moreover, what is clear enough is that, at the time a man makes a promise, his heirs, who do not exist, make no such promise: on his part, then, there is a covenant, which the sovereign, by adopting, turns into a law of which he the covenantor is the agible subject: but on the part of his heirs there is no such covenant: if, in consequence of the act of their ancestor, they are bound, it is not by a covenant that they are bound, but by a mandate: by a mandate or recommendation or request, no matter what in that stage it is called, which, by being adopted by the sovereign, is turned into a law: in other words, by a conveyance which the covenantor is allowed to make of a right to such and such services to be render'd in certain contingencies by his heirs to the party in whose favour the covenant is made.

If a man has any power over his assigns as such, it is in virtue of a power of conveyance: the power of limiting the interest that any one in future shall have in a proprietary subject which, at the then present time, happens to be in his possession or *pro tanto* at his disposal, in such manner that, if they acquire that interest, it shall be on condition of their being subjected to such or such an obligation. I covenant for myself and my assigns under a penalty of £5 not to plow up a certain meadow which I am about to rent: that is I promise for my own part that I will not so long as it is in my own possession, and as concerning my power of conveyance I limit it in such manner that, were I minded to dispose of the meadow to any person, such person could not acquire it without subjecting himself to the same obligation, sanctioned by the same penalty.

the law to which a conveyance of this nature appertains be consider'd in respect of the persons who are bound, it is usually general, and that in the highest degree: if the de-imperative part be consider'd, which is the part in which the force of the conveyance more particularly resides, it may be particular in this respect or general according to the quality of the party or parties who are favoured by it: that is to whom the right in question is convey'd.[a] In other points the law may be general or particular as it may happen.

When the corporeal proprietary subject is of the class of persons, insomuch that the right convey'd is a right to the service or services of a person or class of persons, no regard being had to any particular subject of the class of things, the conveyance is a mandate which, in respect of the party bound, may be general or particular as it may happen. Instances where it is general are a right of toll; a title of honour; a copy-right; or any other kind of monopoly.[b] Instances where it is particular are a pecuniary debt, a right to the services of an apprentice.

Use of the distinction between general laws and particular.

[8.] The distinction between a general law or mandate and a particular law or mandate, as here explained, is more material than at first sight might be imagined. Developped and applied, it will afford us a clue without which it would be scarce possible for us to find our way through the labyrinth of constitutional jurisprudence. Correspondent to the distinction which respects the laws themselves is that which respects the power of making them. The power of enacting particular laws, the power as it may be called of imperating *de singulis*, is one sort of power: the power of enacting general laws, that is of imperating *de classibus*, of making laws in general terms, is, as we shall see, another and a very different sort of power. The latter power, although it be susceptible of a degree of extent of which the former is not susceptible, is, on the other hand, liable to peculiar limitations by which its force may be diminished or even utterly destroy'd. These limitations give room for other powers which, in many cases, form a necessary complement, as it were, to imperative power when modified as here supposed. Adding to these the autocheiristic power, and dividing each into the shares into which any lot of political power, upon being distributed among several hands, is liable to be divided, we have the sum total of all the powers whatever, constitutional as well as private, that can have existence in a state.

[a] They may be an individual or a body corporate.

[b] Speaking according to the current language, we should hardly look upon a law conferring upon a man any of these possessions as coming in any respect under the notion of a general law.

Of the complemental powers above alluded to, it will be necessary to give a variety of examples, without which the peculiar nature of a general law in contradistinction to a particular one could hardly be understood. If the several powers thus introduced for example sake should themselves receive illustration from the occasion on which they are brought to view, the information thence derived will be a kind of collateral acquisition. In this way, a sort of side glance will be given, as it were by anticipation, of the structure of the constitutional branch of law: some glympses will be afforded, however incompleat, of the connections and dependencies of some of the principal parts of that complicated whole: and those oppressive ideas of immensity and incommensurability which have hitherto hung over the subject will, even at this early period, have been in some measure dispelled.

Power of legislation is but a part of the whole power of imperation in any given case.

9. To the words power of legislation we naturally annex the idea of the power of enacting general laws: laws that shall be general in all points: such laws of which the bulk of the statutes, by whatever name termed, which, emaning from the sovereign authority and being consigned to the press, are handed down from age to age, appear to be composed. The power of issuing such laws in all cases, in such sort that no man has authority to render them invalid, and every man is bound to submitt to them or obey them, would naturally, upon first mention of it, appear to be the same thing with absolute uncontrolled power. Such a power one would naturally suppose must involve in its texture, must absorb, as it were, into its substance, every other power that could have existence in a state: insomuch that he who had this power would have every thing, and that no one without his appointment could have any thing. The possible powers in a state are reducible to two: the power of contrectation or impressive power[1] as we have termed it, and the power of imperation: which latter again may be distinguished into the power of *imperation properly so called*, and the power of *de-imperation*. But of the power of legislation, that is when confined to generals, it will appear that, so far from being equivalent to or co-extensive with both these powers, it does not include so much as what is contained in the power of imperation properly so called. This we shall presently perceive. Let a field of dominion be conceived of given amplitude, embracing a given tract of land, a given number of persons and a given assemblage of valuable things which have become, or are capable of becoming, proprietary subjects. It

[1] In the margin, Bentham has noted at this point: 'autocheiristic'.

might naturally enough be supposed that there were two ways in either of which a person might have all the power which it would be possible for a man to exercise over this land, these persons and these things: by taking the persons in classes, commanding them or setting them at liberty to perform such and such acts in classes, with or without relation to such and such things taken in classes, or by taking them individually and commanding each person to do so and so, (the particularity will hardly bear to be carried any farther) as it shall be thought proper: in a word, that the power of imperating *de classibus*, and the power of imperating *de singulis*, were but two different ways of exercising the same power. But, upon examination, this will be found not to be the case. Neither of them of itself includes the power of doing every thing that is to be done by commanding and countermanding. Let a man possess either of them in the amplest extent, there will always be something which he can not do without the other. To form the compleat power of imperation, there needs the union of both these powers. The power of imperating *de classibus* at any rate: to which must be added either the power of imperating *de singulis* or what is equivalent to it. To demonstrate this, we shall first state what it is that the power of general legislation *de classibus*, or the power of legislation ordinarily so called, wants of being compleat: next, what it is that is wanted by the power of particular legislation, or the power of issuing the sort of mandates which are commonly called *orders*.

To begin with the deficiencies to which the power of general legislation or legislation *de classibus* is exposed.

The *power of aggregation* or *accensitive power* is the other.

10. The commands of a sovereign will, like any other communications, be liable to receive a tinge from the channel through which they are convey'd. The channel through which alone the bulk of a sovereign's commands can be convey'd is that assemblage of conventional signs which, taken collectively, are called *language*. A legislator, in uttering a law which shall be general, must, in as far as it is intended to be general, make use of general terms or names. By these general terms or names, things and persons, acts, and so forth are brought to view in parcels; which parcels are the larger and more comprehensive in proportion as the extent or logical amplitude (if so it may be called) of such names is the more considerable. This being the case, the legislator in the grouping of the persons, things and acts which he takes for the subjects and objects of his laws is limited to such parcels as correspond to the generic names which are furnished by the language.

Conceive him, then, on any occasion to have taken up any such generic name. By this name, a class, suppose, of subjects (no matter what) is brought to view. This class taken at a given period is composed of a certain number of individuals. As to these individuals, then, by what means is it that they have come to be aggregated to this class? to be looked upon as belonging to it? to be the individuals who are deemed to have been had in view upon the mention of this name? By whatever means the event of their belonging to this class has come to pass, such event either depended or did not depend upon the will of a human being: if it did, such person has thereby a power: in the [latter][1] case, whatever limitation the power of the legislator be subject to on this account, the power which remains to him, whatever it be, is still so far his own, that no other person is a sharer in it. In the other case, the power of imperation does not belong to him alone; he has a sharer or partner in it: and this partner is the person on whose will the event abovementioned has a dependence.[2] The share which this person has in the entire power of imperation may be termed the *accensitive*[a] power, or power or right of *aggregation*, with regard to the class in question.

11. This power, according to the different applications that may be made of it, according to the nature of the subjects or objects to which it may be applied, will admitt of so many modifications or specific subdivisions. It may be applied to persons, to things, to acts, to places, or to times. It may, accordingly, be distinguished in the first place according to these several applications: and may, accordingly, be termed accensitive power *in personam, in rem, in actum, in locum,* or *in tempus.* Of these several branches of accensitive power, examples will be given farther on. But first, it will be proper to push the division of accensitive power *in personam* a little farther.

Accensitive power—its five branches.

12. To begin with accensitive power *in personam*. To every class of persons who in any manner stand affected by a law, a certain condition or station in life is attributed by the fashion of the language: a person being said to be of such or such a condition in virtue of his belonging to such or such a class. To aggregate a man, then, to a class is the same thing as to invest him with a condition: the accensitive power *in personam* has, therefore, the

Accensitive power *in personam* has the effect of *investitive*.

[a] From *accenseo*, to aggregate to a class; from whence the word Censor.

[1] MS 'former'. Bentham is alluding to the case where the event did not depend upon the will of a human being.

[2] In the margin, Bentham has noted at this point: 'Thus, by giving a power to a man and his *assigns*, the sovereign may give it to his mortal enemy.'

same effect as the power we have already had occasion to allude to in speaking of investment and non-investment.[a] [b]

Modifications of the accensitive power *in personam*.

13. Now we have seen what the possible ways are in which a man or any class of men may be affected by the law:[c] by any given law, and thence by the sum total of the laws put together: if affected by it at all, he must be either favoured by it, bound by it, or exposed by it to suffer: in the first case, the condition that belongs to him in consequence may *pro tanto* be spoken of as an advantageous one, in the two others as a disadvantageous one: in the first case, he stands invested with a *right*, which in certain circumstances may be also termed a *power*: in virtue of which right or power other men owe *services* to him: in the second case, an obligation is incumbent on him, and he owes services to other men: in the third case, no obligation is incumbent on him on this score, but he may be said to be *obnoxious to impressions* which other persons have the right, and perhaps are under the obligation, of causing him to undergo. Now, in all these cases the power of aggregating a man to the class to which the condition in question belongs, may, as we set out with observing, be stiled a power of investment, or an investitive power. But in some of these cases, owing to the particular figure it is apt to make in those particular instances, it may be worth while to give it a particular name. Accordingly, where the condition is accompanied with a right, it may be of use to distinguish the power of investing a man with it by some such name as that of *juris-dative*[d] or

[a] v. Ch. 16. {Division}.[1]

Difference between accensitive power *in personam* and investitive power.

[b] Notwithstanding what is said in the text, we are not to conclude that accensitive power *in personam* and investitive power are precisely the same thing; that is that the two expressions may in all cases be used interconvertibly for each other. True it is, that he who exercises this branch of accensitive power may in all cases be said thereby to exercise investitive power. But it is not in every case that accensitive power is exercised by the exercise of investitive. The exercise of this latter power includes not that of the former, in any other case than where the person who is invested with the condition does, in virtue of that condition, acquire a particular denomination such as on a similar account either hath been applied or is about to be applied to other individuals. A particular commission of an unprecedented nature, unaccompanied with any official name, whatever powers it may invest a man with, does not aggregate him to any known class of persons, unless it be some such vague and general one as that of *commissioner* or *power-holder*.

[c] supra §8. {Parties}.[2]

[d] In Latin *juris* is already used in composition with *dictio* subjoined to it; and *datio* with *satis* prefixed to it.[3]

[1] See, for instance, *An Introduction to the Principles of Morals and Legislation* (*CW*), Ch. XVI, para. 27, pp. 214–21, and para. 35, pp. 226–32.

[2] See pp. 75–93 above.

[3] i.e. *jurisdictio*, 'legal authority' or 'administration of justice', and *satisdatio*, i.e. 'satisfaction of a creditor' or 'bail'.

dicaiodotic[a] power: and where that right amounts to a power, the power of investing a man with it may again be distinguished by some such name as *potis-dative, dosidynamic*[b] or *endynamistic.*[c] This *jurisdative* power (if the term may be allow'd) is neither more nor less than the power of making conveyances, when the word *conveyance* is taken in the largest sense which it will admitt of: a power which, when the rights conferred are powers of a public or constitutional nature, comprehends one of the grand divisions of the powers of government.

14. As to the accensitive power *in rem*, this, though different in its name and in its first appearance, comes, when examined, to the same thing as the accensitive power *in personam*: inasmuch as the things in question are in the number of the subjects of some law by which the persons in question are affected. Now, it hath been shewn, that there is no way in which a thing can be mentioned but [that][1] it is in some way or other the subject of the law: indirectly[d] at least, if not directly. To cause a thing that before appertained to a class of things which did not belong to a man to appertain to a class of things that does belong to him is in effect to invest him with a power over that thing. The case is the same with all the other branches of accensitive power: with accensitive power *in actum, in locum,* and *in tempus.* This will be render'd sufficiently apparent by the examples which will be found a little farther on.

The other branches of accensitive power are productive ultimately of the same effects.

15. Opposite in a certain sense to accensitive power is a power that may be termed *disaccensitive*: of this it will be convenient to give some explanation before we proceed to give examples. Conceive a person to belong to a certain class of persons, characterised by a certain name: either, then, there is a power in some other person or persons to cause him to belong no longer to that class, or there is not: if there is, the power possessed by such person or persons may be termed *disaccensitive* power. This, then, is an accidental concomitant which may exist in regard to any class, or not exist, and which, when it exists, may exist in the same hands with the accensitive, or in different hands, as it may happen.

Disaccensitive power, what.

[a] From δικαιοδοτης compounded of δικαιον, right, and δοτης, a giver.

[b] This form of composition is exemplified in the words δοσιδικης, Δοσιθεα.

[c] From ενδυναμιζω, to confer power on a man or, as we say, *empower* him to do so and so: a word that may be made from εν and δυναμαι, to possess power: as πλουτιζω, to enrich or confer riches, is made from πλουτεω, to possess riches. In the same manner, βαδιζω, to cause to go, is derived from βαινω, to go.

[d] v. supra §6. {Subjects}.[2]

[1] MS 'what'.

[2] See §6, paras. 9–10, pp. 63–5 above.

In like manner, the power which is opposed to investitive may be termed *divestitive* or *disinvestitive*, and more particularly, that which is opposed to juris-dative, *juris-ademptive*, that which is opposed to endynamistic, disendynamistic power.

Correspondency between investitive power, power of conveyance, power of *jurisdation* and endynamistic power.

16. It appears, then, that these three expressions, *investitive power* when it regards a right (that is when it is the power of investing a man with a right), *power of conveyance*, and *power of jurisdation* are but three names for the same thing: they each of them consist in the power of *accensing*, if we so say for a moment, or aggregating a man to some division or other in the wide-extending class of *right-holders*. In particular cases, which are so various that it is impossible to comprise them under any concise description, the right is also termed a *power*: in these cases, the power of investing a man with it, the power of conveying it to a man, may be stiled *endynamistic* power, *dosidynamic* power, or power of *potisdation*. When the right or power which is convey'd is one that is exercisible on a private account, that is for the benefit either of him alone who exercises it or of some other individual or subordinate class of individuals, the power of conveyance is a private proprietary power: when the right or power which is convey'd is one that is exercisible only on a public account, that is for the benefit of the public at large, the power of conveyance is a *constitutional* power, for public powers differ no otherwise from private fiduciary powers than in respect of the scale on which they are exercisible: they are the same powers exercisible on a greater scale. Correspondent, then, to the rights and powers which may be convey'd, are so many branches of the power of conveyance: as also of that branch of disaccensitive power which may be stiled juris-ademptive.

Now, of the several rights and powers which may be convey'd, a pretty detailed enumeration was given in a former chapter,[a] in which it became necessary to mention them as capable of giving occasion to so many species of delinquency. It should seem, therefore, that to the exemplifying of the several branches of the power of conveyance nothing more can be requisite than to give a brief indication of the hands in which, in certain instances, they are lodged.

Instances of the exercise of accensitive and disaccensitive power:

17. The matrimonial contract, whatever covenants may be annexed to it, is at any rate a conveyance, if it were only in virtue of the autocheiristic or contrectative powers it conveys to

[a] Ch. 16. {Division}.[1]

[1] See, for instance, *An Introduction to the Principles of Morals and Legislation* (*CW*), Ch. XVI, paras. 25–30, pp. 205–22, and paras. 38–55, pp. 234–70.

the husband commonly over the property of the wife, and necessarily over her person. The power of conveying these powers belongs to the several parties whose concurrence, collectively or disjunctively, is necessary and sufficient to the validity of the marriage: such as the parties, the parents or guardians, the priest or magistrate who performs the ceremony, the magistrate who grants the license, and so on. The divestitive or potisademptive power belongs to the several persons whose concurrence is necessary and sufficient to the validity of a divorce: such as the parties or one of them, and the Judge or Judges having cognizance in that behalf. To the former set of parties, then, belongs the *accensitive* power with regard to the class of persons who are stiled husbands: to the latter, the *disaccensitive*. It would be easy enough, but can hardly be necessary, to apply the same method of exemplification to the powers belonging to the other conditions of the domestic kind. In virtue of the obligations or other burthens which may stand annexed to any of those conditions, the same example may also serve for such branches of investitive power the exercise of which has the effect of subjecting a man to obligations and of rendering him obnoxious to the exercise of powers of contrectation or, as they may be otherwise termed, *impressive* powers.

1. as applied to the matrimonial condition;

18. Let us pass on to constitutional powers. Taking examples from that country alone in which I write, I shall lessen the trouble of citations, and the danger of mistakes. In Great Britain, the King possesses, with respect to the chief of the great offices to which judicial power is annexed, the investitive or endynamistic, and, with respect to some of them, the divestitive or disendynamistic, power. With respect to the offices of Chancellor [and] Privy-Councillor, in both of which the judicial power forms a considerable part of the authority that belongs to them, as also with respect to the humbler office of Justice of the Peace, he has the divestitive power as well as the investitive: with respect to the offices of Member of the House of Lords, the 16 Scotch Peers excepted, and with respect to the Magistrates included under the collective appellation of the twelve Judges, as also with respect to some other Judges of inferior note, he has the investitive power only. In regard to Military offices, he possesses the investitive and divestitive power both: though in the former there are other persons who by custom have in some instances a share[a] at the same time. The divestitive power it

2.—to various constitutional powers, such as that of appointing and displacing officers of various sorts.

[a] The Lord Lieutenants of counties sign all the commissions in the militia.

belongs to him to exercise *mero motu*: at the same time there are other persons, I mean the members of Court Martials, who have the power of doing the same thing *propter quid*, that is for delinquency.

Declaring war and making peace.

19. To him alone belongs the power of declaring war: that is of aggregating large denominations of men to the disadvantageous condition of enemies: a condition which, depriving them of a variety of rights and laying them under a variety of disabilities, subjects them and the things which otherwise would be their properties to various applications of contrectative or impressive power: and the converse of this account will serve for the power of making peace.

Convicting delinquents.

20. To Juries, in many cases, belongs, in conjunction with the regular Judges, also with prosecutors, witnesses, ministerial officers of justice, and other persons whose share in this power, however inconspicuous, is not the less real, the power of aggregating persons to the disadvantageous class of delinquents, a class which is branched out into the various classes we have seen.[a] They thence become the persons from whom the legislator has taken such and such rights, whom he has subjected to such and such obligations, and render'd obnoxious in the way of punishment or for other purposes to such and such applications of the *impressive* power. This branch of the accensitive power is a distinct power from that of issuing judicial mandates, at least in as far as a part is distinct from the whole. Take the instance where a man is to be hanged for robbery or any other crime. To authorise any person to perform such an act of violence on the body of another, a warrant or order issued by a magistrate of a certain description is made necessary. In the issuing of this warrant or order, no Juryman has any direct participation. The order is signed not by the Jury, but by certain other magistrates who are called Judges. But to the validity of such order, or at least to the indemnity of those who issue it, a variety of conditions are made requisite: among which are a previous declaration made on the part of a certain number of the abovementioned occasional magistrates called Jurymen, importing that such or such a person, the person who afterwards is taken for the passible subject of such an order, belongs to one of those classes of persons out of which, and which alone, the Judges are allow'd to select the individuals on whom such violence shall in pursuance of their orders be committed.

[a] Ch. 16. {Division}.[1]

[1] For the division of offences into five classes see ibid., Ch. XVI, §i, pp. 187–91.

All these are instances of accensitive power *in personam.*

21. An instance of accensitive power *in rem* is the power of assigning value and giving currency to coin. This power applies itself to, and modifies the effect of, that part of the body of the laws which relates to the offence of wrongful non-investment of property in the case where the proprietary subject in question consists in money, or in goods which require to be marked out by weights or measures. On the 1st of January 1780 Peter enters into a covenant which obliges him to pay to Paul, on the 1st of Jan:y 1781, the sum of 20s. On the 1st of Jan: 1780 a shilling contains 93 grains of silver. The King has the power of determining what pieces of money shall be understood to belong to the class of things called *shillings.*[1] Before the 1st of January 1781 he issues a number of pieces of money which he calls shillings, but which in fact contain each of them but half the quantity of silver that was contained in any of the pieces of money which on the 1st of January 1780 went by the name of shillings. What is the consequence? that Peter is exempted from so much of the obligation as concerns ten out of the twenty shillings he had covenanted for. A covenant to pay twenty shillings may be consider'd as consisting of two covenants each for the payment of ten shillings. Each of these covenants, by means of the standing declaration made by the sovereign concerning the validity which he gives to covenants, is turned into a law. What, then, is the influence of the act of accensitive power in question upon these two laws? The one of them indeed it leaves standing: but the other it repeals. So mighty is the force of this single branch of the accensitive power. Supposing it exercisible without controul, and the force of the legislative power in all money matters may be reduced to nothing. Pecuniary engagements may be annihilated at pleasure: taxes may be levied upon the creditors of the public to the amount of almost the whole of what is due to them. All laws whatsoever, which have no other punishment than what is pecuniary to corroborate them, may be render'd of no force. These are but two out of a multitude of revolutions which might be brought about by the exercise of this single power.

Regulating the coin—an instance of accensitive power *in rem.*

Another power of a nature nearly approaching to the former is that of regulating weights and measures. Revolutions similar to those just mentioned may accordingly be made by an alteration in the import of such terms as the words *yard* and *bushel.* This will be easily enough conceived without farther explanation.

[1] In the margin, Bentham has noted at this point: 'Qu. how this stands by actual[?] law and state it. He certainly had it once.'

Accensitive power *in actum* needs no separate exemplification.

22. Of the accensitive power *in actum* no separate examples need be given. One way in which a person may aggregate himself, or render himself liable to be aggregated, to a class of persons is by performing such or such an act. In this way to aggregate any act which a man has peformed to such or such a class of acts is virtually to aggregate him to such or such a class of persons. Thus it is that, by pronouncing an act to be an act of robbery, the agent is pronounced a robber: by pronouncing an act to be an act of lunacy, the agent is pronounced a lunatic, and so on. Accordingly, the instance above given of the power exercised by Jurymen might as well have been applied to the illustration of this branch of accensitive power as of the other.

Instances of accensitive power *in locum*.

23. Instances of accensitive power *in locum* are the power of consecrating churches and other places of religious worship. Even by this power, if exercised without controul, revolutions might be effected not less extraordinary than any which the preceding branches of accensitive power are capable of producing. By this power we have seen property usurped, debts render'd irrecoverable and crimes dispunishable.[a]

Accensitive power *in tempus*.

24. There remains only that branch of accensitive power which concerns *time*. Of the exercise of this power we have an instance in

[a] In the reign of Rich. 2[d] of England,[1] an ecclesiastic, if he happen'd to see any land that lay convenient for him, used to turn it into a churchyard: an act of parliament became necessary to put a stop to these metamorphoses.[2] The abuses that have been introduced by the establishment of asylums are known to every body. Asylums are mostly of a religious origin, but in some instances they have owed their establishment to the secular authority. In some places it has been thought for the honour of God that crimes should go unpunished: in others for the honour of the King that debts should go unpaid. In England the verge of the court, as it is called, together with certain other privileged places, are a sort of imperfect asylum for insolvent debtors.

Long before the Clergy had begun to possess themselves of the estates of individuals by turning them into churchyards, the King had been used to swallow them up in much larger masses by turning them into forests. Had it not been for the successful struggles of the other states, the kingdom might by this time have consisted of nothing but forests and churchyards. See the history of England during the 12th and 13th centuries, *passim*; particularly the reigns of William Rufus, John, and Henry 3[d].[3] See also, among the statutes, that called *Carta de Forestâ*.[4]

---

[1] Richard II (1367–1400), King of England 1377–99.

[2] The conversion of land to a churchyard was brought within the scope and penalties of the Statute of Mortmain of 1279 by 15 Ric. II, c. 7 (1391).

[3] William II (*c.* 1060–1100), King of England from 1087; John (1167–1216), King of England from 1199; and Henry III (1207–72), King of England from 1216.

[4] The Charter of the Forest was first issued in 1217 as a supplement to *Magna Carta* of 1215, which had itself contained several clauses dealing with the forest laws. For *Magna Carta* see p. 256 n. below.

the regulation of the stile. Exercised without reason and without measure, even this power might be productive of revolutions as extensive as any which we have seen produced by an abuse of the right of coinage. Interest of money might be diminished or encreased, bonds forfeited, proprietary terms protracted or curtailed, minors emancipated, adults subjected to the disadvantages of minority, and the effect of an infinite variety of covenants, conveyances and other legal dispositions perverted or destroy'd: and that without the designation of the legislator or the intention or expectation of the parties. As great changes might be made by it, and as much mischief done, as by a general abolition of debts, or an agrarian law.[a] These general illustrations will, I suppose, be thought sufficient: demonstrations more particular it were easy enough, but can hardly be necessary, to bring to view.

Imperfection of the power of imperation *de singulis.*

25. It is by this time, I suppose, sufficiently manifest that the legislative power ordinarily so called, I mean the power of legislating *de classibus,* even though it be supreme, can never of itself be absolute and unlimited. It can never so much as amount to the entire power of imperation: it will fall short of being equal to that power by so much as is contained in whatever powers of aggregation or disaggregation are established in the state. We have seen what the points are in respect of which a law may be general or particular: in whatever of those points it happens to be general, there may be room for the intervention of those other powers.

It now remains to shew that the power of imperation in particular terms, the power of imperating, as we may say, *de singulis,* how extensive and unlimited it may be in itself, can never possess all the efficacy that is capable of being exerted by this and the preceding power put together. The principal article to be consider'd in this view is that of the person or persons whom the law has principally in prospect, whichever be the purpose of the sovereign concerning them; whether to favour them, to coerce them, or to make them suffer. Whichever, then, be his purpose, the intercourse he has with particular persons can never, comparatively speaking, be very extensive. Few will be the individuals whom he can find motives for selecting or the means of describing. We even see families so large as to include more servants than

[a] Care was accordingly taken to obviate these inconveniences in the British act (24 G. 2. c. 23) for the adoption of the new stile.[1]

[1] Chesterfield's Act of 1751, which introduced the Gregorian Calendar (the New Style) from the following year, stipulated that commercial transactions would continue to be based on the Julian Calendar (the Old Style).

come individually under the master's notice: in how much greater a degree must this be the case in empires? Thus limited by the nature of things is the power of the despot (to use the term in the indifferent sense which first belonged to it) in comparison with the power of the legislator: I mean, even with relation to their contemporaries: and in regard to posterity, the difference is still more conspicuous. With posterity the despot, as such, has no means whatever of communication. He has no names to call them by: he has no language in which to converse with them. But to the power of the legislator, time has no barrier to oppose: the *nati natorum et qui nascentur ab illis*[1] form but a small part of the multitude he has under his care:[a] so that in this line alone, the power of the latter is, to that of the former, as infinity to one. Were power indeed to be consider'd in no other light than that of an instrument of private satisfaction to the possessor, and the measure of its magnitude were the tendency it has to contribute to that end, farther discussions might perhaps be requisite: but in this quality, it does not concern us here.[2]

[a] In the act above referred to, express and separate provision is made for the concerns of the years 2| | and 2| |.[3] It is curious and not unpleasing to observe [the] providence of the legislator taking so large a stride.

---

[1] Virgil, *Aeneid*, III. 98, i.e. 'sons of sons and those who shall be born from them'.

[2] The following continuation, with the marginal heading 'Recapitulation', has been crossed through by Bentham: 'At any rate, it appears that the power of the legislator and the power of the despot are not even, when put together, equal to the whole power of imperation in a state: that a chasm is still left, to supply which requires the addition of the several modifications of power which may be included under the names of accensitive and disaccensitive.'

Bentham has noted after this paragraph: 'Go on with the distinction between the power of accensition &c. *in classis* and *in singulis* and *singula*.

'Endynamistic power of the 1st, 2d &c. orders: electors of Members of Parliament, electors of the first electors.'

[3] Chesterfield's Act of 1751 stipulated that the years 2000, 2400, and 2800 would be leap years, whereas the remaining hundredth years would have 365 days only.

§ 12. *Aspects of a law.*[1]

[53.][2] *prohibition* or *forbiddal*: and the act is said to be prohibited or forbidden.[a] In both cases the expression of the will is stiled

[a] To make use of the words *command* and *prohibition* to denote the mere aspect of the will, without regard to the motives which it may happen to relie on for its accomplishment, is, it must be confessed, an impropriety. But there are no other words that could have been made use of for the purpose without giving into a still greater degree of impropriety: constituted, then, as language is at present, the impropriety was unavoidable: and being immediately confessed and held up to view, it will not, it is hoped, be productive of any mistake. Imperfection of the nomenclature relative to expressions of the will.

To obtain a clear view of the ideas that are included or liable to be included under the notion of a law, it will be necessary to take them one at a time: the aspect, for example, now, and the motive by and by. As to the act which is the object of the will in question, it is evident enough that, if it be a voluntary act, some motive or other to give it birth, it must have had. As to the will, however, which may have taken that act for its object, it is possible for it to have been conceived without averting to that motive, or even to any motive at all; the will, the *wish* as it is called, may even be expressed, without particularizing any thing of the motive. As the two objects, viz: an expression of will, and the expression of the motive relied on for the accomplishment of that will, may actually exist the one without the other, of course may they be conceived to do so.

The business, then, is to find words that will convey the one idea without the other: the former without the latter. This is what the word *command* will not properly do: for it limits the nature of the motive relied on, intimating it to be of the coercive kind, and thereby excluding every expression of will which does not place its reliance on that motive: and the word *prohibition* is in the same case.

Now, true it is, that where the will in question is, as here, the will of a sovereign, the motive, or at least one of the motives, which it relies on, is commonly of the coercive kind: the reasons of this will be stated in their proper place.[a] True it is, therefore, that whatever be the motive actually relied on, any will the expression of which appears to come from such a source will in general be apt to appear as if it were accompanied with an intention of employing such motives for the purpose of providing for its accomplishment. This, however, is not necessarily the case: the two circumstances of sovereignty, and an intention to coërce, though closely connected, are not by any means inseparable. Hold up to view a motive of the alluring kind, and no other, the connection will be much weaken'd: disclaim in express terms all intentions of a coercive kind, it will be entirely dissolved: and it can not so much as have been formed, where the act is such that it is plain, from the nature of it, no intentions of that kind could ever have been entertained: as is the case, for instance, where, if the act be not performed, there is no harm done, and at the same time the probability is against its being in a man's power to perform it.

[a] infra 93 n.[3]

---

[1] For a later, alternative draft on this topic see Appendix C, pp. 250–67 below.

[2] The following text is the latter part of paragraph 53 of the 'principal draft'. As well as the preceding part of paragraph 53, the manuscripts for paragraphs 51–2, which together formed the beginning of the discussion of 'Aspects' in the 'principal draft', and consisted of six pages, have not been located. The discussion here deals with the case where the aspect of the will is 'active'.

[3] See pp. 144–5 n. below.

sometimes a *command*: and for distinction's sake it may be termed, in the former case an *affirmative*, in the latter, a *negative*, command. To prevent ambiguity, where both cases are meant to be included, instead of the word *command*, we may make use of the word *mandate*. Moreover, in either case the provision made by the law may be said to be *imperative* or *obligative*: or the mandate itself may be stiled an imperative or obligative provision.[a] 'Every man shall export corn:'—this may serve as an example of a command. 'No man shall export corn:'—this may serve as an example of a prohibition.[b]

Conceive a law to this effect—'Give information against all such as you shall suspect to be deserters.' This, as coming from the sovereign, might carry the appearance of an intention to punish in case of non-compliance, although nothing were mentioned about punishment. Let it go on and say—'and you shall have 40[s] for each,' such intentions may possibly indeed be apprehended, but it is not provable. Let it go on still farther and say, 'but whether you do or no, you shall not be punished,' it is certain no such intentions can be apprehended: I mean so long as any confidence is put in the declaration of the law. But take another act, and let the law be, 'Exert yourselves, ye men of science, and let the longitude be discovered.' It is plain enough that not the smallest apprehension of punishment could ever be excited by an address like this; even although no reward were proffer'd nor indemnity proclaimed.

It appears, then, that strictly speaking it does not follow that, where the aspect of the will is active and affirmative, the expression of it must, because it is the will of the sovereign, be of that limited species which is commonly brought to view by the word *command*: and so *vice versâ* with regard to a *prohibition*.

These, however, are the only words we can make use of: unless we were to invent an entire set of new expressions and lay aside the current language altogether.

The word *invitation*, for instance, if that were used, would be as bad on the other side: it would intimate that the motive relied on were not of the coercive kind, but of the alluring.

The word *requisition*, indeed, stands pretty clear of the idea of a motive: but then there are no words for expressing any of the correlative aspects: nor has it any *conjugates* (as the logicians call them) for expressing the states of the act which correspond to them. No words which are to *requisition* what *prohibition* and *permission* are to *command*. We could hardly say 'an act required': and even if we could, still [there][1] are no phrases which are to the phrase 'an act required', what the phrases 'an act prohibited', and 'an act left free', are to the phrase 'an act commanded'.

The like or stronger objections would, I am pretty well satisfied, appear against any other terms that could be assigned.

[a] The difference between what I mean by a legislative provision and what I mean by a law is as follows: A legislative provision may be a whole law or only a part of a law. Every law contains one or more legislative provisions: but it is not every legislative provision that amounts to a law. See infra 84.[2]

[b] The provisions here exemplified, while they remain thus unqualified, appear

[1] MS 'they'.

[2] See pp. 137–8 below.

54. Next let the aspect be inactive. Here, then, there is nothing to express: there is neither command in the case, nor prohibition: and the act, being on the one hand not commanded, and on the other hand not prohibited, may be said to be *left free*.

Aspect inactive—a non-command—an inactive permission.

This, however, seems to be one of the cases in which the word *permission* has been employ'd: what others there are we shall come to presently. A man is about to perform an act, no matter what; you, being in authority, do not prohibit him: he may thereby be said in a certain sense to have your permission for doing it. In this case, to distinguish it from another which we shall come to presently,[a] the permission may be stiled an *original* or *primordial* permission: and it may be said to be *inactive*.

To match with this it is plain there should be some word opposed in like manner to *command*. But there does not seem to be any such word in use: to answer the purpose of it, there seems to be as yet no other expedient than that of having recourse to circumlocution, and saying *a permission not to perform* or *a permission to forbear performing* such or such an act. But how then to distinguish this sort of permission from the former? it might be stiled, perhaps, though not very characteristically, a negative permission. But if on any occasion an univocal appellative (I mean an appellative comprised in a single word) should be necessary, we must make one for the purpose: such, for example, as the word *non-command*.[b] This would tally pretty well with the word *countermand*: a word already in use, for which we shall have occasion presently.[c] Moreover, as a command or a prohibition may either of them be termed indifferently a mandate or provision obligative, so a non-command or an inactive permission may be termed indifferently a *non-mandate* or a provision *unobligative*. 'No man is obliged to export corn:'—this may serve as an example of a

equally absurd when consider'd in the character of laws actually enacted: but the absurdity of the law is a matter that need not be regarded. It seemed conducive to perspicuity to take the same act throughout for all the modifications of which the aspect of the will is susceptible: and it would be singular indeed if there should be any act towards which the law could, without absurdity, bear indifferently all sorts of aspects. The argumentative logicians in their explanations of the forms of syllogizing exhibit every form that is conceivable; absurd as well as rational. The act here specified was preferred as being simple in its conception.

[a] infra 57.[1]

[b] A little farther on we shall see there is as much occasion for finding a name for the expression of these inactive aspects, as for any of the others. See infra 73.[2]

[c] infra 60.[3]

[1] See pp. 118–19 below for the confirmative or re-iterative provision.

[2] See pp. 129–30 below.

[3] See §11, p. 120 below.

non-command. 'Every man may export corn:'—this may serve as an example of a permission, which in the present case is supposed to be a primordial one.

Aspect superventitious—superventitious provision confirmative—alterative.

55. So much for the case where the aspect of the will is *primordial*: let it now be *superventitious*. This superventitious aspect is either conformable to the primordial one or unconformable: in the former case the expression of the superventitious aspect may be said to be *consentaneous to* that of the primordial: in the latter case, *alterative* of it.

Primordial aspect active, superventitious provision, if consentaneous, a command or a prohibition

56. Let us begin with the former: and first let the primordial aspect have been active: the expression of it was, then, either a command or a prohibition: the expression of the superventitious aspect will, therefore, be either a command or a prohibition likewise: and the act is commanded or prohibited as before.

—and it may be re-iterative *in genere* or *in specie*.

An expositive provision, what.

57. Again: let the superventitious provision be consentaneous to the primordial one as before. In this case, the superventitious aspect, in applying to the class of acts which was the object of the primordial, either applies itself to the whole class undivided or applies itself to some subordinate class or classes of the number of those which are included in the class in question: in the former case, the superventitious provision may be stiled confirmative *in genere*, or *confirmative*, or re-iterative with reference to the primordial: in the latter case, confirmative *in specie* or *expositive*. Let the primordial provision be: No person shall export corn. The superventitious provision may say, in the same words as before: No person shall export corn; or in different words: let no person export corn: in this case, it is simply re-iterative of the primordial one. Or it may say, no man shall export corn, or no woman shall export corn, or no merchant, no factor, or no husbandman: or no person shall carry corn out of the country, or employ another to carry it out of the country: or no man shall export corn by land or by sea, on a waggon or in a cart: in a ship or in a boat: or no man shall export wheat, or rye or barley. In any of these cases, the superventitious provision may be said to be expositive of the primordial one.[a]

If, without repeating the words particularly expressive of volition, the exposition be confined to the words made use of in the primordial provision, it will come to the same thing: as thus: It

[a] To give an exposition in this manner of the whole provision at length is to break down the general provision into so many subordinate specific ones.[a]

[a] v. infra §| |.[1]

[1] MS del. '4.' See, for instance, §12, para. 85, pp. 138–9 below.

matters not who the exporter is: whether a merchant, a factor, or a husbandman: nor what the corn exported, whether wheat, rye or barley . . . and so on.

If the species mentioned under each head are intended to include the whole genus, the mode of exposition may be termed *enumeration*: if not, *exemplification*.[a]

It is evident that any exposition given of the words employ'd in the provision illustrated is *pro tanto* an exposition of the provision itself.

58.[1] Again: let the primordial aspect have been inactive: the expression of it, then, was either a non-command or an inactive permission: the expression of the superventitious aspect, being consentaneous to the other, will, therefore, be either a non-command or an inactive permission likewise: and the act, as before, is in either case left free.

Primordial aspect inactive, superventitious provision, if confirmative, a non-command or inactive permission.

59. Next, let the superventitious aspect be unconformable to the primordial. Now it may be unconformable in either of two ways: in the way of simple *contradiction*:[b] or in the way of *contrariety*:[b] in this latter way in certain cases only, as we shall presently

Superventitious aspect unconformable, superventitious provision contradictive—contrariant.

[a] Various other modes of exposition might be distinguished: such as definition, paraphrasis,[*a*] archetypation,[*b*] etymologation, division, &c.: these, however, I pass over as belonging rather to metaphysics or logic in general, than to the logic of imperation in particular.

Let the subordinate classes contained under a given superior class of acts that are the objects of a law be enumerated, the superior class itself not mentioned by its name at first, but mentioned afterwards, the provision in which it is mentioned will be the converse of the expositive provisions before mentioned: it might be termed a *concentrative* provision. As if, instead of mentioning corn as the article of which the exportation was prohibited, the law had at first mentioned wheat, barley, rye, and so on, and then by another provision it had declared by name the same will as to corn in general: this latter provision might be said to be concentrative of the three former. Except in a digest, a provision of the concentrative kind will scarcely occur, since, if a superior class of acts and a number of acts which are subordinate to it should both be mentioned, the more general term will naturally be mentioned either first or alone: the more particular being either left out altogether; or subjoined, in the form of an exposition, to the more general.

[b] Saunderson's Logic, Lib. II. cap. 5.[2]

[*a*] See Fragm. on Gov. Ch. v. par. [6.] n.[3]

[*b*] See supra 40 n.[4]

[1] An earlier draft of paragraphs 58–9, and the first part of paragraph 60, is at UC lxxxviii. 184[v].

[2] Robert Sanderson, *Logicæ Artis Compendium*, 11th edn., Oxford, 1741, pp. 70–3. This was the edition that Bentham studied when at the University of Oxford.

[3] MS '7. n.' is a slip. See *A Fragment on Government* (*CW*), pp. 494–6 n.

[4] See p. 67 n. above.

perceive.[a] Accordingly, in the former case the superventitious provision may be said to be *simply contradictive* or *revocative* of the primordial one; in the latter case, *contrariant* or *reversive*.

Primordial aspect active, superventitious provision, if contradictive, deobligative—a countermandate—a countermand—a repermission.

60. Let us begin, then, with the case where it is simply contradictive or revocative: and first, let the primordial aspect have been active. If, then, it was affirmative, the expression of it was a command: the expression of the superventitious aspect, then, being revocative of such command may be stiled a *countermand*: and the act may be said to be countermanded: it is accordingly left uncommanded and made free again.

Next, let the primordial aspect (being active still) have been negative: the expression of it, then, was a prohibition: the expression, then, of the superventitious aspect being contradictive of the other is what is stiled a *permission*; and the act is said to be permitted: it is accordingly left unprohibited and made free again. Moreover, the permission, wherever there is occasion to distinguish it from the inactive original permission above spoken of, may be termed a *superventitious permission* or a *repermission*: it may likewise be said to be *active*: and the act may be said to be repermitted. Also, whether the provision be a countermand or a repermission, it may in either case be termed a *countermandate* or a *de-obligative* provision.

Primordial aspect inactive, superventitious provision, if contradictive, a command or a prohibition.

61. Again, let the primordial aspect have been inactive. The expression of it, then, was either a non-command, or an inactive permission. The expression, then, of the superventitious aspect will accordingly be either a command or a prohibition.

Primordial aspect active, superventitious provision, if contrariant, a prohibition or a command.

62. We come now to the case where the expression of the superventitious aspect is doubly alterative or reversive of that of the primordial. And first let the primordial have been active. The superventitious, then, will be active likewise: only on the opposite side. If, then, the primordial aspect was affirmative, and consequently the expression of it a command, the superventitious aspect is negative, and the expression of it a prohibition: if the primordial aspect was negative, and the expression of it a prohibition, the superventitious aspect is affirmative, and the expression of it a command. Between command on the one hand and prohibition on the other, inactivity lies midway. The superventitious provision, then, takes in either case two steps instead of one: one from command or prohibition down to inactivity: another from inactivity

[a] infra 63.[1]

[1] See p. 121 below, where Bentham states that, where the primordial aspect is inactive, the superventitious aspect can not be opposite in the way of contrariety.

up to prohibition or command. A reversive provision may accordingly be resolved into two provisions, both having for their object the same act: the one destroying the obligation imposed by the primordial provision, the other imposing a new obligation, but of the opposite nature.

63. Lastly, let the primordial aspect have been inactive. In this case, the superventitious aspect can not be opposite to it in the way of contrariety: it is only in the way of simple contradiction that it can be so. Let it take one step and it becomes unconformable: but let it take another, and it falls back again into conformity. The expression, therefore, of the one can not be reversive of that of the other. Contradict a non-command and you have a command: but contradict the command, and you have a non-command as before. Contradict a permission and you have a prohibition: but contradict the prohibition, and you have a permission as before.[a]

Primordial aspect inactive, superventitious provision can not be contrariant.

[a] The correspondence here observable between the word *countermand* and the word *permission* does not hold throughout: it does not hold good with respect to all their conjugates: nor even throughout all the phrases into which the words themselves may be introduced. A man may be said to *be permitted* to do a thing: to have a *permission given him* to do it: but he can not be said to *be countermanded not* to do it, to have *a countermand given him not* to do it. The word *permission* again, as we have seen, is used as well where the aspect is primordial as where it is superventitious: the word countermand can not be used where the aspect is primordial: it necessarily supposes a command preceding.

Countermand—does not match in every case with permission.

This want of symmetry is not confined to the English language. It will be found, I believe, to prevail in most other languages that deal largely with the Latin. Perhaps the cause is of a more extensive nature: and is grounded in the nature of the acts themselves that are in question. The case seems to be that, in general, there are more acts which men have need to be restrained from doing, than there are which they have need to be constrained to do. I mean more sorts of acts. Moreover, let the sort of act be in the main ever so innocent, beneficial, or even necessary, it is only at certain seasons that it is so.[a] The moments which give a man the opportunity of performing any positive service to the community are separated by long and frequent intervals: but mischief a man may do almost at any time. The great crimes, such as murder, robbery, incendiarism, perjury and so forth, are almost always committed by acts of the positive stamp.[b] Mankind, then, take the sum of their conduct throughout life, have much greater need of a bridle than of a spur. Since prohibitions, then, come oftener in question than commands, there will be more frequent occasion to grant re-permissions, that is to countermand prohibitions (I mean in particular cases that are excepted), than to countermand affirmative commands.

Cause of this want of symmetry in language.

The word *dispensation* may be used in some cases either instead of the word countermand or instead of the word re-permission: but it is scarcely used where the description of the persons whose acts are the objects of the superventitious

Dispensation, what.

[a] infra 64 n.[1]

[b] See infra 93 n.[2]

[1] See p. 122 n. below.

[2] See the sixth point at pp. 144–5 n. below.

Command &c. conditional—unconditional.

64. We come now to speak of the appellations that a provision may receive in consideration of the relation it bears to the specificant circumstances which may be made use of for the purpose of determining and characterising the act.

Let the aspect be active, and that primordial. If an act, then, is commanded, either it is commanded purely and absolutely, without the mention of any specificant circumstances, or it is commanded *in* such or such circumstances, or in other words when accompanied by such and such circumstances; in the former case, it may be stiled an *unconditional* command; in the latter, a *conditional* one. And so in the case of a prohibition.

Every man shall maintain his children: This may serve as an example of an unconditional command.[a] 'No man shall export wheat out of the country:' This may serve for an example of an unconditional prohibition. 'Every man shall maintain his children, *so long as* they are unable to maintain themselves:' This may serve as an example of a conditional command. 'No man shall export wheat out of the country *when* the market-price at the place from whence it is meant to be exported is more than 44[s] a quarter:'[b] This may serve as an example of a conditional prohibition. 'No man is obliged to maintain his children:'[c] This may serve as an example of an unconditional non-command. 'Any man may export corn out of the country:' This may serve as an example of an unconditional permission. 'No man is obliged to maintain his children, if they are weakly or deformed:'[d] This may serve as an example of a

provision is co-extensive with that of the persons whose acts are the objects of the primordial provision. It is most commonly applied only to individuals. This word, too, is very imperfectly supplied with conjugates.

[a] It must be confessed that the idea belonging to the word *maintain* as applied to children is very changeable and vague: it includes a vast variety of different acts, to be performed upon different occasions. But there was no finding any such thing as one unvaried physical act that could pass even for a moment as a proper object for an unconditional command. The reason is that there is no positive physical act of any sort the performance of which could in all circumstances be of a beneficial nature to any one: nor on the other hand, if there were, would there be any act which it could ever be expedient that any person should be obliged under all circumstances to perform.

[b] British Statute 13 Geo: III. c. 43. §. 5.

[c] A liberty allowed by the law of Athens and many other Grecian states. Potter's Antiq. B. IV. Ch. 14.[1]

[d] A liberty allow'd by a law of Sparta. Ib.[2]

[1] John Potter, *Archæologica Græca: or, the Antiquities of Greece* (first published 1697–9), 9th edn., 2 vols., London, 1775, ii. 318–35, esp. 333–4.

[2] See ibid., ii. 333: '[the Triers] carefully view'd such [children] as were brought to them; if they found them lusty and well favour'd, they gave Orders for their Education, and allotted

conditional non-command. 'Any man may export wheat out of the country when the market-price &c. is under 44^{s} a quarter:' This may serve as an example of a conditional permission.

65. When a command is unconditional, that is when the act which is commanded is mentioned by itself without the mention of any circumstances, the intention of the legislator (at least for any thing that is expressed) is that it shall be performed, whatever circumstances it be attended with, that is in any circumstances or cases whatsoever: in other words, that every individual act of the class of acts signified by the generical words in question shall, without exception, be performed. So likewise, *mutatis mutandis*, where the act is prohibited or left free. Let the command now be conditional; let certain circumstances be mentioned as those in which it is his will that the act should be performed: what is his intention now? what is the effect which the mention of those circumstances may be attended with?[1] Either it has none at all, and then the import of the command is neither more nor less than what it would have been if no such circumstances had been mentioned, or it has the effect of intimating that in these circumstances indeed it is his intention the act should be performed, but in these *only*: and that in cases where the act is not accompanied by these circumstances, he means not to express any such will about the matter: that where the act is not of the class to which the genus is reduced by the specificant terms in question, it is not the object of his will. The effect, then, of introducing a specificant circumstance is to set *limits* to the case in which it is his will that the act should be performed. These circumstances, then, may, with reference to the case in which the act is commanded to be performed, be stiled *limitative circumstances*: the words by which they are made to have that effect, *limitative words* or *words of limitation*: the assemblage of those words, a limitative clause: and that clause, if it be in such a manner detached from the rest of the words in the law as to form an entire proposition, may be termed a limitative proposition or provision.

Limitative circumstances—words—clause—proposition.

66. By the same operation, every case which does *not* lie within the case composed of the same circumstances is *excepted* and

Exceptive circumstances.

a certain Proportion of Land for their Maintenance; but if weakly or deform'd, they order'd them to be cast into a deep Cavern in the Earth near the Mountain *Taygetus*, as thinking it neither for the Good of the Children themselves, nor for the publick Interest, that they should be brought up, since Nature had both denied them the means of Happiness in their own Particular, and of being serviceable to the Publick, by not enduing them with a sufficient Measure of Health and Strength.'

[1] In the margin, Bentham has noted at this point: 'A new species is made by the addition of specific circumstances. A command in this case extends only to this species.'

thrown out, as it were, of the case in which it is his will the act should be performed: the same circumstances may, therefore, with reference to the case in which the act is commanded to be performed, and all the cases in which it is not commanded to be performed, be stiled *exceptive* circumstances; to wit as taking these last cases out of the limits of the former.

The words, then, are virtually words also of exception: the clause, an exceptive clause: the proposition, an exceptive proposition.

In what cases the words are limitative; in what, exceptive.

67. There are other words, however, by means of which the same effect may be produced in a more explicit and conspicuous manner. This is done by describing in positive terms the case which it is meant should *not* be regarded as included within that to which the expression of will has already been applied, at the same time mentioning the former as meant to be taken out of the latter. This is commonly what is done where such words as the words *exceptive clause* and *exceptive proposition* may be made use of. It is one and the same import which may be couched in either of the two forms of expression. In both ways the general and unlimited case which is constituted by the entire assemblage of all the circumstances with which the performance of the act can by possibility be attended is divided into two subordinate and more particular cases: one of which *is* that which the act must be in so as to be of the sort which the legislator commands to be performed; the other, *not*. Of these two subordinate cases, it is the one or the other that is expressly mentioned, according as the clause is in the limitative form, or in the exceptive: if in the limitative form, the former: if in the exceptive form, the latter. A limitation, then, is an indirect exception: an exception, an indirect limitation.

Example of a conditional law reduced to the unconditional form.

68. To give an example: suppose a prohibitive law to this effect,[a] *No man shall export corn out of the country, when the market price* (at the place from whence it is meant to be exported) *is more than 44^{s} a quarter.* This is a conditional prohibition: the act is that of exporting corn out of the country. This act, then, is capable of taking place in either of two cases: in the case where the market price at the place in question is greater than the sum specified: and in the case where it is not greater than that sum. When the act,

[a] The difficulty of finding an example of an unconditional law of the affirmative kind has been already noticed (supra. 64).[1] It was scarce possible to find a clear specimen but what, if totally divested of all limitative as well as exceptive clauses, would appear too absurd to pass even in the way of supposition.

[1] See p. 122 & n. above.

then, is in the first of these cases, it *is* the lawgiver's intention that the prohibition should take place and that the act should *not* be done: he accordingly subjoins the words 'where the market-price' &c., and by so doing he narrows the unlimited extent which the prohibition had while it was general, so as to confine or limit its application to that particular case. Where the act is in the other particular case, it is *not* his intention that the prohibition should take place: the act, for any intention that he has to the contrary, may be performed or not performed as a man pleases: narrowing, then, the general case to the above particular and *limited* one, the other case is tacitly excepted and thrown out. Here, then, it is the limitation that is expressed; the exception being only implied. But the same provision might have been expressed in the opposite way; so that the exception should have been expressed, and the limitation only implied. 'Any man may export corn out of the country: except where the market price is'—so and so.

Circumstances &c. whether limitative or exceptive may be termed qualificative.

69. It appears, then, that the same species of act, the same compartment of the logical or generic whole, may be expressed in either of the two ways; viz: by words of limitation or by words of exception. But although words of either import may, by a particular mode of application, be made to produce the same effect, yet in themselves those words are different. As, therefore, on some occasions it may be requisite to distinguish them, so on other occasions there may be a conveniency in characterising them indifferently by one common name: accordingly, whether it be by words of the one kind or of the other that the sort of act denoted by the generic name is narrow'd and the species in question extracted out of it, the words may in either case be termed words of *qualification*: the circumstances denoted by them, qualificative circumstances: and the clause composed of them, a *qualifying* or *qualificative clause*.

Provisions unconditional and conditional interconvertible.

70. It also appears that a conditional provision (a conditional prohibition, to keep to the same example) is convertible into two provisions: a general unconditional permission, and a particular exceptive clause which stands opposed to it: and it is the exceptive clause that wears the aspect of which the provision, when in the conditional form, is expressive. Thus in the example above put—'*No man shall export corn*' &c. is a prohibition: accordingly the general clause '*Any man may export corn*' being a permission, the particular exceptive clause, '*except where the market price is so and so*,' operates as a prohibition likewise. In other words, a permission with an exception is equipollent to a prohibition with a limitation.

In like manner, a conditional command may be converted into a general non-command and a particular command in exception to it: so that a non-command with an exception is equipollent to a command with a limitation: a conditional non-command into a general command and a particular countermand in exception to it: so that a command with an exception is equipollent to a non-command with a limitation: a conditional permission into a general prohibition and a particular permission in exception to it: so that a prohibition with an exception is equipollent to a permission with a limitation.[a]

The qualificative matter may be placed all of it on either side.

71. It may also happen that a law, although it be conditional, and thereby provided with limitations, may be provided with exceptions likewise: which, indeed, is most commonly the case. Even when in this form, it may be converted into either of the simple forms above-mentioned: viz: that of an unconditional law with exceptions, or that of a conditional law without any. In short, the qualificative matter may be placed either on both sides, or on one side only: and when on one side only, on either side indifferently. All this, as may easily be imagined from the examples already given, depends upon the turn and phraseology of the sentence. In some cases, one of these forms is the most natural and commodious: in other cases, another. This may be easily enough imagined: farther details and distinctions would take up more room than can be allotted to them here.

An unqualified law to be explicit must be translated into a qualified one.

72. It has been observed already that, in the unconditional form, specimens of affirmative laws are hardly to be found:[b] with laws of a negative aspect, this is not altogether the case. Of laws of this kind a number of specimens, such as they are, might be produced: specimens in which the mandate is apparently not only unconditional, but altogether unqualified: having to appearance at least[c]

Words of limitation and exception various.

[a] As to the words and turns of expression by which a clause may be made to have the effect of a limitative or that of an exceptive clause, they are too numerous and too various to be here enumerated. Among words of limitation are, *where, when, only, if, so that, provided that*: among words of exception are *except, without, unless, except where, except when, but, yet, but not, but not if, if not, nevertheless, however, notwithstanding*; and the like. The way in which they may respectively be made productive of these effects depends upon the turn and fashion of the sentence.

[b] supra 64 n., 68 n.[1]

[c] I say to appearance: for, strictly speaking, even the laws here alluded to, concisely as they are expressed, must be acknowledged to be accompanied with limitations. Take, for instance, this law: 'Let no person committ theft.' The expression is, grammatically speaking, an elliptical one: to render it compleat, instead of *theft*, we must say *act of theft*: 'let no man committ, i: e: perform, an act of

---

[1] See pp. 122 & n., 124 n. above respectively.

neither limitations nor exceptions. Take for examples the cases of murder, theft, embezzlement, extortion, peculation, rape, robbery, adultery, and so on.[a] Offences, however, which are characterizable in this manner bear but a very small proportion to the whole number of the acts which might be, or of those which ought to be, created offences. Moreover, even in these few, while the prohibition continues in this simple and inexplicit form, it can hardly answer the purposes of a law. Expressions of this kind may be compared to those literal symbols which, in order to expedite the business of calculation, are substituted by algebraïsts in the place of a long line of figures. Of themselves they signify nothing; they present no determinate idea any otherwise than through the medium of some other signs which they serve to bring to view. A proposition thus scantily expressed is rather an index to a law than a law itself. To render it explicit enough to be understood by those who are to obey or execute it, it must be taken to pieces, as it were, and made up again according to a fuller pattern: the short name given to the act must be laid aside and a definition substituted in its stead. Now, when a definition is given in such case instead of the term to be defined, another term, the name of some superior genus, is exhibited: and this superior genus, in order to be narrow'd down to the dimensions of the act in question, must be diminished by the application of a certain assemblage of qualifying clauses, applied to it in the shape either of limitations or

theft.' It is not here as in the case of the law against exporting corn, where *corn* was the passible subject of the act signified by the verb *export*.[a] Here, no passible subject is expressed at all: which is one cause of the obscurity of the law. All that is expressed is the agible subject '*person*', and the abstract act or motion, which in the first instance is here no otherwise characterised than by the *genus generalissimum act*: to specificate which and reduce it within the intended compass, the words '*of theft*' are immediately subjoined: No person shall perform any act of that sort which is known by the name of an *act of theft*. In this particular instance, indeed, and a few others, the law may be expressed in a form which is strictly unconditional: 'let no person steal:' so likewise 'let no person murder: let no person rob.' But among the laws here alluded to, there are others with which this is not the case; for instance those against adultery and treason. This depends upon the idiom of the language. In English, we can not say, let no man adulterize: but in Latin, we may say, *non moechaberis*:[1] and in Greek, μη μοιχευσεις.

[a] Among the laws made against these offences there are a few which, in certain cases, the appellation of the act remaining still the same, may apply to positive offences as well as negative. Thus the law against murder will include the law against starving to death, which may be performed without any positive act, as in the case of a mother leaving her infant child to perish.

[a] supra 68.[2]

[1] See Exodus 20: 14 in the Vulgate. [2] See pp. 124–5 above.

exceptions. To take, for example, the law against theft. 'Thou shalt not steal:' or 'Let no man commit theft.' This may be taken for a law against theft exhibited *in terminis*. It is expressed without any sort of qualification:[a] and so, without any impeachment on the score of integrality, it may be: for whatever circumstances relative to it may be brought to view may be considered as included under the word *theft*. But what, after all, is theft? it is an idea the composition of which is so far from being determinate, that to this hour no tolerable definition of the word seems ever to have been given.[b]

[a] I mean, taking the law to be framed, as here, according to the simplest pattern:[*a*] so as to stand in the shape of a mere directive law, without any punitory law to give it force. It, therefore, needs no inculpative nor exculpative clauses: but apply a punitive law to it, together with a comminative clause, and then, as to exemptive clauses, it will stand upon the same footing as every other law.

[b] I do not mean to say but that the idea entertained of this offence by the generality of the people is in most cases clear enough for use: but for this idea, whatever it may be, they are indebted to their own observation, not to any explanation that has been ever given them of it by men of law.

Furtum is defined by Justinian (Inst. de obl. quæ ex delict) *contrectatio fraudulosa* &c.[1] But what is meant by '*fraudulosa*'? this is shifting off the difficulty, not explaining it: he might as well have said *furtiva*.

English Lawyers, to make the matter clearer, add to the word *fraudulent* the word *felonious*:[*b*] but this again is only a roundabout way of saying *furtive*: Theft is the taking of a thing in circumstances in which the taking of it is punished by a certain punishment, which is the punishment inflicted on the act of taking when accompanied with circumstances which make it theft. L[d] Hale is honest enough to confess he does not know what those circumstances are.[*c*] This, however, was

[*a*] v. infra 123.[2]

[*b*] I. Hawk. 89.[3] Burn, Larceny.[4]

[*c*] I. H. H. 509.[5]

---

[1] *The Institutes of Justinian*, ed. J. A. C. Thomas, Cape Town, 1975, IV. i. 1: *Furtum est contrectatio rei fraudulosa vel ipsius rei vel etiam usus eius possessionisve quod lege naturali prohibitum est admittere*, i.e. 'Now theft is the fraudulent meddling with a thing, whether the thing itself, the use or possession of it which one is barred from countenancing by natural law.'

[2] See p. 168 below.

[3] See William Hawkins, *A Treatise of the Pleas of the Crown: or, A System of the Principal Matters relating to that Subject, digested under their Proper Heads*, 3rd edn., 2 vols., London, 1739, Bk. I, Ch. XXXIII, § 1, i. 89: 'Simple Grand Larceny is a felonious and fraudulent taking and carrying away, by any Person, of the mere Personal Goods of another, not from the Person, nor out of his House, above the Value of twelve Pence.'

[4] See Richard Burn, *The Justice of the Peace and Parish Officer*, 7th edn., London, 1762, ii. 345–63, at 345, which repeats the definition given by Hawkins.

[5] Matthew Hale (1609–76), Chief Baron of the Exchequer 1660–71, Chief Justice of King's Bench 1671–6, in *Historia Placitorum Coronæ. The History of the Pleas of the Crown*, 2 vols., London, 1736, i. 509, writes: 'But in cases of larciny the variety of circumstances is so great, and the complications thereof so mingled, that it is impossible to prescribe all the circumstances evidencing a felonious intent, or the contrary, but the same must be left to the due and attentive consideration of the judge and jury, wherein the best rule is *in dubiis* rather to incline to acquittal than conviction.'

It is the taking (that is the beginning to occupy) a thing under certain circumstances. To make the law against theft intelligible enough to exhibit an idea of the offence, it must accordingly be translated into a law that forbids the taking under certain circumstances; which circumstances, when specified, will constitute so many limitations or exceptions to the general prohibition against taking.[a]

73. We are now in a condition to apprehend the use and effect of non-commanding and originally-permissive provisions. Of themselves, it is manifest, they can have none. A law of either kind, if that were all of it, would be nugatory and inoperative:[b] since, after the establishment of such a law, the condition of the subject would be not a whit altered from what it was before. 'Any man may export corn out of Attica.'—To what purpose would such a law have been to the Athenians? So might any man have done as soon as Triptolemus had taught them the arts of husbandry,[1] and before ever they had learnt from Theseus to bear the bonds of government.[2] It might, indeed, have happened that Theseus or some of the intervening powers had previously to this allowance consider'd the traffic in question an object of prohibition: but then the law would have been not an unobligative, but a de-obligative one. The only use of a provision of either of the unobligative kinds is to introduce some provision of a more active and efficient nature: the former serving as a basis to which the latter, in the shape of a limitation or an exception, may adhere. When regarded in this point of view, every efficient law whatever may be consider'd as a limitation or exception, grafted on a pre-established universal law of liberty: and thus a kind of medium of connection may be established in the mind, whereby the idea of every law that can be conceived may be confronted with, and rendered, as it were, commensurable to, that of every other. Under the single term *acts* are included all the possible modifications of human conduct: add

Use of non-commanding and originally-permissive provisions.

no hindrance to his hanging men for theft. It is one thing to conceive an idea, it is another thing to express it: it is one thing to form a particular idea on a particular occasion, it is another thing to abstract from it a general idea for all occasions.

[a] See B. I. Tit. {Theft}.[3]

[b] Provisions of either kind might accordingly be termed provisions *inefficient per se*: in contradiction to which, provisions expressive of any of the other aspects may be termed *efficient per se*.

[1] Triptolemus was one of the legendary princes of Eleusis to whom the goddess Demeter gave corn and the arts of agriculture.

[2] Theseus, a legendary king of Athens, was credited with combining a number of small towns to create the unitary political state ruled by Athens.

[3] A cross-reference to Bentham's projected penal code.

the several possible aspects or phases of the will, and you have the whole possible assemblage of laws as well as of autocratic ordinances. The will of the legislator, like that of any other person, may be consider'd as a uniform, unvaried surface: susceptible indeed of as many different colours as it may have aspects: but in other respects deriving its distinctive character no otherwise than from the various images, which are reflected upon it, as it were, from the several modes of conduct towards which it turns itself. The non-commanding and permissive phases of the law placed side by side and turned towards the universal system of human actions are expressed by the before-mentioned universal law of liberty: a boundless expanse in which the several efficient laws appear as so many spots; like islands and continents projecting out of the ocean: or like material bodies scatter'd over the immensity of space.

Limitations and exceptions to preceding limitations and exceptions.

74. As any kind of provision which happens to take the lead, whether it be obligative, unobligative or de-obligative, may have its limitations and exceptions, so again may any of those limitations and exceptions have *their* limitations and exceptions; and so on through any number of alternations. In such case, every such limitative or exceptive provision, having the effect of narrowing the dominion as it were of that which stands next above it, widens in the same proportion that of the next but one: a qualification to a limitation widens the provision first limited: a qualification to an exception widens the provision first excepted from, just as in arithmetic, substraction from a subtrahend is an addition to the minuend. Let the following chain of provisions serve for an example. 1. Leading[a] provision in the form of a general permission: 'Any man may export corn out of the country.' [2.] Exceptive clause having the effect of a particular prohibition: '*Unless* the market price be above 44^{s} a quarter.' 3. Exceptive clause of the 2^{d} order, having the effect of a re-permission: 'and even then, if it be for the subsistence of the King's armies.' 4. Clause limitative of the last mentioned exceptive clause, and thereby re-extensive of the first prohibition—'and provided a license from the first magistrate of the place have been previously obtained.'

Here the chain of provisions has four links in it. Convert the law into the conditional form and it has but three. 1. Leading provision in the form of a conditional prohibition—'No man shall export wheat out of the country where the market price is above 44^{s} a

[a] v. infra 81.[1]

[1] See pp. 134–5 below.

quarter.' Exceptive clause having the effect of a particular permission—'Unless it be for the subsistence of the King's armies.' Limitation to the above exception—'*and* a license from the first magistrate of the place have been previously obtained.'

The same limitation converted into an exception to the same exceptive clause: 'nor then, [unless][1] a license from the first magistrate of the place have been previously obtained.'

75. When an act is taken for the object of a legislator's will, and that will is declared, the opposite act (in the case where such declaration is meant to be enforced by motives of the coercive kind) is thereby render'd an offence: if the object of such will be an act of the positive stamp, then it is the opposite negative act that is converted into an offence: if that object were an act of the negative stamp, then the offence so created is the opposite positive act. In other words, where the provision of the law is a command or a prohibition, it creates an offence: if a command, it is the non-performance of the act that is the offence: if a prohibition, the performance. The effect, then, which a limitative clause has upon such a provision is to take all other particular cases but the one marked out by the limitation out of that general one in which the performance of the act is an offence: as the effect of an exceptive clause is to take out of the general case the particular case itself to which the exception is applied. In either way, then, a circumstance is introduced which has the effect of taking the act, in some particular case or other, out of the general case in which the non-performance or the performance of it is an offence. Such circumstance may therefore be termed an *exculpative* or *justificative* circumstance: a circumstance *of exculpation* or *justification*: and the clause or provision which invests it with that character, an *exculpative* or *justificative provision* or *clause*.[a] Moreover, the law, in constituting any act an offence, is said to impose thereby an *obligation* on the persons in question not to perform it: which obligation, upon the act's ceasing to be an offence, is taken away. The same circumstance may, therefore, be termed also upon occasion a *de-obligative circumstance*, and the clause a *de-obligative*

An offence what—Circumstances and clauses justificative, exculpative or de-obligative.

[a] It might also be termed *exemptive*. But this word we shall have occasion for by and by,[2] for the purpose of expressing an idea which is different from that which it is here intended to bring to view by the word *exculpative*; and to which this latter word would not be applicable: I mean the idea of a circumstance which takes an act out of the case in which it is thought proper to punish it, without taking it out of the case in which it is wished it were not done.

The word 'exemptive' why not used.

[1] MS 'without'.

[2] See §13, paras. 107–13, pp. 156–60 below.

clause: that is provided the exception in taking the act out of the case in which it is commanded or prohibited stops there, and does not go on to place it in the case in which it is forbidden, and so *vice versâ* in the case of a prohibition: in short, provided the exception be simply contradictory and not contrariant[a] to the clause to which it is applied: in this latter case the succeeding provision might, with reference to the preceding one, be termed *reversely-obligative*.

Circumstances and clauses &c. inculpative or criminative.

76. So on the other hand, when the leading provision of the law is a non-command or a permission (which is the case where the command or prohibition is conditional), there is no offence created by it: the effect, then, which a limitative clause has upon such a provision is to take all other particular cases but the one marked out by the limitation out of that general one in which neither the non-performance nor the performance of the act is an offence: as the effect of an exceptive clause is to take out of the general case the particular case itself to which the exception is applied. In either way, then, a circumstance is introduced which has the effect of taking the act in some particular case or other out of the general case in which the non-performance or the performance of the act is *not* an offence. Such circumstance may, therefore, be termed an *inculpative*, and in some cases a *criminative* or *criminalizing*, circumstance:[b] and the clause which mentions it, an inculpative, criminative, or criminalizing clause.[c]

[a] supra 59. infra 112.[1]

The word *criminative* not applicable to all cases.

[b] Of these three words, the words *criminative* or *criminalizing* would in all cases be the clearest were it not for the appearance they have of excluding all offences of inferior magnitude. This forms such an objection to the applying it to those offences as seems to be insurmountable. See infra §. 5.[2]

Objection to the term *inculpative* cured.

The objection to the word *inculpative* is that, owing to the uncertain and ambiguous signification of the particle *in* in the language from which it is taken, it may appear doubtful whether the idea meant to be annexed to it is that which it is here put to signify, or the opposite idea which is here denoted by the term *exculpative*. But this objection vanishes as soon as it is perceived that the former word is put in opposition to the latter. It must be confessed, indeed, that the sense here attributed to the word does not seem to be warranted by any Latin writer: it is made use of, however, in this sense by the French law. See Dict. de Trevoux verbo *Inculpation*.[3]

The word *Delinquefying* or *Delinquefactive* proposed.

The term that would point in the clearest manner to the idea in question would be some such word as *delinquefying* or *delinquefactive,* if a term so novel and uncouth could be endured.

[c] It may be worth while just to mention, that the absence of an exculpative

[1] See pp. 119–20 above, 159 below respectively.

[2] i.e. §19, pp. 201–6 below. This cross-reference was inserted at an early stage in the composition of the work, when the discussion of civil and criminal law formed the fifth section: for further details see the Editorial Introduction, p. xxviii above.

[3] *Dictionnaire Universel François et Latin, vulgairement appellé Dictionnaire de Trévoux,*

77. According, then, as the mandate of the law is unconditional or conditional, the circumstances which make their appearance first are of the exculpative kind, or of the inculpative: if it be unconditional, of the exculpative kind; there being no room in the first instance for any that are inculpative: if conditional, of the inculpative kind: for the offence must first of all be created, before any limitations or exceptions can be applied to it: a *genus* of acts must first be expressed, before any species can be excluded or taken out of it.

In what cases exculpative circumstances come first; in what, inculpative.

78. Now the case is, as hath already been observed,[a] that by far the greater part of the mandates that occur in a body of laws will be in the conditional form. In general, then, the circumstances that stand first in order in the texture of a law will be of the inculpative kind: there will come a certain number of circumstances of this nature before there come any that are exculpative.

Inculpative circumstances to be found in most laws.

79. Exculpative circumstances, then, are limitations or exceptions to an obligatory or inculpative clause: inculpative circumstances, to a de-obligatory or exculpative one. If in an unconditional law, after the first set of exculpative circumstances, there come any that are inculpative, they are so many limitations or exceptions to preceding limitations and exceptions: so likewise, if in a conditional law, any that are exculpative come after the first set of inculpative ones. In this way, then, it is plain that sets of exculpative and sets of inculpative clauses may, like any other limitations and exceptions, follow each other alternately without end.[b] To distinguish, then, a clause of any such sort from another clause of the same denomination, they might be number'd according to the order in which they make their appearance. Upon this

Exculpative and inculpative circumstances of the 1st, 2d, &c. orders.

circumstance is equipollent to the presence of one that is inculpative: and *vice versâ*. This proceeds from the interconvertibility of limitations and exceptions. v. supra 70.[1]

[a] supra 71.[2]

[b] By way of illustration, the cases constituted by the above circumstances might, in conformity to the archetypation above suggested,[a] be represented under the similitude of a nest of boxes of opposite colours inclosed one within another: where the law is unconditional, first a black box; within that a white box; then a black one again; and so on: where it is conditional, first a white box; within that a black one; and then a white one again; and so on.

[a] supra 74.[3]

7 vols., Paris 1752, vol. iv: 'Inculpation . . . Terme de Palais, qui s'emploie lorsqu'on attribue quelque faute à quelqu'un, qu'on l'accuse d'avoir fait quelque action reprehensible'.

[1] See p. 126 above.

[2] Bentham probably had in mind para. 72, rather than para. 71: see p. 126 above.

[3] MS '74 n.' appears to be a slip, as para. 74 has no note. See pp. 130–1 above.

plan they will stand thus: Where the mandate is unconditional; 1. exculpative circumstances of the first order: 2. inculpative circumstances of the first order: 3. exculpative circumstances of the 2[d] order: 4. inculpative circumstances of the 2[d] order: and so on: Where the mandate is conditional; 1. inculpative circumstances of the 1st order: 2. exculpative circumstances of the 1st order: 3. inculpative circumstances of the 2[d] order: 4. exculpative circumstances of the 2[d] order: and so on.[a]

In unconditional mandates, inculpative circumstances may be termed re-inculpative.

80. Where the mandate is unconditional, the offence is created without the help of any inculpative circumstances: the effect, then, of the first set of inculpative circumstances that occur is not to place the act for the first time in the case in which it is an offence, but to bring it back into that case after it has been taken out of it by circumstances of the exculpative kind. In this case, then, the inculpative circumstances may all of them, even those of the 1st order, be termed *re-inculpative*. This will serve to shew all along that the mandate is unconditional, and thereby distinguish the case from that in which the mandate is of the opposite complexion.

Principal or leading provision, what.

81. A legislative provision either contains a law of itself, or only goes towards the making up of a law by the help of others. Now, of every groupe of legislative provisions making all together a law, one at least must be so expressed as to present the name of the act which is the object of the will, in conjunction with words expressive of the aspect of the will towards that act: a provision so expressed may be termed the *principal* provision. If there are several so expressed, then the appellation of principal provision may be given to that in which the name of the act is of the greatest

Pleadings in a cause explained.

[a] In the mutual allegation of circumstances thus militating one against another (that is of the existence of such or such a circumstance in the case in which the individual act in question was performed) consists what are called the *pleadings* in a cause: the *actionis intentio, exceptio, replicatio, duplicatio,* &c. of the ancient Roman Law: the *declaration, plea, replication, rejoinder*, &c. of the English Law. This is to be understood of the cases in which the plaintiff alledges a wrong to have been already done to him. In the cases where there is no complaint of that sort, the cause being of a purely civil nature, there it is plain the words *inculpative* and *exculpative* do not apply. Thus it is where the plaintiff does no more than claim to be invested with a right as yet not created or not liquidated: or what comes to the same thing, demands that others shall be subjected to the obligation of doing or forbearing to do something or other for his benefit. In this case, the terms *inculpative* and *exculpative* must be changed for some such words as *investitive* and *divestitive*. See Ch. 19. {Corpus Juris}.[1]

---

[1] For the projected Chapter entitled 'Corpus Juris' see the Editorial Introduction, p. xii above.

amplitude:[a] and of which what other provisions there are in the law are but so many qualificative or expository clauses. This is to be understood of the case where the provision of the greatest amplitude is of the obligative or efficient kind:[b] where it is not, there the amplest of those that are obligative may be consider'd as the principal provision. These rules may easily be illustrated by turning to the examples already given.[c] In this latter case, it is not the principal provision that stands first, but an un-obligative one, which, were it not for the use it may be of in serving as an introduction to some obligative provision, would be inefficient, and, in the way of original imperation at least, whatever purpose it might answer in the way of instruction or information, nugatory. But in other cases, the principal provision will commonly stand first, and may on that account be also stiled the *leading* one.

82. We set out with supposing the superventitious provision to regard all along such a class of acts as is included within the same bounds which limit the primordial. But it may happen, that the primordial aspect may regard one act, and the superventitious another not comprehended by the primordial: and yet, either on account of the identity of the two aspects themselves, or on account of some circumstance which enters in common into the description of the acts which are respectively the objects of them, the provision expressive of the latter will may be consider'd as connecting with, and exercising a sort of influence over, the provision expressive of the former will. As to the acts, there are three descriptive circumstances any two of which they may have in common without belonging to the same genus, viz: the agible subject,[d] the passible subject,[d] and the bare act which is the object.[e] Hence it happens that when, upon the back of a provision which has already been expressed, there comes another relating to a distinct act in the description of which some of the circumstances are made use of that served to give the description of the former act, the two acts may be consider'd as being both of them comprised under the first provision: which, however, as of itself it

Provision extensive.

[a] v. supra 49 n.[1]
[b] supra 73.[2]
[c] supra 74.[3]
[d] v. supra 37.[4]
[e] v. supra 38.[5]

[1] The corresponding paragraph in the 'principal draft' has not been located, but it would have formed the first paragraph in §9, pp. 94–5 above.
[2] See pp. 129–30 above.
[3] See pp. 130–1 above.
[4] See p. 58 above.
[5] The relevant part of the 'principal draft' has not been located: see pp. 58–9 n. above.

comprized only the first of them, is not consider'd as having been alter'd and *extended* for the purpose, by the operation of the second provision. This second provision may in such case be spoken of as *extensive* with reference to the former.[a] To recur to the old example. Let the primordial provision be—'No merchant shall export barley.' A provision extensive of this might stand thus:—'The same provision which was made concerning the non-exportation of barley by merchants shall extend to the growers.' In like manner, importation might be added to exportation: or wheat to barley.

It is evident that the extension in all these cases might more clearly as well as more concisely be expressed by a distinct superventitious provision unconnected with the primordial. As thus: 'No merchant shall export barley:'—'no grower of barley shall export barley:'—'no merchant shall import barley:'—'no merchant shall export wheat.' A circumstance, however, that may render it convenient sometimes to make use of an extensive provision, rather than of an independent law, is that by this means the qualifying provisions and subsidiary laws belonging to one law may be taken up as they stand and applied all together to another law: and thus a considerable saving may be made in point of words.

It is evident that an extensive provision may apply to one provision of a law as well as to another: to any qualificative clause as well as to the principal: if it applies to a qualificative clause of the first order, it joins with it in narrowing the amplitude of the principal; if to one of the second order, in extending it: and so on through any number of alternations.[b]

Provisions indirectly or virtually extensive.

83. There is also another way in which a provision becomes entitled to the appellation of an extensive one. This is the case wherever there is a qualification of the second order narrowing one of the first: that which narrow'd the principal provision being itself narrow'd, the principal provision is thereby of course extended. In this way, all qualificative clauses after those of the first order are extensive: extensive according to the order they are of, either of the principal provision, or else of the qualification of the first order by which the principal provision is narrow'd: in which latter case they are restrictive of the principal provision. But in this way, the extension that is applied to the principal provision is not applied in a direct way, nor by any such formulary as carries

[a] v. infra 130.[1]
[b] v. supra 74.[2]

---

[1] See pp. 174–6 below.
[2] See pp. 130–1 above.

the idea of extension upon the face of it. They may, therefore, for distinction's sake be termed *indirectly* or *virtually* extensive.

84. Provisions, consider'd with respect to the relative times of their enactment, may have been issued *uno flatu* or *diverso*. This distinction it may on various occasions be of use to bear in mind. Two or more provisions may be said to be issued *uno flatu* when they are authenticated[a] at one and the same time: *diverso flatu*, when at different times. Upon this distinction turns the difference between the object to which it is all along proposed to appropriate the term *law*, and that which is commonly known by some such names as *edict, ordinance*, or *statute*. A legislative provision, as we have seen,[b] is by possibility the whole, but generally a constituent part only, of a law: a statute is either one or any other number of provisions which, with respect to one another, are issued *flatu uno*, with respect to all other provisions, *diverso*.

Provisions may be issued *uno* or *diverso flatu*—difference between a provision, a law and a statute.

We have frequently had occasion to bring to view the distinction between the primordial aspect of the will and the superventitious. Where, of two provisions that stand in connection with one another, the aspect expressed by the one is superventitious with respect to that of which the other is expressive, this does not necessarily imply that they were issued *diverso flatu*; that they are provisions of different statutes. They must, indeed, if they are repugnant *in toto*, and are both allow'd to have a meaning: otherwise the legislator must be supposed to have been willing contradictions: willing that the same act shall be performed and not performed at the same time. But if repugnant *ex parte* or *pro tanto* only, that is if they be qualificative one of another, in short if they be any thing but repugnant *in toto*, no such consequence follows: a repugnancy thus limited may as naturally take place within the limits of one single statute as within the compass of ever so many different statutes. Indeed, without going into such a repugnancy as this, there are in general no means of making the dimensions given to the act upon paper quadrate with those under which it presents itself to the will. There are few cases, as hath been observed, in which there are any single phrases by which the act (I mean always the class of acts) can be expressed exactly of its

[a] Any ceremonies employ'd as signs for the purpose of making known to the people that such or such a discourse is expressive of the will of the legislator may be stiled *ceremonies of authentication*: and a legislative provision upon the fulfillment of such ceremonies may be said to be *authenticated*.

[b] supra 72.[1]

[1] Bentham discusses the distinction between a law and a legislative provision at para. 53 n., p. 116 n. above.

proper shape and size: in all other cases, the only expedient is to begin with a class that is too large, and so reduce it to the requisite degree of amplitude, by a number of different provisions which, though in the order of conception they may perhaps have been contemporary and thereby all of [them] equally primordial, must in the order of enuntiation be successive, and thereby one after another superventitious.

Provisions expositive and qualificative, how reducible to independent provisions.

85. As to qualificative provisions, and such expositive ones as apply only to single words, from the account that has been given of them,[a] it will appear that so long as they possess the precise form from which they take their name, they can not by themselves convey any intimation of the legislator's will. Yet some share in the expression of that will it is evident they must have. To estimate the amount of this share, it must be extracted from the rest, and deliver'd in separate propositions. Now, a superventitious provision, we may remember, if not re-iterative of the primordial, must be alterative. Being re-iterative, if it is not re-iterative *in toto*, it is re-iterative *pro tanto*: being alterative, if it is not revocative *in toto*, it must be revocative in part. Accordingly, a provision of the expositive kind may be render'd into an independent provision, re-iterative as far as it goes with respect to the primordial one of which it is expositive: this is but the converse of what has been shewn already.[b] So on the other hand, a provision which is qualificative may be render'd into an independent provision, revocative, that is destructive as far as it goes, of the primordial one which it qualifies. This with respect to an exceptive provision is seen immediately: and it is equally true of a limitative provision; since there is no limitation, as we have seen,[c] but may be render'd into an exception.[d]

[a] supra 57.[1]
[b] supra 57.[2]
[c] supra 70.[3]
[d] Accordingly, what has been said of qualificative provisions lying one within another in alternation,[a] may be said of provisions of the same purport when thrown into the independent form. Independent provisions of one and the same aspect respecting acts standing in logical subalternation under one and the same *genus generalissimum* are boxes of the same colour inclosed one within another: independent provisions of different aspects respecting acts that are in like manner subalternate to one another are boxes of opposite colours enclosed one within another in the same manner: the general law of liberty, which for its

[a] supra 74; 79 n.[4]

[1] See pp. 118–19 above.
[2] See ibid.
[3] See pp. 125–6 above.
[4] See pp. 130–1, 133 n. above respectively.

'No man shall export wheat when the market-price &c. is more than 44[s] a quarter—*except* it be for the use of the King's armies:'— Here the leading provision (which is a conditional one) is obligative: the exception, therefore, being revocative *pro tanto* of the principal provision, is not obligative: 'Any person may export corn for the use of the King's armies.'

It may be observed that, in passing from the dependent to the independent form, the provision is changed from a de-obligative one into one that is simply un-obligative, by which means the reference it bears to the principal provision which it was employ'd to qualify is no longer apparent upon the face of it. In this case it would appear an absurdity, were two provisions that were thus related to be placed close together in the same statute, without the insertion of some adversative particle or other (such as *but, nevertheless, provided always*, and the like) for the purpose of giving notice of such relation: it would look as if the legislator himself could not see what he was doing.

86. Thus much concerning the several aspects of which the will of a legislator is susceptible, and the several sorts of provisions in which they may display themselves, when expressed in words. In order to present a summary view of their mutual relations and dependencies, their several agreements and diversities, the following analytic sketches, framed according to the exhaustive method, may be not without their use. Recapitulation.

First, then, with regard to the aspects of which any single provision may be expressive, no regard being had to the connection it may have with any other provision.

The will of any man (and, therefore, of a legislator), with relation to any act is susceptible of four aspects: of which four there are in two cases two, in the two remaining cases either one or two, as it may happen, and in no case more than two, that are presented to the act at the same time, the aspects going together most commonly in pairs. 1. The act may be commanded: it is, then, left unprohibited: and it is not prohibited, nor left uncommanded. 2. It may be prohibited: it is, then, left uncommanded: and it is not commanded, nor permitted (that is left unprohibited). 3. It may be left uncommanded: it is, then, not commanded: but it may be either prohibited or permitted: yet so as that, if it be in the one case, it is

object has the *genus generalissimum* indicated by the word *act* without addition, being, as it were, the outside box which encloses all the rest.[a]

[a] supra 79 n.[1]

[1] See p. 133 n. above.

not in the other. 4. It may be permitted: it, then, is not prohibited: but it may be either commanded or left uncommanded: yet so as that, if it be in the one case, it is not in the other.

A command, then, includes a permission: it excludes both a prohibition and a non-command.—A prohibition includes a non-command: and excludes both a command and a permission.—A non-command of itself does not necessarily include either a prohibition or a permission: but it excludes a command: and as a prohibition and permission exclude one another, it can only be accompanied with one of them at a time.—A permission of itself does not necessarily include either a command or a non-command: but as a command and a non-command exclude one another, it can only be accompanied with one of them at a time.

Secondly, to consider a provision with regard to the dependence it may have on other provisions.

A provision is either significant (as such) of itself, or not but by reference to others. A legislative provision that is significant of itself stands either insulated or in connection with others: if insulated, it makes a whole law: if in connection with others, it makes a part only of a law.

Provisions that are significant of themselves are either unobligative or obligative, otherwise termed imperative. Provisions that are significant only by reference to others are provisions extensive, expositive, de-obligative, limitative and exceptive.

Thirdly, to consider a provision with relation to the differences of aspect and the connection it may have with other provisions, both at once.

A legislative provision, then, is either *primordial* or superventitious.

A primordial provision is either obligative or unobligative.

A primordial provision, when obligative, is either an original command or an original prohibition.

A primordial provision, when unobligative, is either a non-command or an original permission.

A superventitious provision is either un-alterative of the primordial one, or alterative.

If unalterative, it is either re-iterative of it (viz: *in toto*) or expositive (viz: re-iterative *pro tanto*).

If alterative, it is either unextensive of it or extensive.

If unextensive, it is either destructive (viz: *in toto*); or qualificative (i: e: destructive *pro tanto*).

If destructive, it is either revocative or reversive.

If revocative, it is in itself either de-obligative or obligative.

If de-obligative, it is a countermand or a re-permission.

If obligative, it is either a command, as before; or a prohibition, as before.

If reversive, it is either a prohibition or a command: a prohibition instead of a command: or a command instead of a prohibition.

If qualificative, it is either limitative or exceptive.

Fourthly, to consider it with relation to the effects which a law, as far as it is conformed to, may have upon a man's *liberty*: that is the liberty of the person whose conduct is the object of it.[a]

The effects which a law has upon a man's liberty are either to coerce him, or to leave him free; if coerced, he is laid either under compulsion or under restraint: under compulsion, by command; under restraint, by prohibition: if left free, he remains neither under compulsion, nor under restraint.

[a] supra 38.[1]

[1] Only part of the relevant paragraph of the 'principal draft' has been located: see pp. 58–9 n. above.

§13. *Force of a law.*

Motives a law relies on, alluring or co-ercive—reward or punishment.

87. [Tenthly],[1] with respect to the *force* of the law: that is, with respect to the motives it relies upon for enabling it to produce the effects it aims at. Motives of some sort or other to trust to, it evidently must have: for without a cause, no such thing as an effect: without a motive, no such thing as action. What, then, are motives? we have seen that they are but the expectations of so many lots of pain and pleasure, as connected in a particular manner in the way of causality[a] with the actions with reference to which they are termed *motives*.[b] When it is in the shape of pleasure they apply, they may be termed *alluring* motives: when in the shape of pain, *coercive*.[c] It is when those of the alluring kind are held up as being connected with an act, that a *reward* is said to be offer'd: it is when those of the coercive kind are thus held up, that a *punishment* is said to be denounced.

Sources from whence they may issue—the moral, religious, or political sanctions.

88. The next question is from what source these motives may issue. Now, it has already been observed,[2] that of the four sources from whence pain and pleasure may be said to take their rise, there are three which are under the influence of intelligent and voluntary agents; viz: the political, the moral and the religious sanctions. The legislator, then, may, in the view of giving efficacy to his laws, take either of two courses: he may trust altogether to the auxiliary force of the two foreign sanctions, or he may have recourse to motives drawn from that fund which is of his own creation. The former of these courses is what has sometimes been taken with success:[d] there seem even to be cases in which it is to be preferred to any other. These cases, however, are in comparison but rare. For the most part it is to some pleasure or some pain drawn from the political sanction itself, but more particularly, as we shall see presently,[3] to pain, that the legislator trusts for the effectuation of his will.

[a] Ch. 7. {Actions}.[4]
[b] Ch. 10. {Motives}.[5]
[c] Ch. 16. {Division}.[6]
[d] See Ch. 18. {Indirect Legislation}.[7]

---

[1] MS 'Sixthly'.

[2] See pp. 91–2 above.

[3] Bentham has indicated his wish to insert a cross-reference here, but has failed to do so.

[4] See *An Introduction to the Principles of Morals and Legislation* (*CW*), Ch. VII, pp. 74–83.

[5] See ibid., Ch. X, pp. 96–124.

[6] See ibid., Ch. XVI, pp. 187–280, where the distinction between coercive and alluring motives is mentioned at para. 27, p. 220.

[7] For the projected Chapter entitled 'Indirect Legislation' see the Editorial Introduction, p. xii above.

89. This punishment, then, or this reward, whichever it be, in order to produce it's effect, must in some manner or other be announced: notice of it must in some way or other be given, in order to produce an expectation of it, on the part of the people whose conduct it is meant to influence. This notice may either be given by the legislator himself in the text of the law itself, or it may be left to be given, in the way of customary law, by the judge: the legislator, commanding you, for example, to do an act: the judge, in his own way and according to his own measure, punishing you in case of your not doing it, or, what is much less frequent, rewarding you in case of your doing it. As to the particular nature of customary law, more will be said of it by and by.[a]

When from the political, they may be announced by written or by customary law.

90. But the most eligible and, indeed, the most common method of giving notice is by inserting a clause on purpose: by subjoining to that part of the law which is expressive of the legislator's will, another part the office of which is to indicate the motive he furnishes you with for complying with such will. In this case, the law may plainly enough be distinguished into two parts: the one serving to make known to you what the inclination of the legislator is: the other serving to make known to you what motive the legislator has furnished you with for complying with that inclination: the one addressed more particularly to your understanding; the other, to your will. The former of these parts may be termed the *directive*: the other, the *sanctional* or *incitative*.

When by written law, it consists of two parts: 1. the directive, 2. the incitative or sanctional.

91. As to the incitative, this, it is evident, may be of two kinds: when the motive furnished is of the nature of punishment, it may be termed the *comminative* part, or *commination*: when it is of the nature of reward, the *invitative* part or *invitation*.

The incitative may be [1. comminatory; or 2. invitative].[1]

92. Of the above two methods of influencing the will, that in which punishment is employ'd is that with which we are chiefly concerned at present. It is that, indeed, of which we hear the most and of which the greatest use is made. So great, indeed, is the use that is made of it, and so little in comparison is that which is made of reward, that the only names which are in current use for expressing the different aspects of which a will is susceptible are such as suppose punishment to be the motive. Command, prohibition, and permission, all of them point at punishment: hence the impropriety we were obliged to set out with, for want of words to remedy it.[b]

It is more frequently the former than the latter.

[a] infra | |.[2]
[b] supra | |.[3]

[1] MS '1. invitative; or 2. comminatory'.
[2] See §17, pp. 185–97 below.
[3] See §12, para. 53 n., pp. 115–16 n. above.

Why—punishment the only force that can be depended on.

93. The case is that for ordinary use punishment is beyond comparison the most efficacious upon the whole. By punishment alone it seems not impossible but that the whole business of government might be carried on: though certainly not so well carried on as by a mixture of that and reward together. But by reward alone it is most certain that no material part of that business could ever be carried on for half an hour.[a]

Why government can not be carried on by reward alone.

[a] The reasons why the principal part of the business of government can not be carried on any otherwise than by punishment are various: among which there are several which would each of them be abundantly sufficient of itself.

1. In the first place, any man can at any time be much surer of administering pain than pleasure.

2. The law (that is the set of persons employ'd for this purpose by the legislator) has it still less in it's power to make sure of administering pleasure than particular persons have: since the power of administering pleasure depends upon the particular and ever-changing circumstances of the individual to whom it is to be applied: of which circumstances the law is not in any way of being apprised.[a] In short, the law seems to have no means of administering pleasure to any man by it's own immediate operation: all it can do is to put the instrument in his way, and leave him at liberty to apply it himself for that purpose if he thinks proper: this is accordingly what the law does when it is said to give a man a pecuniary reward.

3. The scale of pleasure, supposing it actually applied, is very short and limited: the scale of pain is in comparison unlimited.

4. The sources of pleasure are few and soon exhausted: the sources of pain are innumerable and inexhaustible. It has already been observed that the only means the law has of administering pleasure to a man is by placing the instruments of it within his reach. But the number and value of these instruments is extremely limited. Any object in nature may be converted into an instrument of pain: few in comparison and rare are those which are calculated to serve as instruments of pleasure.

5. The law has no means of producing pleasure without producing pain at the same time: which pleasure and which pain being consider'd by themselves apart from their effects, the pain is more than equivalent to the pleasure. For, an instrument of pleasure, before it can be given to one man, must have been taken from another: and since *cæteris paribus* it is more painful to lose a given sum than it is pleasurable to gain it, the pain produced by the *taking* is upon an average always more than equivalent to the pleasure produced by the *giving*.

6. The insufficiency of rewards is more particularly conspicuous when applied to acts of the negative kind. The acts of a positive kind of which it is necessary to enjoin the performance are always made referable to some definite passible subject, and included within a definite portion of time: such as to pay money on a certain occasion to a certain person: to lend a hand to the repair of a certain road for such a number of days; and so forth. But acts of a negative kind are commonly comprised under no such limitations. Take, for instance, the not stealing, and the not doing damage to the roads. Now, by not stealing is meant the not stealing

[a] See Ch. | |. {Sensibility}.[1]

[1] See *An Introduction to the Principles of Morals and Legislation* (*CW*), Ch. VI, pp. 51–73.

94. The sense of mankind on this head is so strong and general, however confused and ill developed, that where the motives presented to the inclination of him whose conduct it is proposed to influence are of no other than the alluring kind, it might appear doubtful perhaps whether the expression of the will of which such conduct is the object could properly be stiled a law. The motives which the law trusts to being in most cases of a coercive nature: hence the idea of coercion shall in their minds have become inseparably connected with that of a law. Being then an invitation, that is an expression of will trusting for its efficacy to the motives not co-ercive, they will conclude that it can not with propriety be stiled a law.[a]

Hence the idea of punishment is difficultly separable from that of law.

from any person any stealable articles, at any time: but persons are numerous, stealable articles still more so, and time indefinitely divisible. If, then, Paul, for example, were to be rewarded for not stealing, it must be in some such way as this: for not stealing from Peter a farthing at 12 o'clock, one shilling: for not stealing another farthing from the same Peter at the same time, another shilling: for not stealing another farthing from the same Peter at a moment after 12, another shilling: for not stealing from John a farthing at such a place at 12 o'clock, another shilling: the same sums to be given also to Peter and John for not stealing from Paul: and so on for everlasting.[a] [1]

[a] In the nomenclature as well as in the practise of the law, it is upon punishment that every thing turns: nothing, upon reward. Try, for instance, the words *obligation, duty, right, power, title, possession,* and *conveyance*. Take away the idea of punishment, and you deprive them of all meaning. A set of fictitious entities analogous to these might indeed be conceived to be generated by reward. But they would evidently be of a very flimsy consistence in comparison of the objects men have hitherto been accustomed to call to mind upon the mention of those names. The obligation would be a cobweb; the duty, a feather; the right, power, title, possession, conveyance, not worth a straw.

The phraseology of law refers uniformly to punishment, not to reward.

[a] v. supra [63] n.[2]

[1] The remainder of the note has been crossed through by Bentham: 'With regard to the plain fact that the general business of government can not be carried on but by punishment, lawyers, as it happens, are pretty well agreed: indeed the disputing it is what no man could attempt for a single moment without running into the most palpable absurdities. But the reasons seem not as yet that I can find to have ever been settled upon any conspicuous and solid footing.'

The final sentence above is an MS alt. for the following passage: 'But as to the reasons, wonderful are the difficulties that men have been at in finding them out. One of the latest we have seems to have got a general idea of that which turns upon the insufficiency of the fund: which insufficiency he seems notwithstanding to have fixed upon its proper footing. "It were impossible," it seems, "for any state to furnish stock enough for so profuse a bounty." [1 Comm. 56.] It looks, then, as if the impossibility of governing by reward alone were placed to the account rather of the poverty of the states we are likely to be acquainted with, and the impolicy of profusion, than to any other cause: so that if the national debt, for instance, were ever to be paid off, and trade rendered a certain number of times more flourishing, the penal method of governing might be laid aside. A later writer, not satisfied with this reason, although reinforced with that of the superior efficacy of punishment, looks farther. To wheedle men into the performance of their duty is to be too indulgent: if they won't perform

 [*See p. 146 for n. 1 cont. and note 2*]

An invitative or præmiary law.

95. The conclusion, however, seems not to be a necessary one. For as these invitations are as much the expressions of the will of a lawgiver as commands themselves are, as they issue from the same source, tend to the same ends, are susceptible of the same aspects, applicable to the same objects, and recorded indiscriminately in the same volumes with those expressions of will which beyond dispute are entitled to the appellation of a law, it should seem that, without any great incongruity, they might be established in the possession of the same name. To distinguish, however, a law of this particular kind from the other, it should never be mentioned but under some particular name, such as that of an *invitative* or *praemiary* law; or it might be stiled a *legislative invitation* or a bounty.

A law with an alternative sanction.

96. As a law may have sometimes a penal sanction to back it, sometimes a sanction of the præmiary kind, so may it (as is obvious) be provided with two opposite sanctions, one of the one kind, the other of the other. A law thus provided may be stiled *a law with an alternative sanction*. In this case, the mode of conduct with which the one of these sanctions is connected is the opposite to that with which the other is connected. If the one sanction is connected with the positive act, the other sanction is connected with the correspondent negative act. Take the following example. Whoever comes to know that a robbery has been committed, let him declare it to the Judge: if he declares it accordingly, he shall receive such or such a reward: if he fails to declare it, he shall suffer such or such a punishment.

Law principal—subsidiary.

97. We are now arrived at the notion of an object which might in a certain sense admitt of the appellation of a law. It may even be looked upon as constituting a law and something more: since there are to be found in it two distinguishable parts: the directive part, which may of itself be a compleat expression of will, and an article of a different nature, a *prediction*.[a] But nothing hath as yet been

[a] A prediction is the expression of an act of the understanding, whereby a man declares it to be his opinion or belief that such or such an event is certain or more or less likely to happen in time future.

---

it willingly, they should be forced. It is thus that, irritated as it were by the idea of refractoriness on the part of those in whom obedience is a duty, he grounds the demand for punishment on the principle of antipathy.—What then? with pain and pleasure at your command, if you could govern men as well by soothing as by hurting them, would you choose to vex them?'

Bentham's references are to Blackstone, *Commentaries on the Laws of England*, i. 56, and possibly to [Samuel Johnson], *Taxation no Tyranny; An Answer to the Resolutions and Address of the American Congress*, London, 1775 (see, for instance, pp. 77–8, 81).

[2] MS '61 n.' appears to be a slip. See §12, pp. 121–2 n. above.

brought to view by which the efficacy of the directive part, or the verity of the predictive, can have been established upon any solid footing. Let the law stop here, and let the influence of the two auxiliary sanctions be for a moment set aside, what has been done by the law as yet amounts to nothing: as an expression of will, it is impotent; as a prediction, it is false. The will of the legislator concerning the matter in question has indeed been declared: and punishment has been threaten'd in the case of non-compliance with such will: but as to the means of carrying such threat into execution, nothing of this sort hath as yet been made appear.[1]

Now, there are three sources, as hath been often observed, from whence punishment may be expected to flow: I mean the three sanctions so often mentioned:[a] of which the political only is that which has its origin in the will of the legislator. But the force of the moral and religious sanctions may as well be expected to be annexed to a law, that is to a dictate of the legislator, as to a dictate of any other kind: and when this is the case, the law, it is evident, may possess a certain degree of efficacy in virtue of its directive part, and even without an incitative. This, indeed, will actually be the case as often as the dictates of those two auxiliary sanctions coincide respectively with the dictates of utility, at the same time that the dictates of the legislator appear to co-incide likewise with the dictates of that principle. Let it appear to a man that the law in question is, upon the whole, a beneficial one, or even that, upon any other ground, the not obeying it would, upon the whole, be attended with pernicious consequences, and at the same time let him be accustomed to take the influence of an act on the happiness of the community as the measure of his approbation or disapprobation with regard to it, in such case the influence of the moral sanction, as far as depends upon his suffrage, acts in favour of the law and gives a force to it: the moral sanction adopts the law, and adds it to the number of it's dictates. If, then, it appears to you that a considerable number of those whose good or ill will is an object of concern to you are likely to be in these sentiments, a proportionable quantity of the force of the moral sanction will act upon you in favour of the law. So in regard to the religious sanction, let it appear to you that the non-observance of the law would, on the above ground or any other, be displeasing to the supreme being, and that punishment of any kind, here or here-

[a] supra p. 135.[2]

[1] The following two paragraphs have been crossed through by Bentham.

[2] See para. 88, p. 142 above. The text sheet in which this paragraph appears (UC lxxxviii. 281) may, at one point, have been paginated 135.

after, would be the consequence of such displeasure, in such case the observance of such a law will appear to you to be a dictate of religion, and the force or influence of the religious sanction will also act upon you in favour of the same law. Take, for example, a law against theft, or a law of taxation: let the force either of the religious or of the moral sanctions act in the manner that has been mentioned, and a certain degree of efficacy may be possessed even by a simple expression of will requiring theft to be abstained from, or money to be paid.[a]

It is, however, but too evident that in ordinary cases the forces of the two auxiliary sanctions, even where added together, are too uncertain to be depended upon: and hence the occasion there is for subjoining to the directive part of most laws an incitative part holding up to view a punishment drawn from the political sanction itself as about to result in case of non-compliance.

What course then can the legislator take? There is but one, which is to go on commanding as before: for as to taking upon himself the infliction of the punishment with his own hands, this, were it practicable in every case, which it manifestly can not be, would be overstepping the bounds of his own function, and exercising a different sort of power.[b] All he can do, then, in his

[a] Instances are not wanting in which a general tax laid on in this singular way is said to have been productive. See Smith on the wealth of nations | |:[1] an anecdote which, if it be true, is much to the honour of human nature in general, and those of whom it is related in particular.

Of perfect dominion power of imperation is but one half; power of contrectation being the other.

[b] What, then, is this unnamed sort of power, which is different from, and the necessary complement, to the imperative?[2] This we must see presently: for without it our notions of dominion, whether private or public, beneficial or fiduciary, in short all our notions about government and property, would be imperfect. Meantime, whatever it be, it is plain that if it be any thing, the power of legislation, though it be supreme and unlimited legislation, nay even the entire power of imperation, though that too be supreme and unlimited imperation, is not self-sufficient and compleat. It is in fact but half the power which those by whose submission and obedience dominion is constituted are capable of conferring, and which must be exercised ere property can be enjoy'd or government carried on.

Dominion consists in the exercise of power. The faculties by which a being of any kind, rational or irrational, animated or inanimate, is capable of being the subject of power are all reducible to two classes, those which are merely passive, and those which are active or self-moving: the former are common to beings animated and inanimate, the latter belong to such as are animated alone; that is to

[1] See Adam Smith, *An Inquiry into the Nature and Causes of the Wealth of Nations* (first published 1776), ed. R.H. Campbell, A.S. Skinner, and W.B. Todd, 2 vols., Oxford, 1976, ii. 850–2, describing such instances of taxation in Hamburgh, several Swiss cantons, and Holland.

[2] In the margin, Bentham has noted at this point: 'Work this up with the rest of what concerns imperation under title Generality.' See §11, pp. 98–114 above.

capacity of legislator is to issue a second law, requiring some person to verify the prediction that accompanied the first. This secondary law being issued in aid of the primary may, with reference thereto, be termed the *subsidiary* law: with reference

such only as are endued with the faculty of volition. Power which is exercised over the passive faculties may be stiled in a large sense *power of contrectation*; that which is exercised over the active or self-moving faculties, *power of imperation*. Power of contrectation, (for by this name I am reduced to call it for want of one more apposite and comprehensive) must be distinguished into that which is properly, and that which is improperly, so called: or the former might be termed the power of *physical* contrectation; the latter, the power of *hyperphsyical* (that is *super-physical*) contrectation. The former is that which is exercised over the body of the subject, and may be exercised as well over inanimate as over animated subjects: the latter that which is exercised over the faculties, meaning here the passive faculties, of the mind; and can of course be exercised over animated beings alone. As to the inferior animals, their pathological faculties being commonly disregarded more than is consistent with humanity, and their intellectual faculties than is consistent with just reasoning, they are commonly spoken of as being subject to no other power than that of contrectation; and stand accordingly degraded into the class of things. Instead of the *power of contrectation*, we might say, making use of a term more familiar but less apposite, the *power of action*: or making use of a term more apposite, but altogether new and unfamiliar, epergastic power: επι upon, εργαζομαι to act.

Power of contrectation is, in private dominion, the power which a man exercises over the land he walks over or cultivates; the bread he bakes or eats; the coat he wears or brushes; the child or the servant he feeds, beats or reprimands: in public dominion, the power of the soldier over the persons, and occasionally over the property, of those whom he is commanded or allow'd to treat as enemies: of the executioner or other inferior minister of justice over the persons and properties of those who come under the controul or censure of the law: and indirectly the power of the public gunsmith, the public gunpowder-maker, the public storekeeper, and so forth, over the things they make or keep or use for the benefit of the public.

Power of imperation is, in private dominion, the power which the master exercises over the will of his servant, the parent over that of his child, the husband over that of his wife, the guardian over that of his ward: in public dominion, that which the sovereign exercises over the will of all his subjects, the general over that of his soldiers and occasionally over that of other persons who come within the sphere of his command, the judge over that of the persons who are subject to his jurisdiction.

Power of contrectation is most apt to be the power of the many: power of imperation, to be the power of the few.

Power of imperation, as we have seen already, (§. 11)[1] may in an infinite variety of ways be broken into shares: in the same manner may the power of contrectation: the latter, however, is not so apt to be thus broken, as the former.

Power of imperation, as we have seen in the text, rests ultimately upon the power of contrectation; since all punishment is an exercise of the power of contrectation; those punishments excepted which apply themselves to the active

[1] See pp. 98–114 above, esp. paras. 9–12, pp. 103–6 above.

to which the primary law may on the other hand be termed the *principal*.

The subsidiary law addressed commonly to the Judge.

98. To whom is it, then, that this subsidiary law should be addressed? It can never be to the same person to whom the principal law was addressed: for a man *can* not reward himself; nor *will* he punish himself. It must, therefore, be to some other person: a circumstance which of itself is sufficient to shew that the principal and subsidiary are two distinct laws, and not parts of one and the same law. It may be any other person indefinitely. Commonly, however, it is to some particular class of persons, who, occupying some particular station or civil condition instituted for the purpose, such as that of Judge, are presumed on the one hand to be properly qualified, on the other hand to be previously disposed, to execute or cause to be executed any such commands when issued by the legislator.

Who must have assistants—hence more subsidiary laws.

99. But neither can the hand nor the eye of the judge reach every where: to be in a condition to discharge his functions he must be provided with a variety of assistants: which assistants must for various purposes be of various ranks and occupations and descriptions: witnesses, registers, court-keepers, jail-keepers,

faculty, such as banishment; and even these depend for their efficacy upon those which apply to the passive faculty.

Finally, in an established commonwealth, of the power of all subordinate power-holders, the ultimate efficient cause is the command or allowance of the sovereign: of the power of the sovereign himself, the constituent cause is the submission and obedience of the people.

As to rights, they are either rights of dominion, or mere liberties, rights of exemption from dominion: rights of dominion are either entire powers (for every power is a right) or shares of powers: for every right is not a power. See supra, §.11.[1]

The plan of arrangement in which *powers* and *rights* are the leading terms is more particularly adapted to the civil branch of the law; and more especially to that subordinate branch of it which may be termed the constitutional: as that in which laws and offences are the leading terms is more particularly adapted to the penal. By what is here said of the power of contrectation, added to what has been said in §. 11[2] of the power of imperation, the limits of the private part of the civil branch, and more clearly those of the constitutional part, are marked out, and the possible modifications of constitutional power, and the possible combinations of these modifications, viz: the possible forms of government, brought within our grasp.

The power of imperation being the same thing with the power of creating offences, it is thus that the two plans abovementioned coincide: the power of contrectation is the power of doing those acts which are necessary, amongst other purposes, for that of punishing offences, and which, where this power is wanting, are offences of themselves.

---

[1] See paras. 13–25, pp. 106–14 above.

[2] See pp. 98–114 above.

bailiffs, executioners, and so forth. Of these there are many who must begin to act in their respective characters even before the matter is submitted to his cognizance: consequently before they can be in a way to receive any commands from him. On this and other accounts they too must have their duties prescribed to them by the law itself: and hence the occasion for so many more subsidiary laws or sets of subsidiary laws of which they are respectively the agible subjects, and their acts the objects.

100. It is evident that the number and nature of the subsidiary laws of this stamp will be determined by the number and nature of the different sorts of acts which, on the part either of the same person or of different persons, it is thought proper should be performed or abstained from in the course of the *procedure*. Now, by the procedure is meant on the present occasion[a] the suite of steps which are required to be taken in the view of ascertaining whether a man has or has not done an act of the number of those which stand prohibited by some principal law: and thereby of ascertaining whether he is or is not of the number of those persons on whom a punishment of the sort denounced by the principal law in question is required to be inflicted.

On what circumstances the number of them depends.

101. Amidst this various train of laws subsidiary, that which is addressed to the judge and contains the command to punish may for distinction's sake be termed the punitive or *punitory* law: and, with reference to the rest, the *proximate* subsidiary law: the rest may indiscriminately be termed *remote*. Where the principal law is of the præmiary kind, the proximate subsidiary law may be termed *remunerative*.

Subsidiary laws proximate—remote:— the proximate punitory or remunerative.

102. Now, it is evident that in like manner as a principal law must have it's subsidiary laws, so also must each of those subsidiary laws have a train of subsidiary laws to itself, and that for the same reason. This is a circumstance that belongs alike to every law which takes it's support from the political sanction. A. committs an offence: it is thereupon render'd the duty of B. to contribute in such or such a way to the bringing of him to punishment in the event of his proving guilty: and a particular

Laws substantive—adjective.

[a] All Judiciary or contentious procedure, as there will be occasion to shew hereafter,[a] is divisible into procedure *delicti causâ* and procedure *petitionis causâ*. The former comes nearest to what is commonly meant by penal procedure, the latter to what is meant by civil procedure. The former is that with which we are concerned at present.

[a] infra §§19 or 20.[1]

[1] See §20, pp. 207–18 below.

process is appointed to be carried on for ascertaining whether he be or no. In the course of that process, such and such steps are required to be taken by C. in such and such contingencies: such and such others by D. and E. and F.: and so on indefinitely. But what if B. also prove refractory? a similar process must thereupon be carried on, and a similar provision made by the law, for the bringing of him also to punishment: and so on if any failure should arise on the part of D. or E. or F. In this way must commands follow upon commands: if the first person called does not obey, the second may: if the second should not, yet a third may: if even the third should fail, yet there may be hopes of a fourth. If it is not expected that any one will obey, the law is plainly impotent and falls to the ground: but let obedience be but expected from any one of the persons addressed, at whatever distance he stands from him who was addressed first, this expectation may prove sufficient to keep all the intermediate persons to their duty. If an offence, then, be committed, untill obedience takes place[1] on the part of some one or other of the persons thus connected, the law is, as it were, asleep, and the whole machine of government is at a stand: but let any one law in the whole penal train meet with obedience, let punishment take place in any quarter, the law awakens out of its trance, and the whole machine is set a-going again: the influence of that law which has met with obedience flows back, as it were, through all the intermediate laws till it comes to that principal one to which they are all alike subsidiary.[2]

To every law, then, subsidiary ones as well as others, there must be others which, with reference to it, are subsidiary: so far all laws which, for their support, depend solely on the political sanction are upon a footing. There are, however, certain laws in particular which, and which alone, although like the rest they have their set of subsidiary laws belonging to them, do not themselves stand in that relation to any other laws. In this predicament stand those which we set out with mentioning under the appellation of principal ones. There are, then, two sorts of laws: one of which are altogether principal without being subsidiary to any: the other subsidiary and principal at the same time. As to these latter, however, the subsidiary character is that in which they can not but appear in the first instance. They not only could not have any effect, but they could not be understood, nor even have existence,

[1] In the margin, Bentham has noted in relation to the opening part of this sentence: 'Polish.'

[2] In the margin, Bentham has noted at this point: 'Take notice that this is not a certain consequence. State here the instance of the Sheriff, Coroner and Elizors.'

without having a principal law to refer to: the idea of such a law being included in their very essence. 'Punish him who refuses to bear his part in bringing to punishment those who committ murder,' is a law which supposes the existence of a law against committing murder. On the other hand, a law which forbids the committing of murder is not only possible and intelligible, but may even possess a certain degree of efficacy, although there were no such thing as any other law in the world: to wit by the help of the two auxiliary sanctions. Those laws, then, which can not stand alone, but require to be preceded by some other to which they may adhere, may on that account be stiled *adjective* or *enclitic* laws:[a] those of the opposite description, *substantive* or *self-subsisting*. To the adjective class belong all laws relative to the course of judiciary procedure.[b]

103. To consider the proximate subsidiary law, it is evident that between that and the principal, distinguishable as they are, there can not but be a very intimate connection and dependence. On the one hand, the principal law, by it's comminative part, has an essential reference to the subsidiary; of the contents of which, if that reference be expressed, it must necessarily give some general intimation. The business of the former is to predict that same evil which it is the business of the latter to endeavour to produce.

Connection between the principal law and its proximate subsidiary.

On the other hand, the description and texture of the subsidiary law must of course be determined in great measure by that of the principal. There is always one person who is concerned in both: the person whose obedience is required by the principal law, and for whose punishment, in case of his not obeying, provision is made by the subsidiary law. This person, after having been consider'd in the light of an agent in the one, is consider'd in that of a patient by the other. Or to speak more exactly, the class composed of the persons who are the passible subjects of the subsidiary law is taken out of the class composed of those who are the agible subjects of the principal: for the persons on whom the punishment is to be inflicted are not all such persons to whom the mandate of the principal law has been addressed, but such of them

[a] {Enclitic} By the Greek and Latin grammarians, certain particles (such as τε, δε, que, ve), which never stand alone, but are always tacked on to the end of some other word, are termed *enclitic* particles.

[b] In the language of the English law, the word *procedure* is not much in use: questions which arise in the courts with relation to laws of this stamp are stiled *questions of practice*: cases which give rise to such questions, *cases of practice*: and the subordinate laws which are made by Judges with relation to this head, *rules of practice*. The word *procedure*, though not so familiar, seems more characteristic and determinate.

only by whom it has been transgressed: nor in fact even all these, but such of them only against whom such and such persons, or such and such appearances, shall have deposed; or more generally, in the proceedings against whom such and such formalities can have been, and actually shall have been, observed.[a]

By this dependency, the nature and description of the subsidiary law is limited in divers manners. The aspect which the legislator's will bears upon the occasion can scarcely be other than affirmative: the act which it commands, of course a positive one: the expression given to it, an affirmative command: moreover, as hath already been observed in other words, the act is, in respect to its pathological termination,[b] confined to the particular sorts of persons who shall have appeared to be delinquents as against the principal law. In this respect, then, the description of the subsidiary law is influenced and narrow'd by all the circumstances which contribute to narrow the description of the act commanded by the principal law: the definition of the former is determined by the definition of the latter.

One expression may serve for both principal law and subsidiary.

104. The unity of the law, it is to be observed, is not to be determined by the unity of the proposition or grammatical sentence which expresses it. So close is the union between a principal law and the subsidiary law which stands next to it, that one proposition is frequently enough to hold them both. Indeed, the principal law is commonly thought sufficient of itself to answer the purpose of the first subsidiary law that belongs to it: that part which is incitative to the one set of persons being directive to the other. Let it be once known that there is a Judge appointed for trying such and such offences, and murder among the rest, a Law which says 'whoso committs murder shall be put to death,' is sufficient intimation to the Judge that, in case of a man's being convicted before him of that crime, it is the will of the lawgiver that the judge should cause that man to be put to death. So on the other hand were a law to say 'let the Judge cause every man that committs murder to be put to death,' the prohibition thereby given would be not awhit less intelligible than if it were to say, 'let no man, on pain of death, committ murder.' The ways of expressing a will are infinitely various, many of them such that nothing can be more indirect. There is no trusting, therefore, to mere words. To understand any subject thoroughly, but more

[a] v. infra 109.[1]
[b] supra 37 n.[2]

[1] See pp. 157–8 below.

[2] See p. 58 n. above.

particularly that of law, to have a clear perception of the ideas that belong to it, we must strip them of their fallacious covering and judge of them by themselves.[a]

105. These two methods of abbreviation are both of them perfectly natural and intelligible: so much so that not to make use of one or the other of them would be such an instance of unnecessary diffusion as is perhaps scarce any where to be found exemplified. The first, however, is of the two by much the more natural and the more eligible: since the party whose conduct it is the first and principal design of the law to regulate, and against whom in case of disobedience the punishment is denounced, is the person who of all others has the first and greatest occasion to be informed of it. That done, one general notice to the Judge will serve for as many principal laws as there are in the whole code. A very short one will suffice. 'The various punishments which stand denounced against the various classes of offenders, let such and such Judges see inflicted:' or in a less explicit though more usual way, 'let such and such Judges have cognizance of such and such offences.'[1]

The principal most commonly serves for both.

106. It has just been observed that instances are now and then to be met with of laws in which the sanction, if such it can be called, is purely of the remunerative kind. But laws of this kind can not be strung together, one upon the back of another, like laws of the ordinary penal mould. If the principal law is of the former kind, the

To a præmiary law when principal, the next subsidiary must be penal.

[a] It is to be observed that the principal law which is here comprised in the same sentence with the subsidiary consists itself of two distinguishable parts, the directive and the incitative (see supra | |),[2] and which are so distinguishable that the former is frequently to be found without the latter. In the same manner, where the law has no armature from the political sanction, a particular turn of the phrase, an insertion or alteration of a single word, may be sufficient to give it an armature from the moral.[3] It should be remember'd once for all, that there is no judging of the logical divisions of a law from the grammatical divisions of the discourses in which it may happen to be contained.[4]

---

[1] In the margin, Bentham has noted at this point: 'Shew how a whole system of substantive law is indirectly contained in a system of constitutional law through the medium of a system of procedure. v. Russian Code. British India regulating act.'

For the 'Russian Code' issued by Catherine II (1729–96), Empress of Russia from 1762 see *Réglements de Sa Majesté Impériale Catherine II, pour L'Administration des Gouvernements de l'Empire des Russies*, Liege, 1777. The Regulating Act of 1773 (13 Geo. III, c. 63) was a wide-ranging measure which reformed the administration of the East India Company in London and its system of government in India.

[2] See para. 90, p. 143 above.

[3] In the margin, Bentham has noted at this point: 'Refer to Indirect legislation.' For the projected Chapter entitled 'Indirect Legislation' see the Editorial Introduction, p. xii above.

[4] Bentham has commented in relation to this note: 'Insert this supra.' He has not, however, indicated precisely where the note should be placed, and its insertion at this point is, therefore, conjectural.

very next subsidiary law that is applied to it, or at farthest the next but one, must be of the latter. You are a legislator: you wish to have the longitude discover'd: you offer a reward, suppose in money, for the discovery.[1] So far all is right: the course you take is not only a proper one, but the only one that could be so. Here, however, you are obliged immediately to change the sanction: to proceed farther in the remunerative track, and as a means of getting the Judge to pay the money, to offer him a reward for paying it, without appointing any punishment in case of his omitting so to do, would be but an indifferent expedient. To pay for the trouble of receiving and telling the money is again no more than right: but if this were all, the money would be received indeed, but when it came to be told, it would be rather extraordinary if none of it were told into the wrong purse. There are cases, then, in which the law may not without advantage step aside into the remunerative path: but it can scarce ever take more than a single step at a time. Although the principal law be of the præmiary kind, the proximate subsidiary law, though stiled remunerative,[a] will commonly have something in it that is of a penal nature.[b]

Exemptive circumstances.

107. It is this notion of the distinction between a principal law and its subsidiary that must lead us to the notion of those circumstances belonging to a law which may be stiled *exemptive*. Exemptive circumstances are circumstances which limit the application of the punishment, without limiting the description of the offence. We have seen already that the connection between delinquency and the demand for punishment, however close, is not inseparable: but that there are cases in which, though guilt even in the highest degree be indubitable, yet punishment would be improper.[c] Wherever, then, there is a circumstance which, over and above any influence it may have on the mischief of the act, has the effect of taking it out of the case in which it would be expedient

[a] supra | |.[2]

[b] It might, indeed, consist in a mere exemption. But even a law of this kind has a necessary reference to punishment: it consists in abrogating the punishment he would otherwise be liable to in case of his not doing what he is exempted from.

[c] See Ch. 13. {Cases unmeet}.[3]

---

[1] The Longitude Act of 1714 (12 Ann., c. 15) established the Board of Longitude and offered a prize of £20,000 for the invention of an accurate means of determining longitude. The problem was effectively solved by a series of sea clocks constructed by the horologist John Harrison (bap. 1693, d. 1776). Harrison, however, was never awarded the prize, although he did eventually receive an equivalent sum from Parliament.

[2] Bentham perhaps has in mind para. 91, p. 143 above, where he uses the term 'invitative' rather than 'remunerative'. He does, however, introduce the term 'remuneratory law' in *An Introduction to the Principles of Morals and Legislation* (*CW*), Ch. XI, para. 2, p. 126.

[3] See ibid., Ch. XIII, pp. 158–64.

to punish it, such circumstance is fit to be invested with the character of an exemptive circumstance: and at any rate, however the matter may stand in point of expediency, if in fact a circumstance of any sort is made to operate in that manner without obliterating or outweighing the mischief of the offence, such circumstance may with equal propriety be characterized by that name.

Difference between exculpative and exemptive.

108. Exemptive circumstances are distinguished in several particulars from exculpative. The latter must have had their existence at or before the time of the performance of the act which, had it not been for them, would have been an offence: among the former are such as can not take place till a long time afterwards.[1] Exculpative circumstances apply as well to laws which have no other force than what they derive from the two auxiliary sanctions, as to those which are armed in the ordinary way from the political sanction: exemptive circumstances apply only to the laws last mentioned.

It hath already been observed[a] that the principal law and the punitory law which is subsidiary to it, are two essentially distinct laws: exculpative provisions, then, are qualifications to the principal: exemptive ones, to the punitory.

How laws of procedure apply exemptions to substantive laws.

109. To ascertain what circumstances are in point of utility proper to be invested with the character of exemptive circumstances comes not within the design of the present chapter: our business here is to represent the mere matter of fact: in what manner a circumstance which has this effect is made to have it. For this purpose it is to be observed, that wherever in the course of the procedure a person is required to perform such or such an act, upon the non-performance of which the party accused is acquitted or the process put an end to so as not to begin again, such non-performance is thereby constituted, with regard to the principal law, an exemptive circumstance; and the person by whom the act in question is required to be performed is thereby virtually invested with a power of dispensing with the principal law, upon the terms of running the chance of the punishment annexed to the violation of the subsidiary law. This is the case, for instance, where, in order to warrant a conviction, an instrument of accusation couched in a certain form is render'd necessary. In such case, the person invested with this power is the officer or other person

[a] supra 98.[2]

[1] In the margin, Bentham has noted at this point: 'Not so: ex. g. insanity.'

[2] See p. 150 above.

to whom it belongs to draw the instrument: in order to exercise such power he has nothing to do but to draw the instrument in a form different from that required. So where the appearance of a witness within a certain time, or his taking a certain oath within a certain time, are render'd necessary: he has but to keep out of the way or to refuse the taking oaths during that time; and upon these terms he may save whom he will from punishment.

Disexemptive circumstances.

110. As there may be circumstances to which the legislator has given the effect of taking an offence out of the case in which it is punishable, so there may be others which are attended with the effect of re-instating it in that case, after it's having been taken out of it as above. Circumstances of this stamp, if any should occur, may be termed dis-exemptive circumstances.

As exemptive provisions are qualifications of the punitory law,[a] so disexemptive are qualifications of the aforesaid original qualifications: re-enlarging the law after the defalcations which, by virtue of such original qualifications, have been made in it.

Limitations which are annexed of course to a punitory law

111. Upon considering the matter with a little attention, it will be evident that, provided any tolerable regard be paid to justice, there are a certain string of exemptions by which every punitory law will of course be qualified: I mean those which, antecedently to the infliction of the punishment, require the fact of the delinquency to be ascertained by the result of a particular process to be instituted for that purpose. The form in which a qualifying clause to this effect presents itself will naturally be that of a limitation rather than an exception: expressing at first in general terms the sort of process which is in question: of course by means of some word of limitation,[b] the connection which is meant to be established in point of causality[c] between the event of such process and the act of punishment. 'Whosoever' (let the imperative provision say) 'has been a thief, let the Judge cause him to be hanged.' Thus far the imperative provision: provided, says the limitative provision, that he have been duly convicted and sentenced in course of law.

This very general provision, in order to be expressive of all the effects which the institution of a system of procedure can have

[a] supra 107.[1]
[b] supra [70] n.[2]
[c] See Ch. 7. {Actions}.[3]

---

[1] See pp. 156–7 above.
[2] MS '69 n.' appears to be a slip. See p. 126 n. above.
[3] See *An Introduction to the Principles of Morals and Legislation* (*CW*), Ch. VII, paras. 23–5, pp. 80–1.

upon a punitory law to which it is annexed, must be consider'd as including in its bosom an immense string of qualificative clauses, some indeed after the manner of the general one narrowing the extent of the imperative provision, but others again, re-extending it. Exemptive clause: 'provided he be convicted upon trial:'—disexemptive clause: 'unless upon non-appearance he be outlawed:'—exemptive clause of the 2[d] order: 'and the outlawry shall not have been reversed.'

112. But a limitation, as hath been observed, is always convertible into an exception:[a] and that exception is again convertible into an independent provision,[b] destructive *pro tanto* of the imperative provision which is excepted from. Being destructive, then, it may be either simply revocative or reversive. In the present case, it is always, as of course, reversive. Leading provision a command: 'Whosoever is a thief the Judge shall cause him to be hanged:' exemptive provision in form of a limitation: 'provided he have been duly convicted and sentenced in course of law.' The same turned into an exception: 'except he have not been duly convicted and sentenced in course of law.' This exception turned into an independent provision simply revocative of the imperative: 'The Judge need not cause a thief to be hanged when he has not been duly convicted and sentenced in course of law.' This, were it to stand thus, would leave it to the Judge's option altogether, when a thief (that is a person whom he believed to be a thief, for the Judge's belief is what the question must always turn upon) when a thief, I say, is not duly convicted and sentenced, whether he shall be hanged or not: the Judge is not obliged to cause him to be hanged: he may, however, if he pleases, for any thing that the law says to the contrary. This option, however, is what it is never thought fit to leave to the Judge: accordingly the provision goes a step farther and becomes imperative on the opposite side: 'The Judge shall not cause a thief to be hanged unless he have been duly convicted and sentenced in course of law.'

— and which are made obligative on the other side.

113. If this be every where the case, it follows that, wherever there is a punitory law established on the one side, there is another law established to controul it on the other. For this other law, the standing antagonist[c] of the punitory, there is as much need to find

Law anætiosostic, the antagonist to the punitory.

[a] supra 70.[1]

[b] supra 85.[2]

[c] In anatomy muscles which counteract each other are spoken of as antagonists to each other, and termed antagonizing muscles.

---

[1] See p. 125–6 above.

[2] See pp. 138–9 above.

a name as for the punitory itself. It may be termed the *anœtiosostic*.[a] The punishment of guilt is the object of the former: the preservation of innocence that of the latter. The provisions that have been stiled exemptive may be consider'd as clauses expository of the anætiosostic law: those which have been stiled disexemptive, as clauses expository of the punitory law.[b]

[a] From αναιτιος, one who is innocent, and σωστικος, having the property of saving.

[b] v. supra 57.[1]

---

[1] See pp. 118–19 above, where Bentham discusses the way in which a superventitious provision may be expository of the primordial one.

§ 14. *Signs of a law.*

114. [Eleventhly],[1] with regard to the *expression*. A law is an *expression* of will; that is an assemblage of signs expressive of an act of the will. These signs, then, may by possibility be any signs whatever which are capable of expressing such a will: the behaviour of him who, instead of saying, put to death the chief leaders of the people, smote off the tallest heads among a parcel of poppies,[2] might, instead of being an advice, have been a command. But the only signs which can answer this purpose in a manner tolerably commodious are those conventional signs the assemblage of which forms what is called *discourse*. Now, the signs of which discourse is composed may either be of the *transient* kind, of which those most in use are articulate sounds: or they may be a sort of secondary symbols, permanent signs of the before mentioned transient ones, composing what is commonly called *written*, and what by a more comprehensive mode of appellation might be stiled *graphical*, discourse. Of the last description of all are what are commonly called statute or written laws. Of the first kind,[3] if laws they are to be called, are what in the English language are usually styled *common* or *unwritten*, but which might more aptly be stiled *customary*, laws. For the second,[4] it being for so many ages out of date among civilized nations, no distinct denomination seems ever to have been in common use: they might be stiled *traditionary* statute laws; or more shortly *traditionary* laws.

Signs by which a law may stand *expressed*. Law written—traditionary—customary.

115. When the nature of those laws which are here called customary comes to be precisely understood, which it seems hardly to have been hitherto, the doubt above expressed will not be wonder'd at. These laws are nothing but so many particular autocratic acts or orders, which, in virtue of the more extensive interpretation which the people are disposed to put upon them, have some what of the effect of general laws. Here it is to be observed that all verbal discourse is out of the question. Perhaps there shall have been no verbal discourse made use of on the occasion: but if there be, it is not this verbal discourse that makes the law. For the verbal

Customary laws are expressed by acts only, not by words.

[1] MS del. 'Thirdly'; MS alt. 'Eighthly'.

[2] See Livy, *Ab urbe condita*, I. liv. 5–9, where Lucius Tarquinius Superbus (d. 495 BC), traditionally the last King of Rome 534–510 BC, having been asked for advice by a messenger sent by his son, lopped off the heads of the poppies that were taller than the rest. A similar story appears in Aristotle, *Politics*, 1284a, 26–34, and Herodotus, *History*, V. xcii, where Thrasybulus, Tyrant of Miletus, advising Periander, Tyrant of Corinth (*c.* 627–587 BC) how to deal with rivals, walked through a field of corn lopping off the tallest ears.

[3] i.e. laws composed of signs neither spoken nor written.

[4] i.e. laws composed of signs spoken, but not written.

discourse containing the mandate of the judge is in point of extent particular, being confined to the assignable individuals to whom it is addressed: whereas what there is of law in the case must be general, applicable to an indefinite multitude of individuals not then assignable. A magistrate exercises some act of power over a particular individual: the assemblage of acts by which this is done serve as a sign to the people at large, expressing that the like act of power will probably be exercised in future in a like case. A Cadi comes by a Baker's shop, and finds the bread short of weight: the baker is hanged in consequence. This, if it be part of the design that other bakers should take notice of it, is a sort of law forbidding the selling of bread short of weight under the pain of hanging. Whether the Cadi makes a record in writing, attesting that the Baker has sold bread short of weight, and issues an order to a public executioner to strangle him, or whether the Cadi himself, without saying a word, strangles him on the spot with his own hands, is what to this purpose makes no difference. The silent act of hanging, when thus made a consequence of the offence, has as good a title in point of extent to the appellation of a law as any thing that could be made out of a whole shelf-full of pleadings put together. Written law, then, is the law of those who can both speak and write: traditionary law, of those who can speak but can not write; customary law, of those who neither know how to write, nor how to speak. Written law is the law for civilized nations: traditionary law, for barbarians: customary law, for brutes.

No assignable laws to be found in books of customary law.

116. Not but that there are plenty of books purporting to be books of customary, or as it is more frequently called *unwritten*, law: for if the written law is written, so is the unwritten too. But what are they? Books written not by the legislator, but by private individuals: Books not of authoritative, but of unauthoritative, jurisprudence.[a] In none of all these books is there so much as a single article which can with propriety receive the appellation of *a* law. It is owing rather to an imperfection which, as we have seen,[b] is peculiar to the English tongue, if in that language they can with any degree of propriety be termed books of law: they contain *jus* indeed, but not *leges*: *du droit*, but not *des loix*.

If in all that has been ever written of this nature there be a single paragraph which (not being a passage copied from some statute) is seriously meant to pass for a paragraph of *a* law, I mean in the

[a] supra §2.[5]
[b] supra | |.[6]

[1] See §2, para. 22, p. 16 above. [2] See §2, para. 23 n., p. 16 n. above.

sense in which the word *law* is used in contradistinction to the word *order*, it is a forgery. Whether there be any thing in it or not that has been marked with the stamp of authority, makes no difference: if authoritative, it is particular;[a] and, therefore, no law: if general, it is unauthoritative: and, therefore, again no law. But of this a little farther on.[b]

117. Where words are the signs made use of to give expression to a will, the form of words in which this may be done admitts of a great variety of modifications. A slight sketch of the principal distinctions observable among them is all that can be afforded here: to give a regular display of them in all the formalities of the exhaustive method would take up more room than can consistently be allotted to such a purpose. Taking for a thesis the old example of a law against the exportation of corn, I shall exhibitt some of the principal forms of which a command to that purpose is susceptible, arranging them in such manner that the mode of expression grows gradually more and more inexplicit or oblique in proportion as each formulary is more distant from the first.

Various modes of expression that may be given to the same written law.

1. The command expressed at full length—the party to whom it is addressed (the agible subject) spoken to in the 2[d] person. It is my pleasure that you do not export any corn.

2. The command in the ordinary elliptical form: the verb expressive of the act being put in the imperative mood. Export no corn.

3. The verb, in the future tense. Ye shall not export corn.

4. The party, spoken of in the 3[d] person. Let no man export corn. No man shall export corn.

5. The idea of the passible subject, put foremost. Let no corn be exported.

6. The command, expressed in the way of commination. All persons who export corn shall be punished. Every person, any person, exporting corn shall be punished. If any person export corn, he shall be punished. Whosoever exports corn shall be punished.

7. The legislator speaking, as it were, in the person of another man, who is consider'd as explaining the state which things are in, in consequence of the arrangements taken by the legislator. It is not permitted to any man to export corn. It is unlawful for any man

[a] It is an act of punishment or other act of coercion exercised, not upon a class of persons, but upon a particular individual.

[b] infra §| |.[1]

[1] See §17, pp. 185–97 below.

to export corn. No man has a *right* to export corn.[a] The exportation of corn is forbidden.

The first five of the above forms of imperation may be stiled directly imperative; the sixth and seventh indirectly imperative: and for distinction's sake, the sixth, comminative; the 7th, declarative.

Thus much may suffice for the present concerning the different manners in which the connection between the will of a legislator and the act which is the object of that will may be expressed. I pass by a multitude of observations which, however necessary to the compleat explanation of the subject, would be thought misplaced, as belonging to the head rather of grammar than of legislation.

I pass over also, for the sake of brevity, the explanation of the different ways in which the other aspects of the will may be represented in connection with the same act.

As to limitative and exceptive clauses, these, as hath been shewn already,[b] may all be reduced to the form of independent obligative or de-obligative provisions. With regard to the words and phrases that may be made use of for expressing the particular relation they bear as such to the leading provisions to which they are subjoined, enough has also been said already.[c]

[a] Why? because the legislator has forbidden it.

[b] supra 85.[1]

[c] supra [70] n.[2]

---

[1] See pp. 138–9 above.

[2] MS '69 n.' is a slip. See p. 126 n. above.

§15. *Appendages of a law.*

118. [Twelfthly],[1] with respect to the occasional appendages of a law: by which I mean certain subsidiary laws of a less essential nature than the *punitory*, which may or may not be subjoined, in the view of contributing still farther to obviate the mischief which it is the object of the principal law to provide against: the laws I am speaking of may be termed *remedial*.

Appendages or remedial laws—another species of subsidiary,

It has, indeed, been shewn already that against political mischiefs the only remedy that is of universal efficacy is punishment; a stock of which from some source or other[a] every law must be provided with in order to be effectual. But by punishment as such, all that can be attained is the preventing, by the dread of a suffering similar to one which in one instance hath already been inflicted, such similar mischievous acts as might otherwise have been committed subsequently to some given individual instance of delinquency. In some cases, however, not only those indeterminate, uncertain mischiefs may be guarded against as above, but measures may even be taken for obviating the particular mischiefs actual and contingent, which, in the way of causality, are particularly connected with the individual offence. Let an offence of any kind, then, have been committed: a certain quantity of mischief is connected with it. Take, then, any parcel of that quantity, and consider it at any given instant posterior to that of the commencement of the offence: such parcel must at that instant be either past, present or to come. There are, accordingly, three courses which the law may take in obviating the mischief: to make *compensation* for what is past, to cure, that is to put a stop to, what is present, and to guard against what might otherwise be to come. Now the courses which it may be necessary the law should take for these purposes respectively, that is the acts which it may have occasion to command to be performed and the persons by whom they must be performed, will not always be the same. The laws, therefore, will not always be the same: neither with regard to the punitory, nor yet with regard to one another. In some cases, the three purposes may require three different laws, having perhaps as many different sets of persons for their immediate subjects. A law, then, if it has the first of those

[a] supra 88.[2]

[1] MS del. 1 'We come ninthly and lastly'; MS del. 2 'Eighthly'; MS alt. 'Tenthly'.
[2] See p. 142 above.

purposes for it's object, may be stiled *compensative*; if the second, *therapeutic*[a] or catapaustic;[b] if the third, *metaphylactic*.[c]

Nor is it in every case of delinquency that the attainment of every one of these objects is either requisite or possible. As to compensation, what cases do and what do not admitt of it have been already shewn:[d] the cases that require and at the same time admitt of any special precautionary measures to be taken for the purpose of guarding the individual injured against future injuries of the same kind on the part of the same offender[e] will be found to be confined within still narrower bounds: those which require and

[a] From θεραπευω, *to cure*.

[b] From καταπαυω, to put a stop to. *Catapaustic*, when once understood, has the advantage of being more literal and precise: *therapeutic*, that of being less unfamiliar, being in use already among physicians.

[c] From μετα, *subsequently*, and φυλαττω, *to keep guard*: i: e: to guard against certain future parcels of the mischief which might otherwise ensue from the individual offence which is supposed to have been committed. Provisions of this nature are here stiled *metaphylactic*, in order to distinguish them from those which belong to the head of the preventive[a] or *prophylactic*[b] branch of the police. A provision of the metaphylactic kind necessarily supposes some individual offence to have been actually committed, before the occasion which calls for obedience can take place: some individual offence, though perhaps not precisely of the same species as those which it undertakes to guard against: for example, a threat to kill (a species of wrongful menacement) or an attempt to set fire to a house (an accessory offence preliminary to the principal offence of incendiarism), whereas the offences it undertakes to guard against are *wrongful homicide* and *incendiarism*. As to provisions of the prophylactic kind (such for instance as those for the keeping of watch and ward), they do not necessarily suppose the commission of any offence whatever.

[d] Ch. 16. Division §5.[1]

[e] As in case of atrocious offences against person or against person and reputation together; for instance by exacting security for good behaviour, or even by banishing the offender from the presence of the party injured.

Provisions of this nature, however, are applicable, wherever the magnitude of the danger requires them, to semi-public, public, and even to self-regarding offences. To this latter head may be referred the provisions made against prodigality by the Roman law and adopted in the laws of several of the modern nations of Europe.

Positive mischief consists either of actual pain or danger. Private offences produce pain as well as danger; semi-public and public offences as such, danger only. It is, therefore, only the mischief of private offences that can be or requires to be compensated for: but in semi-public and public offences as well as in private, danger which is present may be put a stop to, and that which is future guarded against.

[a] v. Ch. 16. {Division} 17.[2]

[b] ib. 54 n.[3]

[1] See *An Introduction to the Principles of Morals and Legislation* (*CW*), Ch. XVI, paras. 61–6, pp. 274–80.

[2] See ibid., para. 17, pp. 196–201.

[3] See ibid., 'OFFENCES against the PREVENTIVE branch of the POLICE', para. 54 n., p. 262 n.

admitt of any special measures to be taken for putting a stop to the mischief of the offence, are fewer still.[a]

119. These, then, in the cases in which they apply, form another class of subsidiary laws with which any one of a certain number of principal laws may be attended: and which in like manner as those of the punitory class may be distinguished into proximate and remote. Moreover, to each of these series and combinations of laws correspond so many distinguishable tracks or courses of procedure. Procedure against offences may accordingly be distinguished into procedure *ad puniendum* and procedure *ad satisfaciendum*: and this again into procedure *ad compensandum*, procedure *ad compescendum*, and procedure *ad avertendum*. All these several courses will sometimes run separate for a considerable way: at other times they will co-incide: so that one and the same proceeding, and one and the same law enjoining it, shall answer all those purposes.

Procedure *in compensandum—compescendum—avertendum.*

120. In the same manner also, this additional apparatus of adjective laws will require a correspondent prediction to be annexed to the directive part of the substantive law: the clause containing such prediction may be termed *the satisfactive clause*. As the business of the comminative clause of a substantive law is to give notice of the punitory law, so is it of the satisfactive clause to give notice what is done by any or all of the three abovementioned species of remedial laws, with the help of the several trains of remoter subsidiary laws that come respectively in their suite.[1]

Satisfactive clause added to the substantive law.

[a] As in the case of wrongful confinement; by deliverance: of wrongful banishment; by recal: of wrongful non-investment, interception or divestment of trust, property or condition; by investment. These are among the cases in which the offence is a *continued* act:[a] and the *catapaustic* law requires to be executed before the *punitory*.

In regard to public offences, the provisions contained in the British Statute commonly called the Riot Act {1 Geo. 1. stat. 2. ch. 5} (provisions for the suppression of riots upon the spot) are of the catapaustic kind. In the case of wrongful confinement, the provisions in the English statute commonly called the *Habeas Corpus* Act {31 Car. 2. c. 2} are also of a catapaustic nature. There are provisions of the same nature in the same case in the Code of Constitutional Law established by Catherine 2[d] for the government of certain provinces of the Russian Empire. See Reglements de Cath. 2de, Ch. 26. art. 401. Liege. 1777.[2]

[a] Ch. 7. {Actions} 16.[3]

[1] Paragraphs 121–2 of the 'prinicpal draft' have not been located. The pagination indicates that there are four pages missing at this point.

[2] See *Réglements de Sa Majesté Impériale Catherine II, pour L'Administration des Gouvernements de l'Empire des Russies*, pp. 160–1.

[3] See *An Introduction to the Principles of Morals and Legislation* (*CW*), Ch. VII, para. 16, p. 78.

§. 16. *Idea of a compleat law.*

The definition of a compleat law varies according to the fullness of the pattern.

123. We are now prepared for endeavouring to fix what may be termed the *individuality* of a law. Now the individuality of a law results from the *integrality* and the *unity* of it laid together. To fix the individuality of a law, then, is to ascertain what a portion of legislative matter must amount [to] in order on the one hand not to contain less, on the other hand not to contain more, than one whole law. And first with regard to the integrality or compleatness of it.

It may have been observed already that there are laws of different patterns which are of different degrees of fullness: the description of a compleat law will, therefore, depend upon the pattern it is of. 1. It may consist merely of a directive part without an incitative: which is the case where, having no subsidiary laws belonging to it, all the force it has depends upon what it derives from the auxiliary sanctions. 2. It may have an incitative part as well as a directive: which incitative part again may consist, as we have seen,[1] either of a comminative part alone, or of an invitative part alone, or of both together. 3. It may have temperative clauses annexed to it; which again, as hath been shewn,[2] may be either extenuative or aggravative. 4. It may in certain cases have satisfactive clauses annexed to it; which is the case when it has a set of remedial laws for its appendages: which laws again may, as hath been shewn,[3] be any of them either of a compensative, catapaustic or metaphylactic nature. Of all these parts, the only essential one is the directive: as to the rest, it may be provided either with all of them together, or with any one or more of them, as it may happen.

A law of the first or narrowest pattern, in what respects it may be compleat or incompleat.

124. To begin, then, with a law of the first and narrowest pattern; a law which consists solely of a directive part: when is it that such a law can be pronounced compleat? A law is either obligative or de-obligative. These must be consider'd separately: since what is said of the one will not apply exactly to the other.

A law may be consider'd as capable of being compleat or incompleat in either of three respects: in point of expression, in point of connection, and in point of design: it may be compleatly or incompleatly expressed, put together, or imagined. Now, compleatness is a word of reference: it supposes a standard of

[1] See §13, para. 91, p. 143 above.

[2] The subject of temperative clauses has not hitherto been discussed, but for the distinction between extenuating and aggravating circumstances see *An Introduction to the Principles of Morals and Legislation* (*CW*), Ch. VII, para. 27, pp. 82–3, and Appendix D, para. 136, pp. 270–1 below.

[3] See §15, para. 118, pp. 165–7 above.

reference: this standard, then, may be either what actually was the will entertained by the legislator relative to the matters in question, or what on a certain contingency it is supposed would have been his will: his *actual* will as it may be stiled, or his *hypothetical* will. In the first and second case, the standard referred to is of the former kind: in the third case, of the latter.

125. First, then, with regard to the compleatness of a law in point of *expression*: the standard of reference being what is supposed to be the actual will of the legislator. When is it that that will, with respect to any act, is to be deemed to be compleatly expressed? how much of the matter contained in the whole code goes to make up the expression of that one will? Now, in every obligative law there must be an imperative provision: if, with respect to any act, there be no such provision in the code, there is no law concerning it. But this provision may stand unqualified or qualified: unexpounded or expounded. If it be unexpounded as well as unqualified, it is a compleat law of itself: if it has expositions, it is not compleat without those expositions: if qualifications, without those qualifications. As to any such expository or qualificative provision, it is plain it can not, so long as it continues in that form, be a compleat law. It may indeed be thrown, as we have seen,[a] into the form of an independent provision: and then, if it be of the obligative stamp, it is imperative, and as such is capable of being a compleat law; yet, then, not without leaving out of the code all such provisions, if any, as are subalternately or *pro tanto* contradictive with regard to it: that is without leaving out all other provisions in the code, if any, which apply to it in the shape of a qualification. 1. in point of expression.

To recur to the old example. 'It is to be deemed exportation whether the conveyance be by water or by land.'[b] This, it is plain, could never be a compleat law. Nor this, 'where the market price is above 44[s] a quarter.'[c] Nor yet this: 'Unless it be exported for the use of the King's armies.' Nor in short this, 'Provided a license from the first magistrate of the place have been previously obtained.' Indeed, the first of these provisions, which, when applied to the clause 'no man shall export wheat,' is a limitation,

[a] supra | |.[1]
[b] supra | |;[2] see infra Separation.[3]
[c] supra [68].[4]

[1] See §12, para. 85, pp. 138–9 above.

[2] For the 'old example' see, for instance, §12, para. 57, pp. 118–19 above. The distinction between export by sea and by land is also mentioned explicitly in Appendix B, p. 243 below.

[3] See §18, pp. 198–200 below.

[4] MS '63' is a slip. See pp. 124–5 above.

may be converted into an exception.[a] 'Any man may export wheat when the price is not above 44[s] a quarter.' But this provision is not of the imperative stamp, and on that account can not, in the nature of things, constitute an independent law: it supposes some other provision which is imperative and with which it is connected in the capacity either of an introduction[b] or a qualification. For the same reason, neither can the provision 'unless it be exported for the use of the King's armies' appear in the character of a compleat law. The only one of the above provisions which can appear in that shape is the last of all—'Provided a license from the first magistrate of the place be previously obtained.' This, being a limitation to a former provision which was de-obligative, may be thrown into the form of an exception, which, when placed upon an independent footing, will turn out to be obligative, that is imperative. 'No man who has not obtained a license &c. shall export wheat, where the market price &c. is more than 44[s] a quarter.' This is capable of standing in the capacity of a compleat law. So, likewise, is the leading unqualified provision: 'no man shall export wheat:' and it will actually be a compleat law, however improvident and inexpedient, if in the whole code there be no other provision respecting the exportation of that commodity.

In a compleat code there can be no law that is not compleat.

126. It follows that, were a legislator to take a book of any size whatsoever, containing any quantity of imperative matter whatsoever, and exhibit it as comprehending a compleat collection of all the laws he thinks proper should be looked upon as being in force, as many imperative provisions as it contained would, with the help of such qualifications as were to be found, be all and every [one] of them compleat laws: I mean always in point of expression: in this point, the laws in a compleat code, such as they are, can not be otherwise than compleat. For from what other sources can his will be collected, than from the signs, and those the only ones, which he has made choice of to express it? In searching after his will, there may be occasion indeed to travel from one passage of this instrument to another: but out of this instrument, so long as the words of it are intelligible, there can be no pretence for travelling. If, indeed, there should be any words in it which, notwithstanding every thing that can be done in the view of collecting the import of them from the instrument itself, still continue ambiguous or unintelligible, in such case, as a means of finding out the sense

[a] v. supra | |.[1]
[b] supra 73.[2]

[1] See para. 69, p. 125 above.

[2] See pp. 129–30 above.

of them, it may indeed be necessary to have recourse to some other instrument. But such explanatory instrument can not be said to detract from the compleatness of the principal one consider'd as a book of law. If it could, then a common dictionary might be consider'd as a book of law. The evidence derived from any such foreign source, being only presumptive evidence, can never be consider'd as outweighing any direct intrinsic evidence that may be to be had from the body of the code itself. To recur to the old instance of a law against the exportation of corn. A doubt arises what sort of articles are to be understood under the name of corn: whether *maiz*, for example, is to be looked upon as included in the number. The opinions of persons conversant in the trade being doubtful or divided, a dictionary of commerce or a dictionary of botany is recurred to; and it there appears that maiz is looked upon as a species of the commodity in question. The law being totally silent, the interpretation thus obtained may be consider'd as conclusive, without any disparagement to the compleatness of the law. This, however, could never be the case if the contrary sense could justly be collected from any passage contained in the law itself. In such case, to decide according to the dictionary would be to deny the compleatness of the code, and recognizing the author of the dictionary as being *pro tanto* the superior legislator.

127. Secondly, with regard to the compleatness of a law in point of *connection*. A single law, even of the narrowest pattern, may consist, and as we shall see more particularly hereafter,[a] will usually consist of a great multitude of provisions: a greater multitude by far than from any thing that has hitherto been observed would easily be suspected. These provisions, in order to have the effect they are designed to have, it is necessary that the influence they are meant to have on one another should, by some means or other, be made appear. This there are two ways of doing: the one is by making them follow one another in the same instrument without interruption: this may be stiled connection by juxta-position: the other is by sending the reader from the place at which the chain of provisions is broken off, to the place where it is resumed again: this may be stiled connection by reference.[b] In the first case, the order [2. in point of connection.]

[a] infra | |.[1]

[b] I say nothing here of the connection that may be established by the use of the particles called conjunctions (as mentioned above[a]) between a leading provision

[a] supra [70 n.][2]

[1] A cross-reference, perhaps, to para. 131, pp. 176–8 below.

[2] MS '69' is a slip. See p. 126 n. above.

in which it is meant the ideas should occur is pointed out by the order of the signs: in the latter case, by instructions given on purpose. The first is neither usual, nor in general, for reasons that will appear hereafter,[a] is it practicable: to the other method there can be no objection. A law, then, how compleat so ever in itself, is never compleatly adapted to its purpose, whatsoever that purpose be, until it be compleatly put together. This operation, which ought so evidently to be practised upon all laws, has never yet been performed perhaps upon any: why? because the idea of such a body must first have been formed, before the members of it can have been put together. At present, open what code you will, pitch upon what law you will, the parts of it lie scatter'd up and down at random, some under one head, some under another, with little or no notice taken of their mutual relations and dependencies.

3. in point of design: which may happen through want 1. of discrimination: or 2. of amplitude, original or residuary.

128. Thirdly, with regard to the compleatness of the law in point of *design*: that is with reference to what would, it is supposed, have been the will of the legislator had such or such a case been present to his view. Every law that is made may be said to have been made upon the consideration of some mischief:[b] of a sort of mischief regarded as being apt to ensue from the sort of act which the legislator is thereby induced to prohibit: which general idea of mischief must originally have been suggested by the idea of some particular mischief which appeared to result from some particular act of the sort in question.[c] In as far, then, as the general idea

and a limitative or exceptive clause that qualifies it: these will not answer the purpose unless the principal and the qualificative clause be contiguous.

[a] infra §. 5.[1]

[b] I say of some *mischief*: for on whatever principle he acts, something or other which, to him at least, presents itself in the light of a mischief it must be his design to obviate: else he would be acting without a motive. This motive, if he abuses his trust, may be a merely selfish one: still, however, it is the view of something which, with reference to himself at least, appears in the character of a mischief that is his motive.

To avoid embarassment, I forbear making any separate mention of a law of the *agathopoietic* stamp;[*a*] I mean a law of which the sole object is to make an addition in some way or other to the quantity of positive good there is in the community: in this case, the absence of the good as yet unattained may be consider'd as the mischief.

[c] Our ideas originate all of them from the senses: our ideas of mischief and the causes of it, as well as any other. Imagination may do something: but it must

[*a*] See Ch. 16. {Division}.[2]

---

[1] This theme is discussed in §18, pp. 198–200 below, which Bentham at one point intended would form §5 of the text.

[2] See *An Introduction to the Principles of Morals and Legislation* (*CW*), Ch. XVI, OFFENCES against the POSITIVE INCREASE of the NATIONAL FELICITY, para. 54 n., p. 262 n.

which (to judge from the act as described in the prohibition) he appears to have formed to himself of the mischief of the case deviates from that which, from the view of that case, it is thought he should and might have formed to himself, in so far the law may be looked upon as incompleat in point of design. If, then, the law be consider'd as deviating from the standard thus assigned, it must be consider'd as deviating from it in one or other of two ways: as falling short of it, or as stretching beyond it: in the former case, it may be said to be deficient or incompleat in point of *amplitude*; in the latter, in point of *discrimination*. Now, the amplitude of a law depends jointly upon the several constituent parts of it: that is upon the imperative provision, and upon the qualifying clauses. If, then, in point of amplitude the law is deficient, it may be so from either of two causes: because the class of acts which is taken for the object of the imperative provision is originally too narrow; or because, although originally perhaps it was wide enough, it has been render'd too narrow by the improper bearing and extent of some qualifying clause or clauses. In the former case, the law may be said to fall short in point of original amplitude; in the latter case, in point of residuary amplitude.

Example of a law incompleat in point of design.

129. 'Whoso draweth blood in the streets shall be severely punished.'[a] This is a law which may serve at the same time as an example of every fault in point of extent of which a law is susceptible: want of original amplitude; want of proper discrimination: and want of residuary amplitude through improper discrimination. 1. Want of original amplitude. For drawing blood is but one out of a great variety of ways in which a mischief the same in substance may be produced: a bruise, a scald, a burn, and so forth

always have experience or observation or report, that is it must have sense, as a ground to work upon. It follows, then, that there never can have been such a thing as a law which did not owe it's establishment originally to the view of some particular mischief: the mischief resulting from some individual occurrence. In a nation of Struldbruggs,[c] there would be no such thing, we may presume, as a law against homicide: in a republic of angels, against angelicide: nor in one of devils, against diabolicide. The laws which are to be found in the Jewish code against certain impurities are a conclusive proof, as hath been observed, of the prevalence of them among that people, or else, it should have been added, among some of the nations they were acquainted with.

[a] It is given as a law of Bologna, by Puffendorf, B. v. Ch. 12. §. 8. who quotes for it Everhard. *loc. legal.* 8. *ab absurdo*.[1]

[c] Gulliver's Voyage to Laputa.[2]

---

[1] Samuel Pufendorf, *De jure naturae et gentium*, Lund, 1672, p. 718, citing Nicolaus Everard, *Topicorum seu de locis legalibus Liber*, Louvain, 1516, fo. XXI.

[2] In Jonathan Swift, *Gulliver's Travels* (first published 1726), Part III, Ch. X, the Struldbruggs, who live in the kingdom of Luggnagg, are immortal.

may be as hurtful as a wound. 2. Want of proper discrimination. For how many disorders are there with which a man is as liable to be seized in the streets as any where else for which instant bleeding is the only remedy?[a] And what if a man has no other way of defending or otherwise saving his life or limbs, or a woman her chastity? 3. Want of residuary amplitude through improper discrimination. For why must the act be confined to the streets in order to come within the censure of the law? Is it less mischievous if committed in the market-place, or in a church? These cases are but a few out of a multitude which might be alledged under every one of the above heads of imperfection.[b] This instance I chose not as an uncommon but as a simple one: for the difficulty (I might have said the impossibility) is not to find laws that are incompleat in this point, but to find such as are compleat.

Interpretation strict—liberal—liberal, extensive—restrictive.

130. These distinctions may enable us to form an idea somewhat more precise perhaps than has ever yet been given hitherto of what is commonly meant by interpretation: of the real nature and proper limits of that practise, of the necessity of it, of the mischief of it, and of the method to be taken for obviating the mischief by superseding the necessity.[c]

If the will which a legislator manifests with relation to a given act fails of being what it ought to be, such failure (want of power being here out of the question) must arise from one or other of two causes: the state of his understanding, or the state of his affections.[d] In the former case, it must be owing either to inadvertency, or to wrong judgment: the facts which may go to constitute, or those which may serve to controul, the mischief may not have been, all of them, present to his *apprehension*: or being present, the judgment formed by him concerning their existence or their tendency may have been a wrong one.

[a] In the case quoted by Puffendorf, a passenger being taken ill in the streets, a Surgeon bled him: and for so doing was prosecuted upon that Statute. Under the same Statute, the good Samaritan, had he made use of bleeding, might have met with the same fate.[1]

[b] For cases that call for provisions of an exemptive nature see Ch. 13. {Cases unmeet}.[2]

[c] v. infra §. [21].[3]

[d] v. Ch. 16. {Division}.[4] Ch. 18. {Indirect Legislation}.[5]

---

[1] For the parable of the Good Samaritan see Luke 10: 25–37.

[2] See *An Introduction to the Principles of Morals and Legislation* (*CW*), Ch. XIII, pp. 158–64.

[3] MS '8'. See pp. 219–33 below. For the renumbering of the sections of the work during its composition see the Editorial Introduction, pp. xvi–xviii above.

[4] See *An Introduction to the Principles of Morals and Legislation* (*CW*), Ch. XVI, pp. 187–280, though this precise point does not appear to be made therein.

[5] i.e. Bentham's projected Chapter of that title: for further details see the Editorial Introduction, p. xii above.

Interpretation may be distinguished into *strict* and *liberal*. It may be stiled strict where you attribute to the legislator the will which, at the time of making the law, as you suppose, he really entertained. It may be stiled liberal where the will you attribute to him is not that which, you suppose, he really entertained, but a will which, as you suppose, he failed of entertaining, only through inadvertency: insomuch that, had the individual case which calls for interpretation been present to his view, he would have entertained that will, which, by the interpretation put upon his law, you act up to, as if it had been his in reality.

I say through inadvertency: for to attribute to the legislator a will which you suppose him to have failed of entertaining through any other cause than inadvertency, that is from wrong judgment or perverse affections, and to act accordingly, is not to interpret the law, but to act against it: which, in a judge or other officer invested with powers of a public nature, is as much as to over-rule it.[a]

[a] It is a common thing among lawyers to speak of the power of interpretation as a power that may be exercised by some persons and not by others: *Cujus est condere ejus est interpretari*:[1] or that ought to be exercised in some cases but not in others. Espr. des loix, L. VI. ch. 3.[2] The persons they had in view must have been persons in authority: persons invested with the judiciary, or some other branch of public power. The mode of interpretation they had in view must also have been that which is here distinguished by the name of liberal: for that which is here called strict is no more than what every man must put upon a law in order to obey it.

A liberal interpretation built on any other ground than that of inadvertency, approaches very near to an act of autocratic power, and thence also in some measure to an act of legislation: to an act of autocratic power, in virtue of the effects of any particular order which, in consequence of the interpretation, comes to be issued in the particular cause in the course of which the law supposed to be interpreted came to be referred to: to an act of legislation, in as far as the decision grounded on such particular interpretation is likely to be adopted as a standard of decision in succeeding causes. By what restrictions an order thus irregularly grounded would be distinguished from a perfectly autocratic order, is a point that could not be settled without entering into details that belong to the head of constitutional law.[a] These restraints, whatever they were, would be very apt to be

[a] The executive power thus exercised approaches to the nature of autocratic power in as far as the effects of it, when exercised, are confined to the individual case in which it is exercised: to that of legislative power in as far as the exercise of it in that instance comes to serve as a rule of decision in subsequent cases which are deemed of the same sort. It thereby gives birth to a rule of customary law, which, in order to be conceived, must be represented in the form of a statutory provision connecting in some way or other with the law interpreted.

---

[1] i.e. 'He that makes the law ought to interpret it', a maxim of Roman law based on *Code of Justinian*, I. xiv. 12. 2.

[2] See Montesquieu, *Spirit of the Laws*, trans. Nugent, Bk. VI, Ch. III, entitled 'In what Governments and in what cases the judges ought to determine according to the express letter of the Law.'

It appears, then, that to interpret a law according to the liberal mode of interpretation is *pro tanto* to apply to the imperative provision either an extensive or a qualificative clause: interpretation, when liberal, may accordingly be distinguished into extensive and restrictive. To interpret it liberally is accordingly to charge it with being deficient either in point of amplitude, or in point of discrimination: in point of amplitude, if the interpretation be extensive; in point of discrimination, if restrictive.

In either case, thus to interpret a law is to alter it: *interpretation* being put by a sort of euphemism for *alteration*. Now, to extend an old law is in fact to establish a new law: as on the other hand to qualify the old law is *pro tanto* to destroy it. The only circumstance that can serve to distinguish the alteration itself when made in this way from alteration at large is, that the alteration goes no farther than from what it appears was the legislator's will to what, it is supposed, would have been his will had the case in question been present to his view: from his actual to his hypothetical will. If, then, there is a new law made, it is made, however, upon the pattern, and with some of the materials, of the old: if there is part of the old law destroy'd, it is such part only as he himself, it is supposed, would have destroy'd, had the particular case in question come before him.

A law takes more words to compleat it than an ordinary command—why.

131. From what has been said, it appears that, with regard to completeness, whether in point of expression, in point of connection, or in point of design, a law of the pattern here in question, viz: the narrowest pattern, stands on precisely the same footing as any ordinary command: whatever is necessary to give compleatness to any such command, just so much and no more is necessary to give compleatness to a law.

If this were the case, it might be objected that any trifling command whatever which any private person, in consequence of any of the most trivial incidents of private life, have occasion to give, for example to his servant, might stand as a model of a compleat law: and that such phrases as 'light the fire,' or 'put the fire out,' or 'open the window,' might be as proper as any other: but what similarity, it will be said, between commands so simple and the long-winded and voluminous expressions of will which there will hereinafter[1] be occasion to allude to in the character of laws? The case is that, with regard to the extreme simplicity observable in the

removed by artifice and collusion: such, for instance, as was practised by the Decemvir Appius in order to get possession of Virginia.[2]

[1] Presumably in the projected penal code.

[2] Livy, *Ab urbe condita*, III. xliv–lviii.

commands just specified, it is to their individuality that they are indebted for it: the act which they seek to have performed is the act of a determinate individual performable on a given and determinate occasion. Now, the individual occasion on which you command an individual act to be performed being given, the circumstances (I mean the material circumstances) with which it is attended may be all of them before your eyes: seeing what they are, you have no need to particularize them: seeing that, whatever other circumstances there might be which, if present, might give a different turn to your inclination, there are none, however, that in fact *are* present, you give command accordingly: and that without saying any thing about the circumstances: to say what it might have been your pleasure should have been done in a case which you see does not exist would be idle and superfluous. But legislative command can not do less than extend to a class of persons:[a] it therefore extends to a class of acts not individually assignable and, therefore, to be performed, if at all, in circumstances, that is on occasions, not individually assignable. Being, then, a legislator, you can not tell what individual circumstances, what individual incidents, every individual act of the number of those which you command to be performed, it actually *will* be accompanied with: you must, therefore, consider what incidents it *may* be accompanied with, and if you find any upon the happening of which you would not think proper to have the act performed, you must set them down in the character of exceptive circumstances.

History affords two examples, the one of a particular command, the other of a general law to the same effect, which, when laid together, will be well enough suited to [illustrate] this. Philip 3[d] of Spain, sitting one day by the fire side and finding himself too hot, called to one of his Lords in waiting, and said to him, 'Put out the fire.'[b] Here, then, is a command which might very well be utter'd in the same concise and unqualified form of words in which it is here exhibited: and that without affording the least proof of any want of circumspection. But if it be true what is related of William the

[a] supra 49.[1]

[b] The Marquis de Pobar. Upon the Marquis's excusing himself on the score of the etiquette which did not admitt of his interfering in a business of that sort, Philip, thinking it beneath his dignity to stir, sat on till he contracted a disorder of which he died. Bielfeld Instit. Politiques, tom. IV. ch. 3. §47.[2]

---

[1] This paragraph of the 'principal draft' has not been located: see p. 94 n. above. The subject is, however, discussed extensively in §11, pp. 98–114 above.

[2] See Baron de Bielfeld, *Institutions politiques, ouvrage Où l'on traite de la Société Civile; Des Loix, de la Police, des Finances, du Commerce, des Forces d'un État; Et en général de tout ce qui a rapport au Gouvernement* (first published 1760), 4 vols., Paris, 1762, iv. 176–7.

Conqueror, that in the same peremptory and unqualified manner, and with the same silence with regard to exceptions, he commanded all his English subjects without distinction at a certain time at night to do the like,[a] a law to that effect would hardly be produced as an example of one compleat in point of design. What if a man be sick in the house and fire be necessary to prepare physic for his relief? what if money be coining at the mint, what if arms be forging in the arsenal, and the exigencies of the state admitt of no interruption in the process? These and a variety of other exceptions that might be imagined serve to shew how great a difference there must be in point of simplicity between a general law and any individual command of the number of those which might be included under it, before the former can, in point of design, be as compleat and perfect as the latter.

Unity of a law. **132.** So much with regard to the compleatness or integrality of a law of the pattern in question: the unity of it is a matter that follows of course. Let a certain quantity of discourse be recognized as constituting one compleat law, if any thing more be added, it makes it a law and something more. This something more will either be of the nature of law or not: if it be, it admitts of the following variations.

1. It may amount to one other entire law, and no more.

2. It may amount to a certain part or parts of one other entire law and no more.

3. It may amount to several laws all of them entire.

4. It may amount to several parts of laws without including any entire ones.

5. It may amount to one entire law, and a part or parts of one other entire law.

6. It may amount to one entire law, and a part or parts of so many other laws together.

7. It may amount to several entire laws, together with a part of some one entire law.

8. It may amount to several entire laws, together with a part or parts of so many other laws together.[1]

Language on this head unsteady. **133.**[2] This detail it may be of use to advert to on occasion as a

[a] Spelmann's Gloss[y] *verbo* CURFEW.[3]

---

[1] For a later draft of the remainder of the section see Appendix D, pp. 268–73 below.

[2] MS orig. '109' represents an earlier sequence of paragraph enumeration. The text which constitutes the remainder of this section and § 17 carries the earlier enumeration, which, for the sake of clarity, has been silently amended in order to form a continuous sequence with the preceding part of the 'principal draft'. For further details see the Editorial Introduction, p. xxvii above.

[3] Spelman, *Archæologus. In modum Glossarii*, p. 195.

clue to the process of analyzing the contents of any given quantity of legal matter. A consideration, however, that must never be lost sight of is that the integrality and unity of a law is dependent in a great measure on the choice of the words that are made use of to express it: that the unity of the law will depend upon the unity of the species of act which is the object of it: consequently, that the description of the former will be liable to all the unsteadiness to which that of the latter has been shewn already to be liable.[a] According, for example, to the words that are employ'd, the several articles in a cluster of offences, whereof one or more are consider'd as principal and the rest as accessory, might be spoken of as coming under one and the same law, or under so many different laws, and that whether they be offences of one and the same person or of so many different persons. Assassination is forbidden: the hiring of assassins is forbidden also: is it by one and the same law that these offences are forbidden, or by two? In like manner, fabrication of spurious deeds and the publication of them: perjury and the subornation of that crime. No genus of offence however narrow but may be distinguished into species: the genus was comprised under one law; do the species come under one law or under several? Frauds are forbidden in the lump: among frauds are distinguished defraudment by short weight or measure, defraudment by bad coin, defraudment by forgery of deeds, defraudment by imposture in the way of begging, defraudment in the way of gaming, defraudment in the way of insurance, and so on; is it by one law that this is done, or by several? The instability of language is a source of doubt and controversy against which the legislator can not be too much upon his guard.

A law with a comminative part, when compleat in point of connection.

134. Let us now consider the laws which are made upon the second of the patterns abovementioned: where the directive part is armed, as it were, by a commination.[1] As the directive part is an expression of will: a declaration of what it is the wish of the legislator should take place: so the comminative part is an expression of an act of the understanding, an expression of belief; a declaration of what, according to the belief of the legislator, will take place, in consequence of certain measures which, if he says true, he himself has taken. As the former, then, in order to be compleat, must be a full and faithful picture of the legislator's

[a] See Ch. 7. {Actions}.[2]

[1] See para. 123, p. 168 above.

[2] See *An Introduction to the Principles of Morals and Legislation* (*CW*), Ch. VII, pp. 74–83, esp. para. 20, p. 79.

mind, so the latter must be a full and faithful picture as to what regards the probability of the event predicted, in as far as futurity can be the subject of a picture. The commination is a prediction of an event which it is designed should take place in consequence of a man's committing the offence: of an event which is to happen not at any rate, but only in case such and such other events do, and such and such others again do not, take place: that is in case all the several regulations of procedure are complied with, the observance of which is necessary to the legality of the sentence and the execution of the punishment: in case none of those events happens to take place, the happening of which is invested by the law with the character of an exemptive circumstance: and so on with respect to circumstances dis-exemptive and re-exemptive, through as many alternations as there shall be found occasion to establish.

The directive part of the law forbids a man to steal: the comminative part says if he does, he shall be hanged. The punitory subsidiary law goes on and says, that such or such a kind of Judge shall cause him so to die. What, then, is a thief sure to be hanged *at any rate*? no, says the comminative part as applying to a law of procedure, he shall *not, if* a clerk in drawing the instrument of accusation chances or chooses to write one word instead of another: *unless*, says another law, the court chooses to let the wrong word be struck out and a proper one inserted in the room of it. The directive part of the law forbids a man to committ perjury: the comminative part says if he does, he shall be pilloried. Yes, says a law of procedure, and so too shall a man who is innocent of theft if, being charged with it and sent for in order to answer, he does not appear: unless, says another law of procedure, the King's advocate will let him put himself upon his trial.

So many exemptive circumstances as are established, so many incidents there are that may fall out between the cup of punishment and the lip of the offender. Say, then, that an offender will be punished at all events, and you say what is not true. He will not be punished, not a grain of the punishment will ever reach him, if any of those events take place the happening of which is invested by the law with the quality of an exemptive circumstance. It follows that the prediction which the comminative clause consists of, that this prediction, I say, if utter'd absolutely, is not true: to bring it within the pale of truth, qualifications limiting in a proper manner the generality of it, qualifications holding up to view the events in question in the exemptive character which they are invested with, must in some way or other be subjoined to it. One way of doing this, and that as natural an one as any, is by making references to the several laws of procedure by which they stand invested with that character.[1]

135. So much with regard to the integrality of a law made according to this second pattern. As to the unity, it may be sufficiently made out from what has been said already.[a] Unity of an obligative law of the 2[d] pattern.

136. With regard to the integrality or the unity of a law made upon either of the two last of the four patterns above specified, nothing in particular need be remarked. A law, if it has temperative provisions annexed to it, to be compleat must exhibit those provisions: if it has remedial appendages, it must contain a satisfactive clause or clauses referring to those appendages. Integrality and unity of obligative laws of the two remaining patterns.

137. We come now to the case where the law is of the de-obligative kind; that is either a countermand or a repermission. Where the law bears either of these aspects, it is evident enough that the first of the four patterns abovementioned is the only one to which it can be made conformable.[2] In this case the integrality and unity of it are so intimately connected that it will be sufficient to speak of them together. A law of this sort presupposing the existence of a preceding law, the amplitude of it is of course determined by the amplitude of that which it presupposes. — of a de-obligative law.

The application, then, of a superventitious de-obligatory law to the primordial obligative one in respect of unity is susceptible of the four following cases: either

1. The former covers the latter exactly: or

2. It covers it in part only, and without any where over-hanging it: or

3. It covers it throughout, over-hanging it at the same time: or

4. It over-hangs it in one quarter, while it falls short of it in another.

In the first case, the act which before was commanded or prohibited being now left free, all the apparatus of qualifying clauses, of punitory and remedial laws and the laws that are respectively subsidiary to them, and consequently of comminative, exemptive &c., and of satisfactive clauses belonging to the substantive law, as also whatever temperative clauses may belong to it, fall to the ground of course.

[a] supra | |.[3]

[1] In the text, Bentham has written the following note, bearing the marginal heading '—in point of design', at this point: 'To be compleat in point of design, all the exemptive clauses expressive of all the grounds of exemption (cases unmeet &c.) should be set down.'

[2] Bentham has crossed through the remainder of the paragraph, and noted in the margin: 'If the superventitious law is not de-obligative *in toto*, it is only qualificative: if it is, then by destroying the mandate, the qualifications fall to the ground of course, or rather reign in its stead.'

[3] See para. 132, p. 178 above.

In the second case, the de-obligatory law in question operates only in the light of a qualification to the primordial: investing some circumstance or other with the character of a limitative or exceptive circumstance with reference to the act commanded or prohibited by the primordial mandate: and consequently with the character of an exculpative circumstance with reference to the offence constituted by that mandate: As to its effects upon the punitory and remedial laws that may be subsidiary to the substantive law in question, they may be analysed in the same manner by considering them as so many distinct laws: and so likewise with regard to any temperative clauses.

In the third case, to analyse the effect of the de-obligatory law, it must be resolved into two: the one destructive of the primordial mandatory law in question as in the first case: the other either destructive or qualificative of some other mandate or mandates.

In the fourth case, the effect of it is the same as in the third: with only this difference, that it is qualificative only of the primordial law in question, instead of being destructive.

Obligative laws the only standards to measure by.

138. Thus much with regard to the case of a de-obligative law, that nothing might appear to be left unnoticed. To have a clear conception, however, of the state of the whole system of legislation at any period, it is upon the obligative laws alone that the spectator should fix his eye: it is by them that he should measure the number and extent of the laws that are in force during a given period in a given state, and thereby of the obligations to which the members of that state are subject. It is owing merely to the changes which the will of the legislator is liable to undergo with respect to the same act at different periods that laws of the de-obligative kind are susceptible of any separate consideration: were it not for this, the effect produced by them might be produced in a better manner by more simple methods: where the primordial law or any determinate part of it is destroy'd, declare it repealed and throw it out of the code:[a] where the former is made to receive a

[a] I pass over the temporary provisions that may be requisite to be established, in order to prevent the abolition from having the effect of an *ex post facto* law, upon acts done under the authority of that which is abolished. For these see Append. tit. {Digestion} and {Conservation}.[1] Meantime, lest it should be found [too][2] difficult to apprehend how any danger should result from a law which of itself does no more than leave a man at liberty, it may be proper just to hint, that in many cases there are obligative laws which are commonly looked upon as annexed of course to de-obligative: thus a law exempting a man from punishment is understood to include, as it were, a law forbidding all other persons from

[1] i.e. projected Appendices to the penal code.

[2] MS 'to'.

qualifying clause, insert the clause in the same manner as if that and the rest of the law so qualified had from the very beginning made but one.

This is not only the most eligible method, but the most simple: the most common, however, is to let the new and the old lie all in a confused heap together, the de-obligative and the obligative, the slaying and the slain. To what causes, then, is so slovenly a practise to be ascribed? to the nature of the things themselves? by no means; but to causes more accidental and less irremediable: to the want of exertion or skill on the part of the legislator, where there is but one:[1] to the same causes, added to the want of concert, where there are many. Now, for supplying the second of these deficiencies there can not be a more effectual expedient than the laying down, if possible, a precise idea of the integrality and unity of a law. This done, the legislator's task will be comparatively a light one. He may then with ease penetrate to the bottom of the whole mass of law, distinguish the several laws which enter into it's composition, extricate them from their mutual entanglements, and determine at any time by a glance which are and which are not affected by any new provision that presents itself.

What is necessary to make it appear compleat.

139. Thus much in the way of description: a word or two here may not be amiss in the way of caution. It is not enough that the law be really compleat: to have the effect of a compleat law, it should be made to appear such in the eyes of those who are concerned in it: to the subject citizen who is to take it, that is to take the whole of it together, for the measure of his conduct; to the Judge who is to take it for the measure of his decision: and to the legislator, who, in order to know whether any thing that is requisite remains to be done, should be able to see at a moment's glance what it is he hath done. It ought accordingly to be consigned to paper, and that in such a form that any one who opens a volume of the code may lay his finger upon it and say, this is one law: and that is another: here the first of them begins, and there ends: here are all the parts, and these together are what make the whole of it.

In what respects laws are apt to fail of being compleat in this point.

140.[2] This being the description of a compleat law, where, then, it may naturally be asked, is there a specimen of such a law to be

inflicting on him the punishment he is excepted from. There is no punishment, the infliction of which, were it not for the law which expressly commands it to be inflicted, would not be an offence.

[1] In the margin, in relation to the preceding part of this paragraph, Bentham has noted in pencil: 'Qu.', i.e. 'Quere?'

[2] In relation to the whole of paragraph 140, Bentham has noted: 'Qu.'

met with? I answer—nowhere. Before any such specimen can be found, a perfect plan of legislation must first have been produced: perfect in point of method at least, whatever it be in point of matter. If, in this view, we cast an eye over the current systems of legislation, and observe the laws that are contained in them, we shall find them marked, all of them, more or less with the following deficiencies.

1. The inculpative circumstances, being in many instances lumped together in one word along with the description of the physical act, have in those instances perhaps never, and in others but seldom, been perfectly developped: this is the case, for instance, with such words as theft, murder, robbery, fraud, extortion, peculation: words of which no tolerable definition seems ever yet to have been given.[1]

2. Of the circumstances to which the effect of exculpative circumstances ought to have been given, a great part have remained unheeded.

3. Of the punishment, instead of it's being chosen and fixed by the legislator according to the nature of the offence, it has often happen'd that no mention has been made: so that the law would have remained impotent had not the judge assumed the place of the legislator.

4. To many circumstances the legislator has given or suffer'd the Judge to give the effect of exemptive, disexemptive, convictive or [re-integrative][2] circumstances, without placing them formally to that account, and frequently, as it would seem, without so much as perceiving them to be attended with that effect.

5. For want of observing the many differences which the intervention of so many different circumstances may make in the mischief of the offence, or by other means in the demand for punishment, he has invested few or none with the character of aggravative or extenuative circumstances: so that either no temperament at all has been applied, or none but what has depended upon the casual observation and fluctuating discretion of the judge.

[1] In the margin, Bentham has noted at this point: 'either the generic term has not been well chosen or the exculpative and inculpative circumstances have not been developped and expressed'.

[2] MS 'redintegrative'.

§17. *No customary law compleat.*

141. If it be thus with the statute law, how is it, let any one imagine, with the customary?[1] A customary law is not expressed in words: in what words should it present itself? it has no parts: how should it exhibit any? It is one single indivisible act, capable of all manner of constructions.[a] Under the customary law there can

A customary law can never be compleat.

[a] supra [115.][2]

---

[1] Bentham has failed to indicate precisely where the following passage at UC lxxxviii. 341, which is intended for a footnote and carries the marginal heading 'Unaccommodatingness of the customary law', should appear in the text: 'This is not a place to enter into a compleat detail of the imperfections of the customary law: for such a discussion the proper place seems to be the title of *Digestion*; since in proportion to the imperfections of such part of the law as is in this form will be the benefits of the salutary operation which consists in reducing it to the form of statutory law. The imperfections which are here brought to view are no others than what transpired, as it were of themselves, in the course of the discussion which seemed necessary in order to give a view of the characteristic nature of this modification of the law. One other capital imperfection may just be hinted at in a few words. I mean that which consists in the *unaccommodatingness* of its rules. Every decision that is given is spun out of some vague maxim conceived in general terms without exceptions, and without any regard to times and circumstances: a maxim conceived in words which, whenever put together, were put together, a thousand to one else, by persons who had no such case as the particular one in question present to their view. It admitts of no temperaments, no compromises, no compositions: none of those qualifications which a legislator would see the necessity of applying. Even when it aims at utility, which perhaps is now and then, it either falls short of the mark or overshoots it. [In the margin, Bentham has noted at this point: 'For an illustration, take the case of the Proculeians and Sabinians. The Eng. law giving no specific remedy does better: one imperfection palliating the mischief of another. Or the law which makes the goods of under-tenants distrainable.'] A sort of testimony or recognition of this truth is contained in the magnificent and well known adage—*fiat justitia ruat coelum*. Though heaven were wreck'd, let justice be obey'd. Heaven may always be preserved when the law that governs is the work of the legislator. Hence the hardness of heart, which is a sort of endemical disease of lawyers, where that part of the law which is in the customary form is predominant in the system. Mischief being almost their incessant occupation, and the greatest merit they can attain being the firmness with which they persevere in the task of doing partial evil for the sake of that universal good which consists in a steady adherence [to] established rules, a Judge thus circumstanced is obliged to divest himself of that anxious sensibility, which is one of the most useful as well as amiable qualities of the legislator. An empire shall run to ruin, and the lawyer drive on in the same track, as if nothing were the matter.

'Familiarized with the prospect of all those miseries which are attendant on poverty, disappointment, and disgrace, accustomed even to heap those miseries on the heads of those by whom he knows them to be unmerited, he eases himself by habit of the concern which the prospect of them would produce in an unexperienced mind: just as a man whose trade is in blood becomes insensible to the sufferings which accompany the stroke of death. It must be no common share of humanity that can induce him, nor any common share of wisdom that can enable him, to keep this rigour within the bounds which are presented by utility, and the necessary regard to uniformity of decision. By men of ordinary mould, the dictates of utility may in these circumstances be easily lost sight of altogether: and a precedent the most absurd and mischievous conformed to with as much tranquillity as an equally apposite precedent of a complexion the most reasonable and salutary.'

Two abandoned sentences follow at this point.

For the Proculian and Sabinian schools see p. 193 n. below.

[2] MS '98' refers to the original enumeration of §14, para. 115, pp. 161–2 above.

scarcely be said to be a right or a wrong in any case. How should there? right is the conformity to a rule, wrong the deviation from it: but here there is no rule established, no measure to discern by, no standard to appeal to: all is uncertainty, darkness and confusion.

It is evident enough that the mute sign, the act of punishment, which is all there is, properly speaking, of a customary law, can express nothing of itself to any who have not some other means of informing themselves of the occasion on which it was given: that the act of hanging, for example, is no definition of the act of stealing: and that a blow which is given to a dog (for here dogs and men are put upon the same footing[a]) is no lesson to the dog who is in the next yard, or to the whelp that will have been begotten by one of them a year hence. If, then, it can serve as a rule to any distance or for any length of time, some account of the case must be taken and handed down by somebody: which somebody stands then in the place of a legislator. But of the boundless groupe of circumstances with which the act punished must necessarily have been attended, how many and which of them were consider'd as material? what were received as inculpative? what were not suffer'd to operate in the way of exculpation? to what circumstances was it owing that the punishment was so great? to what others that it was no greater? These and a multitude of other circumstances, which it would be needless to repeat,[b] must all be taken into the account in the description of the case. But let the case be delineated ever so exactly, it is still but that individual case that is delineated: to make a rule that can serve for cases yet to come, a new process must be carried on: the historian must give place to the metaphysician: and a general rule must be created by abstraction out of this particular proceeding. And by whom, then, shall this abstraction be performed? by every man for himself, or by some one for all the rest? In the latter case that one man, if his rule comes to be adopted and adhered to, that one man, be he who he will, becomes in effect the legislator.

Sources of customary law—Records.

142. Under these circumstances, the state of the branch of law in question is apt to stand upon some such footing as the following.[c] The Judges, who perhaps at first did take, and are

[a] supra [115.][1]

[b] v. supra | |.[2]

[c] The picture here given of it is local, because it could not well be otherwise. The statute law of a country is upon paper, and may be seen all the world over: the

[1] MS '99' refers to the original enumeration of §14, para. 116, pp. 162–3 above, though it is at para. 115, pp. 161–2 above, that customary law is said to be 'for brutes'.

[2] See, for instance, §12, para. 72, pp. 126–9 above.

still supposed, or rather pretended to be supposed, to take, an account of every case that came before them and of their proceedings on it, never trouble their heads about the matter: the business is left to certain officers who are under them. These officers give what is called the history of the case, which history is termed by some such name as a *record*. This record, being copied from precedents of the darkest antiquity, instead of being a compleat history of the case of which it purports to be the record, is in fact a partial and imperfect history of a different case that was determined upon some hundreds of years before: applied to the case in question, it is in consequence partly imperfect, partly false, partly irrelevant, and partly unintelligible: and is in many instances much the same sort of history of that case as a chapter of Bede or Orosius would be of the present war.[1] [a]

state of the customary law is comparatively a secret, depending in a great degree upon habits which are not perceptible out of the particular circles in which the practise of it is carried on. It was necessary, therefore, to take up with a single model and to copy from the only system of jurisprudence to the interior history of which I had any opportunity of access. If, in the slight sketch here given, any of the lines should seem peculiar to the particular original from whence they were copied, the bulk of them will, however, be found, I believe, to be applicable to all nations, being imprinted on the very essence of this species of law.

Having fixed the idea of a law, shewn what might be its parts, and when it might be looked upon as entire, I perceived what any body may perceive, that, in the case where the law is of the permanent kind, it was applicable only to a statute law: and that, as to *a* customary law, there was no such thing existing. It became necessary, therefore, to shew how this happen'd to be the case, and since there were here no laws (no *leges*), of what sort of materials it is that the aggregate body stiled the customary law (*jus consuetudinarium*), consider'd as a body of permanent regulations, is made up.

The picture I am about to give will, I trust, be found a faithful one[2]—a pleasing one, indeed, it is not: but who is [it] that is in fault? I paint things as I find them: if bad, it is in order that they may be made better. Meantime, let not my design be mistaken; nor let a picture of the law be misconstrued into a satyre against individuals. My business is not with individuals, but with nations: not with the year, but with the age. The dark spots which I am about to exhibit are accordingly inveterate evils, not recent grievances: nor do I believe that other period will be found, at which the constitutional diseases of the law itself have met with so powerful a palliative as they find at present in the talents and virtues of its professors.

[a] More particularly in actions of *ejectment*, by which the title to landed property is tried, and which are the causes of the greatest importance of any in the civil line.

---

[1] Both authors undertook wide-ranging histories within a relatively short compass. Bede (673/4–735), monk, historian, and theologian, completed *Historia ecclesiastica gentis Anglorum* in 731. Paulus Orosius (*fl.* 414–17), theologian and historian, probably from Braga, undertook his *Historiarum adversus paganos libri VII*, a world history written from a Christian perspective, at the request of Saint Augustine (354–430). The 'present war' was, of course, the American War of Independence 1776–83.

[2] In the margin, Bentham has noted at this point: 'Paint objects in their natural colours, it

These documents, such as they are, are written in a form the most inconvenient for reading or consulting of any that could have been devised: and being by many a waggon-load too bulky for publication, they are kept locked up in places where not one in ten thousand of those whose conduct is to be guided by them, and whose fate depends on them, can know how to find them: much less to make any thing of them when found. The trouble of finding them out is so great, and the information to be got from them so scanty and undecisive, that it is not above one time in a hundred that even the Judge, who professes to take the decisions given in the cases of which they purport to be the histories for the measure of his own, can endure to look at them. Whether they have weight in any case or whether they have none, depends therefore upon accident: if a fit of curiosity happens to take the judge, such an one as shall not take him thrice perhaps in a twelvemonth, they are hunted down: if not, they are let alone: one out of a thousand becomes a law: the nine hundred and ninety-nine others remain waste paper.

Reports—their deficiencies

143. These documents being become to such a degree useless, another set of documents came gradually into use under the appellation of *Reports*. In these reports, taking them all together, about one third or one tenth or one twentieth or one hundredth part of the cases are made public, which, if they were equally known, would be equally entitled to make law. Here you have a little of the history of one court; there of another: sometimes the history of a court goes on pretty well for several years together: then comes a blank for twenty or thirty years during which all is darkness.[a] Sometimes you have the history of

[a] Of cases determined in the court of Chancery, there have been none reported from the year 1755 to the present year 1782:[1] of cases in the Exchequer, none from the year 1741:[2] a very few excepted relative to a very narrow branch of practise: and those not published till last year but one—1780.[3] The first mentioned court is that which exercises a greater share than all the other

must appear that a quarry is not a palace; that a lay-stall is not a garden; that a wen or a scab is not a beauty.'

[1] See John Tracy Atkyns, *Reports of Cases Argued and Determined in the High Court of Chancery, in the time of Lord Chancellor Hardwicke*, 3 vols., London, 1765–8, which reports cases from 1736 to 1754.

[2] See William Bunbury, *Reports of Cases in the Court of Exchequer, from the Beginning of the Reign of King George the First, until the Fourteenth Year of the Reign of King George the Second*, London, 1755, which reports cases from 1713 to 1741.

[3] Bentham perhaps had in mind *The Law and Practice of Writs of Error, in the Courts of Common Pleas, King's Bench, Exchequer Chamber, and Parliament*, London, 1780, though this dealt with Exchequer Chamber rather than Exchequer, and was published in 1781 rather than 1780.

the middle of a cause; sometimes of the beginning; sometimes of the conclusion. Sometimes you have the argument without the decision: sometimes the decision without the argument: sometimes the decision of the inferior court without that of the superior which reverses it.

These reports are published by any body that pleases, and by as many people as please; and where nobody publishes, nobody cares. If a lawyer who can get no practise happens to think of this method of making money: if the executor of a lawyer happens to find a manuscript among his papers: if either of these or any other such accident happens to throw a copy into the hands of a bookseller: the bookseller, without being aware of it and without caring about it, becomes a legislator.

Sometimes by commission from the same high authority, a judge, who had been dead and forgotten for half-a-century or for half-a-dozen centuries, starts up on a sudden out of his tomb, and takes his seat on the throne of legislation, overturning the establishments of the intervening periods,[1] like Justinian brought to life again at Amalfi.[2][a]

tribunals in the nation put together in the disposal of the property of that nation. In matters which are there cognizable, the statute law has scarcely any thing to do: every thing turns upon customary law, which in that court has assumed the particular name of *equity*. Respecting these matters, the public has been six-and-twenty years, respecting matters cognizable in the other court (which is also a court of Equity), it has been forty years, without a guide.

[a] L[d] Chancellor Freeman's reports were first published in 1742: there are cases in them so old as the year 1670. Peere Williams's (the most generally esteemed perhaps of any) were first published in 1740: there are cases in them of the year 1695. Judge Croke's (held also in the highest estimation) in the year 1657: there are decisions in them of the year 1582. Serjeant Maynard's Yearbook was first published in 1679: there are cases in it prior to the year 1306. In the first-mentioned of these books, the cases were brought to light many of them 72 years after they were agitated: in the second, 45: in the 3[d], 75: in the last, upwards of 370.[3]

In the customary law, a great, perhaps the greatest, part of the business is done

[1] In relation to this paragraph, Bentham has noted in the margin: 'The difficulty is to make out the relation the matters[?] of procedure bear to the mandates of the substantive laws.'

[2] According to Blackstone, *Commentaries on the Laws of England*, i. 81, a copy of Justinian's *Digest* was found at Amalfi 'about the year 1130'. Barrington, *Observations on the Statutes*, 1st edn., 1766, p. 54, gives the date as 1127, but in *Observations on the more ancient Statutes, from Magna Charta to the Twenty-first of James I. Cap. XXVII. With An Appendix, being a proposal for new modelling the statutes*, 3rd edn., London, 1769, p. 76, the date is revised to 1137. The copy is now known as the Florentine Pandects.

[3] See Richard Freeman, *Reports of Cases in Law and Equity: From 1670 to 1706*, London, 1742; William Peere Williams, *Reports of Cases Argued and Determined in the High Court of Chancery, and Of some special Cases Adjudged in the Court of King's Bench*, 2 vols., London, 1740; *The Reports of S[r]. George Croke Knight; Late, one of the Justices of the Court of Kings-Bench;*

— redundancy and confusion. If the series of the cases that are published is broken and interrupted, the deficiency is made up by the multitude of reports there are of the same case: all perhaps contradicting one another and contradicting what little there is of truth in the record.[1]

Treatises. **144.** Meantime, out of these scatter'd atoms, be the collection of them ever so copious and exact, nothing, it is plain, so long as they continue in the order in which they happen to be brought to light, can be made, that shall wear the face, I do not say of a law, but of any thing that bears any perceptible relation to any thing that is entitled to that name. To give them any sort of connection with one another and with the rest of the matter of which law is made, a set of general rules must be abstracted from them and worked up into the form of a treatise. A set of treatises accordingly start up: and here again the bookseller gets another share in the prerogative of legislation.

It is plain these general rules can have no foundation in authority any farther than as they are the necessary result of some particular assignable decisions: if they deviate but a hair's breadth from that standard, they become laws *suo jure*, and the author, if they are adopted and acceded to, becomes *pro tanto* as much a legislator as the sovereign. Accordingly the writer, while living, has no such independent authority: he has none even so long as his book can be deemed a modern one. But in proportion as he is more ancient, that is in proportion as the age he writes in is more barbarous, he stands a better and a better chance of setting the law: insomuch that at a certain period his authority shall often prevail not only without the authority of preceding cases to ground it upon, but

in the way of *ex-post-facto* law. The decisions, being formed on grounds that were inaccessible to the party previous to the act for which he was made to suffer, carry with them a great part of the mischief of the *privilegia* against which Cicero inveighs with so much justice.[2]

And formerly, one of the Justices of the Court of Common-Bench, of such Select Cases, as were adjudged in the said Courts, the time that he was Judge in either of them: Collected and written in French by Himself; Revised and published in English, ed. Sir Harebotle Grimston, London, 1657; Sir Jehan' Maynard, *Les Reports des Cases Argue & Adjudge in le Temps del' Roy Edward le Second, Et auxy Memoranda del' Exchequer en Temps le Roy Edward le Primer*, London, 1678 (not 1679 as Bentham states). Bentham's calculations respecting the interval between the earliest cases reported and the date of publication are correct, except in the instance of *Croke*, where the earliest case reported is in 1625, making an interval of 32 years. However, the edition of 1661 (*The First Part (Though last Publish't) of the Reports of Sr George Croke K^t, Late one of the Justices of the Court of King's-Bench, And formerly one of the Justices of the Court of Common-Bench; of Such select Cases, As were adjudged in the said Courts, from the 24th to the 44/45th of the late Queen Elizabeth*, ed. Sir Harbottle Grimston, London, 1661) does contain cases from 1582, which is 75 years before the publication of the edition of 1657.

[1] In the margin, Bentham has noted at this point: 'Soften.'

[2] See Cicero, *De legibus*, III. xix. 44; and *De domo*, XVII. 43.

even against the authority of such preceding cases. The treatise is confused and barbarous: still yet less so than the cases; so much less, that out of pure weariness and despair the authority of the treatise is preferred to that to which alone it stands indebted for all the weight that could originally have belonged to it. First in point of original authority comes the record: then comes the report: last of all comes the treatise: the shadow of the shadow of a shade: and it is this shadow that is worshipped as the substance.

Manuscript Reports.

145. To supply the deficiencies in the reports, men of the profession have a resource: men out of the profession, the people whose lives and fortunes are at stake upon the decisions which ought to have been or are supposed to be related in the reports, have none: no matter: the demand for the lawyer rises in proportion to the ignorance and helplessness of the client. While decisions are yet young, before any reports of them can have been published and [lest][1] none should be published, such lawyers as happen to be present will naturally be taking notes for their own use. These notes are circulated from hand to hand: and happy is he who has his bookcase full of them. But no one man can be in half-a-dozen courts at once: nor in any one court before he is born. Every lawyer, therefore, if he would make a collection of these recondite treasures, must be beholden to his brethren. By this means two monopolies establish themselves, one within another: a monopoly by the profession against the rest of the people: and a monopoly of the illustrious in the profession itself against the obscure: a monopoly by the seniors against the juniors: a monopoly by men of extensive connections against men of small connections.

Formularies or Precedents.

146. It has already been intimated that the description of the formularies made use of in judging, prosecuting and defending enters in a certain manner into the description of every law whatsoever: the invalidity of a formulary exhibited on the part of an accuser or of an order in prejudice of the defendant having the effect of an exemptive circumstance: the invalidity of a formulary exhibited on the part of the defender or of an order in his favour, that of a condemnative or dis-exemptive circumstance.[2] In a similar manner does the description of the formularies made use of in covenanting or conveying enter into the description of those particular laws which, by lending their sanction to such contracts or dispositions, convert the several violations of which they are susceptible into so many species of delinquency: the invalidity, then, of a covenant has the effect of an exculpative or exemptive circumstance to the law which makes the non-performance of the

[1] MS 'least'. [2] See §13, paras. 109–10, pp. 157–8 above.

service stipulated for by that covenant an offence: as hath the invalidity of an acquittance from such contract, that of a re-inculpative or of a convictive circumstance. In like manner, the invalidity of an investitive conveyance has the effect of an exculpative or exemptive circumstance with regard to the law which makes the invasion of the property or interest disposed of an offence.

Accordingly, so long as the validity of these formularies rests upon the customary law, and untill a sufficient stock of them has been framed and authenticated by the proper legislator, a collection of such of them as have been drawn into question and confirmed, or past unquestioned through the scrutiny of lawyers of eminence concerned for parties interested in their downfall, forms another branch of the customary law. The possession of such a collection becomes an object of value: and the access to it, like the use of any other object of exclusive property, may form an object of sale. Hence arise a multitude of little subordinate monopolies, carved out of the great monopoly possessed by the profession at large: the proprietors of each branch having a valuable property in the ignorance of the rest of the profession, as the rest of the profession have in the ignorance of the people.

Preference not settled.

147. A report, in order to furnish the matter that laws are to be made of, must at least be permitted to be cited in debate. But it is not every printed report that is always permitted to be cited: and there is no list of such as are not. The Judge A will hear the reporter A: he will not hear the reporter B: the Judge B will hear the reporter B: he will not hear the reporter A: the judge A will sometimes hear the reporter A, and sometimes not. Reports become distinguished into citeable and unciteable: and the citeable into good and bad: those which are citeable to one judge, are not so to another; nor to the same judge at a different time: those which are good to one judge are bad to another.[1] Every judge has his own gage: and each man's gage may be set sometimes one way and sometimes another.

It is evident that inedited reports must be in a case nearly similar.

In both classes, some are avowed by their authors, some anonymous. Some are the better for having a name: others are the worse: to some the names of the authors add authority: from some they take it away. And the same reporter who mostly reports

[1] In the margin, Bentham has noted at this point: 'If such are the variations in the authority of printed reports, such as are inedited must at least be liable to the same.' A further comment which is illegible follows.

well, will sometimes report ill: and the same who mostly reports ill, will sometimes report well.

Utility secondary—primary: original—derivative.

148. But the rule extracted, no matter how, from these particular *data*, and which, if there were a law in the case, would be the law, is after all absurd and mischievous: perhaps it was so from the very first: that is the decisions on which it is grounded were so at the first moment of their being made. But at any rate it would be so if applied now to the matter at present in dispute. To decide, then, according to *this* rule would be mischievous in one way: but to depart from *any* rule which is to be deemed to have been established would be mischievous in another way. It is only in as far as subsequent decisions are render'd conformable to the rules that are fairly to be drawn from prior decisions that such prior decisions can answer, in any even the most imperfect degree, the purpose of a law. Whenever the chain of conformity, such as it is, is broken, the anomalous decision, whatever it is, does all the mischief that can be done by an *ex-post-facto* law. If the question be of a penal nature, in the one way it absolves without reason, in the other way it punishes without warning: in a matter of purely civil competition, it subjects the unsuccessful party to a privation or to a burthen which, as far as they go, have the effect of a punishment without cause. This it does by its own single efficacy: add to which, that in the way of example it gives a shock which, from hand to hand, is felt by the whole fabric of customary law. Nor is the mischief cured, till a strong body of connected decisions, either in confirmation of the first anomalous one, or in opposition to it, have repaired the broken thread of analogy, and brought back the current of expectation to it's old channel. I speak in metaphors: since in metaphors only on a subject like the present can one speak. This being the case, whenever any past decision, in itself apparently absurd, is brought in the character of a law to govern the proposed decision in the case in litigation, there are two maxims that point different ways and press for opposite determinations. As this dilemma is occurring at every turn, lawyers are of course continually called upon to embrace the one side of it or the other. Accordingly, then, as the inconveniences on the one side or those on the other have been accustomed to press upon their imaginations with the greatest force, they insensibly contract a general propensity to lean on the one side or on the other. They form themselves like the Proculeans and the Sabinians of old,[1] though on a ground of much greater extent and importance, into

[1] i.e. the Proculian and Sabinian schools of lawyers, named after the mid-first-century Roman lawyers Sempronius(?) Proculus and Masurius Sabinus respectively.

different parties: *Stare decisis* is the maxim of the one; *salus reipublicæ*, or some thing like it, the motto of the other: both perhaps partizans of utility, though of utility viewed through a different medium: the one of the general utility which results from the adherence to established precedents: the other of the particular utility which results from the bringing back the current of decision at any rate into the channel of original utility from which the force of precedents, they suppose, had drawn it aside: the one enamoured of uniformity, the mother of security and peace: the other, of Natural Justice or Equity or Right Reason, or by whatever other name the phantom is best known.

Competition between documents of different orders.

149. Given the documents from whence the law that is to govern a given case is to be abstracted, it is required to find that law. A question arises concerning the title to an article of property. A deed copied from one drawn by a conveyancer of great name, and since copied by a thousand others, but now impeached for the first time, a decision badly reported upon the face of it but taken from a printed book of high authority, a decision well reported upon the face of it but taken from a printed book of low authority, a decision indifferently reported and taken from a book without a name, a corresponding string of unprinted cases, an antient treatise, and the decisions which it quotes and which when examined make against it, these, together with the dictates of utility in the abstract, are all candidates for the prerogative of legislation at the same time:—which of all these contending authorities ought to carry it? When the circle has been squared, this problem will be solved.[a]

Other authorities omitted.

[a] There are various other species of authorities, which it would be to no purpose to insist upon: for example

1. Maxims: which are unconnected scraps of general treatises.

2. Opinions of counsel: which are treatises on the particular cases laid before them.

3. Pleadings (that is formularies of procedure) settled by counsel: which carry with them their opinions concerning the validity of those pleadings.

There are also various circumstances which may give different degrees of weight to authorities of the same species.

1. The reputation of the counsel who advised; or of the Judges who decided.

2. The rank and fulness of the court: was it before the Master of the Rolls, or before the Chancellor: at a Judge's chambers, at Nisi prius, *in Banco*, or at the House of Lords?

3. The solemnity of argumentation—how many times argued? by how many counsel on a side?

4. The solemnity of decision—did the Chief Justice deliver the opinion of the Court: or did the Judges give their opinions *seriatim*?

5. The number of stages in the cause.—Was it a decision acquiesced in, or a decision confirmed upon an appeal?

150. From a set of *data* like these, a law is to be extracted by every man who can fancy that he is able: by each man, perhaps a different law: and these, then, are the *monades* which, meeting together, constitute rules which, taken together, constitute that inimitable and unimproveable production of enlighten'd reason, that fruit of concord and pledge of liberty in every country in which it is found, the common or customary law.[1] Uncertainty of this branch of law.

Caligula published his laws in small characters: but still he published them: he hung them up high, but still he hung them up.[2] English Judges neither hang up their laws nor publish them. They go farther; they will not suffer it to be done by others: and if there be any dependence to be placed in any rule of common law, whosoever takes upon him to do it, well or ill, he may be punished. The rule is indeed falling into desuetude: but it has lately been recognized;[a] it has never been disclaimed; and it may be enforced at any time. Whosoever takes upon him to do any such service to his country does it, like the Grecian lawgiver, with a halter about his neck.[3]

151.[4] It appears, then, that the customary law is a fiction from beginning to end: and it is in the way of fiction, if at all, that we must speak of it. Uncertainty of this branch of law.

The customary law, you say, punishes theft with hanging: be it so. But by what law is this done? who made it? when was it made? where is it to be found? what are the parts that it contains? by what words is it expressed?

Theft, you say, is taking under certain circumstances: but taking by whom? taking of what? under what circumstances? taking by a person of such a sort, taking of a thing of such a sort: taking under such and such circumstances?—But how know

These are but a part of the topics which may occasionally be thrown into the scale, all adding to the perplexity of the enquiry, and to the uncertainty of the result.

[a] See Preface to Reports of | |.[5]

---

[1] In the margin, Bentham has noted at this point: 'A rule of customary = a law, *quasi*-command—*quasi*-prohibition—every thing *quasi*.

'No speaking of it without fiction.'

[2] See Suetonius, *De vita Caesarum*, IV. xli; Cassius Dio, *Roman History*, LIX. xxviii. 11.

[3] Demosthenes (384–322 BC), the Athenian orator, in his speech *Against Timocrates*, 139–40, contrasts the incessant legislative changes at Athens with the permanence achieved at Locri in Italy, where anyone proposing a change in the laws of Zaleucus must do so with a halter round his neck, which is either removed or tightened till he dies according to the approval or disapproval with which the proposal is received.

[4] Bentham gave the same enumeration and heading to this paragraph as to the previous one. The following passage was, therefore, possibly intended to supersede para. 150 above.

[5] Bentham's source has not been identified.

you this?—because so it has been adjudged.—What then?—not if it be a taking by any other person, nor if of any other thing, nor if under any other circumstances? O yes, in many other cases—if by whom then? and if, of what? and if, under what circumstances? if—*by* a person of such another sort, if—*of* a thing of such another sort, if—*under* such and such circumstances? But how do you know this is the case? because I think it ought to be so, because I believe it would be so: because such and such persons believe it ought to be so or would be so. But how *came* you to think so? and how came *they* to think so? and what if I and as many people with me, *quorum ego judicium* (as saith the courtly Cicero, to his friend)[a] *longe antepono tuo*, happen to think differently? tell me, I say, where is your law then?

But for peace sake, let your notion be the right one: no matter why nor wherefore. I am content to abide by it, and to acknowledge that all others ought and are bound to do so, too. Be pleased, then, to give it words for us to know it by.—And are these, then, the words? is this paper the standard we are to measure an act by in order to see whether it be an act of theft or no?—Then is this a law, and you the legislator.

A quasi-law—quasi-provision &c.

152. In short, if there be still a man who will stand up for the existence and certainty of a rule of customary law, give him every thing he asks, he must still have recourse to fiction to produce any such rule: if it appears in any shape, it must cloath itself in the similitude of some particular provision of the nature of statute law: it must purport to be, it must pretend to be, a provision of statute law, although it be no such thing.[1] To enable ourselves to conceive and express the influence which a rule of this sort may have over the whole system of law, and at the same time to distinguish it from the real entity whose semblance it usurps, it may be called after the name of that provision which it would be, if it were any thing, with the particle *quasi* prefixed to it, according to the usage of the Roman Law.[b] Upon this plan, a rule of customary law describing,

[a] Tuscul. Disput. in principio.[2]

[b] Fragm. on Gov.[3]

[1] In the margin, Bentham has noted at this point: 'To conceive a quasi-law we must put it into words: which words will be such as a man happens to think would be most suitable to it were it a real law.'

[2] Cicero, *Tusculan Disputations*, v. iv. 12: *A. Non mihi videtur ad beate vivendum satis posse virtutem. M. At hercule Bruto meo videtur, cuius ego iudicium, pace tua dixerim, longe antepono tuo*, i.e. 'A. It does not appear to me that virtue can be sufficient for leading a happy life. M. But, I can assure you, my friend Brutus thinks it sufficient and with your permission I put his judgment far above yours.'

[3] See *A Fragment on Government* (*CW*), Ch. I, para. 12 n., points 10–11, p. 430 n.

for example, what is to be looked upon as theft, may be stiled a quasi-law against theft: which quasi-law will accordingly have its quasi-imperative, quasi-limitative, quasi-exceptive provisions, and so on.

153.[1] A quasi-provision aboriginal—excretitious.

[1] The text has been abandoned at this point. In the margin, Bentham has noted: 'The aboriginal the result of autocratic or judicial power: the excretitious of executive-judicial exercised in the way of interpretation either strict or liberal.'

§18. *Separation of the civil branch from the penal.*

The generality of laws have each a penal as well as a civil branch.

We may now, perhaps, be able to find an answer to the question we set out with[a] concerning the distinction between the penal branch of law and the civil: and we may say at once that in every law (at least in every law that is comparatively speaking of any importance[b]) there is one part which is of a penal, and at the same time another part which is of a civil, nature: and that, after the few exceptions which have already been marked out, there is no such thing as an entire law which is penal only and not civil, nor as one which is civil only and not penal. The truth of these propositions, if it be not clear already, will presently be made appear. What the cases are in which a law may possess a certain degree of efficacy without having any punishment provided by the legislator for it's support have been already stated:[1] they are 1. where the law has for its support the apprehension of a punishment issuable from both or either of the two auxiliary sanctions: 2. where it has no punishment at all to support it, but only reward. In all other cases, if it has any support, any efficiency at all, it is to punishment provided by the sovereign that it stands indebted for it: to a subsidiary punitory law or what is equivalent, announced by a comminative clause (or what is equivalent) in the principal law. Now, it manifestly is not upon either of the slender pillars abovementioned that the main parts of the fabric of political society are supported: for example those laws which provide for the preservation and circulation of property. In every one of these, therefore, be they what they may, there must be a penal part as well as a civil; so that a law of property which, being entire, shall have nothing in it of a penal nature is a law which either does not exist or, if any where it exists, is nugatory: nor at any rate is it of a piece with the bulk of those which, in speaking of the laws of property, men are wont to bear in mind.

Law-books in which no mention is made of punishment accounted for.

All this while it can not but have been observed that nothing is more commonly to be met with [than] not only whole chapters, but whole volumes, and those authoritative too, in which, from the

[a] supra 29.[2]
[b] supra | |.[3]

[1] See §11, pp. 98–114 above.
[2] See pp. 21–3 above.
[3] See *An Introduction to the Principles of Morals and Legislation* (*CW*), Ch. VII, para. 3, p. 74 & n., where the consequences of an act are said to be '*material*' or '*of importance*' insofar as they 'either consist of pain or pleasure, or have an influence in the production of pain or pleasure'.

beginning to the end, there is not so much as a syllable hinted about punishment, and which, notwithstanding, are full of a sort of matter which is called law. This makes a seeming inconsistency, which it will be well worth our while to endeavour to remove: but which could not, however, have well been removed upon any other terms than that of travelling through the long and intricate details that have occupied the . . . . last chapters.[1]

The cause of it is neither more nor less than this: the want of coincidence or conformity between the typographical arrangement and the logical: between the order of the ideas about which the several laws in question are conversant, and the order of the signs which are made use of to express them.

According to the order of the ideas, the penal and civil branches would stand together.

To consider the several laws separately without regard to the exigencies of the whole, without regard to the form into which it might be necessary to cast them, for the sake of the form which is requisite to be given to the whole, the natural course to take would seem to be as follows: to take each law by itself, beginning, suppose, with the law against personal injuries, and under the head of that law to insert all the words whatsoever, and how many soever they be, which are requisite to give a clear expression of the various ideas that enter into the composition of that law. This plan shews mighty fair upon the first opening: but before a man had got to the end even of this single title he would find, perhaps to his no small surprize, that after a due attention paid to the several limitations and exceptions which the case requires, he would have set down matter enough to fill a volume. When, after having got thus far, he came to consider that the title upon which he had bestow'd a volume was but one out of perhaps some hundreds which remained, how great would be his amazement and despondency? 'At this rate,' he would say to himself, 'hundreds of such volumes may have been travelled through, and yet the work not done.'

But must be separated for the convenience of discourse.

If, however, after this it would be possible for him to muster up courage enough to go on with the next offence, he might be as much surprised perhaps another way: he would find that, with the exception of a page or two, he would have that same volume to write over again and insert under this second title. This being the case, it would naturally enough occur to him, that there could be no use in inserting these same words twice, either to himself who was to write or to the people who were to read them: but that to both parties it would, on the contrary, be equally irksome and inconvenient. He would, therefore, collect this common matter and

[1] MS del. 'sections'. Bentham presumably has in mind §§3–17.

set it down in a third title by itself: which third title, by the simple expedient of a set of references, might be adopted into and made, as it were, parcel of each of the two others.

Foundation of the penal and civil codes.

If, then, with a view to the distinction between the penal and the civil branches of these two laws, he were to look over them and examine their contents, he would find that such clauses as were in the imperative or comminative form took up comparatively but a small space: that at the same time these were the clauses which, after the separation, adhered to the two original titles: that these were in each of those titles different: and that it was the qualificative and expositive matter, as being common to both titles, that took its station under the new one: and, in short, that in the two first titles thus reduced he had laid the foundation of a *penal* code, as in the third he had of what would be called a *civil* code.

§19. *Distinction between civil law and criminal.*[1]

1. Thus much concerning the meaning of the word *penal* when applied to a branch of law, and put in opposition to the word *civil*. But there is another word, the word *criminal*, which is also put in contradistinction with the word civil, and which at the same time is in many cases used interconvertibly with the word *penal*. In some cases, that is, but perhaps not in all. Therefore, although no very explicit line of distinction is to be drawn between the civil branch and the penal, may not there, however, be a line somewhat more explicit drawn between the *civil* branch and the *criminal*? Let us see, then, what is to be understood by the word *criminal* as applied to a branch of law.

Is *criminal* law more distinct from [*civil*, than *penal* is?][2]

2. The criminal branch of law is that which concerns crimes. What, then, do we mean by crimes? do we mean offences? but we have seen that there is no law whatsoever which does not terminate in the creation of an offence.[3] If the word criminal, then, is to distinguish the branch of law it is applied to from any other, it is only some particular class of offences that can be meant by the word crimes. I know of but three circumstances that seem ever to have served as marks to distinguish them from other offences: 1. the magnitude of the mischief they occasion or are thought to occasion: 2. the quantum of displeasure or disapproba tion which is annexed, or thought to be annexed, to them by the community in general: 3. the punishment annexed to them by the law. An offence is spoken of as a crime sometimes under the notion of its being *very* mischievous, sometimes because it is *very* odious, sometimes because the punishment for it is *very* heavy. The circumstances are apt not unfrequently to concur in one and the same offence: more especially on account of the tendency which the one of them has to produce the other. The notion of an act's being mischievous is one cause at least, as it ought to be the only cause, which makes it odious: and it's being odious is perhaps the most frequent, though never otherwise than improper, cause of it's being made punishable.

Three senses of the word *crime*—it imports 1. *mischievousness*: 2. *odiousness*: 3. *penality*.

3. As to the magnitude of the punishment, it is evident that from this circumstance no mark of distinction can be taken to separate one division of offences from another for the present purpose. For the business here is to consider in the first place what the offences

Magnitude of the punishment alone no source of distinction between offences

[1] This section formed the original continuation of the material presented here in Appendix A, pp. 237–41 below, which in turn formed the original continuation of §1, pp. 3–15 above. For further details see the Editorial Introduction, p. xxviii above.

[2] MS '*penal*, than *civil* is?'

[3] See §5, para. 4, p. 57 above.

consider'd with a view to punishment.

are in themselves, and it is from thence that we are afterwards to determine what treatment ought to be given to them. As to the treatment actually given to them, this, as every one knows, is in great measure different in different countries; so that it never can come under any one single description whatsoever.

—Nor the degree of odiousness.

4. The degree of popular odium under which an offence lies is also in a high degree variable, to say nothing of the difficulty of measuring and collecting it.

—Nor the degree of mischievousness.

5. The degree of mischievousness of an offence, though liable to some variation, is, however, liable to less variation than either of those other circumstances.

Whether an act be a crime depends on all three circumstances together.

6. It has been already observed that these circumstances are found frequently to attach in conjunction upon an offence: as it were to be wished they always did. It is not, indeed, without some force put upon language, and some appearance at least of impropriety, that an offence can be called a crime if any one of them be wanting. If it be mischievous without being odious, if it be not proportionably odious, you would scruple to call it a crime for fear of being understood to represent it in the light of an offence which was actually odious; a fact which, by the supposition, is not true. Are you persuaded of it's being odious, without looking upon it as mischievous, you would not without reluctance call it a crime lest you should be understood to represent it as being mischievous, and thereby join in exasperating an odium which you look upon as unjust. Were the case even such that you deemed it mischievous at the same time that you were sensible of it's being odious, yet if it were not treated with severity by the laws, you would scarce perhaps think yourself warranted in point of verbal accuracy in speaking of it as a crime. To call it a crime would seem to be a trick of oratory.

Easier to point out some acts that are crimes, than to say what are not.

7. If the word *criminal* is to be employ'd, it seems impossible, therefore, so far to mark out the boundaries of the criminal branch of the law as to determine with precision what offences it shall *not* extend to. To find some which it may not improperly be determined to extend to seems, however, not to be alike impossible. Such, for instance, are the offences of Robbery, Incendiarism, certain species of Homicide, and calumniatory Perjury: these being offences to which it is not likely that, on any of the three grounds abovementioned, any person will be disposed to deny the appellation of crimes. Several articles more might perhaps be added to the catalogue: it would be impossible, however, to proceed any great length in it without getting into controversy: a controversy which, as there is no assignable standard to appeal to, would be indeterminable.

8. What makes this the more indisputable is that, in drawing the line between offences which are crimes and offences which are not so, the consideration of *degree* enters every where into the question; it was for this reason that it seemed necessary a little higher up to make use of the word *very*. In point of mischievousness, to entitle an offence to the appellation of a crime, it is not enough that it be mischievous, it must be *very* mischievous: in like manner, it must be *very* odious: so also must the punishment be *very* severe: at least, it is not any *very* slight punishment that will suffice. This consideration alone is enough to make the application of the word crime altogether uncertain.

Particularly inasmuch as it depends upon degree.

9. It seems, therefore, that the word criminal will not serve to characterize any branch of law as subsisting in contra-distinction to that which is called the civil. It seems, therefore, that we must come back to the word penal after all. But the word penal as applied to this purpose does not seem to have as yet acquired any determinate application, as we have already shewn. To settle the matter and save ourselves from the inconvenience of running into continual contradictions and obscurity, there seems to be no remedy but to propose a new and in some measure arbitrary line. To the civil branch, therefore, may be understood to belong exclusively such offences as it is not judged necessary to punish with any extra-ordinary degree or species of punishment: to the criminal, such offences as it is judged necessary to punish with some extra-ordinary degree or species of punishment.

Offences if punished with an ordinary measure of punishment may be deemed civil offences; if with the extra-ordinary, criminal.

10. Let the immediate standard, then, be the supposed demand for the punishment. The punishment, consider'd in respect of it's quantity, may be distinguished into *ordinary* and *extra-ordinary*. Under the name of ordinary punishment may be comprised the least proportion of punishment that can in any case be made use of in point of quantity, and consequently of the mildest quality: that is pecuniary punishment: and that in such proportion as but just to outweigh the profit of the offence: for less than that, as has been shewn,[1] would only do harm, and could not possibly be of any use: to which must be substituted, in case of the offender's not having wherewithal to undergo this sort of punishment, some other punishment, such as imprisonment, of the next mildest nature that can be devised.[2] By extraordinary punishment may be understood any quantity or mode of punishment which it may be proper

Punishment ordinary, and extra-ordinary.

[1] See *An Introduction to the Principles of Morals and Legislation* (*CW*), Ch. XIV, paras. 8–9, pp. 166–8.

[2] In the margin, Bentham has noted at this point: 'and this where there is a special party favoured: and where the punishment is absorbed by compensation'.

to substitute in certain cases to the ordinary mode and measure of punishment.

Grounds for extra-ordinary punishment.

11. As to the grounds upon which it may be proper to have recourse to extra-ordinary punishment, these [have been] hereinbefore hinted at:[a] viz: 1. any extraordinary mischievousness on the part of the offence, when it is so great as may make it necessary and worth while to hazard an extraordinary expence in point of punishment for the sake of purchasing the better chance of combating it with effect: 2. the deficiency of the punishment in point of certainty as resulting from the difficulty of detection: which difficulty depends in great measure, as is evident, upon the nature of the offence: 3. the presumption which the offence may afford of the offender's having already been guilty of other offences of the like nature: 4. the accidental advantage in point of quality of a punishment not strictly needed in point of quantity: [5.][1] the use of a punishment of a particular quality in the character of a moral lesson: [6.][2] an extraordinary want of sensibility on the part of the offender to the force of such standing tutelary motives as are opposed to the offence, whether on the part of the law itself, or on the part of the other auxiliary sanctions.[3] [b]

Punishment must be extra-ordinary, where the profit is not pecuniary.

12. It is to be observed that it is only where the profit of the offence is all of it pecuniary that there can be any very entire certainty of outweighing it by a given quantity and mode of punishment. When what a man gets by his offence is money and nothing else, take from him that money and so much more, and you may be certain enough of not leaving him a gainer. But when the profit is any part of it not pecuniary, there the case is different. Take, for example, the case where the motive, or one of the motives, is ill-will, and the profit of the offence is the gratification of the irascible appetite. A man falls upon you and beats you: what

[a] See Ch. 14. {Proportion} 27.[4]

[b] See Ch. 11. {Dispositions} 31, 32, 33.[5]

It will be observed that, with a view to the aggregating an offence to this or that branch of law, this last circumstance can operate no otherwise than as far as the nature of the offender's disposition may be indicated by circumstances comprizable in the description of the *species* of offence. Circumstances that happen by accident to accompany the offence in this or that instance can not, for this purpose, be taken into consideration.

---

[1] MS '6.'

[2] MS '7.'

[3] In the margin, Bentham has noted at this point: 'Or any punishment, however slight, where there is no individual party favoured. For that circumstance draws away the attention from punishment.'

[4] See *An Introduction to the Principles of Morals and Legislation* (*CW*), Ch. XIV, para. 27, pp. 172–3.

[5] See ibid., Ch. XI, paras. 31–3, pp. 135–6.

pecuniary loss is there that you could be sure would give him just so much pain as the satisfaction of giving vent to his ill-will promised to afford him pleasure? It is plain that, between quantities so incommensurate, there is no striking a sure balance. In such cases, therefore, it will not be safe to trust to pecuniary punishment altogether. Some other punishment, therefore, must be allow'd of as applicable to such offence: which other punishment, according to the line of division here assigned to the two branches, will exclude the offence from the civil branch by aggregating it to the penal. And this is one among other reasons why the slightest offence against a man's person, though frequently of less mischief than even a very trivial offence against property, can scarcely be referred to any other than the penal branch of law.

The directory part of every law belongs to the civil branch—the comminatory to the criminal.

13. Thus far, then, we are arrived, that any offence may be deemed a civil offence, to which there seems to be no need of annexing any extraordinary species or degree of punishment. So much, then, as concerns an offence of this description belongs to the civil branch of the law, and not to the penal. On the other hand, every offence to which it seems to be necessary to annex any extraordinary species or degree of punishment may be termed (it would be too much to say a crime, but, however, for want of any less inapplicable expression) a criminal offence or misdemeanour. Is it, then, true accordingly that whatever part of the law goes to make up the description of a criminal offence, belongs to the penal or criminal branch of law? Here, we see, the correspondency must fail. In many articles it is a part only of what belongs to the description of a criminal offence that can be included with any degree of propriety or convenience within this latter branch. For wherever the directory part of any law, of which the comminatory part threatens an extraordinary degree of punishment, runs out into details, those forming long and separate titles, those titles, carrying nothing that belongs to punishment upon the face of them, must be aggregated to the civil branch of law. The necessity of this will appear the more manifest in the instances where we see an offence which, by the change or addition of a single circumstance, may be attended with such diversity of effects, as in the one case shall rank it under the head of civil, in the other under the head of criminal, offences.

Intentionality makes the difference between civil and criminal offences.

14. The circumstance I am speaking of is of one sort, a circumstance respecting the state of the offender's mind with reference to the obnoxious event: a circumstance relative to intentionality and consciousness: the circumstance that takes place where the offender is conscious of his being acting against the law, and intends accordingly to avoid if possible the being amenable to law for what he has done. It is this consciousness, and the intention which is in a manner inseparable from it, that added together make up the idea which seems hitherto to have been but vaguely expressed under some such terms as *dolus, prœva intentio, malus animus, malitia*, and the like.

Influence which this has on the mischief of the act.

15. That this circumstance is intimately connected with the mischief of the act will be readily apprehended by any one who recollects what is said on that subject in a preceding Chapter.[a] There are two ways, then, in which this circumstance may enhance the demand for punishment. One is by enhancing the mischief of the act: the other is by diminishing the certainty of the punishment. When a man is conscious beyond a doubt that the act he is about to committ is within the prohibition of the law, that accordingly it is of the number of those acts which are marked out for punishment, his ingenuity will of course be set to work to escape detection. The punishment will, therefore, be attended with every degree of uncertainty which he can give it: for which uncertainty it is necessary, as has been already intimated, to make up in magnitude.[1]

This uncertainty is an additional circumstance which contributes afresh to encrease the mischief, to wit the secondary mischief, of the offence. For the better chance an offender learns to give himself of concealing the offence, the more apt he will be to committ it; and the more apt men are to committ offences, the more those offences will be dreaded: the more secret the offence may be from the nature of it, the more will people be afraid of it.[2]

[a] Ch. 12. {Consequences} §. 2.[3]

[1] See ibid., Ch. XIV, paras. 16–18, pp. 169–70.

[2] The corresponding marginal contents sheet at UC xcix. 98 adds the following four marginal contents, for which no text has been identified: '**16.** Intentionality with respect to amenableness supposes the absence of intentionality with respect to mischievous consequences.

'**17.** These in offences through ill-will only are directly intentional—in offences of self-interest, obliquely.

'**18.** The distinction between civil and criminal is material chiefly in its application to the subject of Procedure.

'**19.** Yet not explicit even there—better to substitute that between ordinary and extraordinary.'

[3] See *An Introduction to the Principles of Morals and Legislation* (*CW*), Ch. XII, §ii, pp. 152–7.

§20. *Distinction between penal and civil procedure.*[1]

The nature of the power exercised by a judge depends upon the nature of the cause or case in which it is exercised. In every cause there must be at least two parties, a plaintiff and a defendant: and if there are more parties than two, the cause may be consider'd as a complex one; and may accordingly be resolved into a proportionate number of simple causes, in each of which there shall be but one plaintiff and one defendant. The nature, then, of every cause depends upon the manner in which the interest of the defendant is affected by the last act, the ultimate or definitive act, which comes to be performed on the part of the magistrate in the course of the proceedings relative to that cause. This act may be termed the judgment.[2]

Division of judicial procedure into penal and competitional or disceptative or dejudicative.

[1] The material which forms the text of this section was originally written for the projected Chapter entitled 'Corpus Juris'. For further details see the Editorial Introduction, pp. xxviii–xxix above.

[2] The text was originally continued by the following passage at UC lxxxviii. 351–2: 'This judgment will either be unfavourable to the defendant or favourable. If unfavourable, either he is treated by it as having already, i: e: previously to the commencement of the cause, committed an offence or he is not: if he is, the cause is of a penal nature: if not, it is of a civil or non-penal nature. Now, whatever is done in the way of law has reference to delinquency: it supposes delinquency either past or future, either actual or possible: it supposes either that an offence has been committed or may be committed. When the cause is of a penal nature, the judgment supposes that an offence has actually been committed and punishes a man for having committed it accordingly: when the cause is of a civil or non-penal nature, the judgment supposes (not that an offence has actually been committed, but) that an offence may be committed, and has the effect of prohibit[ing] it accordingly.

'In other words, every judgment has reference to some obnoxious act; which is a name that may be given in common to an act which, having actually been committed, is actually an offence, and an act which, were it committed, would be an offence. This obnoxious act, then, at the time of instituting the suit, either had been committed or had not: if it had, the object of the suit, and the business of the judgment belonging to it, may be to punish it: and if it was, the suit was a penal suit: if it had not, the object of the suit, and the business of the judgment in that same suit as such, can not have been to punish it: it can only be to prohibit it.

'To consider the matter in another point of view. On what occasion soever the law does any thing in favour of any person, it thereby conferrs on that person a right.[a] But there is no law whatsoever that does not operate in favour of some person or other:[b] consequently there is no law whatsoever that does not confer on some person or other a right. Now, the violation of a right is an offence: nor is there any thing else but the violation of a right that is an offence. In other words, by whatever act an offence is committed, a right is violated: and vice versâ, by whatever act a right (meaning always a legal right) is violated, an offence is committed. Whatever judgment, then, has relation to an obnoxious act has thereby also relation to a right. This right, then, which the judgment has reference to is either created by the judgment itself or it is not: if it be created by the judgment, it could not have been violated before the judgment, consequently there could not have been any offence created or committed on the score of that right previously to the judgment; if it be not created by the judgment, it must have subsisted before, it may have been violated, and the judgment may be stiled a judgment of adjudication. Now in general, such a judgment is not given but in consequence of an application made on the part of him in whose favour it is given: such an application may be termed a *forensic claim* or *petition*, and, where there is no danger of ambiguity, for shortness sake, a claim or a petition simply; and by analogy, the party by

This judgment may be consider'd either with respect to its influence on the interests of the plaintiff or with respect to its influence on the interests of the defendant.

—with respect to the Defendant.

To consider it first in the latter point of view. Affecting the interests of the defendant, it will affect them either in a favourable or an unfavourable way. Let it be in an unfavourable way: either, then, the intention is that it should affect him in the way of punishment, or it is not: in either case, if it affects him at all, it must operate on him either with or without the intervention of his will:[a] if with such intervention, it may be said to affect him in respect of his active as well as his passive faculties; if without, in respect of his passive faculties merely. If, then, the intention is that the judgment should affect him in the way of punishment, in such case, by what means soever it affects him, the judgment may be stiled a punitory or penal judgment or judgment of conviction: if not, by what means soever it may affect him, it may be stiled, in conformity to common usage, a *civil* judgment: taking the word civil in one of the many senses in which this very vague and ambiguous appellative is employ'd. We shall enquire a little further [on][1] whether some other epithet somewhat less uncharacteristic may not be found.

Judgment of conviction.

Next, let the judgment be in favour of the defendant: of this case little need be said: it is only in a negative way that a defendant can as such be favoured by it.[b] If the judgment, had it been against him,

Judgment of acquittal.

[a] v. supra {Division}.[2]

[b] I am speaking here all along of one simple cause independent of every other that may by accident be combined with [it]. A sort of accessory suit which in most cases is combined with the principal one is that concerning costs: the costs incurred on each side, in the carrying on of the principal one. In as far as the business of a judgment is to give costs to the defendant, it may be consider'd *pro tanto* as a judgment given in a cross cause in which he is not the defendant, but the plaintiff.

---

whom it is preferred, a *claimant at law* or *petitioner at law*, and for shortness, a *claimant* or a *petitioner*. In like manner, where there is any person by whom the claim is contested, such person may be stiled the *repugner* or *defendant*. In such case, both parties are of course petitioners: the claimant requesting that a judgment of adjudication to such or such an effect should be given, the defendant that it should not be given: they may, therefore, both of them be indifferently stiled *competitors*: and by analogy, the branch of procedure which concerns the steps that may respectively be taken by them for the purpose of obtaining the object of their respective petitions may be stiled competitorial procedure—an epithet which, it should seem, would be somewhat more characteristic than the word civil.'

[a] It follows that a power is a species of right.

[b] See | |. [i.e. pp. 77–8 above.]

[1] MS 'one'.

[2] See *An Introduction to the Principles of Morals and Legislation* (*CW*), Ch. XVI, pp. 187–280, though the precise point does not appear to be discussed therein.

would have been a penal one, a judgment of conviction, being in his favour, it may be termed a judgment of acquittal or absolution. To find a name for a judgment given in favour of the defendant in a cause in which, had it been against him, it would have been not a penal, but only a civil, judgment, we must consider it in respect to the influence it may have on the interests of the plaintiff.

First, then, let it have been given in his favour. Whatever is done by one man, whether a magistrate or not, in favour of another, whether a plaintiff or not, is done with or without the assistance of a third person: if without such assistance, the magistrate or other person may be said to have done it with his own hand, *manu propriâ*: if with such assistance, he may in so far be said to have done it by the hand of another, *manu alienâ*. Now, what is done by a judgment can never be done *manu propriâ*: for a judgment, in the sense in which it is an expression of will, is a kind of occasional law, an order made upon such or such persons requiring them to do so and so: requiring them in the present case to comport themselves so and so for the benefit of the plaintiff. It is, therefore, from the conduct that is maintained by the persons in question in consequence of such judgment, and not from the judgment itself independent of such conduct, that the advantage accruing to the plaintiff takes its rise: it is not ever *manu propriâ* that a judge acts as such, but always *manu alienâ*. It is not, therefore, by any action of his own that the judge produces the effect resulting from his judgment, any farther than by means of some action which it produces on the part of some one else. The action, then, which is produced on the part of some one else must be produced either by physical or by moral influence: by physical influence it is not, by the supposition: for, then, it might be said to be produced *manu propriâ* by the judge himself. It must, therefore, be by moral: that is by the force of certain *motives*. Now, motives must be either of the coercive or the alluring kind:[a] those of the latter kind are, as hath been shewn already,[1] inapplicable to the purpose in question; there remain those of the coercive kind. But to give birth to action of any kind on the part of any person by the force of coercive motives is, in other words, to lay him under an obligation: which obligation is, by the supposition, in the case in question, a legal one: and the judgment by which it is imposed may be consider'd as a kind of

Judgment of adjudication.

[a] v. Ch. | |. {Motives}.[2]

[1] See §13, para. 93 n., pp. 144–5 n. above.

[2] See *An Introduction to the Principles of Morals and Legislation* (*CW*), Ch. X, pp. 96–124, though the distinction between coercive and alluring motives is made explicitly at Ch. XVI, para. 27, p. 220.

law. Now, this obligation under which the party is laid is, by the supposition, imposed on him for the sake of another person. But when in favour of one person an obligation is laid on another, such other person is said to have a right conferred on him or to be invested with a right. Since, then, the effect of the judgment is to *invest* the plaintiff with a right, it may be termed a *judgment of investiture*: and since the investment in question is performed by a person acting in the capacity of a judge, it may be termed a *judgment of adjudication*.

Judgment of non-adjudication. Lastly, let the judgment have been given *against*, that is in disfavour of, the plaintiff. Of this case little need be said. As all that it could do in favour of a plaintiff as such is to invest him with a right, so all that it can do against a plaintiff as such is not to invest him, or in other words to refuse to invest him, with a right: it may, therefore, be termed a judgment of *non-investiture* or *non-adjudication*.

Recapitulation. It appears, then, that every legal judgment by which a period is put to a cause is either a penal or a civil judgment: if a penal judgment, a judgment of conviction or a judgment of acquittal: if a civil judgment, a judgment of adjudication or a judgment of non-adjudication.[1]

Let us try whether it might not be possible to find out some epithet which, in its application to the subject of procedure, might be opposed to *penal*, and which might be somewhat less uncharacteristic than the word *civil*. In a civil suit, the two parties are both of them of course petitioners: the plaintiff or claimant requesting that a judgment of adjudication to such or such an effect may be given in his favour, the defendant or repugner that it may not be given: they may, therefore, both of them indifferently be stiled *competitors*: and by analogy the branch of procedure which concerns the steps that may respectively be taken by them for the purpose of obtaining the object of their respective petitions may be stiled *competitorial procedure*.

It cannot be denied but that in every cause, penal as well as civil, there is a competition, so that neither that which is here in question, nor probably any other epithet that could be found, would be quite so characteristic as could be wished: all that can be said in favour of it is that, where the suit is of a penal nature, the circumstance of the punishment which is peculiar to it is of so striking a nature as to eclipse, as it were, and put out of sight the other circumstance which is in common.

[1] MS alt. 'denegation'.

It has been already stated, that to give a judgment of adjudication in favour of one man is to impose an obligation on some other. The person on whom this obligation is imposed is in most instances the defendant. Let it have been a right of property, for instance, that is adjudged to the plaintiff: to confer on him that right, the defendant is inhibited from performing any act the effect of which would be to disturb him in the enjoyment of that property: or let it have been a condition or station in life: the defendant is inhibited from performing any act the effect of which would be to disturb him in the enjoyment of the advantages belonging to that condition. But there may be cases in which the obligation is imposed not on the defendant but on other persons: usually on the special ministers of justice. Let it, for instance, have been a right of guardianship which is adjudged to the plaintiff as against the defendant, who is thereby treated as a lunatic: to give effect to this adjudication, it may be necessary to lay an obligation on other persons to lay hands on the defendant and deliver him into the plaintiff's custody; in such case, to trust to the effects of any obligation laid on the defendant himself, to trust altogether to the effects of mental coercion on the mind of one on whom such coercion may perhaps have no hold, would be evidently absurd. So, where a delivery is to be made of the physical possession of a thing which, perhaps, the defendant has no longer in his possession, or where a nusance is to be removed, which, perhaps, were he ever so well disposed, it exceeds his power to remove. In both cases, indeed, it is the defendant whose interests are principally affected: but in as far as the obligation is laid on himself alone, it is through the medium of his active faculties that he is affected: in as far as it is laid on third persons, it is through the medium of his passive faculties merely.

All suits reducible to the above standards.

In fixing the idea of a suit at law, the business is to pitch upon such a model as shall be at once compleat and simple. To this model, if properly delineated, every other less regular specimen may be reduced and made conformable: if imperfect, by completion, if complex, by decomposition or resolution.

Suits defective by the want of a plaintiff.

In some cases it may be proper or customary or both for the Judge to take up the matter of himself: in this case he may be consider'd as acting himself in the double capacity of plaintiff as well as judge, untill the former function be made over to a third person. This is the case, for instance, where the investitive event in a civil concern, or the act of delinquency in a penal concern, happens under his eye, so that there is nobody can tell him any more of the matter than he knows already: as where a lunatic is seen raving, or a rioter doing mischief, in the court in which the judge is sitting.[1]

Many accusations in one—many claims in one. Incidental suits arising out of the principal.

But the cases are much more frequent in which a suit, in order to be reduced to the ideal standard, requires to be decomposed. Thus, in matters penal, many distinguishable offences may be included in one accusation: as in matters civil may divers rights be included in one claim. This may be the case even from the very commencement of the suit; from the date of the first step that happens to be taken in it. Besides this, there is scarce an instance of a principal suit but what gives birth to a number of incidental contestations, which may be reckoned as so many collateral suits growing out of the principal one, and which are successively determined by judgments which in this case are stiled *interlocutory*.

Moreover, there are few accusations of a penal nature which are not either originally or incidentally intermixed with claims of a civil nature. This is the case in most of the instances where there is room for the operation of any of those subsidiary laws which we have had occasion to characterize under the names of catapaustic, metaphylactic and compensative laws.[a]

Cross claims.

Lastly, in many or perhaps most civil causes, there are cross claims; the defendant insisting not only that the right in question ought not to be conferred upon the plaintiff, but that some other right ought to be conferred upon himself. In this case, also, there are two suits going on together in which the parties are the same: only he who appears in the one capacity in one cause appears in the opposite capacity in the other.

The judgment may be the same in a civil suit as in a penal one.

It should be understood that in many, perhaps in most, instances, it is precisely the same judgment that is given in a penal suit and in a civil one: at least the interests of the defendant are affected by it in precisely the same manner: the only difference lies in the *cause* for which, and the intention with which, it is so given. Thus where money (that is a right to the absolute use and disposal of a sum of money) is given to the plaintiff at the expence of the defendant: if the event on account of which it was given, the event by means of which the plaintiff stands invested with the right of calling upon the judge to make over to him or compel the defendant to make over to him [a sum of money], if this event was

[a] See Ch. | |. {Limits}.[2]

[1] In the margin, Bentham has noted at this point: 'So in case of a contempt of court.'

[2] See §15, para. 118, pp. 165–7 above. As noted above (p. 207 n.), this material was originally intended to form part of the projected Chapter entitled 'Corpus Juris', hence the cross-reference to the text in which it now appears.

one that happen'd so much without the consciousness of the defendant as not to subject him to the imputation of delinquency, the suit can be called nothing but a civil one, for instance where the cattle of the defendant, without any default of his, do mischief to cattle belonging to the plaintiff: if, on the other hand, that event was of such a nature as to subject him to the imputation abovementioned, as if he had driven the cattle purposely into the plaintiff's field, the suit may be termed a penal one: in short, the delinquency of a defendant is but one out of a vast variety of *titles* on which, under any system of laws in being, a plaintiff may ground himself in praying a judgment of the nature in question against the defendant.[a]

Recollecting that, upon the plan here given of the law, every thing that is or can be done by law supposes an offence, it may still be asked, perhaps, how is it that the judgment in a civil suit, in a suit in which nobody is held up to view in the character of a delinquent, has any thing to do with any offence? The answer is, by creating one: by turning into an offence the act of any one who, according to the nature of the judgment whatever it be, should not comply with it. What it is that civil suits have to do with offences.

A judgment although by its name it should be nothing but an act of the understanding, yet before it can have any effect must be understood as having been transformed into a mandate, which is an act of the will. A judgment, then, if it be a civil one, must, if it does any thing, create an offence: it must pitch upon some act or other as one which, in case of its coming to be performed in future, is to be A judgment must pass into an act of the will.

[a] Writing on the law in the English language, I am not writing in the language of the English law. Under the English law in certain cases (for instance in case of the beating of a clergyman), by judgment of three different courts on three different accounts, a man may be made to pay a sum of money to the same amount three different times for one and the same offence: by the Court of Common Pleas, ten pound, for example, to the plaintiff in satisfaction for the injury: by the Court of King's-Bench, a second ten pound to the Crown for the punishment of the offence: by a court called an ecclesiastical court and filled by laymen (the Court of the Dean of the Arches),[1] a third ten pound to the officers of the Court, for the good of his own soul. The founders of the English law were unable to conceive how the being made to pay money should be any punishment to a man when his adversary is to receive it: how the seeing a man punished should be any satisfaction to his adversary, although it should be all he prays for: or how the being made to pay money to any body but the officers of the pretended ecclesiastical court should be of any service to his soul. This same act, forbidden as it is by the law, yet when a man is sued for it in the Common Pleas, they will not allow to be an offence: or if they allow it to be an offence, they will not allow the suit to be a penal one.

---

[1] In the text, Bentham has noted at this point: 'Qu.'

treated in that light. All the difference is that (according to the distinction here laid down) where the judgment is of a civil nature, what offence there is in the case comes after it; there is none to ground it upon: if it is of a penal, an offence is alledged to have been committed against a mandate already subsisting at the time: and it is this offence which is the ground of the judgment, in consequence [of] which judgment, if not complied with, another distinct offence will have been committed, just as there would in the case where a civil judgment is not complied with. In short, in a penal judgment, there are two offences supposed: one precedent and therefore certain, the offence on which it is grounded: the other consequential and contingent as to any individual instance of it, the one which it creates: in a civil judgment, there is but one offence concerned; viz: that consequential contingent one which it creates.

Rights unliquidated and liquid.

Rights, then, may for this purpose be distinguished into two kinds: the one which may be termed *inchoate, inconsummate, unliquidated* or *liquidable*: the other *consummate, liquid* or *liquidated*. The latter is the only one which is susceptible of being violated. A right of the former kind is nothing but a right which a man has to the being invested with a right of the latter kind by the hands of some other person: in some cases, in the first instance by the judge: in other cases, by a private individual in the first instance, but depending always ultimately for its effectivation upon the assistance of the judge: the former is a right to a right: the latter is the immediate right itself. This immediate right may in many, or indeed most, cases be violated by any body whatever: the more remote right is of such a nature as not to be violated but by the Judge or other person by whose hands the right-holder of the first right ought to be invested with the second. In a penal suit as such, the plaintiff's complaint is that some right of his which is already liquid, and needs not the intervention of any one to liquidate it, has been violated; the which violation is of course an offence. In a civil suit as such, he does not allege that any liquid right of his has been violated; but says, that he has a right not yet liquid which he prays the Judge to liquidate. Now, the liquidation of this as yet unliquidated right would be a *service* render'd him by the judge: this service, he says, the Judge, upon his demanding it, already owes him: so that to this service he has already a liquid right; which, if the Judge in due time refuse to render him, will have been violated by the Judge.

Sometimes the suit may be indifferently a civil or penal one.

It is not to be wonder'd at if it should be frequently a matter of doubt whether a right does or does not stand in need of liquidation;[1]

[1] In the margin, Bentham has noted at this point: 'it may also be made to require liquidation by a new law where it did not before'.

and consequently whether the suit proper to be brought by a man who wants to enjoy in future the benefit of the right should be of the penal or of the civil kind. The natural partiality of men in their own favour, and their natural propensity to be angry with those who oppose their wishes, will naturally dispose them to prefer the penal course to the civil. They will, therefore, be apt to institute a penal suit in cases in which, considering the doubtfulness of the title and the *bona fides* of the defendant, the civil might have been the more proper remedy. This propensity may be so strong that in certain cases suitors may desert altogether the path of civil procedure, and give every application they make relative to the right in question a penal form. Judges, who as such can follow no other course than what is marked out to them by the suitors, will be apt to give in to the same propensity, will swim naturally with the stream: so that in certain cases, titles, instead of being tried by a civil, will be tried by a penal action, the judge being supposed to have done that which, if called upon by the plaintiff in a civil way, he would in so clear a case, in spite of the reclamation of the defendant, have deemed himself obliged to do: or to speak more unexceptionably, the plaintiff's unliquidated right being supposed so clear that the Judge, if called upon, could not (as must have been manifest to the defendant) have refused to liquidate it. By this means, there might, in the cases in question, be no other means of trying a civil claim than by a penal action; nor of obtaining the liquidation of a claim but by supposing it already liquidated: insomuch that, if two men living in perfect amity, but having rights which, for the sake of persons connected with them, perhaps, rather than their own, they wished to have liquidated by some impartial hand, but which they could not of themselves contrive to liquidate, wished to obtain the decision of the judge, they had no other way left for it than to agree that one of them should pretend the other had (to his prejudice) committed an offence. In this way, a penal suit may come without difficulty to be employ'd indifferently instead of a civil action, provided the punishment be reduced so low as not to amount to any greater inconvenience than in a civil action the unsuccessful party would be obliged to bear on the account of costs: in which case, the defendant would have no motive for contesting the propriety of the one rather than the other.[a]

A suit may be tried either way when there is no punishment.

[a] To take an example or two from the English law. Originally titles to land were tried by what were called *writs of right*: these came under the notion here given of civil actions: these having been spoilt for use by impertinent niceties and delays, succeeding judges, instead of clearing them of their defects, abandoned them and suffer'd plaintiffs to bring the same question to trial, or one that answer'd the

Example in claims to land.

Cases where there is no ground for a penal suit—1. where the right claimed has not been violated.

Where no act has yet been performed which would be a violation of the right which the plaintiff claims, supposing it to belong to him, it is plain there can be no true ground for a suit of the penal kind: and if his claim be tried in such an action, it can only be done by means of a false representation given of the matter of fact, in which falsity the defendant must concur.

2. Where it is as yet unliquidated—as in the case of a *debt*

So likewise where it is clear the plaintiff can derive no title but through the intervention of the Judge. Thus in the common case of a debt. A man is indebted to you ten pound: of what nature is the right you have in this case? it is not that any one specific thing that once was his belongs now to you: there is not a single thing in the world that, in virtue of this debt, you have as yet any right to meddle with: all the right you have is a right to call upon him to pay you money to that amount:[a] or in his default to call upon the judge to take measures either for compelling him so to do, or for doing the same thing in your favour out of his effects by authority of the court. Now, which ever of them it is that discharges the debt by making over to you the money, whether the debtor himself in the first instance, or the Judge at his expence, by the payment of the money you acquire a new right which you had not before, a right to the exclusive disposal of the individual pieces of coin in which you are paid. Now, then, the pieces of coin being your's, you may count them over and keep them or throw them away, and in short do almost what you will with them, without committing an offence;

purpose nearly as well, by an action of *novel disseisin*: this was what, according to the principles here laid down, we should call a penal action: this also becoming clogged with difficulties was dropt in its turn, and the actions of trespass and ejectment (two other sorts of penal actions) substituted in the room of it. These not answering the purpose after all of securing to either party a quiet and uncontrovertible title, the ingenuity of their advocates directed them to a new court of date comparatively modern, called a court of equity, where at length they obtained the security they sought for in a civil action under the name of a bill for a perpetual injunction. Other instances might also be mentioned in which titles to land may be tried in the court last mentioned still in a civil way by methods which it would here be to no purpose to insist upon.

Thus also, partial rights to the use of land in certain cases in which originally they used to be tried in a writ of *quod permittat prosternere*, a civil action, are now tried in an action on the case for a nuisance, a penal action: and where the public is a party interested on one side, by an indictment, a mode of proceeding so decidedly penal as to be stiled a criminal one: in which latter mode also, it is common to try the right of the public to compel an individual or a parish or other corporate body to render those services which consist in the repairing of a road.

[a] v. Ch. | |. {Division}.[1]

[1] See *An Introduction to the Principles of Morals and Legislation* (*CW*), Ch. XVI, para. 35 n., pp. 227–8 n.

which he who has paid them over to you can no longer do without your leave. But till the payment was made, it was he that had the right of keeping the money and so forth: you had no such right.

Had you offer'd to meddle with any of them, it would have been an offence, an act of wrongful occupation. For him to meddle with them was *no* offence: at least no *such* offence. If, indeed, he was bound to make the payment in question to you without your demand, his keeping them, or rather his forbearing to make over to you the right of keeping them, was an offence: it was the offence of wrongful non-investment; but then it was an offence that had no more relation to the individual pieces of money in question than to any other.

—unless it be for the offence of not conferring the right.

It is plain, then, that where a debt is due to you, which debt, if paid at all, can no otherwise be paid than by making over to you the ownership of certain pieces of money, no title can be derived to any of those particular pieces of money but with the concurrence of the debtor or by the intervention of the Judge. In this case, there can be no pretence for charging the defendant with the commission of that sort of offence which a man would commit who should violate the right demanded by the suit: viz: the right of exclusive ownership with regard to certain pieces of money to be determined by the Judge. This, then, is a claim which can not properly be prosecuted in any other manner than by a civil suit: unless it be in a penal suit where the offence alledged is the offence of wrongful non-investment; the offence of forbearing to render a man those services which are necessary to be render'd to him in order to his being invested with the right to which he has a right.

Even this foundation fails where the right which a man seeks to be invested with could not be convey'd to him otherwise than by the judge himself in consequence of the very suit by which it is claimed. The suit itself is instituted in order to obtain it: if the judge deems him to have a right to it, a right to this right, a preliminary right to this conclusive one, he gives a judgment investing him with this conclusive right. This right, then, takes it's commencement from the end of the suit: it, therefore, had no existence at the beginning: it, therefore, never could have sustained a violation. Previous, therefore, to the judgment, there neither is nor can have been any offence whatever in the case.

There is no ground at all for a penal suit where the right, being unliquidated, is not liquidated but by the Judge.

The cases, therefore, where a claim may, at the option of the plaintiff and consistently with the truth of things, be made to wear either a penal or a civil form indifferently, are these: viz: where in

Recapitulation.[1]

[1] In the margin, Bentham has noted at this point: 'N.B. Not to stand as being but repetition.'

point of law the right claimed is such an one as is capable of subsisting without the intervention of the judge: and where at the same time in point of fact an act has really been committed in violation of such right. You have, as you think, a right: which right an adversary of your's has already violated: perhaps advisedly; perhaps through mis-supposal.[a] For this violation, you have a right to have him punished: but this right you are at liberty to desist from just as you might from any other: you may forbear taking any notice of what is past and confine your endeavours to the securing yourself against violations of the like kind in future.

A civil and a penal suit are distinguishable even where either may be brought indifferently, and where the steps taken in them may be the same.

There are many instances, therefore, in which a penal action and a civil action are equally competent to the case: and what is more, where the steps proper to be taken in the one differ but little from those proper to be taken in the other. This, however, does not throw any obscurity over the distinction between the two actions themselves. A man may have recourse to the one of them only or to the other, as he pleases: but whichever he does recur to, it will always be known whether it is that he recurrs to or the other.

Conclusion.

To conclude, then, whatever right is capable of being determined upon in a penal action is equally capable of being determined upon in a civil action: but there are cases proper for a civil action, which can not, without a departure from truth, be determined in a penal action.

Wherever a man has a right to a penal suit, he has already a right, not perhaps to a civil suit, but to all the benefit that is attainable from a civil suit: unless 1. the right violated is expired; and unless 2. in the case the civil suit is of a definitive nature: viz: of the nature of a bill of injunction to quiet possession.

The judgment in a suit strictly civil may be as burthensome to the defendant as the judgment in a penal suit: and even much more so.

[a] v. Ch. | |.[1]

[1] On mis-supposal see *An Introduction to the Principles of Morals and Legislation* (*CW*), Ch. IX, paras. 6–13, pp. 90–3.

§21. *Uses of this chapter.*[1]

[1.] To conclude, and at the same time apologize in some manner for this long-winded and abstruse discussion, it may be not amiss to give some account of the uses that may be made of it. These may be as follows.

After so abstruse, so long-winded, so fatiguing a discussion, something may be expected by way of apology from the writer, something by way of satisfaction to the reader. Labour is sweetened by utility.

1. To draw some sort of line between the penal and the civil branches of the law-system.

2.* To lay the foundation for the plan of a compleat body of laws, supposing it to be constructed *ab origine*, according to a method of division grounded on natural and universal principles.[2]

3.† To exhibit a plan to work upon, a standard to be guided by, in digesting or reducing a body of customary law, or a mixed body of customary and statute law together, into a pure body of statutory law.

*Form.

†Form.

Matter.

4. In point of matter—to exhibit a clue whereby the legislator may be guided in his endeavours to avoid the great imperfections which a body of laws is exposed to fall into: weakness on the one hand, tyranny and oppressiveness on the other.[3]

[1] At the head of this section, Bentham has noted, 'Settled as far as p. 19 inclusive', i.e. to pp. 224–5 below.

[2] In the margin, Bentham has noted at this point: 'field of legislation a trackless wild which, how often so ever traversed, has never hitherto been survey'd by rule'. A fragment on this theme, headed 'Uses. Plan', is at UC lxxxviii. 374–5: 'In a system thus constructed upon this plan, a man need but open the book in order to inform himself of the aspect borne by the law to every imaginable act that can come within the possible sphere of human agency: what acts it is his duty to perform for the sake of himself, his neighbour or the public: what acts he has a right to do, what other acts he has a right to have others perform for his advantage: whatever he has either to fear from the law, or to hope. In this one repository, the whole system of the obligations which either he or any one else is subject to are recorded and display'd to view: delineated either actually by the commands it pronounces, or potentially by the powers it confers: powers of manual governance, powers of issuing commands either permanent in the shape of laws or transient in the shape of executive mandates.

'The acts to the performance of which a man is actually obliged are embraced by the commands that are delineated upon the face of the law itself: the acts to the performance of which a man may *come* to be obliged are embraced by the powers of imperation which are conferred by the law. The commands issued in virtue of these powers will be either of the permanent or of the transient kind: those which are of the former kind go in augmentation of the body of the laws: the latter quit the stage one after another and vanish altogether in proportion as the purposes they are designed to answer come to an end.

'In a map of the law executed upon such a plan, there are no *terræ incognitæ*, no blank spaces: nothing is at least omitted, nothing unprovided for: the vast and hitherto shapeless expanse of jurisprudence is collected and condensed into a compact sphere which the eye at a moment's warning can pervade and traverse in all imaginable directions.

'Such are the fruits of a method planned under the auspices of the principle of utility, in which the laws are ranged according to the ends they have in view.'

[3] In the margin, Bentham has noted at this point: 'From want of principal provisions comes weakness; from want of qualifications, tyranny. From want of clearness, the one or the other as it may happen.'

Matter. 5. To restrain the licentiousness of interpretation.

Legislators may travel with their eyes open over a plain and level road: instead of groping their way blindfold through an un| |wood.

Expository jurisprudence, the art of finding clear ideas to annex to the expressions of men whose ideas were not clear, instead of being the only branch cultivated, would be thrown aside. The legislator might need a censor, but would need no interpreter. He would be himself his own and sole interpreter: the task of censure he would leave, and the exercise of it he would give encouragement to, in others.

Form and Matter. 6. To exhibit a common standard, to which the several systems of law prevailing in every country may respectively be compared, and thereby their mutual agreements and disagreements represented, their comparative excellencies and defects exhibited to view: to the end that what is excellent in one system may be transferred into every other, that improvements in the most important art of all, the art of legislation, may like other arts make the tour of the globe, and that each legislator may add to his own wisdom, the wisdom of his neighbours and co-temporaries.

Form and Matter. 7. That the method of teaching the art of legislation may be improved, or rather that such a method may be invented, and thereby an acquaintance with the principles of this art may be diffused and render'd more common among the body of the people. It is thus that in time the imagination of the legislator may make room for the judgment and industry of the Professor: and the fruit of Invention be made the subject of Science.[1]

Use 1. It gives the plan of a compleat body of statute law

2. First, then, it gives the plan of a compleat and regular body of statute law:[2] and thereby, as we shall have occasion to shew in the next place, a compleat body of law for every purpose. Laws are either obligative or de-obligative: commands or countermands. As to de-obligative, in a regular body of law there will be neither need nor room for them: their only business is to destroy others: and they perish when they have performed their office. There remain such as are obligative: and such alone we shall henceforward speak of under the denomination of a law. Every law turns an act into an offence: and one law creates but one offence: so many offences, so many laws: for every law there is an offence: for every offence there is a law. Now, of the several sorts of acts which it may

[1] In the margin, Bentham has noted at this point: 'Parsing—applied to the rules of grammar. This but a higher kind of grammar.

'Expository is taught—censorial not.'

[2] Bentham does not discuss the first 'use' listed at p. 219 above, presumably because this topic has been covered in §18, pp. 198–200 above. He does, however, add a discussion of 'Alterability' as a further 'use': see pp. 223–4 below.

be proper to invest with the character of offences, an account has been already given: thereby, therefore, an account was also given, though without announcing it, of the purport of the several laws which it might be proper to establish. Take this chapter, then, and the preceding one,[1] lay them together and we have, such as it is, a compleat and pretty detailed plan for a compleat body of the laws. The former chapter, taking the lead, gave an idea of the nature, purport and *substance* or matter of the laws: the business of the present has been to give an idea of the *form* into which it might be proper that substance should be cast: of the expositions or masses of discourse with which it seems necessary that the several laws, as determined by the principles contained in the preceding chapter, should, as it were, be clothed, in order that the true nature and mutual connections of those laws might be made apparent; and of the order in which it seemed most convenient those masses should be arranged. It is to be remember'd that, by thus parcelling out what relates to the several offences, the whole law is parcelled out. Not but that every law may have, and it will probably be found convenient that every law should have, a civil branch as well as a penal: a part which holds an act up to view in the character of an offence: and a part which holds not up to view any act in any such character. But the civil branch of each law, as hath been shewn, is but the *complement* of the penal: it is on the penal that every proposition which can be found in a book of law depends for its obligative force. When the imperative clause or clauses to which a clause that is not imperative relates is traced out and understood, the true nature and efficacy of such clause is clearly understood: till then, it remains in darkness. Not that the order in which these two branches follow one another in point of importance is necessarily determined by that in which it is most convenient they should follow one [another] in idea for the purpose of intellection. In point of importance, the civil branch (if it be possible to draw a line between matters so intimately and inseparably connected) might possibly be found to precede the penal: but it is the penal at any rate that claims the lead in the order of intellection and enuntiation.

Every law may, then, be distinguished from every other. Indeed, as the same division of civil or expositive matter belongs in common to a multitude of divisions of penal or mandatory matter, many laws, any two laws almost, will have a vast portion of their substance in common: they will be like contiguous

[1] i.e. the present work together with *An Introduction to the Principles of Morals and Legislation*, Ch. XVI.

triangles, like the diagrams of pyramids represented as standing upon the same basis: but the matter of each will be separately describable: as in pyramids so represented the parts of each are separately assignable.

The several laws that in a new code shall be established, or that in an old one may be conceived to be established, upon this plan will be the integrant or aliquot parts of that vast and complicated whole: the several parts of a law as herein above described[1] being the constituent parts of the above-named integrant ones. The number and description, then, of the several laws of which the system is composed being once given, the whole code will be given likewise: the parts or contents of it will be an object of arithmetic: the lineaments and limits of it an object of mensuration. They may be placed contiguous: they may be connected together: and one book will hold them. On that one book any man may lay his hand and say: 'Within this cover is the sole basis of my rights, the sole standard of my duties. Duties and rights together, here I shall be sure to find them: elsewhere I have no need to look for them.'

[2.][2]—which includes a compleat digest of the customary law.

3. In the second place, it will exhibit at the same time a plan for the digestion of the customary law. The customary law, as hath been shewn,[3] is not any essentially distinct branch of the body of the law, it differs not from statute law in substance, but, in as far as it is at all intelligible, in as far as it has any force or efficacy, it must be consider'd as a miscellaneous branch of statute law ill-expressed and ill-defined. To speak of it at all, it must be spoken of, though inaccurately and in the way of fiction, as if it were a portion of statute law. It must be spoken of under the same language as the statute law of which it is the precarious and delusive substitute: as paper is brought to account under the heads of pounds, shillings and pence like sterling money. It must be represented, if at all, as containing such and such parts; as containing imperative, expositive, limitative, exceptive, and extensive clauses. And what, then, are these clauses? if apt in point of expression as well as of substance, they will be nothing more than so many portions of discourse which are proper to be adopted into the body of the statute law: that is into the body of the code: blanks of sterling bullion, which want nothing but the stamp of authority to give them currency. Whatever, then, antecedently to the enactment of a new code was customary law, the same being stamped with the seal of authority, becomes statute law with the

[1] See §§ 3–15, pp. 24–167 above.

[2] MS '3.'

[3] See § 17, pp. 185–97 above.

rest. At present we may boldly affirm that, among all the systems of law which prevail among the several nations of the world, there is not one which does not exist more or less of it in the form of customary law: so that as yet no instance of a compleat code of statute law is any where to be found. It follows not, however, by any means that if a compleat code of that kind were given to any nation it must thereby be deprived of so much as a single article of those antient and respected institutions to which the people, in many instances with great reason, are so strenuously attached. If they lose their present form by such a change, it is only in order to be invested with a better: if the unessential parts of their nature are changed, it will be only in proportion as the essential parts are brighten'd and improved. Conceive a compleat code to be established *uno flatu*. If in any point it be re-enactive of the old law, it will *pro tanto* be a digest of such old law: if the old law were in the statutory form, of the statute law: if in the customary form, of the customary law.

The customary will thus be destroy'd indeed: but how? as the old King in the fable by the pious care of his children was destroy'd: by changing a life of decrepitude and deformity into a life of strength and beauty.[1]

It gives room for making amendments without inconvenience—with greater ease kept from growing worse and rendered better.

4. In the third place, it gives room for making alterations without inconvenience.

No system of laws will ever, it is probable, be altogether perfect: none so good but that a greater share either of information, of judgment or of probity might make it better. Even if, at any given instant, it were really perfect, at the next instant, owing to some change in national affairs, it might be otherwise. Every system of law, then, may from time to time be requiring alterations: and though it never were to require any, yet owing to the fluctuation of human counsels, alterations would in fact be made in it. In a body of laws, as in every other complex piece of mechanism, a great part of it's perfection depends upon the facility with which the several parts of it may be alter'd and repaired, taken to pieces, and put together. But such a system, if constructed upon a regular and measured plan, such as that appears to be which we have been attempting to sketch out, would not only have the advantage of every other while both remained untouched, but alterations, whenever any were made, would give less disturbance to it: provided that such alterations, as often as any were made, in point of form were accommodated, as they easily might be, to that

[1] In Greek mythology, Pelias, King of Iolcus, was cut up and boiled by his daughters, having been persuaded by the goddess Medea that, as a result, he would be rejuvinated.

of the original groundwork.[a] The effects and influence of every fresh provision, whether it were an entire law, a provision expositive, limitative or exceptive, might then with certainty and precision be traced on and coloured out by reference throughout the whole body of the laws. At present, such is the entanglement, that when a new statute is applied, it is next to impossible to follow it through and discern the limits of its influence.[b] As the laws amidst which it falls are not to be distinguished from one another, there is no saying which of them it repeals or qualifies, nor which of them it leaves untouched: it is like water poured into the sea.

To distinguish different things, we must give them different names: of that which has no name, nothing can be said.

4. It will serve to ensure their propriety in point of matter.

[5.] In the fourth place, the regularity which it would give to the laws in point of form would be a test, and by that means a sort of pledge, of their propriety in point of matter.

It is plain that, in a body of laws, the main object, and the sole object of intrinsic importance, is the matter: what it is in point of form is no otherwise of importance than in virtue of the influence which the form has on the nature or efficacy of the matter. But it is the particular use and design of the plan here in question to exhibit and display the matter of the law in the clearest light and in its genuine colours. The fundamental principle which is the basis of the system of laws here sketched out is the principle of utility: and the method here proposed is particularly calculated to shew how far that principle has been deferred to, and where, if any where, it has been deviated from. It is the business of that principle to mark out all along the proper line for the steps of the legislator to pursue: it is the design of a plan like this to throw the strongest light upon those steps, and to shew on every occasion in the clearest manner how far they have been governed by, been kept in conformity to, that line.

The list of the laws is made out from the list of the acts which are held up to view in the character of offences: the acts which are thus held up, being selected on account of the mischief they seem calculated to produce, are ranged according to the different modifications[1] of which that mischief is susceptible. In the cases in which an act is deemed mischievous upon the whole, it is made the object of the imperative part of a law: in the cases in which it is deemed not to be mischievous upon the whole, it is made the

[a] See Append. tit. {Conservation}.[2]

[b] supra 127.[3]

[1] Page 19 begins at this point: see p. 219 n. above.

[2] A projected Appendix to the penal code.

[3] See §16, p. 171–2 above.

object of a qualificative part of the same law. The amplitude of a law is as the amplitude of the act which it makes an offence: the original amplitude of the law as the original amplitude of the act, antecedently to the qualifications by which it is narrowed: the residuary amplitude of the law as the residuary amplitude of the act, deduction made of what is defalcated from it by those several qualifications. Now, the amplitude which is given to a law manifests itself in the imperative provision: the discrimination which is given to it, in the qualificative provisions. Take, then, on the one hand all the imperative provisions belonging to the several laws that compose the code, add together their respective amplitudes; take on the[1] other hand all the qualificative provisions belonging to the same laws, add together in like manner their respective amplitudes on the other side; from the sum of the one combined with the sum of the other results the general character of the whole system. If it be weak and insufficient in any part, it is owing to the total absence or narrowness of some imperative provision: if it be tyrannical and oppressive, it is owing to the absence or narrowness of some qualificative clause. Consider'd in a general view, to the imperative clauses[a] it owes it's vigour; to the

[a] Under this head we must include those clauses which give to one set [of][2] men power over another: because whatever acts of authority a man to whom such a power is committed may exercise in virtue of such power, the law allows of; whatever mandates he may issue, it adopts. When exorbitant powers are unnecessarily bestowed, and those powers are exercised in the performance of tyrannical acts, or the issuing of tyrannous mandates, it is the same thing as if so many tyrannous laws had been established *ab initio*.

In[3] an idea so general as this of the dependency of the character of the law upon the extent of the imperative and qualificative provisions in it, perfect clearness and exactness must not be expected. It should be understood, for example, that a law which gives powers or authorities of any kind exerciseable over persons or over things that in the main are the property of other persons adopts in effect all the acts of coercion that can be exercised by the person in authority over the persons subjected to it without abuse of trust: and has, therefore, *pro tanto* the effect of an obligative provision. It is in this way that the law may incur the charge of tyranny merely by conferring powers: which, indeed, is the most formidable and vexatious kind of tyranny: and yet powers will upon this plan have been constituted, as may have been observed,[a] rather by the exceptive, that is by the qualificative matter of the code, than by the imperative.

Moreover, it is by obligations, partly compulsive and partly restrictive, and, therefore, by matter of the imperative kind, that the powers mentioned above are

[a] supra §| |.[4]

[1] Page 19 ends at this point: see p. 219 n. above.
[2] MS 'a'.
[3] In the margin, in relation to this and the following paragraph, Bentham has noted: 'Qu. if not expressed before.' Bentham may have intended the previous paragraph to supersede this and the following paragraph.
[4] See §12, pp. 115–41 above.

qualificative, its mildness: to a happy proportionality and correspondency between the two, its wisdom, and thence whatever share of utility remains to it upon the ballance.

Moreover, in proportion as the law is deficient in any of those qualities which are necessary to it in order to its being present in its proper form to the conceptions of those whose concern it is to be apprised of it, such as the qualities of precision, perspicuity, conciseness, and aptitude for promulgation, it becomes chargeable with one or other of the foregoing imperfections, as it may happen. If, from a failure in all or any of those respects, a substantive law escapes altogether the apprehension of all parties whatsoever who are concerned in it, of those who are to *execute* it as well as those who are to *obey* it,[a] the whole code becomes *pro tanto* weak and simply insufficient: if it escapes the apprehension of those alone who should obey it, without losing the obedience of those who are to *execute* it upon the others in case of its being disobey'd (the frequent and deplorable lot of laws too complicated and obscure to be sufficiently promulgated), it becomes insufficient and oppressive both at once: insufficient in the first instance, tyrannical and oppressive in the second.

Now, the qualities of precision, perspicuity and conciseness in the parts are all connected, either in the character of causes or effects, or both, with the regularity of the method which happens to be adopted for the whole. As to promulgation, this indeed is in itself an operation distinct from that of composition. Though distinct, they are, however, to such a degree connected that, unless composed upon a regular plan, the whole code, take it all together, never can possess a hundredth part of the publicity it ought to have. A plan, therefore, however excellent in other respects, would be very imperfect after all, unless it were composed with a particular view to promulgation: that essential and much neglected branch of administration, by the abandonment of which the greater part of the legislative matter that subsists is

guarded against abuse. The quality of mildness, then, with reference to the subject at large depends partly upon the slackness of such part of the obligative branch of the code as relates to them, partly upon the strictness of such part of that branch as relates to their subordinate rulers: remembering always, that the same person who to some purposes is a ruler is to other purposes a subject.[1]

[a] To obey a punitive law is to execute the substantive. v. supra | |.[2]

[1] In the margin, Bentham has noted at this point: 'A tyranny of men, it has often and justly been remarked, though less discernible, yet when once discerned, is more formidable and at any rate more baneful than a tyranny of the laws. A tyranny of men is that which is established by permission to command or, what is equivalent, by vague mandates.'

[2] See §13, para. 102, pp. 151–3 above.

continually rendering itself worse than useless. Now, to disentangle one law from another, that which concerns one class of persons from that which concerns a different class of persons, a man must know how to describe them separately: the means of doing which it has been one part of the design of this chapter to afford.[a]

Use 5. It tends to check the license of interpretation

6. In the fifth place, it tends to check the license of interpretation.

I mean, of course, what has been distinguished by the name of *liberal* interpretation:[1] that delicate and important branch of judiciary power, the concession of which is dangerous, the denial ruinous.

Now, this necessity, supposing it to exist, from whence does it arise? From the want of circumspection or advertency, from the want of amplitude or discrimination, in the views of the legislator. In the beginning, one might almost say till now, legislators have felt their way rather than seen it, taking up the ground by bits and parcels and without so much as attempting any general survey of the whole. In consequence, no order, no connexity: no steps taken for guarding against oversights and omissions. The best-imagined provision might perhaps have done more mischief than good unless moulded into form by the prudence of the Judge. On the one hand, the obligative part was not wide enough to embrace the mischief: on the other hand, the qualificative parts were not wide enough to yield shelter to innocence or to afford the necessary range to power. But the incidents which foresight could not present to the legislator, experience would from time to time be presenting to the Judge. What was to be done? Was the continual recurrency of partial evil to be suffer'd to reduce, to fritter away into nothing, the hopes of general good? This was not to be endured. Here, then, in the very cradle of legislative empire grew up another power, in words the instrument of the former, in reality continually its censor and not unfrequently its successful rival. How difficult to distinguish what the legislator would have adopted had he adverted to it, from what he did actually advert to and reject? How easy to establish the one under pretence of looking for the other? especially when, if truth refused her aid, fiction was ready at their call. The legislator, perhaps an unletter'd solider, perhaps a narrow-minded priest, perhaps an interrupted,

[a] See farther Ch. 19. {Corpus Juris}.[2]

---

[1] See §16, para. 130, pp. 175–6 above.

[2] For the projected Chapter entitled 'Corpus Juris' see the Editorial Introduction, p. xii above.

unwieldy, heterogeneous, unconnected multitude: the judicature, a permanent, compact, experienced body, composed of connected individuals, participating in the same affections and pursuing the same views. And thus sprang up by degrees another branch of customary law, which, striking its roots into the substance of the statute law, infected it with it's own characteristic obscurity, uncertainty and confusion.

For disorders proceeding from the want of plan, a regular plan may at length, it is hoped, provide a powerful palliative at least, and in time, it is hoped, a compleat and effectual remedy. To supersede as far as may be the necessity of discretionary interpretation, the business is to give amplitude enough in the first place to the imperative matter in the code: and it is for this purpose that a general survey of acts fit to be made offences taken upon an exhaustive plan was presented in the last chapter:[1] in the next place to the qualificative matter: for which purpose an analysis of the possible grounds of justification conducted in the same manner will be given farther on.[a] By these processes when laid together, such a degree of comprehension and steadiness might one day perhaps be given to the views of the legislator as to render the allowance of liberal or discretionary interpretation on the part of the judge no longer necessary.

But in an analysis of so extensive and intricate a nature, errors would unavoidably insinuate themselves: nor supposing it perfect would there be any assurance that the lights afforded by it should always be steadily pursued: and even though a plan were eventually to prove perfect, yet antecedently to experience, it would be rashness to proceed upon the presumption of its proving so. Human reason does not seem to be yet [far][2] enough advanced to warrant the laying the discretionary mode of interpretation under an absolute interdiction in all cases whatsoever. It remains, therefore, to think of some expedient for guarding that power from abuses, clearing the exercise of it from the inconveniences it is attended with, and confining it within it's proper limits. For these purposes, a plan is contrived, which will be developped at length in a subsequent part of the work.[b] Let the judge be required, where-

[a] See Ch. 20. {Plan} and B. I. Tit. {Justifications}.[3]

[b] See Appendix tit. {Interpretation} and {Conservation}.[4]

[1] See *An Introduction to the Principles of Morals and Legislation* (*CW*), Ch. XVI, pp. 187–280.

[2] MS 'farther'.

[3] i.e. the projected Chapter entitled 'Plan of Book I' (the first Book of the penal code) and one of the projected 'titles' in that Book respectively. For further details see the Editorial Introduction, pp. xi–xii above.

[4] i.e. Appendices to the projected penal code.

soever he determines in the way of liberal interpretation, to declare openly his having done so: at the same time drawing up *in terminis* a general provision expressive of the alteration he thinks the case requires, which let him certify to the legislator: and let the alteration so made, if not negatived by the legislator within such a time, have the force of law. By this means the legislator would see what the Judge was doing: the Judge would be a counsel to him, not a controul: the sceptre would remain unshaken in his hands: the experiments of the one would be corrected by the experience of the other: the simplicity of the legislative plan would be preserved from violation: the corrective applied would be applied not in the obscure, voluminous and unsteady form of customary jurisprudence, but in the concise and perspicuous form of statute law.

As to the individual cause by which the propriety of the general alteration comes to be suggested, the authority of the Judge in this line should not extend to positive punishment, [but] should be confined to the case in which whatever burthen was thrown upon one party would be so much taken off the shoulders of the other, and that [in which] no man be left in possession of a clear profit reaped in fraud of the old law: for by punishment, past mischiefs can not be recalled, and whatever is yet to come may as effectually be prevented by a new law which may be made on purpose.[a]

—and to facilitate a comparison between the laws of different nations

7. In the sixth place, it would facilitate a comparison between the laws of different nations. At present, not only the jurisprudence of any given nation is a labyrinth in itself, but each one of those systems is a labyrinth of a different form from every other. Few nations who can boast of having any considerable part of the body of their laws reduced by authority to any such order as to bear the appellation of a code;[b] none who can shew the whole of that body reduced to any such form. But of such codes as there are, take any two and compare them together; and run over the list of the

[a] It is a common rule that penal statutes ought to be construed strictly. This, as we have seen, seems consonant to utility as applied to the substantive laws themselves: otherwise when applied to the adjective laws which concern the steps to be taken for carrying them into execution. There is reason why a man who, upon the footing of the old law, was not guilty should not be punished: there is none why a man who, to the satisfaction of the Judge, can be proved guilty should be suffered, on account of a flaw in the process or in the law relative to it, to triumph in impunity.

[b] See the Preface.[1]

[1] This 'Preface' has not been identified. The 'Preface' which was eventually published (see *An Introduction to the Principles of Morals and Legislation* (*CW*), pp. 1–10) was written in 1789, and hence post-dates this passage by up to nine years.

divisions that are respectively contained in them: in no instance will you find the titles of those divisions the same throughout or in the same order: nor where the titles themselves happen to be the same, will the contents of the divisions so entitled be found to be ranged upon the same plan. And yet, if upon any occasion any part of the legal systems of two different nations come to be confronted by any person, some common plan he must necessarily form to himself to which he will reduce them in his own mind. But if that which is taken for a standard is confused, his idea of the other will in like manner be confused: if the parts of the former were indistinguishable, equally so will those of the latter. This, then, is a difficulty the remedying of which will be another advantage derivable from a natural and regular plan of legislation. To every one of these labyrinths it would afford an uniform and consistent clue. By this means a set of tables might be formed exhibiting the provisions made by the several governments in the world (such of them whose policy was thought to be worth attending to) under the several heads included in the natural syllabus in question: a comparative view of the several systems of legislation confronted together in their correspondent parts and digested into one work: a work which, to borrow an expression from Divines, might be stiled a sort of universal *harmony of the laws.*[1] [a]

As to the uses that might be made of such a comparison, these have been already touched upon in the preceding chapter.[b]

[a] In the year 1727, 1162 years after the death of Justinian in 565, Heineccius Heince, a Dutch civilian lawyer, published a digest of the compilations of that Emperor reduced to the order of the Pandects.[2] In the year 1767, 40 years after, Beger, a German lawyer of Ulm in {Franconia}, published a digest of the same compilation reduced to the order of the Institutes.[3] Sad proof of the slow growth of human reason! that, after an interval of so many hundred years, no better idea should have been devised than that of copying the ideas of a sovereign who, for the purpose of pointing out to the subject the line of his duty, has laid before him two different arrangements of the same matter altogether unconnected and incommensurate.

[b] Ch. XVI. {Division} LX.[4]

---

[1] In a theological sense, a harmony is a collation of passages from different sources, for instance the four Gospels, with a view to demonstrating their consistency.

[2] Johann Gottlieb Heinecke or Heineccius (1681–1741), German jurisconsult, Professor of Law at the University of Halle 1721–4, 1733–41, and at the University of Frankfurt 1724–33, published *Elementa iuris civilis secundum ordinem Institutionum* at Giessen in 1727, though the work referred to by Bentham is his *Elementa iuris civilis secundum ordinem Pandectarum*, 3 vols., Amsterdam, 1731.

[3] Eusebius Beger (1721–88), jurist, lived and worked in Ulm from 1748, and published *Corpus iuris civilis reconcinnatum, in tres partes distributum*, 2 vols., Frankfurt and Leipzig, 1767–8.

[4] See *An Introduction to the Principles of Morals and Legislation* (*CW*), Ch. XVI, para. 60, p. 274.

8. In the seventh and last place, it may be made to facilitate the communication and thereby the gradual improvement of the science to beginners.

and to facilitate the communication of the science to beginners.

When once an improvement has been made in any science and the utility of it stands confirmed by the suffrages of the experienced in that line, the next business is to facilitate the communication of it to the rising generation. In its turn every intellectual production undergoes this course of husbandry. If, while in the nursery of invention, it is found to bear the blasts of criticism, it is taken up by somebody, pruned into form and transplanted into the garden of science.

In that department of logical science which goes by the name of grammar (for between what is commonly called logic and what is commonly called grammar there seems to be no clear line of separation), many helps are made use of for the purpose of teaching the rules of speech in general, which might be transferred and adapted, if it were worth while, to any particular branch of discourse in particular. Such is that exercise which consists in ranging particular words and combinations of words under general classes and rules; and which, when applied to words in the light in which they are consider'd by grammar, goes commonly under the name of *parsing*.

The several general propositions or grammatical rules, as they are called, abstracted and abstruse as they are in themselves, being exemplified over and over again upon different models, the purport of them may, as experience [testifies],[1] be enabled by degrees to make a lasting impression upon the least susceptible conceptions. A word being proposed to the scholar, he is required to point out the classes to which it belongs, in virtue of the several grammatical relations it bears to other words that are connected with it. Each word and combination of words is thus referred to a particular class invented and named for the purposes of discourse in general. This process is equally applicable to any other branch of logic as to that elementary branch which is called grammar.

As words of any sort may be *parsed* by referring them to the classes entitled by the words a *verb*, a *noun*, a *verb in the infinitive mood*, a *noun in the accusative case*, and so forth, so words of a particular stamp, consider'd in a particular point of view, may be parsed by referring them to the classes entitled by the words *genus, species, subject, predicate,* and the like: as may also entire propositions of the argumentative stamp by referring them to the

[1] MS 'testified'.

classes entitled by the words *Barbara, celarent, darii,*[1] and so on. In the same manner may propositions of the legislative stamp be parsed by referring them to the classes entitled law against simple personal injuries, law against semi-public offences, law against public offences: imperative provision, qualificative, limitative, exception, justification; substantive law, adjective law, remedial law, punitive law; and so on through all the variety of appellatives above exhibited, as well as of such others as, upon a maturer and more particular examination, it might be found advisable to add or substitute to the foregoing.

School. When these rules and exercises were prepared and brought into order, a sort of school might be established of which the business should be to teach, not the art of forensic disputation for the emolument of individuals, but the art of legislation for the benefit of empires.

Model. If a model of a compleat code, applied for exemplification sake to the circumstances of some one nation in particular, were once framed, and students of various nations were to meet together under one roof (as hath so often been the case in the schools of medicine, of botany, of chemistry and other branches of the physical department of science) a harmony of the laws actually Harmony. in force, upon the plan above mentioned, might form one part of the business of such a school, each student taking in hand the jurisprudence of his own state. By this work, the old laws of each country would be arranged upon a new plan. This being accomplished, the next and finishing atchievement would be to frame for New code. each nation a compleat code new in point of substance as well as form, copied from the general model above-mentioned, with such alterations as shall be deemed requisite to adapt it to the particular manners, sentiments and exterior circumstances of each respect- Apologetica. ive state. If the time when an institution of such a sort could be proposed with any probability of it's adoption is yet at a great distance, the idea of it, however, can not be thrown out too soon: the sooner it is exposed to public view, the sooner it takes rank among those embryo projects which chance will sometimes bring into life, and a happy concurrence of talents and resolution sooner or later brings onward to maturity.

As grammar is taught by sentences thrown on purpose out of regimen, and geography by dissected maps, in like manner might the art of legislation, particularly what may be stiled the mechanical branch of it, be taught by means of shapeless laws, to be taken to pieces, and put together again after the manner of the model. As

[1] For these terms see p. 22 n. above.

to making examples on purpose, it is what there could be no need of here: since enough and enough might be found ready made among the laws that are any where in being.[1]

Connection of this and the preceding chapters with the next ensuing.[2]

9. But to pursue these visions any farther, would be to wander too far from the proper track of this design. It is time we should resume the regular thread of the discourse, which leads, in the next place, into the examination of the different plans which the legislator may form to himself for the attack of the mischiefs which he has to combat, and the steps which it may lie in his way to take for bringing the whole of the force he has at his disposal to co-operate together and act in subservience to the principal design.

Legislation is a state of warfare: political mischief the enemy: the legislator is the commander: the moral and religious sanctions his allies: punishments and rewards (raised some of them out of his own *demesnes peculiaire*, others borrowed from those allies) the forces he has under his command: punishments his regular standing force, rewards an occasional subsidiary force too weak to act alone: the mechanical branch of legislation, the branch we have been treating of in the present chapter, the art of tactics: direct legislation, a formal attack made with the main body of his forces in the open field: indirect legislation, a secret plan of connected and long-concerted operations, to be executed in the way of stratagem or *petite guerre*. All these heads except this last have been discussed already. It remains that we should say something of this irregular system of warfare: a system which, on account of the oeconomy with which it may be carried on and the ingenuity which it is thought to require and which it often gives occasion to display, stands in much higher favour with men in general than that which is carried on by open force.

[1] The following related fragment is at UC lxxxviii. 372: 'A school-boy is thought to have made but a small proficiency in grammar, if, when a grammatical sentence is set before him, there be a word which he is unable to refer to the place that belongs to it in that sentence. If the science of legislation were as far advanced as that of grammar, and it were the custom for legislators to be as well acquainted with their science, as it is for school-boys to be with grammar, a statesman would be thought to have made but a small proficiency in legislation, if, in any book of law that were set before him, there were a word which he knew not how to refer to the place that [it] occupies in some mandate. But to love power is one thing: and to love the studies which alone can qualify a man to exercise it as he should do, is another.'

[2] i.e. *An Introduction to the Principles of Morals and Legislation* (*CW*), Ch. XVI, pp. 187–280, and the present work, the projected Ch. XVII, with what was originally conceived as Ch. XVIII on 'Indirect Legislation'. For further details see the Editorial Introduction, p. xii above.

APPENDICES

APPENDIX A

§2. *Distinction between penal law and civil.*[1]

Limits between penal law and civil undiscernible.

1. So much for private ethics on the one hand and jurisprudence, or rather the art of legislation, on the other. We come now to speak of what is called civil law or jurisprudence on the one hand, and penal law or jurisprudence on the other: or more properly, to the art of legislation in civil matters on the one hand, and the art of legislation in penal matters on the other. Between these two branches, which are so often set in opposition to one another, where then lies the distinction?—No where. They are inextricably interwoven. What individual law is civil and not penal? there is no such thing. What law is penal and not civil? there is no such thing. In every law must be comprised two things: 1. a specification of the cases in which the punishment is to attach; 2. a specification of the punishment itself: without punishment, no such thing as law: without a motive, no such thing as action.

It is not every sentence of the penal law that mentions punishment.

2. The individuation of a law, I mean the description of that which is to be looked upon as constituting neither more nor less than one entire law, is as yet a matter altogether unsettled and obscure: nor is this a place for entering into those details which would be necessary to clear it up. But be it settled any how, still it will be equally impossible to draw any precise line between the penal branch of the law [and the civil branch] as shall discriminate effectually what is delivered concerning the art of treating one of those branches from that of treating the other. Let [every] distinguishable provision or regulation, every assemblage of words that forms a sentence and composes a part of the body of a law, be looked upon as constituting an entire law: the proposition would not be the less true. On this supposition, every such sentence in which no mention was made of punishment should belong to the civil branch of law: every sentence in which punishment was mentioned, to the penal branch. Would this be admissible? certainly not. For never was there a code called a penal one which did not contain abundance of sentences in which there was not the least mention of such a thing as punishment.

Nor is there any command that belongs exclusively to the civil branch.

3. Is law to be deemed a species of command? and is that to be deemed one law which constitutes one command? Neither in this way could we find any distinction between what is called the civil

[1] This section, itself continued by that which eventually became § 19 of 'Limits' (see pp. 201–6 above), constituted the original continuation of § 1 (see pp. 3–15 above). For further details see the Editorial Introduction, pp. xxix–xxx above.

branch and the penal. In this case, if every law must have a punishment to back it, supposing there were two distinct branches of Jurisprudence, part of every law would belong to the civil branch, while the other part belonged to the penal.

A law may be penal without mentioning punishment.

4. Suppose even a law to which no punishment was annexed by the legislator; still, however, a punishment it must have. It might derive it from the moral sanction: it might derive it from the religious sanction: but some punishment at any rate it must have: else it would not be a law: else it would not obtain obedience: else it could not have any of the effect of what is really a law.[a]

The distinction between civil and penal applies not to the laws themselves, but to the books that treat of them.

5. In the law itself, then, there is no such distinction to be met with. What distinction there is respects the books that happen to be written on the subject of the law. That book belongs to the subject of penal jurisprudence, which has most in it about punishment: that book belongs to the civil branch which has least in it about punishment itself, and most about the cases in which punishment is or is not to be applied.

The Book, indeed, may be a large book; it may indeed be of any size, and yet be a book of law, and yet not say a syllable in any part of it about punishment: still, however, it has a tacit reference to punishment: else the law which it delivers or professes to deliver would be nugatory, and the book useless.

Example in the law relative to Wills.

6. A great book, for example, is written about Wills: a subject in fact which has given birth to many a great book. It says a great deal about the nature of a Will: about the sorts of persons who are empower'd to make them: about the cases in which these persons

Ambiguous import of the epithet *civil* as applied to law.

[a] This is so true that there is no such thing as any tolerably significant name for that branch of law which is so often spoken of as contradistinguished from the penal. The only word used for this purpose is the word *civil*; than which nothing can be more inexpressive. The word civil, it must be confessed, is put to very hard duty. It is to be met with every where: and wherever it comes, it brings confusion. The word *civil* comes from *civis*, the member of a commonwealth, a state, a community of people, such as when the word was first framed were frequently collected all together within the walls of one city. *Civilis*, then, means belonging to a commonwealth. In what respect, then, does it characterize that branch of the law which is not penal as contradistinguished from that which is? That which is not penal concerns the community: true: but does not that which is penal concern the community full as much? Sometimes it is used as synonymous to political, which, in it's original signification, has precisely the same meaning in Greek as civil has in Latin. Sometimes it is put in opposition to political, meaning every branch of the law besides what is meant by the political. Sometimes it is put in opposition to ecclesiastical: meaning every branch of law besides what is meant by the ecclesiastical. Sometimes it is put to express the law, the whole jurisprudence, of antient Rome: sometimes so much of that jurisprudence as is adopted into the law of this or that modern state. Other senses doubtless might be found for it besides these.

may, and those in which they may not, exercise that power: about the things that may be thus disposed of: about the different sorts of Wills when made: about the number of witnesses which must attest them: about the places where they must be register'd: about the construction that is to be given them, and so on for evermore: all this while without intimating a syllable about punishment. Has punishment, however, no concern in this? if that were the case, the whole affair would amount to nothing. In fact, all this is of no farther use than as it serves to fix the application of punishment: distinguishing the one person who would *not* be punished in case of his meddling with and using, and perhaps disposing of, the thing in question from the multitude of other persons (amounting in fact to no fewer than all the rest of mankind) who *would*. You claim to be the sole proprietor of yonder house: that is the only person of all mankind who, according to the disposition of the law, in case of his occupying it would not be liable to punishment. You maintain that you are the person named in this behalf by the will of your deceased friend: who possessed the house: who was of the number of those persons who are allow'd to make a Will: who was so circumstanced as to have a right to dispose of this house by his Will: who made such and such a will accordingly in your favour: took care to have it attested by so many witnesses &c, &c. All this is only to give other persons to understand that, were they to offer to meddle with the house, they would be punished: and that you alone are left free to deal with it as you please.

So in the law concerning the appointment of persons to public trusts.

7. All this holds equally good with regard to what may be called the constitutional branch of law, or that which concerns the designation of persons invested with public trusts, and of the powers they are invested with. Are you a King? a Judge? a General? then upon your commanding me to do so and so, in case of my not obeying, I am liable to be punished for it. Are you not a King? a Judge? a General? then in case of your commanding me to do so and so as if you were, I am not liable to be punished for my disobedience: but you perhaps are liable to be punished for your presumption.

The whole business of law reducible to that of creating duties. This takes two operations.

8. Whatever business the law may be conversant about, may be reduced to one sort of operation, viz: that of creating duties. But to create duties, in the first place it must define them: in the next place, it must mark out the punishments to be inflicted for the breach of them.[a] Here, then, are two operations distinguishable in

Rights created by prescribing duties.

[a] It is by creating duties and by nothing else that the Law can create rights. When the law gives you a right, what does it do? it makes me liable to punishment in case of my doing any of those acts which would have the effect of disturbing you in the exercise of that right.

themselves, though for use they must always be conjoined. In point of expression, it may take more words to perform them, or it may take fewer.

Which however may be expressed in one sentence.

9. After a manner, they may be performed, both of them together, in one single sentence: in which case, they will shew as if in substance they were but one.

Instance in a law against theft.

10. 'Whosoever stealeth, shall be hanged.' That might do, after a certain sort, for a law against Theft. In saying thus much, an inexperienced or negligent legislator might think he had done enough. In this stile accordingly were conceived the first crude attempts at legislation.[a] But what is meant by stealing? for the ideas meant to be represented by this word are certainly not so obvious as to present themselves to every man alike without difficulty or danger of mistake. To explain this sufficiently will at any rate take up another sentence. It may take up a paragraph, a page, a volume.

So a part of it may take up volumes. In many of which nothing should be said about punishment.

11. Were a man to put together all that has been ever written in this view, it might perhaps take up a multitude of volumes. Suppose a single one: it is plain that in this whole volume there need not be a syllable about punishment. Yet to punishment it must have a reference: and before it amounts to so much as to any one single law, it must be conjoined with some clause by which punishment is prescribed. It is a part, however, of the mass of jurisprudence: of that which has been written, with or without authority, upon the subject of the laws in general. Is it then a part of the penal branch of jurisprudence? but it contains not a syllable about punishment. Is it a part of the civil branch? but it has a necessary reference to punishment, without which it would be nugatory and unavailing. Will this necessary reference, then, which it has to punishment serve to confine it to the penal branch? Not so neither: for the same necessary reference has every thing else that comes under the head of law. A regulation belonging to the constitutional branch of law has it, as much as any other.[b]

Conclusion— that book relates to penal law, which dwells most upon punishment.

12. What, then, after all is the difference, such as it is, between the penal branch of the law, and the civil? or rather between a book

[a] The stile of the laws of the 12 tables,[1] and of such of the Greek laws as are handed down to us, was as concise and inexplicit, as this example.

[b] supra | |.[2]

[1] According to Roman tradition, the Twelve Tables were compiled in 451–450 BC, and effectively rendered customary law into statute.

[2] Bentham perhaps had in mind *An Introduction to the Principles of Morals and Legislation* (*CW*), Ch. XVI, para. 54 n., OFFENCES against the SOVEREIGNTY, pp. 263–4 n.

written on the subject of penal law and a book written on the subject of civil law? That book belongs to the penal branch which dwells most upon the subject of punishment: that, to the civil, which, without making any mention, or at least without making much mention, of the article of punishment, dwells most upon the cases in which punishment is or is not to be applied.[1]

[1] For the original continuation of the text see § 19, pp. 201–6 above.

APPENDIX B

§7. *Of acts which are the objects of a law.*[1]

Acts may be directly or indirectly the objects of a law.

[1.] Fourthly,[2] with regard to the acts that are the objects of the law. To these, also, the division into direct and indirect may apply, as well as to persons and to things.[3]

Necessity of introducing the words

2. The mention of the word *act* makes it in a manner necessary

[1] This material represents a later draft of the topic, which is discussed in paragraphs 39–48 of the 'principal draft', pp. 66–74 above.

A passage, crossed out by Bentham, which has been superseded by paragraphs 1–2 of the present text, is at UC lxxxviii. 251.

[2] MS orig. 'Fifthly'.

[3] The following continuation of the passage has been crossed through by Bentham: 'Concerning acts in general and the fundamental differences that may be remarked in them, a good deal has been said in a chapter appropriated to that subject.[a] But what is there observed is applicable rather to individual acts, than to classes of acts as marked out by the names that are in use: such more especially as there is occasion to make use of in books of law. Every individual act that imports motion must have a subject in which it begins, subjects through which it makes its progress, and a subject in which it terminates: and yet it is seldom that the name by which it is known brings the particulars of it's progress at all to view. Thus, in every act of killing there must be some variety, and oftentimes there is a great variety, of bodies through which it has made its progress: yet no particulars concerning that progress are brought to view by the word *to kill*. It characterises the progress made by the act no otherwise than by means of the material part of its effects. And the same pathological effects may have been produced by acts which have differ'd infinitely in respect of their progress: by the stroke of a sword, by the impulse of a bullet discharged out of a gun, by a fall into the water and the consequent exclusion of respirable air from the lungs, by poison administer'd to the stomach either at once or in repeated doses, and so on without end. Not that what has been said concerning the progress of an act proves on this account to be of no use: for as often as there is any occasion to obtain an exact idea of any individual act of those that come under the general denomination of killing, it is no otherwise to be obtained than by obtaining an idea of it's progress traced through every stage.

'Sometimes an habit composed of a long and infinitely diversified train of acts is comprehended under one name; each act consisting of motions, but of motions which, in every stage of their progress, are in the different acts altogether different. Let the act or habit of maintaining one's children serve for an example. It is impossible in this case that any uniform idea of the progress of the act should be suggested by the word *maintenance*. And yet, if in any individual instance a failure in such a point of duty were alledged against a man, the particulars of such a progress must on that individual occasion be brought to view: it must appear, for instance, that, on a certain time when the child wanted feeding, he put no food into it's mouth; that, where it wanted cloathing, he wrapped no cloathing about it's body; and so on without end.

'Sometimes a word purporting to be the name of an act includes not one act only, or one succession of acts, but a number of acts consider'd as co-existing, of which one, and but one, being an external or physical act, is susceptible of such a progress as can be described. In the act of theft, for instance, are included three acts at once: a physical act, an act of the understanding, and an act of the will. A physical act, the act of taking the thing in question: an act of the understanding, the act of being conscious or perceiving that one has no title to the thing taken: an act of the will, the act of intending to prevent the owner from having access to it.'

[a] See Ch. 7. {Actions}. [See *An Introduction to the Principles of Morals and Legislation* (*CW*), Ch. VII, pp. 74–83.]

to say something of the words *circumstance* and *case*: since these are words which will continually be occurring, and without which one act can scarcely be either described by itself, or spoken of as being distinguished from another.[1]

circumstance and *case.*

Specificant circumstances in a law, what.

3. The chief use of a circumstance as annexed to the name of an act is to specificate it, that is to distinguish it from acts which in other respects are of the same name. Yet it is not every circumstance that has this effect; or, to speak more properly, it is not on every occasion that a groupe of words expressive of a circumstance has this effect upon the act with the name of which it connects. Circumstances may, accordingly, be distinguished into *unspecificant*, and *specificant*. The unspecificant are mentioned rather for regularity's sake, and [lest][2] it should be asked what we are to think of them, than for any occasion there will be to make mention of them hereafter. The distinction between these two ways of introducing a circumstance may be thus made out.

Conceive an assemblage of words put together by which an act of any sort is expressed under the character of the object of a mandate: this done, any other words that purport to have any thing to do with the description of the act may be consider'd as expressive of a circumstance belonging to it. Suppose the act to be that of exporting wheat out of the country; and let it be mentioned in the character of the object of a mandate in this manner—'No man shall export wheat out of the country.' The sentence, then, as it stands at present may be looked upon as expressive of an act without a circumstance. Add now the words 'that breathes,' and let it stand, 'No man *that breathes* shall export wheat out of the country:' the words *that breathes* are expressive of a circumstance indeed, but of a circumstance which is not specificant: wheat can not be exported by any man but it must be exported by a man that breathes. So if it be said, 'No man shall *in any wise* export wheat out of the country.' But if it be said, 'no man shall export wheat out of the country in any foreign navigable vessels,' here a circumstance is introduced which is specificant, because corn may be exported in navigable vessels of the country, or if the country be not an island, by land carriages. So, likewise, if it be said, 'No man shall export wheat out of the country—*when* the market price at the place from whence it is meant to be exported is more then 44s. a quarter.'[a]

[a] British Stat. 13 Geo. III. c. 43. §5.

---

[1] In the margin, Bentham has noted at this point: 'I could easily write a volume upon it, but the difficulty is to say any thing of it that can be of any use in the compass of a few pages.'

[2] MS 'least'.

To give one instance more. Suppose the law to say—'let no man steal any thing, knowing that he has no title to it:' the words 'knowing that he has no title to it' are expressive of a circumstance; but of a circumstance which is not specificant: for a man can not steal any thing without knowing that he has no title to it: since, if this consciousness be wanting, the taking is not what is meant by stealing. But let the law say, 'let no man steal in a dwelling house' or 'by night' (as where it means to impose an extraordinary penalty on account of the intervention of these circumstances), these circumstances, it is evident enough, are specificant, for the reason that has been given. As to circumstances that are not specificant, it seems pretty evident, that the introduction of them into a law, unless in as far as they answer the purpose of explanation, or some rhetorical purpose, is altogether nugatory.

So much by way of a general direction. As to the framing a set of rules sufficient to point out with accuracy in every case by what assemblages of words an act is described without mention of any such thing as a circumstance, and in what assemblages of words the mention of a separate circumstance is included, this would be a task which, if it could be executed at all, would take up more room than I believe any reader would bear to see bestow'd upon a subject apparently of such small importance: such variety is there in the phrases by which acts of different natures are denoted.[1]

Specificant circumstances are to an act what specificant properties are to a substance.

4.[2] If the import of the word *circumstance* should still be obscure (and difficult indeed it will be found to make it otherwise), it may be made something clearer perhaps by changing it into the word *property*.[3] Not that a circumstance can be said to be a property; they being fictitious entities of a different order. But wherever the word *circumstance* is employ'd with reference to an act, the phrase in which it stands may be changed into another phrase containing the word *property*. An act is attended with such or such a

[1] The following continuation of this passage, in relation to which Bentham has commented, 'Qu.—an inserendum', has been crossed through: 'I know no other single rule that could be given more precise than this: To know whether, among the words descriptive of an act as being the object of a mandate, there are any by which a distinct circumstance is expressed, try whether, upon taking away any word, enough are left to express an act under that character without the subaudition of the word taken away, or some other in the room of it. By this test, it should seem that in the phrase "let no man export wool out of the country," the words out of the country will be found to be not expressive of a circumstance.'

Bentham has added the following note at this point: 'Not finished.'

[2] The first draft of the opening of this section is at UC lxxxviii. 251, and originally preceded the text which follows here. For further details see the Editorial Introduction, p. xxx above.

[3] A related fragment, on the relationship between circumstance and property, is at UC lxxxviii. 250.

circumstance: this upon the present occasion will be found (although the identity of the two meanings may perhaps not be perceptible at first sight) to be the same thing as to say, an act is endued with such or such a property. I will that such an act be done in such or such circumstances; that is if attended with such or such circumstances: this is as much as to say, if possessed of such or such a property or set of properties. This brings us into the beaten paths of common logic. In common logic, indeed, we hear rather more of substances or of fictitious substances than of acts; and, therefore, the word *property* is more frequently made use of with reference to such substances or pretended substances than with reference to acts: but it is likewise occasionally made use of, at least it is evident that it may be made use of, with reference to acts. In its application to substances, it hath passed from the language of the logicians into the language of natural science, and thence into familiar speech: but the word *circumstance* as applied to acts seems to have had its birth originally in familiar speech without passing through the hands of the logicians.[1] While logicians and naturalists made use of the word *property*, people at large made use of the word *circumstance*.[2]

[1] The following sentence has been marked for deletion by Bentham.

[2] The following continuation of this passage, at UC lxxxviii. 252, has been crossed through by Bentham: 'To fix, then, the analogy of the idea belonging to the word *circumstance* to that which belongs to the word *property* the firmer in the memory, I shall for some little time continue to mention them together: after which the term *property* may be discarded, and the term *circumstance*, in conformity to common speech, exclusively employ'd.

'A denominated act being given under its univocal name as the object of a law, and the agible and passible subjects being given either as characterised by their respective univocal names, or as implied under the name of the act, if any words are subjoined to it in such manner as to express a property of the act in question, such property is either to be found in every individual act comprised under the name in question, or in a part only of that number: in the former case, there is nothing in it to merit any special appellation, unless it be the negative one opposed to that which it has in the latter case: in the latter case, the property, in as much as it serves to shew the difference between the part in question and the rest, is termed a *differential property*: in as much as it serves to characterise a subordinate species of acts included under the genus expressed by the univocal name, it is termed a *specific* or *specificant property*.

'To express the same thing, changing only the word *property* for the word *circumstance*. A denominated act being given under its univocal name as the object of a law, if any words are subjoined to it which express a circumstance in such manner that the act, where accompanied with such circumstance, is meant to be taken as the object of the law, such circumstance is either one with which every individual act comprised under the name in question is sure to be accompanied, or one with which a part only of that number are sure of being accompanied: in the former case, there is nothing in it to merit any special appellation, unless it be the negative one which it has in the latter case: in the latter case, the circumstance, for the reasons already given, may be termed a *differential* or *specificant circumstance*. Illustrations will be given presently.'

In the margin, Bentham has noted at this point: 'Qu. should not indirect objects be the acts indirectly mentioned? And so make the circumstances another head?

'Corn exporting—change of place—corn having grown—being done in *some* place—at *some* time—non-specificant circumstances.'

Example. **5.** Let us take the examples above given, and instead of the word circumstance make use of the word property. A certain genus of acts is proposed for consideration: the act of exporting wheat out of the country: out of this a certain species, as distinguished by it's being performed in a certain set of circumstances or, what comes to the same thing, by it's possessing a certain property, is taken and render'd the object of a prohibitory mandate: viz: that species which is performed 'in any navigable vessel belonging to a foreign country.' So, again, in the next case, another species is taken out of the same genus: viz: that species which is performed (that species which comprehends the individual acts of exportation as above mentioned which are performed), when the market price of the commodity in question is at the rate above mentioned.[1] In the same manner, the word *circumstance* may be exchanged for the word *property* in the other examples above proposed.

In the last of the two here given, it may seem that the application of the word *property* is not quite so natural as in that which goes before it: because mere *time* is not commonly taken for the differential character of a species. But the establishment of species and genera and so forth are but so many contrivances for throwing individuals into groupes or parcels; and the groupes may as well be formed upon this principle as upon any other.

6. It may occasion a good deal of perplexity if we are not careful to observe, that the question whether such or such an act as noticed by the law be attended with circumstances, or whether it be not a mere act pure from circumstances, depends altogether upon the wording: insomuch that the same act precisely in one way of expressing it shall be attended with circumstances, in another not. In the few instances in which an act which is the object of a law happens to be characterized by a universal name, such as theft, or by a name which, though multivocal, is simple enough to enter into grammatical construction upon the footing of a univocal one, as wrongful homicide, wrongful occupation of property, in such instances, I say, so long as the name of the act remains in this simple form, there are no circumstances that accompany it: expand it, throw it into the form of a Definition, then circumstances appear: specificant circumstances which, whenever the definition is in the regular form, being annexed to the name of some superior genus, reduce such superior genus to the dimensions of the species expressed by the simple name which is defined.

7. Not that the idea of an act can ever be cloathed in any such expression as the word circumstance will not in some way or other

[1] In the margin, in relation to the latter part of this sentence, Bentham has noted: 'Qu.'

associate with. For here, too, it is with an act and its circumstances as it is with a substance and its properties: you may strip a substance of its properties one by one till you reduce it to nothing: so you may an act by stripping it of its circumstances: an act being made up of circumstances, as a substance is of properties. Such at least seems to be the way of speaking in these cases. But the plain truth of the matter is that, as the description of a substance is performed by the enumeration of particulars which are called properties, so the description of an act is performed by the enumeration of particulars which are called circumstances. The misfortune is that, with these very circumstances, of which the very texture of the act, as it were, is made up, it is said (such is the phrase), to be *attended*; as if the act itself were a thing that subsisted without them, and they something separate from and external to it. This makes such a confusion between these *constituent* circumstances, as they may be called, and specificant circumstances, as is scarcely to be remedied or avoided. Although no circumstances are specified in the law against theft, when couched in these words, 'thou shalt not steal,' or 'let no one steal;' yet no individual act of those that come under the name of theft, can be conceived without the conceiving, or described without the enumerating, of circumstances, which circumstances, when mentioned under that name, are spoken of as circumstances attending or accompanying the act of theft.

8. A word or two, according to promise,[1] concerning the import of the word *case*. The import of this word is nearly allied to that of the word *circumstance*: and, perhaps, there is no occasion on which, if the one may be employ'd, the other may not be employ'd instead of it. Yet of a case it cannot be said, that it is a circumstance, this, as well as *circumstance* and *property*, being fictitious entities of a different order. This will appear by making up the phrase. We speak of an act as being attended or accompanied by or with a circumstance; but we cannot speak of it as being attended or accompanied by or with a case. On the other hand, we speak of an act as being performed *in* such or such a case: but we cannot speak of it as being performed *in* such or such a circumstance. We may speak of it, indeed, as being performed in such or such circumstances: for an assemblage of circumstances may be considered as constituting a case.[a] The A case, what.

[a] What may be called the archetypation of the word *case*, as compared with that of the word *circumstance*, is as follows. In the word *circumstance*, the image is that of an assemblage of objects *standing round* a given object. In the word *case*, it is that of an assemblage of objects *falling*, as it were, around the given object, and by

[1] See para. 2, pp. 242–3 above.

relation which the word case bears to the word circumstance appears to be somewhat of a piece with that which the word *species* bears to the word property: since as a substance or an act, by being possessed of such or such a property, is said to belong to or come under such a species, so an act, by being attended with such or such a circumstance, is said to be performed in or to come under such or such a case.

Use of the above disquisitions.

These disquisitions are of no other use as applied to the explanation of a law, than in as far as they are necessary to ascertain the distinction between a conditional and an unconditional mandate; a distinction which it will be necessary to advert to in considering the different forms which a mandate may assume in respect of the different aspects it may bear to the acts which are its objects. Here, then, we must leave the subject.

The few observations that have been already given may serve to exhibit a slight and general view of the principles to be pursued in investigating the import of these very vague though universal terms, *circumstance* and *case*: to sift the matter to the bottom, so as to guard against all inaccuracies,[a] and to exhibit all the different

virtue of their common relation to that [object][1] cemented, as it were, into one, and forming a ring *in* which the object is said to stand or be.

Case, in Latin *casus*; in French *cas*; in Italian and Spanish, *caso*; in German, *falle*: the image is in all these languages the same. So in Greek, πτωσις; though here the use of it seems to be more confined. In the word *circumstance*, the analogy runs in the same manner through all those languages.

[a] It may be observed, for example, that the word *circumstance* can scarcely, according to the usage of the language, be applied to any real entity: it can be applied to nothing but a fictitious entity. Thus in the groupe of circumstances mentioned upon a former occasion as accompanying the act performed by Felton in the stabbing of the Duke of Buckingham:[a] it is not the bloody knife, the hat found upon the ground, the sentences written in the hat, and so forth that, according to common speech, are the circumstances, but the bloodiness of the knife (that is the existence of the quality of bloodiness in the knife), the finding of the hat on the ground (that is the happening of the act of finding the hat upon the ground) and the writing of the sentences (that is the happening of the act consisting in the writing of those sentences).

This particularity in the use of the word *circumstance* is more than I was aware of on a former occasion in which I was endeavouring to give an exposition of that word.[b]

[a] v. Ch. 7. {Actions} 25.[2]

[b] See Ch. 7. {Actions} 22 n.[3]

---

[1] MS 'objected'.

[2] See *An Introduction to the Principles of Morals and Legislation* (*CW*), Ch. VII. para. 25, pp. 80–1. George Villiers (1592–1628), first Duke of Buckingham, was assassinated at Portsmouth on 23 August 1628 by John Felton (d. 1628).

[3] See ibid., para 22 n., pp. 79–80 n.

applications that may be made of the two expressions, is a task which I shall probably be very readily dispensed with from fulfilling, and which belongs rather to the subject of general metaphysics, than to that of jurisprudence.

APPENDIX C

CHAPTER 12.
ASPECTS OF A LAW.[1]

§ 1. *Plan of this Chapter.*

A law may [take] for its objects either acts alone, or other laws as well as acts.

1. We come in the [ninth][2] place to consider what may be termed the *aspects* of a law: the aspects of which it is susceptible with relation to the articles which it is capable of taking for its *objects*: the aspects or *phases* which the will of a legislator may be consider'd as presenting to those objects in virtue of the different volitions, inclinations, or wishes which he may entertain concerning them, and the different names which may be given in consequence to the expression of such will.

In examining the law with relation to this head, perspicuity requires that we should begin with viewing it in the simplest form in which it can appear. There are two things essential to every law: an act of some sort or other, being the object of a wish or volition on the part of the legislator; and a wish or volition of which such act is the object. When an act of any sort is marked out, as also on the part of a legislator an aspect of any kind as turned or directed, as we may say, towards that act, a law is expressed; let either of these requisites be wanting, the supposed law wants something without which it can not be a law: nothing is enacted; no distinguishable volition is expressed. But to the making up of a law there are no other essential requisites than these; so that if, to

[1] This material is a later draft of the topic of 'Aspects', which constitutes paras. 51–86 in the 'principal draft' (see pp. 115–41 above). By the time that this material was composed, Bentham had decided to divide the present text into Chapters, rather than sections. For further details see the Editorial Introduction, pp. xxx–xxxii above.

Two alternative drafts of 'Plan of this Chapter' are at UC lxxxviii. 164. The second and later of these is as follows: 'Throughout this analysis there will be four particulars, the consideration of which will go hand in hand; but which, on account of the different terms in which there may be occasion from time to time to speak of them, will need to be distinguished. These are: 1. The will or inclination which the legislator bears towards the act or the law which is the object of it. 2. The law or assemblage of words by which such will or inclination may stand expressed. 3. The act which is the object of such will or inclination. 4. The precedent law, where there is one, towards which the law in question bears a reference. These objects will all of them require to be kept in view: and each of them may, in conformity to the changes of which the aspect of the law or laws in question is susceptible, admitt of and require a different appellative. In the catalogue of these appellatives, it will be necessary to exhibit the leading articles: but it would be tedious, and in some measure superfluous, to pursue the enumeration through every article: where the catalogue is defective, analogy will fill up the gap.'

[2] MS del. 'tenth'.

a given law, any thing else be added, such additament is accidental and unessential to its nature. Laws, however, are things which are generally found in multitudes: insomuch that there is no state in which, if there be found one law, there are not found a multitude of others at the same time. Conceive, then, a given law, no matter to what purport, to be established in any state: in the same state, there are also other laws. Of these other laws, take any one at pleasure, this second law either has something, or has not any thing, in common with the law first supposed. If it has not any thing, the two laws are entirely distinct from and independent of one another: each may as well be conceived without the other as with it. On the other hand, if it have any thing, it will be necessary, in order to form any conception of either, so long as they stand thus connected, to consider them together. Now, the essential ingredients in the idea of a single or simple law are, as we have seen, the *act*, and the *aspect*. If, then, the second law have any thing in common with the first, it must be one of these: and it is evident that it may have both or either.

Four heads under which what concerns the aspect of a law may be arranged.

2. This being the case, what we shall have to say with relation to the aspects of a law may naturally arrange itself under four heads, which may be taken for the subjects of so many ensuing sections. Accordingly, in examining the modifications of which a law consider'd in this point of view is susceptible, we shall consider in the first place the case where there is only one mandate applying itself to one act: in the second place, where there is a mandate applying itself to an act to which another mandate of the same aspect has applied already: in the third place, where there is a mandate applying itself to an act to which another mandate of a different aspect has applied already: in the fourth place, where there is a mandate applying to one act an aspect which is spoken of as having been applied already to another.[1]

For these purposes it may be sometimes necessary that not only acts but laws themselves should be spoken of under the name of *objects* of a law. Between these very disparate classes of objects there will always, however, be this conspicuous difference: acts are essentially objects of a law, for without them it could not have existence: laws only incidentally so; since it is not a matter of course for any one law to apply itself to any other.

[1] In this later draft, Bentham considers only the first two of these four 'modifications'.

§2. *Primordial.*[1]

Aspect primordial—superventitious.

1. To begin with considering a mandate in its simplest form: viz: that which it wears when it hath *acts* alone for its objects, not applying itself to other mandates. Wherever this is the case, the aspect which the will of the magistrate bears to the act which is its object may, with reference to other aspects which it might have borne, be termed *primordial*: in the opposite case, *supervening* or *superventitious*. At present, we are to suppose the aspect of the law to be primordial: laying out of the question all other laws or expressions of will with respect to which it might be superventitious.

Aspect decided or neutral: mandate decisive &c. or undecisive.

2. Conceive, then, any act at pleasure: with regard to this act, it is either the wish of the magistrate to influence the conduct of the party in question or it is not: in the former case, the aspect of the magistrate may be said to be decided; in the latter, *neutral* or *undecided*: and as to any mandate whereby such aspect is expressed, it may in the former case be termed a *decisive, operative, influencing,* or *directive*, in the latter, an *undecisive, unoperative, neutral, uninfluencing,* or *undirective*, mandate.

A command—prohibition—non-command—non-prohibition or permission.

3. To begin with the case where the will is decided. The wish must either be that the act should be performed, or that it should not be performed: in the former case, the mandate is what, in the most confined sense of the word, is termed a *command*: in the latter, a *prohibition*. The will being undecided, there is no wish, that can be operative or efficient, to express: all that the mandate can express is the negation of one or other of the two operative kinds of mandates: it is accordingly either what may be termed a *non-command*, or else a *non-prohibition*, that is, to use the common language, a *permission*. 'Every housholder shall carry arms:' this is an example of a command:—'No housholder shall carry arms:' this, of a prohibition:—'Any housholder may forbear to carry arms:' this, of a non-command:—'Any housholder may carry arms:' this, of a non-prohibition or permission.

Example.

Aspect and mandate affirmative—negative.

4. In the first and last of the above cases, the aspect may be termed *affirmative* with relation to the act: in the second and third, negative: and the same distinction may be applied to the mandates by which those aspects are respectively expressed.

A negative aspect towards an affirmative act equipollent to an affirmative towards a negative.

5. In the above definitions, the act is supposed, as of course, to be of the positive kind: let it be of the negative kind, they will of course change places. A negative aspect towards a positive act is equipollent to an affirmative aspect towards the correspondent negative act. To will that during a given period the act of not

[1] This title is taken from the marginal sub-heading on the text sheets.

carrying arms shall be performed is to will that throughout that period the *continued act* or *habit* of not carrying arms should be persevered in. It is in this way that a command may wear the form of a prohibition: and a prohibition that of a command. The law which prohibits the mother from starving her child commands her to take care that it be fed. The one may be at pleasure translated or *converted* into the other.[1] Of these two species of mandates, then, an affirmative and a negative, each one may at pleasure be translated or converted into the other. A mandate prohibiting drunkenness may, without any change in its import, be converted into a law commanding sobriety: a mandate commanding chastity, into a mandate prohibiting incontinence. But amongst names of acts, those of the affirmative class are much more abundant than those of the negative. Accordingly, of the two forms into either of which a mandate may be thrown, the most natural will generally be that in which the name of the act is of the affirmative stamp. In the particular instances, however, where there happens to be a particular name for the negative act, the affirmative and negative form of imperation will appear equally natural in both cases. To command sobriety is as natural as to prohibit drunkenness: to prohibit drunkenness as to command sobriety. It would make little difference, although the substance of the mandate were to be changed. A mandate commanding drunkenness, if a mandate to such a purport were conceivable, would in point of expression be neither more nor less natural than a law prohibiting sobriety. These remarks, in order to be perfectly exact, would need to be pushed to a farther degree of minuteness: it would be necessary that examples of laws should be exhibited *in terminis*: and that a variety of grammatical and other metaphysical discussions should be travelled through. But what has been said already is probably at least as much as will be generally endured.

Mandates imperative, obligative, coercive, or unimperative &c.

6. When the aspect is *decided*, the mandate which contains the expression of it may be termed an ***imperative, obligative*** or ***coercive*** mandate: in the opposite case, ***unimperative, unobligative*** or ***uncöercive.***

Of imperative mandates, as well as of unimperative, there are affirmative as well as negative: and of affirmative mandates, as well as of negative, there are imperative as well as unimperative.

Opposition and concomitancy among mandates.

7. Of the mandates, then, which are capable of being deliver'd with relation to any given act, there are never either more or less

[1] In the margin, Bentham has noted at this point: 'Refer to Saunderson's Logic for *conversion*.'
See Sanderson, *Logicae artis compendium*, 11th edn., Book II, Ch. VII, pp. 75–7.

than four: expressive each of them of a different aspect: a command; a non-command; a prohibition; and a permission. Among these mandates, there subsists such a relation, that with respect to one another some of them are necessarily repugnant and exclusive; others as necessarily concomitant. Examine them in this view, and we shall find that there are, upon all occasions, two of these aspects, and upon none more than two, presented to the act at the same time: the aspects going together constantly in pairs. To represent this the more clearly, let us advert at present to the act: and let us state the condition into which it may be said to be put, the manner in which it may be said to be affected, by being taken for the object of the mandates corresponding respectively to those aspects. First, it may be commanded: it is then left unprohibited: and it is not prohibited nor left uncommanded. 2. It may be prohibited: it is then left uncommanded: and it is not commanded nor permitted (that is left unprohibited). 3. It may be left uncommanded: it is then not commanded: but it may be either prohibited or permitted: yet so as that, if it be in the one case, it is not in the other. 4. It may be permitted: it is then not prohibited: but it may be either commanded or left uncommanded: yet so as that, if it be in the one case, it is not in the other, as before.

A command, then, includes a permission: it excludes both a prohibition and a non-command. A prohibition includes a non-command: and it excludes both a command and a permission. A non-command of itself does not necessarily include either a prohibition or a permission: but it excludes a command: and as a prohibition and a permission exclude one another, it can only be accompanied with one of them at a time: and as they are contradictory to each other, it must be accompanied with one or other of them.

Aspects for which there are no corresponding mandates.

8. In comparing the distinctions here laid down with respect to the mandates by which different aspects of the will may be expressed, it may be observed that they do not in every direction descend so far as to embrace every distinction of which the internal state of the will itself is susceptible. To speak particularly, this is the case with regard to the unco-ercive sort of mandates. When a legislator takes up the pen and says in so many words that any housholder, for instance, may carry arms, or that any housholder may forbear to carry arms, it is out of question that he has taken the matter into contemplation, that he has made up his mind about it, and that he has formed a decided wish that the subject shall enjoy the liberties which in the two cases are respectively allow'd him. Suppose either to be established, and the condition of the subject in respect of the act in question is free as far as they respectively go: and suppose them both to be established, it is compleatly free. But these mandates, take them together, are expressive of but one of three states which the will of the legislator may be in, and the condition of the subject alike free in all of them. It may be in the first place, that the legislator has never so much as taken the act into contemplation: it may be in the second place, that having taken it into contemplation, yet he has made no choice with regard to the question whether the subject shall or shall not have *his* choice as to the performing it: or thirdly, it may be, as in the case above supposed, that, having taken it into contemplation, he has positively chosen that the subject shall have his choice. But of these three states of the legislator's will, there is but one which there can ever be occasion to express: which one is the same which is here last mentioned. The first, supposing it to take place, is what in the nature of things it is impossible for the legislator to express: since a declaration of its existence would carry the proof of its own falsity upon the face of it. The second may indeed be expressed without contradiction: but if expressed in such manner as to distinguish it from the third, the distinction would be of no use. The use of a mandate is determined by the nature of the act or mode of conduct which is the object of it: and where there can be no difference in the conduct of the subject, it is to no purpose to mark out any difference in the mind of the legislator.

The state of the mind may be expressed partly by words, and partly by silence.

9. It has already been observed that, of the various aspects of which the will is susceptible with relation to an act, there can never be either more or less than two presented to it at a time. Accordingly, where the law is silent with reference to any act, insomuch that there is no mandate that applies to it, it is not of one aspect only that such silence is expressive, but of two, viz: the undecided ones both together: so that there are two sorts of mandates, viz: the two undecisive ones, neither of which taken by itself is so expressive as mere silence. Of course, when one only of these mandates is visible upon the face of the law, and at the same time neither of the decisive ones, the state of the legislator's mind with respect to the act is but half-expressed: that is to say, in words. It is not, however, the less effectually determined: the aspect that is wanting being made known, in the manner in which, without the mandate in question, both the undecided aspects would have been made known, by silence.

Use of the undecisive mandates.

10. Here it may be asked,—'since the undecisive mandates taken together express no more than silence, that is than what is expressed without them, and neither of them by itself even so much, of what use, then, can they be made? and to what purpose can it be to take any sort of notice of them?'—The question is natural: but the answers that may be given to it will be found to be satisfactory.

1. In the first place, they are possible and conceivable: which of itself would be a sufficient reason for the mentioning of them: since without them the view of the possible aspects of a legislator's will, with the mandates by which they may respectively be expressed, would be incompleat.

2. More than this, they are actually in use, and that frequently. Instances it is not worth while to exhibit here on purpose: enough will make their appearance of course as we advance. This would of itself be an additional reason why the mention of them ought not to be omitted; although no good reason were to be given for the using them. But the fact is that they have their use, and that, on more occasions than one.

3. They may be of use, for the purpose of removing doubts: where the subject, having seen his liberty infringed in any point or seen cause to apprehend its being infringed, stands in need of an express declaration, an assurance on the part of the law, to ease him of his fears. In this case, indeed, the effect is produced not so much from the literal import of the mandate itself, as from another mandate which is so connected with it that, if not expressed, it may of course be looked upon as implied. I mean, a mandate which, in the form of a prohibition, is addressed to subordinate power-holders in general, restraining them from breaking in upon the liberty of the party whom the unco-ercive mandate in question is meant to favour. Thus much must be inferred of course: to which may be added in some cases a law of a particular kind[a] including the sovereign himself under the same restriction.[b] It is easy to see that some of the most important laws that can enter into the code, laws on which the people found what are called their liberties, may be of this description.[1]

4. A mandate of this stamp may be of use in the way of introduction. Though the purport of it be of no significance, and

[a] v. supra Ch. | |. {Parties affected}.[2]

[b] This may be distinguished by the appellation of a law *in principem*.

[1] In the margin, Bentham has noted at this point: 'A note instancing Mag. Charta &c.' Magna Carta was first issued by John in 1215, reissued in slightly modified form in 1216 and 1217, and attained its final form when reissued in 1225 on the majority of Henry III. For the view that Magna Carta enshrined the liberties of Englishmen see, for instance, Blackstone, *Commentaries on the Laws of England*, i. 123–4.

[2] See §8, pp. 75–93 above, and especially pp. 86–93, for a discussion of laws *in principem*.

the legislator would have done nothing had he stopped there, yet for the purpose of expression there may be a convenience in setting out with a mandate of this stamp, in order to express, in a more easy or pointed manner, a mandate of the opposite or co-ercive stamp. Examples will be found a little farther on.

§3. *Reiterative.*[1]

1. So much for the different sorts of mandates as distinguished by the aspect; no account being taken of their applying to any other mandate. We come now to the different sorts of mandates as distinguished by the manner in which they apply to other mandates: and in the first place to that sort of mandate which not only applies itself to the same act as does the mandate it applies to, but is expressive of the same aspect. A superventitious mandate of this description may, with relation to the primordial mandate it applies to, be stiled *re-iterative*. With relation to the act which is their common object, it requires no particular denomination. Such as the primordial mandate was, such is the superventitious: if a command, a command; if a prohibition, a prohibition: and so on. Mandates reiterative, what.

2. On this occasion it will be requisite to bring to view the doctrine of *subalternation*: that is (to denominate it more fully and precisely) *logical subalternation*. Acts which are the objects of mandates, acts like any other entities, that is the names of acts like names of any other entities, may be said to stand in subalternation, meaning with relation one to another, when they are species one of another: where the ideal compartments which they respectively denominate are included one within another, in the manner that a *species* is within a *genus*. Now, it is evident that, so long as language serves, this sort of connection may subsist amongst any number of acts, that is separate sorts and denominations of acts, forming a *chain of subalternation*, as it may be termed, of any length. As A. is a species of B., so may B. be of C., and C. of D.: and so on indefinitely: or conversely as Z. is a genus with respect to Y., so may Y. be with respect to X., and X. with respect to W.[2] Subalternation of acts.

3. Acts, or rather the ideas that are derived from them, and the names that are given to those ideas, standing in this relation one to Reiteration *in genere* or *in specie*

[1] The title is taken from the marginal sub-heading on the text sheets.

[2] In the text, Bentham has noted at this point: 'Here insert a note on a separate sheet Porphyrian [. . .?].' For Bentham's interest in the commentary on Aristotle's logic provided by Porphyry (*c.* 234–305) in his *Isagoge*, and in particular his definition of man, see *Chrestomathia*, ed. M.J. Smith and W.H. Burston, Oxford, 1983 (*CW*), Table IV, preceding p. 159.

another, it is evident that a mandate, which with respect to another mandate is re-iterative, may be so either *in genere* or *in specie*: *in genere*, where the superventitious mandate applies to the whole of the division or compartment of acts which the primordial mandate has taken for its object: *in specie*, where it applies to but a part of that division.

—*in toto* or *pro tanto*.

4.[1] It is evident that, on this occasion, instead of saying *in genere* and *in specie*, one might with equal propriety say *in toto* and *pro tanto*: but this nomenclature it will be convenient to reserve for a purpose somewhat different. As language is constituted, the same sense may almost in every instance be expressed either in the same or in a different set of words: in whichever way, then, the business of reiteration be performed, the distinction of reiterative *in toto* and reiterative *pro tanto* may equally apply. But as these expressions point more naturally to the very words or tenor of the law, it may be of use to appropriate them to the case where the superventitious provision coincides as well in terms with the primordial one as in effect; using the expressions *in genere* and *in specie* where no account is taken of the words.

Purposes to which re-iterative mandates may be applied—confirmation—continuation—admonition—exposition.

As it seemed with regard to the undecisive mandates in the case where, in point of date, they are primordial, so may it seem with all superventitious mandates in general in the case where they are re-iterative. Judging of them upon a hasty view, it might seem that the issuing of any such mandates were but a nugatory sort of business: that it were but *actum agere*: and, therefore, carried a kind of confession of its own inutility upon the face of it: to what purposes, then, it may be said, can the issuing of any such mandates be applied?—It may be answer'd—To several.

1. To the purpose of *confirmation*: where the title of the lawgiver from whom the primordial law emaned is looked upon as liable to dispute.[a] [b]

2. To the purpose of *continuation*. To this purpose, it may be applied in two cases: where the primordial law was by institution temporary:[c] and where, although the duration of it, as far as depended upon the legislator from whom it originally emaned,

[a] v. Ch. | |. {Source}.[2]

[b] Of this sort were Restoration and Convention Parliaments.[3]

[c] v. Ch. | |. {Durability}.[4]

---

[1] The paragraph enumeration is abandoned hereafter.

[2] See §4, pp. 42–54 above.

[3] The Restoration Parliament, which met in April 1660, recognized the right of Charles II to the Crown, while the Convention Parliament, which met in January 1689, confirmed the accession of William III (1650–1702) and Mary II (1662–94).

[4] See §10, pp. 96–7 above.

were designed perhaps to be indefinite, a doubt comes afterwards to be entertained, whether it be the intention of a succeeding sovereign to adopt it.[a] All the cases hitherto mentioned, and particularly the first, may be consider'd as cases of adoption.[b]

3. To the purpose of *admonition*: where an apprehension appears to be entertained, that the primordial law, though the validity of it be out of question, should remain unheeded.

4. To the purpose of *explanation*: where the terms of the primordial law are looked upon as deficient in any of the three essential points in which a discourse as such is capable of being deficient; viz: perspicuity, explicitness and precision.[c]

A mandate that is re-iterative for the purpose of explanation may also be termed expository. Or, an expository mandate, what. Or, Exposition, what.

When it is for this latter purpose that the re-iterative provision is issued, it may be said to be *explanatory* or *expository* with respect to the primordial one. In the other cases, the two provisions may, for any thing that hinders, be conceived both of them in the same terms. But in this last the terms in which they are conceived must necessarily, in some point or other at least, be different: since it is the supposed unsuitableness of some term or terms of the one that is the very reason for issuing the other.

An expository mandate the only one that must vary in *tenor* from the primordial one.

Here, then, we may note the distinction between a provision which is re-iterative in *tenor* or, as we may say, *in terminis*, as well as in *import*, and one that is re-iterative in *import* or, as we say, in *purport* only. A provision which is re-iterative for any of the three first of the above four purposes may be re iterative in both these points with relation to the primordial one; in other words, may agree with it in both these respects: a provision which is re-iterative for the last of these purposes can not agree with it compleatly any otherwise than in purport. As far as particular words are concerned, the one may be re-iterative of the other *pro tanto*, but not *in toto*.

The re-iteration may be with or without notice taken of the primordial.

For whatever of the three purposes abovementioned the superventitious mandate is designed, it may take notice or not of the primordial mandate of which it is re-iterative. Now, the primordial mandate, if any such thing were ever actually issued, is probably already extant in a certain assemblage of words:[1] which assemblage of words it is strange if there be not some way or other of

[a] v. Barrington.[2]
[b] Ch. | |. {Source}.[3]
[c] v. App. tit. {Composition}.[4]

[1] In the margin, Bentham has noted at this point: '*Aliter* [i.e. 'Otherwise'] in the case of a declaratory law.'
[2] See p. 88 n. above.
[3] See §4, pp. 45–53 above.
[4] i.e. a projected Appendix to the penal code.

describing, shorter than by repeating them. This being the case, either the words are such as the legislator is satisfied with, or they are not: if they are, to what purpose express the proposed import in any other way, than by referring to the instrument by which it has been expressed already? In expressing it over again in other words there can be no good, and there is this obvious inconvenience: an addition is made *pro tanto* to the voluminousness of the body of the laws. Nor is the inconvenience removed by taking for the words of the re-iterative mandate the same terms precisely that were made use of for the primordial. This precaution, though it were taken, would not be sufficient to obviate any of the ill effects which a superfluity of this sort must necessarily be attended with: neither those which apply to the whole body of the law taken together, nor those which apply to the particular part which is thus unnecessarily repeated. Being as much law as the primordial, there is the same occasion for its being inserted. It must be inserted, then, for the second time, that people may be sure it is the same that was issued before: which done, it contributes as largely to the bulk and terrific appearance of the whole, as if it were ever so discordant.[a]

A primordial law, ere notice can have been taken of it as such, must have been distinguished by some denomination.

[a] It is evident that, in order for a law to be re-iterated in the way of reference and not in the way of repetition, by reference to a title which has been given to it and not by repetition of its details, it must at the time of it's first conception have been distinguished by some mark whereby, on any subsequent occasion, it may be described. This is effected by furnishing the body of the laws in it's totality, as likewise the several constituent parts of it separately, with the ordinary apparatus of divisions and subdivisions, entitled by some such denominations as Book, Chapter, Section, paragraph, article number, and the like: expedients which, in didactic works of inferior importance, it would be thought a mark of ignorance or negligence to omitt: which, accordingly, in the codes of perhaps every civilized nation but one, are carefully turned to account; but which, in the written law of a nation which, in matters of jurisprudence, arrogates to itself the pre-eminence over every other, is unaccountably neglected:[1] as if every thing that savours of method ought to be studiously excluded from a work which stands more in need than any other of such assistances to render it intelligible.

In the acts of the British legislature, as much legal matter as is enacted in the course of one session of Parliament, be it ever so much or ever so little, forms what is called, in the technical language, one *Statute*. Of this again, so much as hath happen'd to go through the forms of authentication at one and the same time, so as to have been couched in one and the same instrument, is, in the same

[1] The following passage, in relation to which Bentham has commented 'Alter or leave out', belongs here: 'as if the excellence of a system of laws depended upon their being confused and unintelligible: or as if the laws were to be purposely wrapped up in Ægyptian Darkness, that lawyers, like the Ægyptian Priests of old, might have the exclusive faculty of explaining them: or as if that ordinary portion of intelligence, which is wanting to no man else, deserted a lawyer—so strong is the power of custom over reason—the instant he set his hand to the work of all others to which the greatest measure of intelligence is required, the work of legislation.'

When exposition is the object, a remarkable change in the stile of the mandate naturally and almost constantly takes place. The language of imperation is insensibly dropt, and the discourse slips

How in an expository mandate the stile of imperation is dropped.

technical language, termed one *chapter*; viz: one chapter of the statute. Such a chapter when spoken of by itself, and without reference to the statute of which it forms a part, is termed *an act*: the words '*of parliament*' being understood. Thus the technical title of the famous act commonly called the *Habeas Corpus* act is, The statute of the | | year of the reign of Charles 2^{d}, chapter | |.[1] But in common speech, a single *act*, when spoken of by itself, is also termed *a statute*. There is no lower division than this into *acts* which is authentic: so that an act or chapter is the least integrant part of the whole body of statute law for which the care of legislators has provided a name: an act, then, in English jurisprudence, is like the *point* in mathematics, a thing which has no parts. The editors of the printed copies of these acts do indeed, of their own authority, break them into subdivisions which are termed *sections*. But these subdivisions are not marked upon the original written instrument: it is one entire undivided chaos: accordingly the penner of a superventitious act takes no notice of any such thing as a section in the primordial. These acts in point of bulk are frequently so large, that the matter contained in them is sufficient to fill a moderate duodecimo or even octavo volume: sometimes a single section, or even such a part of a section as still falls short of concluding the sense or compleating the grammatical sentence, shall contain a quantity of matter equal to what is commonly allotted to a shilling or eighteen-penny pamphlet. In the printed copy of so much as is published of the stat. | | Geo. | | ch. | | in Ruffhead's edition, in which neither the first section nor the first sentence is finished, that first sentence occupies thirteen pages and a fraction.[2] These thirteen pages and a fraction I have had *cast*, as the term is with people of the art. The quantity of letter-press they contain is such as, if printed in the form in which the novel of Tristram Shandy is printed, would occupy | | pages. In a volume of Tristram Shandy, the number of pages which, in the several editions that have hitherto (1782) been printed, is upon an average of the six volumes . . . .[3] This fragment of a section, then, contains within $\frac{x}{y}$ th's as much as a volume of the size of those in which books of entertainment are frequently printed.

In point of diversity, in the same act are frequently contained eight or ten sets of provisions of which the purport is as various as that of any eight or ten portions that could be picked out of the whole code. There is a familiar name for such of these acts in which this variety is most remarkably conspicuous: they are termed *hodge-podge* acts. I mention these particulars, lest such readers, if any such there should be, as have never happen'd to turn over a collection of the British acts of parliament, should look upon the supposition of a mass of law which has no name that it can be cited by, as an impossible one.

---

[1] The Habeas Corpus Amendment Act (31 Cas. II, c. 2) was passed in the thirty-first year of the reign of Charles II (i.e. 1679), and was the second Act or chapter so passed.

[2] The statute in question was the Crown Lands—Forfeited Estates Act of 1749 (22 Geo. II, c. 52): see Owen Ruffhead, *The Statutes at Large, from Magna Charta, to the End of the Last Parliament, 1761*, 8 vols., London, 1763–4, vii. 194–216, of which the preamble occupies pp. 194–207.

[3] Laurence Sterne, *The Life and Opinions of Tristram Shandy, Gentleman* was first published in nine volumes between 1759 and 1767. The fifth edition, again in nine volumes, appeared in 1779.

aside into the ordinary didactic or assertive stile. This change is too important, and without explanation too perplexing, to be permitted to pass unheeded. A large portion, commonly even much the largest portion, of the whole mass of law in a compleat code must remain a riddle, without the connection which there is between that part of it which happens to be couched in the one of those forms and that which happens to be couched in the other [being][1] laid open, and the equipollency which there may be between them made appear.

That there should be such a connection and such an equipollency might at first view seem a paradox. The property and very essence of law, it may be said, is to command: the language of the law, then, should be the language of command. For expressing command there is in all languages a particular *mood*, which is stiled the *imperative*. Of what other mood should a law-giver make use? To this it may be answer'd, in the first place,[2] that the only mood to which grammarians have thought fit to give the name of *imperative* is by no means the only one which is calculated to perform the office of *imperation*: the name so far indeed belongs to it with propriety, that being capable of performing that office, it is not capable of performing any other: but it is far from being the only one that possesses this capacity. The future tense of what is called the indicative mood is in truth a stronger imperative than the imperative itself. By way of example, let us take a law or mandate against stealing. How strong soever be the phrase 'steal not;' 'thou shalt not steal,' is stronger still. By the former set of words, all I do is simply to make known my will: in the latter, I not only make known my will as perspicuously as in the former case, but I go farther: I give the party to understand that the motive I trust to for producing the effect I aim at is of such strength as to warrant me in foretelling to the very person I am commanding, that in spite of his free agency my command will be follow'd by his obedience. 'Thou *shalt* not steal' is as much as to say thou *wilt* not steal; but with this addition: that it is the intimation I give thee of my will, and of the motive which makes it thy interest to obey it, that will be the cause of thy not doing so.[a]

Still, it is the language of imperation that is employ'd; though not that particular sort of word to which among grammarians the

[a] In this respect the English has the advantage over the Greek, Latin, French, and probably most other languages.

---

[1] MS 'be'.

[2] In the margin, Bentham has noted in relation to the remainder of this sentence: 'Alter the expression.'

appellation of *a verb of the imperative mood* has been confined. Still, there are *words of volition*: words by which a will on the part of him whose words they are is plainly and palpably expressed. Whatsoever, therefore, be the name which grammarians are in the habit of giving to the verb which is employ'd, the stile of the discourse, to judge of the matter independently of accidental denominations, must be confessed to be essentially and visibly imperative. There is still enough that serves, and that as effectually as in the other case, to distinguish the commanding or imperative from the ordinary didactic, narrative, informative or assertive stile: the language of the will to the will, from the language of the understanding to the understanding.

But in many instances it will be found that the stile of imperation is altogether dropt: no intimation being given in the sentence in question, nor perhaps in the course of many sentences, or even pages, in short or even volumes, that the will of the legislator, or of any body else, has any concern in what is deliver'd: and this may be said of every system of law that has ever yet appeared, or is ever likely to appear. Many are the cases in which this change is apt to take place: and in that which is now before us, the case in which exposition is the object, such change is in a manner necessary. This will be manifest enough, as soon as ever an example of an expository mandate in the imperative form is exhibited. By the verbosity and uncouthness of such a mode of expression, it will immediately be perceived that nothing could be more unnatural or ineligible than to adhere to it. It is not necessary that that part of the discourse by which the concern that the will has in the matter is made known be constantly expressed:[1] it is sufficient if, on the part of the reader, it be perceived, and to that end, if on the part of the writer, it be made perceptible. Let us now proceed with the investigation whereby the manner in which the concern which the will of the legislator has with every thing that comes under the head of law may be developped and ascertained.

In an expository mandate, then, some term or terms at least there must be, as hath been observed, different from some term or terms at least in the primordial one: some term or terms at least of the primordial one must be changed. This may be the case either with all or with less than all. In either case, the re-iteration may be *in genere* or *in specie*. If *in genere*, it may be performed either by one single mandate, as in the primordial, or it may take more mandates than one. If it be re-iterative *in specie*, it may be either

[1] In the margin, Bentham has noted in relation to the remainder of this sentence: 'Alter the expression.'

accompanied with other mandates sufficient to compleat the re-iteration *in genere*, or not. In the latter case, the number of expository mandates need not be greater than that of the primordial: for the case may be that there shall be but one such superventitious mandate. But in the other case, it is evident that there must be more superventitious mandates than one: for there can not be fewer than two specific terms necessary to express the import of one generic one. Where the exposition is performed by a multitude of mandates, which taken separately are but so many mandates re-iterative *in specie*, it is plain the number of these mandates may be multiplied as often as, in the primordial one, there are generic terms: as will presently be seen by an example.

Now, in the description given of the act it is possible, then, that there may be no more than two terms (names of two different sorts of entities) employ'd: viz: the name of the agible subject, and the name of the abstract act itself: as in this mandate, 'let no one steal.' In this instance it is even possible that there shall be but one such term employ'd: viz: the name of the act: as if the mandate were to run thus: 'steal not:' or let not theft be committed. But in most cases, they are much more numerous: nor indeed in the present instance would the number be so small, were it not for an ellipsis or ellipsises: which must be supplied before the logical proposition, before the grammatical sentence, is compleat; in short, before any thing is expressed. In one case the passible subject must be supplied, viz: any thing: let no man steal any thing: in another case, not only the passible subject, but the agible: steal not: that is do thou not steal any thing: let not theft be committed: that is let not theft of any thing be committed by any person. For other examples of similar simplicity take the following: 'let no person carry arms:'—'let no person export corn.'

It is manifest that, where an appellative or title of any kind has once been given to a mandate in such case, in order to re-iterate it, if the re-iteration is to be performed *in toto*, there needs no mention whatever of any thing else belonging to it but the name: there needs no mention of the contents. In this case, how voluminous soever be the mandate, the re-iteration of it is performed in a few words: as thus—'let such or such a law' (naming it) 'stand confirmed:' or 'let it be continued' for such or such a time: or, 'take heed and let it be observed;' according to the purpose for which, as above mentioned, the re-iteration is performed.

As to the question, what is the most convenient form for giving title to a mandate, this is a question of no mean importance: but the discussion of it does not belong to the present subject. It depends, as any one may see, [upon] the method in which the whole body of law, of which the mandate in question forms a part, shall have been disposed, upon the bulk and shape of the divisions into which it is cast.

A declaratory mandate, what.

Here is the place to speak of what is meant by a declaratory law or mandate: an expression which, in certain systems of jurisprudence, is apt frequently to occurr. For this purpose, it will be necessary to anticipate a little in order to introduce for a moment the mention of the customary or unwritten law. The term *declaratory* may perhaps in some instances be employ'd in the cases where the primordial law exists in the form in which we all along suppose it to exist, the form of written as it is called or statute law: in these instances it is synonymous to *explanatory* or *expository*. But the cases in which it is most frequently employ'd are those in which the primordial law (or pretended primordial law) is supposed or pretended to exist in no other form than that of customary law. As the former cases have an appellation of their own, I shall confine the use of the term *declaratory* to these.[1]

It's uses.

It may here be asked, as on former occasions, what use can there be in a mandate of this stamp? For, without entering into any discussion concerning the particular nature of a customary as distinguished from a statutory mandate, either the mandate which is given for a declaratory one exists or it does not. In the former case, the statutory mandate is useless; in the latter, it is not declaratory, but primordial. Let it's existence be even a matter of doubt (a case by the bye which can only occurr where the supposed mandate is an article of customary law), what use can there be in the solving of any such doubt? a business which consists in assertion, not in volition, and which is, therefore, foreign to the nature of a mandate: over acts which have happen'd already the legislator has no power: and over such as have not yet happen'd, his power is the same whatever may have happen'd before: granting him to have power to command an act to be done in future, what use can there be in his declaring whether such a command has or has not been issued heretofore?—Thus far the objection. The truth is, that in this case the discourse in question answers a double purpose. It commands or otherwise expresses volition: and merely by so doing it is not indeed declaratory. But besides that, it asserts a matter of fact; viz: the existence of a mandate of the like purport in time past: by

[1] In the text, Bentham has noted at this point: 'Most wanted for *leges in principem*—whether obligative or unobligative—as declare the matter of fact, viz: the usage or common disposition to obedience, for in laws *in populum* a law *in futurum* / *de futuro* would suffice.'

the former part of its import it is a mandate, by the latter part, it is declaratory.

As to the use that there may be in coupling the declaration with the imperation, this stands upon a somewhat different footing, according to the quality of the party who is the agible subject of it; according as it is a mandate *in principem*, or *in populum*. What use it has is indeed in both cases of the same nature: but in the former case it is much the most considerable. Where the question is between subject and subject, his rights on the one hand and his obligations on the other may, as to their immediate foundation, be grounded wholly on the statute law; on the sum total of the mandates of the sovereign. This might be the case at any time, and would be the case if any where the whole body of the law were reduced into the statutory form, in a word if an entire Code of law were any where established. But when the question is between the subject and the sovereign, this can only be the case where he has become such by an original contract between him and his subjects actually and expressly established. Now, of this state of things the instances are but few. In other cases, the authority of the sovereign is founded originally on, or at least in a great degree influenced by, custom and disposition: on a habit of commanding on one side, accompanied by a habit of obeying on the other: and more immediately in a disposition on the one part to expect obedience, on the other part in the disposition to pay it, according to the course of that custom from whence the disposition took its rise. In such cases, the force and efficacy of the law may depend in a considerable degree on the existence, real or supposed, of some custom. When, therefore, a law *in principem* is established having custom for its foundation, the appealing to that custom is a sort of step taken towards the ensuring the observance of it.

Let us take by way of example two celebrated acts of the British government: the Bill of Rights in the time of William the third, and the American Declaratory Act of George the third: the former an obligative act of the whole sovereignty, the English Parliament, limiting the authority of one constituent part of it, the King:[a] the other, an unobligative act of the English, now by the union with Scotland become the British, Parliament, taking away all limits

[a] 1. W. & M. Stat. 2. c. 2.[1]

[1] The Bill of Rights, based on the Declaration of Rights submitted for acceptance to William and Mary, and outlining the terms on which they were to be offered the throne following the removal of James II, received the Royal Assent as 'An act for declaring the rights and liberties of the subject, and settling the succession of the crown' on 16 December 1689.

from the authority of the whole sovereignty over a part of its subjects, the natives of the British Colonies in North America. By the Bill of Rights, the Lords and Commons, after asserting that the then 'late King James the second' had amongst other things 'assumed and exercised a power of dispensing with and suspending of laws, and the execution of laws without consent of Parliament', aver that that act of authority, amongst others, is 'contrary to the known Laws (meaning maxims of customary law) as well as Statutes of the Realm': they then pray the King and Queen that the right in question, viz: the right of seeing him and his successors restrain themselves from the exercise of the power so condemned, may be '*declared*', amongst others, to be the '*ancient* right of the people of this kingdom': concerning 'all which' their Majesties, with the consent of the same Lords and Commons, are pleased that the same shall be declared, enacted and established: and the same are, by their said Majesties, by the advice and consent of the same Lords and Commons, declared, enacted and established accordingly.[a]

By the American Declaratory act,[b] the British Parliament '*declares*' that it had, hath and of right ought to have full power and authority to make laws and statutes of sufficient force and validity to bind the colonies and people of America, subjects of the crown of Great Britain, *in all cases whatsoever.*[1]

[a] I palliate, as much as is consistent with the fidelity of quotation, the verbosity and perplexity of the English legislative stile.

[b] 6 Geo. 3. c. 12.[2]

[1] The text is abandoned at this point.

[2] The Declaratory Act of 1766 was intended to reaffirm Parliament's right of sovereignty over the American colonies.

APPENDIX D[1]

§16. *Idea of a compleat law.*

Unity of a law to be determined by the occasions for distinguishing offences.

133. By what circumstance determine the unity of the law? by the unity of the class of acts which it takes for its object: by the unity of the offence. That system of provisions is one law which marks out one offence: that system of provisions is more than one law which does more than mark out one offence. But classes of offences, like any other classes of acts, may be distinguished from one another *ad infinitum*: take any class of offences however narrow and it may be made to contain any number of subordinate classes of offences at pleasure: taking, then, the unity of the offence for the standard of unity in the law, the unity of a law is not naturally determinable. If determined then at all, it must be determined by some positive rule: and from whence should this rule be taken but from convenience? So many offences, then, so many *species infimæ* of delinquency, there may be said to be provided against in the code, as there happens to be thought occasion to distinguish: to distinguish in any manner whatsoever, for any purpose whatsoever. Fewer there can not be: more there need not be.

The next question is, for what purposes is it likely that occasions should be taken by the law for making such distinctions? The general answer is, for the purpose of making a distinction in the treatment it gives to some person or other on account of the acts in question.

This rule will require to be developped. Acts, then, which might, by the manner of mentioning them, be consider'd as one have need to be distinguished from one another in the following cases.

1. Where a difference is thought proper to be made with respect either to the quality or the quantity of the punishment. He who exports barley is to forfeit 5^{s} a quarter: he who exports wheat 10^{s}: it is not enough, then, for both purposes to forbid the exportation of corn in general: the offence of exporting wheat must be distinguished from that of exporting barley. He who exports wheat by day time is to forfeit 10^{s} a quarter: he who exports wheat at night is to forfeit all his goods.

2. Where any difference is thought proper to be made in any part of the system of subsidiary laws. If a man is found exporting corn

[1] The text presented here is a later draft of the latter part of §16, intended to follow paragraph 132 of the 'principal draft' (see p. 178 above). It may not, however, be complete, since it does not appear to deal adequately with the second, third, and fourth 'patterns' announced at p. 168 above.

in a waggon, the waggon may be seized: if in a ship, the ship shall not be seized.[1]

It is needless to multiply examples any farther. In short, take any act whatsoever that has a place in the catalogue of offences. If, in any one instance of that act's being performed, any thing is commanded or permitted to be performed or not to be performed, which is not commanded or not permitted to be performed or not to be performed in any other such instance, the act is thereby divided into two separate species of delinquency, which, for the purposes in question, must be distinguished: and the law is thereby divided into so many distinguishable laws. And here we see the difference between the unity of a law and its integrality: a law which was originally one may be divided in this manner into two laws, and yet both of them may be compleat.

A compleat code being given, the number of laws in it is given.

134. The principle of unity in a law being hereby given, it follows that a compleat code being given, the number of the laws there are in it, so long as it continues what it is, is likewise given: not the general purport only, but the precise number: they might be counted, were it to answer any purpose. The number of the laws will, indeed, upon this as well as upon any method of computing, be liable to incessant changes, owing to the continual occasion there will ever be for new laws: still, however, take any one period, at that one period the number is determinable. By this means, then, we may come at the *monades* of which the vast universe of jurisprudence is composed: the idea of infinitude is consequently removed; and the cloud in which that idea never fails to envelop every subject to which it attaches itself, dispelled.

Genera infima of offences.

135. To the *monadic* laws above mentioned, if such for a moment they may be called, or narrowest assignable laws, correspond what may be termed the *species infimæ* in speaking of offences. There is another principle of distinction with the help of which we might mark out, though by a line rather arbitrary, and like the former not exempt from change, what may be consider'd as the *genera infima* with reference to those species. The *genera infima* of offences may be reckoned such and so many classes of offences as are the narrowest in their respective lines of those which happen each of them to be provided with a name: by which I mean not only such names as are strictly univocal, such as theft, murder, adultery and the like, but also any other names which, though compounded, are, like univocal names, capable of entering into constructions and occupying the place of a substantive in a

[1] In the margin, Bentham has noted at this point: 'The provision contains more laws than one, although each of them may be compleat.'

sentence. Of this kind are the greater part of those which, for the purpose of the analysis attempted in the last preceding chapter,[1] I found myself obliged to coin or fix the sense of: such as simple corporal injuries, wrongful confinement, usurpation of the condition of a husband, and so on.[2] Thus, then, the *species infimæ* and the *genera infima* of offences may stand distinguished: the *species infimæ* are the narrowest classes which the law has taken for the separate objects of its notice: the *genera infima* are the narrowest of those which can be made to stand as links in an analytic chain.

To apply this, then, to the laws. A law of which a *genus infimum* of offences is the object may be consider'd as a cluster of laws having for their objects the several *species infimæ* comprehended within that genus.

Species infimæ constituted by circumstances of aggravation and extenuation applied to the above genera.

136. Of the abovementioned sources or grounds of distinction, one of the most material is a difference in respect of the demand for punishment. Conceive an act of any sort to have been constituted an offence, and that offence characterized by a generic name: as, for instance, theft, or wrongful homicide. This offence, upon first consideration, is punished in all cases with one and the same invariable punishment, for instance death. In process of time divers circumstances occur the intervention of which appears to make a difference in the demand for punishment: the act (that is the class of acts as determined by its generic name) remaining in every case the same. Now, the punishment, if varied at all, must be varied either in quality or in quantity: and if it is varied in quality, it can seldom happen but that some variation shall happen in point of quantity. When it varies in quantity, this it may do in either of two ways: in the way of encrease, or in the way of diminution.[a] In the former case, the circumstance in consideration of the effect thus given to it may be stiled a circumstance of *aggravation*: in the latter, a circumstance of *extenuation*. Thus, for instance, in Theft: grounds of aggravation may be, the irreplaceability of the thing stolen, or the

[a] The article of quantity, it is to be observed, includes that of intensity and that of duration: it does not, indeed, strictly speaking include that of certitude or that of propinquity. These, however, are of little account on the present occasion. In these respects punishment ought in every instance to be kept at its *maximum* as of course: and it must be through some palpable error in judgment if ever the legislator should think of making use of intention or remission in these points as a means of producing an intention or remission in point of *value*. See Ch. | |. {Value}.[3] Unhappily, such errors are by no means unexampled.

[1] See *An Introduction to the Principles of Morals and Legislation* (*CW*), Ch. XVI, pp. 187–280.

[2] In a footnote, Bentham has noted at this point: 'Practise of natural historians.'

[3] See *An Introduction to the Principles of Morals and Legislation* (*CW*), Ch. IV, pp. 38–41.

circumstance of it's having been committed under favour of a calamity, such as fire, or shipwreck: grounds of extenuation, the offender's having acted through compulsion, or through necessity for the sake of preserving himself or a person dear to him from the immediate danger of starving: in the case of wrongful homicide, on the aggravative side, the circumstance of it's having been committed with premeditation; in a manner that indicated deliberate cruelty; in a clandestine manner; by poison; upon the father of the offender; for hire; for the sake of succeeding to an estate; in prosecution of a scheme of robbery; in order to stifle evidence; in revenge for something done in execution of justice; and so on: on the side of extenuation, the circumstances of it's having been committed without intention to kill; in a fit of intoxication; through compulsion—or deference to authority; upon high provocation; and the like.

Now then, take any such *infimum genus*, wrongful homicide for example, and add to it any such circumstance of aggravation, premeditation for example, the genus is thereby divided into two species: the one consisting of such individual acts of wrongful homicide as are accompanied with that circumstance, the other of all such as are not accompanied with it: which species, being made punishable with two different species or degrees of punishment, become thereby the objects of two different laws.

Necessity of mixing with *genera infima* those which have others under them.

137. It is evident that the length of any line of *genera*, if one may so say, in the system of offences, and thereby the station in which the *infimum genus* is to be found, must be dependent in great measure upon the accidental differences of language: insomuch that an offence, which stands upon a level with a number of genera each of which are *infima* in their respective lines, shall, however, in its own line have some other genus or genera of offences that stand below it. This may be seen for example in the instance of wrongful occupation; which, though it stand upon much the same level as that of extortion, has another genus that stands below it; viz: theft: for theft is but a species of wrongful occupation: whereas no such genus, as it should seem, would be easily to be found under the article of extortion.

The establishment of *genera* liable to vary in different languages.

138. This will depend likewise a good deal upon the idiom of each particular language. Thus, for instance, in English under the genus *theft*, we have the genus *robbery*: an offence which it seemed requisite to dismiss to another division; viz: that comprized of offences against person and property together:[a] whereas there

[a] supra Ch. 16. {Division} 35.[1]

[1] See ibid., Ch. XVI, para. 35, pp. 226–32.

seems to be no universal appellative that seems exactly to correspond to it in French: in French, to express the idea which in English is characterized by the word *robbery*, people would probably make use of some such phrase as *vol avec force*: theft with force.[a]

Necessity of some such establishments for the purposes of discourse.

139. These *genera infima* of offences, how precarious soever their title to that denomination may appear, it was necessary to establish, otherwise there would have been no such thing as treating to any purpose of the several acts which are taken or appear fit to be taken for the objects of a law: no such thing, in short, as writing a book of the nature of the present work. Were no other appellatives to be made use of than those which have been given to the head classes and their immediate divisions, the distinctions that could thus have been expressed would never have been particular enough for the purpose. Were none to be made use of but what would result from the enumeration of all the circumstances necessary to constitute the description of the *species infimæ*, there would be no such thing as carrying on any discourse upon the subject whatsoever: since, as will be stated more particularly a little farther on, for every one of the generic names now employ'd, it would be necessary to substitute a little volume: so that if half-a-dozen of them came upon any occasion to be included in one sentence, into that one sentence it might be necessary to put words enough to fill the value of half-a-dozen volumes.

Reference of inculpative and exculpative circumstances to such generic names.

140. It is, in short, by means of these alone that we are enabled to speak of any act by name under the character of an offence. It is, moreover, to these names that we refer when we speak of any circumstances under the appellation of inculpative and exculpative circumstances. These terms suppose a class of acts of a certain description to stand invested with a name importing it to be an offence: those which are stiled inculpative serve to bring certain species of acts under the genus characterized by that name: those

[a] The term *brigandage* may perhaps in some cases convey the same idea: but the sense of it seems not to be very determinate; nor does it seem to be employ'd in books of law: indeed, the distinction itself between theft and robbery does not seem in that law to have been very explicitly recognized. See Code penale pp. c. 99.[1] Jousse Nouv. Comment: sur l'ordonn. crim. de 1670, I. 56, 34.[2]

---

[1] Bentham's reference has not been identified.

[2] Daniel Jousse, *Nouveau commentaire sur l'ordonnance criminelle du mois d'Août 1670*, Paris, 1763, Tit. I, Art. XII, with commentary at pp. 56–60, dealing with 'vols faits avec effraction, port d'armes et violence publique', which contains a cross-reference to a discussion of the distinction between 'force publique' and 'force privée' at pp. 34–5.

which are stiled exculpative serve to exclude others out of it. Were it not for this resource, we should have no means of speaking of any act by name in the character of an offence: instead of speaking of clauses inculpative and exculpative and re-inculpative, we could only speak of clauses limitative, exceptive and re-extensive.

Integrality of the laws of the three remaining patterns.

Thus much concerning the compleatness or integrality of a law of the narrowest pattern as well in point of expression as in point of development, connection and design. As to the compleatness of the laws framed according to the other patterns, it is a matter soon determined. Compleatly expressed, a law made upon either of these patterns can not but be if the code, of which they severally make a part, is given for a compleat one. Compleatly developped it will be, if there be such and so many words employ'd as are sufficient to make them readily intelligible. To be compleat in point of connection, they must refer to the several parts of the subsidiary laws whose existence they announce.

Compleat in point of development.

But though in a code which, by being given as compleat, is, therefore, in a certain sense compleat, they must be compleatly expressed, as many as are expressed in it at all, yet it follows not that they are all or any of them compleatly developed.[a]

[a] supra[?] 104.[1]

[1] See para. 104, pp. 154–5 above.

APPENDIX E[1]

§3. *Of a law and its parts.*

[76.][2] expressed, as an object which, if they come into existence, it is designed should give birth to punishment, may be stiled a *penalizing* or *comminatory* or *mandatory*[3] clause or sentence.

An expository clause or sentence.

77. On the other hand, a clause or sentence, the business of which should be to develop in a more particular manner any idea contained in the description of the act, the circumstances of the act, or it's punishment, may be stiled an expository clause or sentence.

A circumstantiative clause—circumstantiative matter.

78. But the punishment, as we have seen, may have it's circumstances as well as the act which is turned into an offence: the punishment (that is the act by which the punishment is to be inflicted) may, as we have seen, have it's circumstances without the accompaniment of which it may not be intended it should be inflicted, as the act may have it's circumstances, without the existence of which it may not be meant that it should give birth to punishment. Expository matter may, therefore, relate either: 1. to the description of the act itself: 2. to the circumstances restraining[4] or enlarging[5] the description of the act: 3. to the description of the punishment: 4. to circumstances restraining or enlarging the description of the punishment: 5. to circumstances influencing the connection in the way of causality[a] between the act and the punishment. Any clause or sentence, then, of which it is the business to develop the idea of any of the above groupe of circumstances may be stiled a *circumstantiative clause or sentence*: and the contents of any such clause or sentence, or of any assemblage of such clauses or sentences broken or entire, may be stiled *circumstantiative matter*.

[a] See Ch. 7. {Actions}.[6]

---

[1] The following text reproduces part of an early version of the text referred to here as the 'primary draft'. For further details see the Editorial Introduction, pp. xxxii–xxxiv above.

[2] The following passage is the final part of para. 76. The immediately preceding text has not been identified.

[3] In the margin, Bentham has noted at this point: 'Mandatory simply where the law is *unarmed*; comminatory, where it is armed.'

[4] Bentham has noted at this point: 'The description of the act is general—circumstances (primary) can not, therefore, but restrain: but circumstances secondary may *enlarge*: viz: by restraining the primary.'

[5] In the margin, Bentham has noted at this point: 'Shew that circumstances (to be *material*) must do one or t'other.'

[6] See *An Introduction to the Principles of Morals and Legislation* (*CW*), Ch. VII, paras. 22–6, pp. 79–82.

Of the expository matter, it is evident, from what has been said already, that that part which concerns the circumstances will naturally take up more room than that which concerns the act: the act being a very simple object: the circumstances, a groupe of objects infinitely diversified.

It is evident enough, also, that the same parcel of circumstantiative matter may apply to divers acts at the same time.

79. It has already been observed that the bare act which is commanded or prohibited is always a very simple object: whereas the circumstances belonging to it constitute an immense groupe of objects which are capable of being infinitely diversified. Now, the more diversified they are in their nature, the more diversified, of course, they will be in their description, wheresoever it is necessary that one should be distinguished from another. The more diversified they are in their description, of course, the more room will the description that must be given of them occupy in the code. The circumstantiative part is, accordingly, that part of the expository matter which will be much the most voluminous.

Of the expository matter, the circumstantiative will be the most copious.

80. Again, it will often happen that the same circumstances which may contribute to render it proper or improper to command or to prohibit one sort of act may contribute to render it proper or improper to command or prohibit another sort of act, or, indeed, many other sorts of acts. Wherever this is the case, the same parcel of circumstantiative will serve for so many different parcels of penalizing matter.

The same parcel of it may apply to divers acts.

81. Now, when a parcel of literary matter of any sort is in such a manner connected with another parcel of literary matter that the one cannot properly be understood without the other, the most obvious method of disposing them is to put them together: placing them in the same instrument, and as close together in that instrument as may be. For this reason, if there were no other to the contrary, where there is one parcel of matter connected in [the] manner abovementioned with a number of other parcels, the most obvious as well as commodious method would be to give to the former the same connection in point of contiguity with every one of them. But were this the case, the former parcel would come to be repeated as many times as there were parcels ⟨to⟩ which it was to be applied. Now, such repetitions, on account of the enormity of their bulk, would soon become impracticable. Some, therefore, of these parcels of penalizing matter there must be to which the quantity of circumstantiative matter that belonged to them could not be placed contiguous. Now, if this might be the case with some, by the same reason might it be with all. It might,

Circumstantiative matter, how it may come to stand apart from the penalizing matter.

therefore, and indeed must often, happen, that a quantity of circumstantiative matter applying alike to divers parcels of penalizing matter, might, instead of being placed contiguous to each, be placed contiguous to none, forming on the contrary a kind of independent parcel of itself. If the parcel were large, it might be made to occupy a distinct volume: if larger still, it might be made to occupy even a multitude of volumes.

The circumstantiative matter forms the civil branch of law: the penalizing, the penal.

82. When the separation in point of material contiguity between parcels of matter which in idea are so inseparably interwoven is once effected and becomes permanent, the two parcels will naturally acquire different names. Thus, accordingly, has it happened in the case before us. Of the circumstantiative matter which concerns the description of the several sorts of acts which are made offences, a great part has been frequently separated from the rest of the body of the law under some such appellation as that of *civil* law or the civil branch of jurisprudence: while the rest, together with the greatest part of what concerns the description of the bare acts that have been made offences, or of the act of punishment, as also the greatest part of what concerns the circumstances affecting the description of the punishment, has been kept together under some such name as *penal* law or the penal branch of Jurisprudence. It will not be wonder'd at, if the boundaries of these two compartments should be in a considerable degree different in different countries: and, indeed, very unsettled in any country. It will not, therefore, be wonder'd at, if the account here given of these boundaries should be found to be neither very particular nor very correct. Loose as it is, it may, however, even at this stage of it, serve to give such an idea of the distinction as shall be rather more precise than any that has been given of it before. To render it, however, still more clear and satisfactory, it may be worth while to give it a more particular application. For this purpose, let us take a short review of the several divisions of the whole mass of law as marked out by the several classes and other subordinate divisions of offences: observing under each division what part of the matter necessarily comprehended under that division is most likely to be referred to the civil branch, and what part to the penal.[1]

[1] In the margin, Bentham has noted at this point: 'To *Signs* and then Integration.' This note perhaps reflects Bentham's decision to reorganize the text: for discussions of the two topics see §§ 14 and 16, pp. 161–4 and 168–84 above, respectively.

§4. *Limits between civil and penal law particularized.*

Circumstantiative matter belonging to the several penal titles.

1. In offences against person—it excepts power.

83. [1.] To begin with offences against person. With regard to a man's person, it may be laid down as a general proposition, that in most cases it is unpleasant to him to have another meddle with it. Every act, therefore, by which the person of another man is affected ought *primâ facie* to be treated as an offence. If he thinks it gives him pain, it does give him pain: if he thinks it is productive to him of any such mischief, it thereby does produce a mischief. Every body knows that, in general, it is unpleasant to a man to have his person meddled with in any way by another. If there be any exception to the above position, it is where you consent that your person shall be dealt with in such or such a manner. Here, your consent (provided it be neither unfreely nor unfairly obtained) shews that the act was not unpleasant to you: and, therefore, that there is no mischief in the case. The case of consent, then, forms one exception to the rule.

But though there should be a mischief in the case, this mischief may be outweighed: it will be outweighed whenever it is the necessary means of a more than equivalent good. This it is presumed to be in the several cases in which the power of exercising such and such acts upon your person, let them prove ever so disagreeable to you, is conferred upon such and such individuals by the law. When the law exempts a man from punishment in case of his dealing with your person in a manner that either stands a chance or is certain of being disagreeable to you, it thereby conferrs on him a *power*: it gives him a power over you; a power over your person. Now, this is what it may find it necessary to do for various purposes: for the sake of providing for the discharge of the several functions of the Husband, the Parent, the Guardian, the Master, the Judge, the Military Officer, and the Sovereign: not to mention those extraordinary and accidental cases in which, for the sake of averting some calamity or other mischief more serious than any which would probably be occasioned by the exercise of the power, it may be expedient to entrust a power of the like stamp to individuals at large. These powers, then, form so many exceptions to the general rule that no man has a right to meddle with the person of another. Accordingly, untill the rule which threatens punishment to him who shall meddle with the person of another has specified and made allowance for such exceptions, it can not be regarded as compleat. The specification, therefore, of these exceptions belongs virtually and substantially to the penal branch of the law. But the collection of the sentences which are necessary to the expression of all these specifications must necessarily occupy a very considerable space. They will constitute the matter of several bulky titles in none of which, perhaps, shall the general word punishment, or the name of any particular sort of punishment, make its appearance. If, therefore, there be any branch of the law which is called the civil branch, these titles will, of course, constitute a part of it. And thus it is that the penal and the civil branches share between them so much of the matter of the laws as regards offences against person.

2. In Offences against Property, it excepts title: viz: power over things.

84. [2.] In offences against property, the distinction between these two branches of law stands upon a somewhat different footing. The objects of property (I mean such as are *corporeal*, into which always may be resolved those other fictitious objects which are stiled *incorporeal*) are either things or persons: things by the uses which they may be put to: persons in some few cases also by the uses they may be put to, but more commonly by the services which they may be obliged to render. Offences against property in things are acts whereby a man goes about to meddle, or does that which has a tendency to exclude another who has a right from meddling, with some object which belongs to the class of things. Now, with regard to things, no such general rule obtains as the above-mentioned one concerning persons. On the contrary, concerning every object of the class of things (concerning every such object at least with which a man's meddling or not can be material), the general rule is that there is always some one person at least who *has* a *right* to meddle with it. So far is it from being true that every act, by which an object of the class of things is affected, ought *primâ facie* to be an offence. You have done so and so with such or such a thing: are you the person who has, or of the number of those persons who have, or are in a way to have, a right to meddle with it? If you are, then you have a *title to* or an *interest in* the thing in question. This lets in all the law relative to the various sorts of *titles*. This branch of the law is commonly an object of infinite variety and prodigious bulk: and may of itself furnish matter for a multitude of volumes. In none of these volumes, unless by accident, will any mention be made of punishment. The very idea of punishment will, therefore, be out of sight: and the whole of this matter will, of course, be referred to the civil branch of law.

Offences against property in the services of persons are acts whereby a man goes about to withhold from another to whom they are due certain services of his own or of a third person, or to cause services to be render'd which are not due. Here, indeed, the general rule is of a piece with that concerning offences against persons: it is that no man has any right to oblige any other man to render him any service. But to this rule there are, of course, a great variety of exceptions. The principal one is that where one man *consents*, or in other words *engages*, to render to another such or such a service. This lets in all that variety of circumstantiative matter which belongs to what is commonly called the Law of *Contracts*: what contracts the law adopts and holds for good: what construction it puts upon them: what it looks upon as a performance of them: what stipulations it looks upon as implied in such as are expressed: what others it holds a man dispensed from observing: and what new obligations it imposes on him in consideration of a change of interests brought about by subsequent events. The answers to these and a variety of other questions that might be exhibited may furnish matter enough for more and more volumes; in all which the punishment by which the performance of the contract is to be enforced, being perhaps of one and the same kind throughout, may lie out of sight as much as ever. Other services may be due to or from a man on account of the civil or domestic condition in life he occupies: of these, then, under the head of offences against condition: others due to public officers for the benefit of the public: of these under some of the divisions of that class.

85. 3. With regard to offences against reputation. Reputation is a fictitious entity: it cannot, in strictness of speech, be meddled with, as a man's person and his property may be meddled with. To meddle with a man's reputation is to propagate some notion to the advantage or to the prejudice of his reputation: to propagate some notion the tendency of which is either to augment or to diminish that portion of good-will which the circle he is placed in may be disposed to bestow upon him. If the tendency of what is done be to augment that portion, no offence is committed: at least no offence against the reputation of that man. If to diminish it, the notion convey'd is either true or false. If true, the general rule is, or at least ought to be, that every man has a right to convey such notion. For the sort of behaviour to which the world in general is wont to annex it's ill will is, for the most part, that sort of behaviour which in some way or other is pernicious to society. To annex that ill will to any sort of behaviour is, in other words, to punish that sort of behaviour with the punishment of the moral sanction. To contribute to the spreading abroad such notion is, at the same time, to prosecute the delinquent, as it were, before the tribunal of the public and to bear a hand in the infliction of that punishment. But

3. In offences against reputation, there is little place for it.

the fear of the punishments, and the hope of the rewards, derivable from this source, or in one word the love of reputation, is one of those standing tutelary motives, of which the regular and ordinary tendency is to restrain men from every sort of behaviour which is pernicious to society: not to mention the tendency which it has to prompt men to actions which are of a beneficial tendency. It is the very best, in point of general tendency, of all the tutelary motives after that of benevolence: and in point of force, it is superior even to that.

There are some cases, however, in which it is not right that a notion to the prejudice of a man's reputation should be propagated, though it be true. These are, in the first place, where the fact charged upon a man, although it be more or less disreputable, is not pernicious to society: the dictates of the moral sanction happening, by reason of some prejudice, to be at variance with the dictates of utility. In the next place, where the fact is of such a nature that the pain given to individuals by the disclosure of it would outweigh the benefit resulting to the public from the punishment of it.

If the notion, being prejudicial to a man's reputation, is at the same time a *false* one, the general rule is that no man has a right to propagate it: and to this there can scarcely be any exception.

Of this complexion are the rules which serve to mark out the acts that are to be deemed offences against reputation. These rules will scarcely take up more words than may, without inconvenience, be included under a single title. The expository matter will take up so little room that there will be no need of sending it to a title apart, and severing it from the mandatory.

4. In Offences against Condition.

86. 4. With regard to offences against condition. In whatever way an offence is committed whereby a man's condition in life is liable to be affected, in such cases, before the description of the offence can be completed, a great many details must be enter'd into which are too multifarious, too minute and too voluminous to be all of them comprised within the penal branch of jurisprudence. Of what description are the persons between whom the relationship by which the condition is constituted can exist? By what means is the relationship formed? by what may it be dissolved? What are the powers which one of the parties has over the person, or which each, perhaps, has over the property, of the other? What are the rights[1] which that one of them has who has no power? What are the duties of each of them towards the other? These and

[1] In the margin, Bentham has noted at this point: 'These correspond to so many cases of abuse of trust or power.'

various other questions belong, all or most of them, to each of the relationships or conditions in question, and form altogether a quantity of matter too bulky to be included within the limits ordinarily allotted to the narrow title of the penal branch of law. Many of them also, we may have observed, must already have been brought upon the carpet under the head of offences against the person: those, I mean, the answers to which exhibit the several *powers* which furnish so many exceptions concerning the general rule against one man's meddling in any way with the person of another. Many of them, likewise, require to have been settled under the head of offences against property; the privileges incident to these relationships being so many means of limiting or extending the power of the parties interested, in respect of their property. To instance in the case of the matrimonial condition. To ascertain what the ceremonies must be by which a marriage is constituted is necessary for three purposes: 1. in order to determine when it is that a man is to be understood to possess that power over a woman's person which constitutes one of the exceptions to the general rule concerning offences against person. 2. in order to determine when it is that a man is to be understood to possess those powers which the law in such a case gives a man over a woman's property. 3. in order to determine when it is that he has a right to cause another to be punished for having carnal knowledge of the woman without marrying her, as in the case of adultery, or by marrying her, as in [the] case of polygamy, and so forth.

Many, therefore, we may see, are the cases in which a number of different mandatory clauses in the body of the law may have one and the same assemblage of circumstantiative clauses belonging to them in common. Now, so long as this circumstantiative matter is upon the carpet, the idea of punishment, though all the while necessarily connected with it, lies concealed, however, and out of sight. It is not to be wonder'd at, therefore, that such a congeries of mere circumstantiative matter should ordinarily be kept apart from the penal branch of the law, and aggregated to the civil.

87. Thus much with regard to private offences. 5. As to semi-public offences, these are determined in a great measure by the relation they bear to private ones: being but so many ways of producing the same mischiefs as are apt to result from private offences, only with less certainty and upon a larger scale. Concerning these, it will not be necessary to be very particular. It may easily be conceived that the matter of the law relative to these offences, like the matter of the law relative to the preceding

5. In semi-public offences, it is of the same tenor as in the corresponding private ones.

offences, will be in some proportion or other divided between the civil branch of the law and the penal.

The truth is, that the same expositive matter that was involved in the mandatory matter relative to private offences, must be involved afresh in the mandatory matter relative to semi-public offences. A man *steals* lead or iron work from off a public bridge. The case must have been, then, that he was conscious of his not having any *title* to the thing so taken. This lets in the whole of the law relative to titles. There are fifty different ways, suppose, of gaining title to a thing: and as many different ways of parting with it. In order, then, for the man to be convicted of theft, it must appear either 1. that in no one of the first fifty ways could he have supposed himself to have acquired a title to the thing: or 2. that if, in any one of those fifty ways, he had supposed himself to have acquired such a title, yet, in some one or other of the other fifty ways, he must have supposed himself to have parted with it.

6. In self-regarding offences.

88. 6. With respect to self-regarding offences. The law relative to acts of this description, such few of them, if any, as it may be requisite to constitute offences, will be apt to wear more of a penal complexion upon the face of it than the law relative to any of the preceding divisions of offences. What little there may be occasion to define, there will be little need, probably, to define for any other purpose than that of furnishing matter for the prohibitions established by the laws relative to this title.

7. In offences against the external security of the state.

89. 7. We come now to public offences. And first, with respect to offences against the external security of the state. Suppose the offence to consist in aiding a foreign power with whom the community in question is at war: and suppose war to have been declared. How does it appear that any such declaration has been made? in what persons is the authority of making such a declaration vested? Suppose the offence to consist in a personal or other injury offered to an alien—who are aliens?—who are denizens? Suppose it offered to a foreign Ambassador. What are Ambassadors? how do they come to be, how may they cease to be, Ambassadors?

[8. In offences against the preventive branch of the police.]

90. 8. With regard to offences against the preventive branch of the Police. Offences of this division will, in the point in question, stand upon a footing very little different from that of offences against justice; to which head, as being the most important of the two, the consideration of them may for the present purpose be referred.

9. In offences against Justice, v. private offences.

91. 9. With regard, then, to Offences against Justice. The power of administering Justice (under which may be included the power of taking the several steps that are requisite to be taken in subservience to the administration of Justice) is a species of trust: a species of public trust. An offence against Justice is an offence against this species of trust. What the possible offences are that are capable of being committed against trust has been already shewn. The mandatory part of the law relative to this division will consist, then, in the designation of these several offences and their punishments. But, under this mandatory matter, a great deal of expository matter will necessarily be involved. A man is guilty of resistance to the orders of a Judge. But what sort of a person is a Judge? How does it appear that the person whose orders are in question, is that sort of person whose orders are, at the time in question in the place in question, with reference to the persons and the things in question, and when issued in the manner in question, to be treated as the orders of a Judge? This lets in so much of the public or constitutional branch of the law as concerns officers of Justice. How and by whom are Judges to be appointed? What are to be their numbers? where are they to sit? Over what extent of territory, over what sort of offences, over what persons and over what things are they respectively to have jurisdiction? Are the orders they give to be regarded as definitive or are they subject to reversal? If subject to reversal, then again come the same string of questions concerning the superior Judges in whom such power of reversal is to be lodged. All this, we see, is so much expositive matter which must be settled before the mandatory matter can have any application.

Let the person offended against be a person employ'd under a Judge or set of Judges, whether to record the proceedings that are carried on before them, or to register their orders. Let the offence consist in disturbing them in the execution of their respective offices. One may easily conceive a similar string of questions to be repeated.

10. In offences against the public force.

92. 10. With regard to offences against the public force. Suppose the offence to consist in the endeavour to withdraw one's self from military service. Military service is the sort of service which is render'd by a soldier. What is a soldier? how is it that a man becomes a soldier? how is it that he may cease to be so? A soldier is a man whose name is enrolled on a certain list as one who is bound to serve the public in a certain way. But who is it that has the power of enrolling soldiers? such or such a military officer? How comes he by that power? by commission from the King, for example: or from such or such a council, &c., according to the nature of the government. This lets in so much of the public or constitutional branch of the law as concerns the appointment and discharge of military officers, and in general of persons engaged in the military service: all which is so much circumstantiative matter as before: and belongs, therefore, to the civil branch of the law in contradistinction to the penal.

11. [In] offences against the positive encrease of the national felicity.

93. 11. With regard to offences against the positive increase of the national felicity. These consist chiefly of offences of which the tendency is to impede or misdirect the operations of certain classes of officers who are invested with so many branches of public trust. What are the respective natures of those offices? by what means does a man become possessed of them? by what means may he cease to be so? The answers to these questions constitute so much expository matter which may be referred to the constitutional branch of the law, and is of a civil nature.

12. [In] offences against the public wealth.

94. 12. With regard to offences against the public wealth. A man omitts, for example, to pay his quota to a tax. What is a tax? who has a right to impose taxes? who is to receive the produce? such or such a person, perhaps, for some purposes: such or such another person for other purposes: the sovereign for all or any purposes. Or let it be an offence touching the office of those persons who have the management of such or such an article of the public stock, moveable or immoveable. What is the nature of those respective offices? By what means does a man acquire them? by what means may he cease to be in possession of them?—More circumstantiative matter belonging to another part of the constitutional branch of the law.

13. [In] offences against population.

95. 13. With regard to offences against population. This is a title which is here inserted rather out of deference to current notions, than with a view to any offences which there will be occasion to place under it. Population (as, in due time, there will be occasion to shew)[1] is a business that will go on extremely well of itself, so long as the legislator does nothing to disturb it. It is scarcely in the power of an individual to do any thing that can materially affect it, unless by offences which come under one or another of the preceding heads. If it were not a solecism to speak of the legislator's committing an offence, one might say, perhaps with some degree of truth, that there is no offence can be committed against population but what is committed by the legislator. Suppose, however, for example sake, the legislator should think fit to have recourse to coercive methods, and, under the notion of favouring population, should command or prohibit certain practises. In the description of those practises, the words *husband*, *wife*, *child* (meaning legitimate child), *nun*, *monk* and so forth, might

[1] Bentham presumably intended to address this point in a succeeding chapter.

probably occurr. It hath already been observed[a] that the circumstantiative matter relative to those several sorts of persons is to be sought for in the civil branch of the law; that which belongs to the words husband, wife, and child, in that part of it which is of a *private* nature: that which concerns the words *monk* and *nun* to that which is of a constitutional or public nature.

96. 14. With regard to Offences against the national wealth. Let the offence consist in exporting goods without a license. The license meant is one that must be given by certain officers: officers belonging to the Customs: officers belonging to the Board of Trade. Who are these Officers? by whom appointed? This introduces another string of questions, the solution of which belongs to another part of the public or constitutional branch of the Law, and is still of a civil nature as before. 14. [In] offences against the National wealth.

97. 15. With regard to Offences against the Sovereignty. Let the offence consist in taking up arms against the sovereignty. In whom does the sovereignty reside? in a single person, or in a number of persons? Whence does he, or whence do they, derive this power? from succession or from election? More civil matter, belonging to the constitutional branch, as before. 15. [In] offences against the sovereignty.

[98.][1] 16. With regard to Offences against Religion. Let the offence consist in usurping the character of a Clergyman. Further repetitions are needless. This, we see, lets in a great abundance of civil matter belonging to the constitutional branch, as before. 16. [In] offences against Religion.

[99].[2] 17. The last division of Public Offences, that of Offences against the National Interest in general, may just be mentioned on this occasion, for the sake of shewing that it has not been forgotten. Let the offence be one that concerns the office of a Privy-Counsellor. What is the office of a Privy-Counsellor? by what events may a man be invested with it, and by what others may he be divested of it: and so with regard to the office of an Ambassador, as hath already been observed.[3] Or let it consist in taking a present from a foreign sovereign, without a license from one's own. This, we see, necessarily refers to so much of the expositive matter as concerns the description of the person or persons from whom the license is to come. 17. [In] offences against the National interest in general.

[a] supra | |.[4]

[1] MS '97.'

[2] MS '98'.

[3] See para. 89, p. 282 above.

[4] See para. 86, pp. 280–1 above.

§5. *Distinction between civil law and criminal.*[1]

§6. *Analysis of the matter of a body of laws.*

Rights, powers, and other fictitious legal entities to be explained by their relation to real entities.

1. The ideas annexed to the words person and thing are ideas copied immediately from the impressions made by real entities. The ideas annexed to the words and phrases, act of the will, sign of an act of the will, physical act or act of the body, event, circumstance, &c. are either like the former, ideas copied immediately from the impressions made by real entities, or copies of the sensible affections of determinable real entities. The ideas annexed to the words command and prohibition are resolvable immediately into ideas of the number of those just mentioned. Now, there can be no such thing as an act which is not the act of some person or some sentient thing: nor can there be any act of law which is not either a command or a prohibition—or the reverse of the one or of the other of those operations: nor, lastly, can there be any command or prohibition which has not for it's object some sort of act. It follows that, whatever other words besides these may be [made] use of in expressing the matter of a law or body of laws and that are not names of real entities or of the sensible affections of determinable real entities, the import of the words just mentioned will serve as a key to the import of such other words: and, while it lays open the import of each, will lay open the connection between that of every one of them and that of every other. By these means alone can the import of such words as duty, obligation, power, right and other names of fictitious moral entities be laid open: by these means alone can a regular analysis of the contents of a body of laws be exhibited. I may be excused for announcing in so peremptory a manner the necessity of the ensuing disquisitions: since nothing less than necessity could have excused the exhibition of so uninviting a detail.[2]

1. continued or inserendum.[3] Power, right, prohibition, property, security, liberty, duty, obligation, burthen, immunity, exemption, privilege—all these and a multitude of others that might be named are so many fictitious entities which the law, upon one occasion or another, is consider'd in common speech as having incessantly to deal with. Not an operation does it ever

[1] For the text of this section see §19, pp. 201–6 above.

[2] In the margin, Bentham has noted at this point: 'It is to these fictit$^{s.}$ entities alone [MS alt. 'this abstract way of speaking'] that the law owes all its obscurity. Avoid them, or explain them by the relation they bear to real ones, and the law is clear.'

[3] It appears that Bentham remained uncertain as to the precise location of the following paragraph in relation to the preceding one.

perform but it is considered as creating or in some manner or otherwise disposing of those it's imaginary productions. All this, it is plain, is the mere work of the fancy: a kind of riddle of which the solution in any case is no otherwise to be given than by giving the history of the operations which the law performs in that case with regard to certain real entities. Would a man know what it is the law really does in every case, and in what condition it leaves the parties that are concerned? He must know in each case the acts which it takes into contemplation, and the aspect which it bears to them. He must know who the persons, and what the things, if any, which are in question: what the acts are of those persons, whether for their termination they look to other persons or to things; and in what circumstances, if in any, the act is prohibited or permitted, commanded or left uncommanded. Knowing thus much, we[1] shall have ideas to our words: not knowing it, we shall have none.[2] These phantastic denominations are a sort of paper currency: if we know how at any time to change them and get sterling in their room, it is well: if not, we are deceived, and instead of being masters of so much real knowledge as by the help of them we mean to supply ourselves with, we possess nothing but sophistry and nonsense.

Legal fictitious entities are created &c. by creating offences.

2. We have already had occasion to shew that the division of offences is in fact the division of the whole law: and that a compleat analysis of all the offences that can be created includes a compleat account of every thing that can be done in the way of law.[3] It follows that, whatever number and variety of these fictitious entities may be created or brought into play, it must all be done in the course of some or other of those operations by which the several sorts of offences are created.

They are a sort of vapours which, during the course of the legislative process, are, as it were, generated and sublimed. By every operation which the law performs, some one of them at least is exhibited or produced: by most operations, two or even three: according to the number of the persons, or rather of the parties, whose interest is concerned and to whom the law during the

[1] In the preceding part of the paragraph, Bentham has altered the first person plural to the third person singular, but has failed to do so from this point.

[2] MS del. follows here: 'The ingenuity of the first authors of language, which, if not compelled by necessity, was at least invited by convenience, has thrown a kind of mist over the face of every science, and over none a thicker than over that of jurisprudence. This barrier it will not be practicable, perhaps not even expedient, altogether to destroy. We must, however, have learnt upon every occasion how to pierce through it at pleasure before we can obtain a clear conception of the real state of things. In a word, these'.

[3] See §1, para. 1, p. 3 above.

process bears a different relation. On the one hand, whatever the law does in any case, somebody or other there must be (if it has any views at all) somebody or other there must be whom it is meant to favour: on the other hand, whatever it does, if in a positive way it does any thing, to somebody or other it must issue prohibition or command: somebody or other, in a word, it must be intended to co-erce. If the party whom it is meant to favour be the same whom it co-erces, there may be but one interest concerned: if different, there must at least be two: and if at the same time that it favours one party, it coerces a second party in one way, and a third party in the opposite way (which we shall see is frequently the case), there may and indeed must be three.

In giving an explanation, then, of the several fictitious legal entities, our plan will be to go over the several heads of delinquency, state the operation which the law performs in creating the offence, and so exhibit the fictitious entity which is the result.

Before the law acts, liberty is universal.

3. As yet there is no law in the land: the legislator hath not yet enter'd upon his office. As yet he hath neither commanded nor prohibited any act. As yet all acts, therefore, are free: all persons, as against the law, are at liberty. Restraint, constraint, compulsion, coercion, duty, obligation, those species I mean of each which issue from the law, are things unknown. As against the law, all persons possess as great a measure of this great blessing of liberty as it is possible for persons to possess: and in a greater measure than any which it is possible for men to possess it in any other state of things. This is the first day of the political creation: the state is without form and void.[1]

As yet, then, you and I and every one are at liberty. Understand always, as against the law: for as against one another this may be far from being the case. Legal restraint, legal constraint and so forth are indeed unknown: but legal protection is unknown also. You and your neighbour, suppose, are at variance: he has bound you hand and foot; in this case, you are certainly not at liberty as against him: on the contrary, he has deprived you of your liberty: and it is on account of what you have been made suffer by the operation which deprives you of it that the legislator steps in and takes an active part in your behalf. Since the legislator, then, takes an active part, how is it that he must demean himself? He must either command or prohibit; for there is nothing else that he can do: he, therefore, cuts off on the one side or on the other a portion of the subject's liberty. Liberty, then, is of two or even more sorts, according to the number of quarters from whence coercion, which

[1] An echo of Genesis 1: 2.

it is the absence of, may come: liberty as against the law; and liberty as against those who, first in consideration of the effect of their conduct upon the happiness of society, and afterwards in consideration of the course taken against them by the law, may be stiled *wrong-doers*. These two sorts of liberty are directly opposed to one another: and in as far as it is in favour of one individual that the law exercises it's authority over another, the generation of the one sort is, as far as it extends, the destruction of the other. In the same proportion in which, and by the same cause by which, the one is encreased, the other is diminished.

Restraint produced on the one part: personal security and protection afforded on the other.

4. The law, after certain exceptions made (of which hereafter), prohibits in me and in others all such acts as it thinks advisable to prevent in consideration of their being liable to produce on your part either bodily imperfection (the source of future pain or of loss of future pleasure), or actual pain of body, or actual pain of mind not proceeding from any of the specific sources that are here mentioned: in other words, all such acts as come under the denomination of simple corporal injuries, irreparable corporal injuries, homicide, menacement or simple mental injuries. What, then, is the result? to me and the rest of the community, restraint: to you, personal security, and protection. To speak more at length, it takes measures for affording you personal security: it makes provision for the security of your person: it affords you it's protection for your person against those injuries: and (to introduce the word right) it gives you, when corroborated by the requisite apparatus of subsidiary laws, a right of being protected by the hands of its ministers against the endeavours of any who would inflict on you such injuries.

Restraint produced on one part—liberty on the other.

5. After certain exceptions, as before, it prohibits in me and in others all such acts as it thinks advisable to prevent in consideration of their being liable to restrain you from doing such acts, from the doing of which it is a prejudice to you to be by such means restrained, or to constrain you to do acts which it is a prejudice to you to be constrained to do: in other words, it prohibits all such acts as come under the denomination of simple injurious restrainment, simple injurious compulsion, wrongful confinement, and wrongful banishment. What is the result now? to you, liberty: to me, restraint as before. Personal liberty is, accordingly, either liberty of behaviour in general or liberty of loco-motion. Liberty of behaviour, again, is either the absence of restraint or the absence of constraint: and liberty of loco-motion, either the absence of confinement or the absence of banishment.

Restraint on the one part—protection of reputation on the other.

6. After the like exceptions as before, it prohibits in me and in others all such acts as it thinks advisable to prevent in consideration of the tendency they appear to have to diminish your reputation. What is the result? to me and the rest of the community, another species of restraint: to you, another species of protection.

To all an inexclusive power over or property in a thing.

7. Thus far we have been treading on plain ground. As to the fictitious entities which are the result of the processes whereby offences against property and offences against reputation are created, these and the processes by which they are produced are of a more various and more complicated nature.

To begin with property. Now, property, before it can be offended against, must be created: and the creation of it is the work of law. To shew how the several modifications of it are created by law we may thus proceed. Conceive any material thing at pleasure: a piece of land, for instance. The law issues no mandate at all to me or any one with respect to that piece of land: on the one hand, it does not command us or any of us to exercise any act upon the land: on the other hand, neither does it command us to forbear exercising such act. It does nothing at all, in short, in relation to the land: and, of course, nothing in your favour. What is the result? on all sides, liberty as before. Moreover, considering that it might have commanded us all not to exercise any acts upon that land, and that such are the commands which to you, to me and to every body but one or a few it actually does give with respect to by far the greatest part of the land under its[?] dominion, it is on that account frequently spoken of as if it had done something in favour of those whom it has left thus at liberty: it is spoken of as having given them, or rather left them, a *power over* the land: it may also be said to have left them a *property in* the land. As this same sort of property is given not to you only, but to me and every body else, no restraint with respect to the use of the land being laid on any body, that which is given to you may, on that account, be stiled *inexclusive*: an inexclusive power over the land: an inexclusive property in the land. The land, in this case, is said to be the common property of us all: and each of us is said to have a property in it in common with the rest: and each man may even be said to have *the* property *of* it, so as this phrase be added '*in common with the rest*'.

A power over a thing, inexclusive as against some, exclusive as against others.

8. Again.[1] The law prohibits me and certain others from exercising any act upon the land: leaving you and certain others at liberty, as before. In this case, it gives you a power or property

[1] In the margin, Bentham has noted at this point: 'Make it first compleatly exclusive, and then mix the cases.'

which, according to the persons with reference to whom it is spoken of, is at once inexclusive and exclusive. It is inexclusive with reference to your own associates: it is exclusive with reference to me and mine. You and they have each of you a power over, a property, an estate, an interest, in the land: we have not any of us any such property or power, nor, for any thing that appears, any interest or estate in it.

A property exclusive with respect to all.

9. The law forbids every body but you from exercising any act upon the land. In this case, it gives you alone a power over the land: it makes the land your property, your estate: it makes you sole owner, sole proprietor, of the land: it gives you not only *an* estate, an interest *in* the land in severalty, but *the* property *of* the land, *the* estate *of* the land, both also in severalty.

This case is never strictly verified.

10. As to this case, it may be proper to be apprized that, in reality, it is never compleatly verified under any system of law: some occasions there are in which, for the carrying on of government, it is necessary that any man's ownership over any object of property should be liable to be suspended: as if, for instance, there were need to make use of the land in question for the encampment of an army. But when these periods are not long, and the commencement of them is casual only and contingent, as in the case just stated, such slight exceptions are not in common speech consider'd as derogating from the general rule.

Power over things, corroborated by prohibition of disturbance.

11. The law, having left you a power over the land, no matter whether in severalty or in common, prohibits me and others from doing such and such acts in consideration of the tendency which they appear to have to annihilate, or at least diminish, the benefit which you might otherwise reap from the exercise of your power over the land. It forbids me, for instance, not only from walking on it, or carrying away turf or stone from it, but also from making a wet ditch all round it though on the outside, or building a wall close to the windows of a house which you have built on it. In this case, the law not only permitts you to exercise such power over the land as, without its interference, you were enabled to enjoy, but interferes itself in your favour, and takes an active part in your favour in securing to you the exercise of that power by taking measures for averting such obstacles as might be opposed to the exercise of it by the enterprizes of other men. The power or liberty you had before as against the law may now be said to be corroborated or assisted by the law: corroborated by the mandate it issues to other persons prohibiting them from exercising such acts as it thinks fit to prevent on the consideration above mentioned. The acts thus prohibited it will be proper to specify.

In general, they will be any acts whatever which appear to possess the tendency above mentioned. But the catalogue of them will require various exceptions, as well in favour of the general interests of the community, as in favour of the liberty and property of other persons whose interests may interfere with those which you have in the occupation of that land.

One though not the only way of corroborating a power over things is by rendering it exclusive.

12. It has been seen that there are acts which interfere with your enjoyment of a piece of land without being acts exercised upon that very piece of land. But among the acts which may interfere with such enjoyment, there are few which are so likely to interfere with it, as any acts of another person when exercised upon the same land. At Athens, there were certain spots which were the common property of the whole Athenian people: such were their amphitheatres or places which among them answer'd the purposes of an amphitheatre. It is evident that the right which was enjoy'd by particular persons of choosing the best station in such an amphitheatre, the *prohedria* as it was called, was a right which, in general, would contribute more materially to narrow and impede the right which another Athenian citizen possessed of fixing himself in the same station than the right of opposing any of those indirect impediments that have been exemplified above. It appears, therefore, that rendering the power which a man has over a thing exclusive is one way, though not the only way, in which the law may corroborate that power. Exclusive power and inexclusive power are both capable of being corroborated, and that without altering their nature: but a power, when exclusive, is already corroborated in some degree by being exclusive: and a power which is as yet but inexclusive can scarcely by any means be so materially corroborated as by being render'd exclusive. Power, when thus corroborated, whether exclusive or inexclusive, may be said to be corroborated by *prohibition of disturbance*, or simply, by *prohibition*.

Powers subservient to powers over things.

13. All this is not enough: in order to give you the compleat enjoyment of the land which is made your property, something more effectual should be provided than the precarious expedient of a legal mandate. In order to give a farther degree of corroboration to a power over things, there are two other powers that have been provided. It is intended you should have the compleat enjoyment of your land; it is necessary, therefore, that if any impediments to that enjoyment should arise, such impediments be removed. Now, the causes, or instruments rather, from which such impediments may arise must be either *things* or *persons*. Hence the occasion for two other sets of powers, the one over other things, the other over persons. These additional powers may be stiled by the common appellation of *subservient* powers: in contradistinction to the power you have over the land itself: which again, in contradistinction to these, may be stiled the *principal* power.

14. First, with regard to things. The things which may be the objects of this power are any things which happen to be in such a situation as to prevent or impede your exercising the power you have over the principal thing, the piece of land, in question. You have a power of travelling over a road: a man sets up a fence across this road: in corroboration of the power which he is thus impeding, the law permitts you to beat down and remove the fence. In this way it is that the law creates a subservient power over impeding things in corroboration of a principal power already given.

Subservient power over things impeding.

15. It is obvious that this subservient power may, in the same manner as that to which it is subservient, be corroborated by prohibition of disturbance. The only point in which it is essentially distinguished from the principal one is that of constancy. The power you have over the land, the power of travelling over it, may either be immediate and unintermitted, or may be constituted so as to be brought to appear or disappear by any variety of events of any sort: on the contrary, with regard to the power you have over the things which may happen to stand in the way of your exercising the power you have over the land, such former power, if subservient to the latter, can be only occasional. Upon all other occasions, perhaps, the only power possessed by any body over the wood of which the fence is composed would have been possessed by your antagonist: no power at least would be possessed over it by you: it is only upon the occasion of it's being so situated as to prove an impediment to the exercise of the power you have over the land, that the law gives you this power over the wood which is upon the land.

It is the essence of such power to be but occasional.

16. Next, with regard to the subservient power over such *persons* as may chance to be circumstanced in a manner to impede the exercise of the principal one. This application of power over persons must be explained in its turn as well as any other: but as this is but one among a great variety of applications and modifications of which that branch of power is susceptible, it will first be proper to give a general explanation of the whole together.

Power over persons is either over their passive or their active faculties.

To understand the nature and possible modifications of that sort of fictitious entity which is called power over persons, it will be necessary to make a distinction between the corporeal or purely passive faculties of man and his mental or active faculties. By the first, I mean those which are common to man's body with the rest of matter: by the second, I mean those which are common to him with other sentient beings only, and which either belong to or constitute his mind. By the first, he is assimilated to the class of *things*: it is by the second only that he stands distinguished from that class.

Distinctions observable in regard to power over the active faculty.

17. In the former case, in order for the power to be exercised, there needs but one person to act, to wit the person by whom the power is said to be exercised, and one act to be performed, to wit the act of that person: in the present case, there must be two persons to act, and two acts to be performed: in the first place, on the part of the person by whom the power is exercised, there must be one act: in the next place, on the part of the person over whom the power is exercised, there must be another: the first of these, when spoken of with reference to the power, may be stiled it's *subservient* or *instrumental* object: the latter, it's *ultimate* or *final* object. The first may be spoken of as the means by which the power operates: the latter as the end in which it terminates. The former may be termed an act of power, the [latter],[1] an act of compliance. From each of these acts, a source of distinction may be derived. From the nature of the act of compliance, the power may be either *productive* or *preventive*: it may be stiled productive if that act be of the positive kind: preventive, if of the negative kind. As to the means whereby the power may operate, these may be either of a *physical* or of a *mental*, in which latter case it may otherwise be said to be of a *moral*, nature: those may be said to be of a physical nature which tend to produce the effect by the influence they exert over his body or the adjacent bodies, independent of any which they may exercise on his will: those may be said to be of a mental or moral nature which tend to produce the effect no otherwise than by the influence they exert upon his will. Now, for acting upon the will of a sentient being, there are but two sorts of means, the prospect of pain, and that of pleasure: those which act by holding out the prospect of pain may be termed *co-ercive* motives: those which act by holding out the prospect of pleasure may be termed *alluring* motives. When the means by which a power of the sort in question operates are such motives of the co-ercive kind as persons in general are prohibited from applying, insomuch that were it not for the creation of such power in favour of the person in question the application of them would be an offence, the power (whether it be of production or of

[1] MS 'former'.

prevention) may be said to be enforced by the *power of punishment*: when they are such motives of the co-ercive kind as persons in general are not prohibited from applying, it may be said to enforce itself by *co-ercive influence*: when they are of the alluring kind, by *alluring influence*. And in particular, when the motives which are applied are of the nature of those which result from a change made in the condition of the body, the power may be said to enforce itself by the *power of corporal punishment*.

Power over the active faculty precarious.

18. It may be observed that, of the two sorts of acts which must be performed in order for a power of this sort to have been exercised, the performance of the former stands upon the whole on a much higher footing in respect of certainty than that of the latter. This footing will again be different according as the act which is the final object of the power is of the positive kind or of the negative. For causing a man to forbear exercising acts which it is intended he should abstain from, there are very effectual expedients: physical means have their application here: and the efficacy of those operations which apply themselves directly to the body is much more certain than of those which, before they can produce any change in the condition of the body, are forced to work their way to it through the mind. The law can be much more certain of giving birth to an [act] which has it's termination in the person of any man than of giving birth to an act which takes it's commencement from that person. Indeed, properly speaking, it is the power of giving birth to the act which is the instrumental object which is all the power that the law can be said to confer upon a man: the power of giving birth to the act which is the final object of the productive or preventive power, it can no otherwise give him than by giving him the power before mentioned. The truth of this observation will be perceived when we come to give an account of these several operations by which these several modifications of power are created and conferred.

Power over the passive faculties of persons, uncorroborated

19. By the general mandate above mentioned,[a] the law has prohibited you from doing any such act to the body of any person as that person does not like. It now takes a certain person in particular under consideration, and, in derogation of that general mandate, permitts you to exercise certain acts on his body, whether it be his pleasure they should be exercised or no. In this case, it gives you a power over the body, or in other words over the passive faculties, of that person. This power, being constituted

[a] | |.[1]

[1] See para. 4, p. 289 above.

by bare permission, is as yet uncorroborated. As all other persons but you are excluded from exercising the acts in question upon the person in question, the power is exclusive, and so entirely exclusive as to belong to you in severalty. It is plain enough that, if the general mandate of which this particular permission is an exception had never been established, every other person in the community would have had this same power over the person in question: as on the other hand, so would that person over every other.

—corroborated by prohibition of disturbance

20. The law, having given you the power above-mentioned, prohibits me and others from doing such and such acts in consideration of the tendency which they appear to have to annihilate, or at least diminish, the benefit which you might otherwise reap from the exercise of your power over the person in question. By this means, the uncorroborated power you had before is now corroborated: corroborated exactly in the manner of a power over things, by prohibition of disturbance. What is the result? To you, a species of liberty as well as of power: the liberty of exercising such acts upon such persons: in other words, a property in the use of his body: to others, restraint. As to the person himself on whom the power is to be exercised, on his part nothing ensues: his personal security, in so far as your power over him extends, is diminished, but his liberty as against the law remains on the same footing as before: you are left at liberty to exercise the acts in question upon his person: but he is left at liberty to resist you.

—by prohibition of disobedience.

21. But now then the law addresses itself to the person himself over whom the power is to be exercised, and includes him under a prohibition similar in it's design to that just mentioned to have been addressed to other persons. By this means, your power receives a farther degree of corroboration: it may be said to be corroborated by prohibition of non-submission, or which comes to the same thing, by command of submission.

Power over the passive faculty includes power over the active. Power over the active faculty constituted by power of punishment.

22. It may have been observed that, in giving you a power over the passive faculty of a man, the same operation gave you virtually a power over the active faculties of the same person. Of this latter power, the amplitude, as far as depends upon that act of your's which is the instrumentary object of it, is in proportion to the uneasiness which can be produced on your part by the acts in which the exercise of the power you have over the passive faculties of the person consists: as far as concerns that act of his which is the final object of the former power, the amplitude of it depends upon the nature of the acts which he can be brought to perform by the apprehension of such uneasiness. On the other hand, the converse of this proposition does not hold good. It is not true that a power over the active faculties of a person involves in it of necessity a power over his passive faculties. This may have been inferred already from the analytical sketch that has been given above: and it will immediately be made appear in a more particular manner by the statement of the several operations by which a power over the active faculties of a person may be given in other ways.

23. Of the number of the sorts of acts which tend to produce uneasiness in a person by the influence they have on his person, reputation, property or condition in life, the law leaves you still at liberty to perform such articles as, in affording him it's protection in those several points, it left unprohibited. In so doing, it gives you such and so much power over his active faculties as is constituted by what may be called co-ercive influence: or more at length, the liberty of applying co-ercive influence: the liberty of endeavoring to determine him to perform or not to perform such and such actions by the application of co-ercive influence to his will.[a]

Power over the active faculty constituted by power of co-ercive influence

24. The law (after such exceptions as it thinks proper) leaves you at liberty to perform what acts you please of the number of those which are attended with such effects as are of a nature to prove agreable to him. In so doing, it gives you that sort of power over his active faculties which is constituted by what may be termed *alluring* influence. Of this permission, and that last mentioned, what is the result? to you, liberty of behaviour as before; to the person over whom the power is given and to others, nothing.

—by power of alluring influence.

25. Upon considering these two last species of power, it will be observed that they are neither more nor less than what every man, in proportion to his physical faculties, possesses of course over every other. Accordingly, they do not either of them constitute any species of what is commonly called property: any more than would

No property constituted by either kind of influence.

[a] It may here be wonder'd what acts of the nature above specified can upon the principle of utility remain unprohibited? The answer is, certainly not many, in comparison at least with those which ought to be prohibited. Of the number of those which affect a man in his person, perhaps none: of those which affect him in his reputation, almost all, provided there be no mixture of falshood in the proceeding. The like may be observed with respect to such as affect him in respect of his property or in respect of his condition in life, but no otherwise than in virtue of the tendency they may have to intercept some benefit which might otherwise devolve on him. Let the law have done every thing for you which it ought to do, every man will still be left at liberty to endeavour to persuade your customers not to deal with you, your mistress not to give you her hand, or your electors not to give you the place you wish for, so long as neither force nor falshood, nor in the last-mentioned case bribery, be employ'd.

Power of co-ercive influence—what sorts of acts (instrumental) it may extend to.

any power over things while it remained inexclusive and uncorroborated, except in virtue of the contrast which the condition a thing is in which a man has this sort of power over makes with the condition of a thing over which no power is left him by the law.

Yet both come under the notion of power.

26. It would have been an omission, however, not to have mentioned them under the head of power: they are commonly comprized under that name: they make as much figure in the world nearly as any other sort of power:[a] and although it requires no express and positive operation on the part of the law to constitute or confer them, yet by the law they may be, and in many instances are, taken away.[b]

By what powers over persons, powers over things may be corroborated

27. Let us return to power over things: we are now prepared for obtaining a precise idea of the manner in which it may be corroborated by an occasional power over persons. As to mere influence, whether coercive or alluring, as hath been already observed, this is no more than every man, unless it be expressly taken from him, possesses of course upon all occasions: it is, therefore, what every man has of course to corroborate any share that may have been given him of power over things: to give it him, therefore, on the present occasion requires no express operation or aspect of the law. There remain power over the passive faculty, and power of punishment.

—by power over the passive faculty

28. First, with regard to power over the passive faculty. The persons who may be the objects of this power are any persons who happen to be in such a situation as to prevent or impede your exercising the power you have over the thing in question: the occasion of its accruing to you is the time at which they are thus employ'd.[c] You have a power of travelling over a piece of land.

[a] In Great Britain, for example, the greatest and most effective part of the King's power is of these two kinds: nor is the efficacy of it thought in general to be too little. The King of Great Britain has abundance of places to put a man into, such as men love to be put into; but he has no Bastiles. Possessing this power, he is the object of a constant and not unsalutary jealousy: without it, he would be a cypher.

It may be said that he has this power from the law: since he possesses it in virtue of his possessing the power of appointment to these offices (a particular species of property of which hereafter) which is given him by the law. True: but it is not by any separate operation on the part of the law: the same operation which gives him those powers gives him this unavoidably and of course.

Power of alluring influence—what acts of power it does not extend to.

[b] For example, where the influence, assuming the shape of *Bribery* or other species of *corruption*, tends to produce a breach or abuse of trust: or where, in the shape of *subornation*, it tends to give birth to any offence at large.

[c] See supra p. 18.[1]

[1] i.e. paras. 14–15, p. 293 above. The cross-reference is to the pagination of the MS.

A man, designing to prevent you, watches the moment when you are making your way through a narrow pass and plants himself in your way: the law permitts you hereupon to push him aside. In this way it is that the law gives a power over the passive faculty in corroboration of a power over things.

29. Next, with regard to a power of punishment over persons. A man is obstructing you as in the case just mentioned: the law permitts you to threaten to beat him, for example, or [do][1] him some other harm which, were it not for this particular occasion, it would be an offence in you to bring upon him: and in case the threat proves ineffectual, the law permitts you to carry it into execution. In this way it is that the law may give you a power of punishment in corroboration of a power over things.[a] —by power of punishment.

30. Thus far the corroboration that has been given to powers by powers whether over persons or over things has been given by operations of which the parties only have been the immediate objects: by permission given to the party favoured: by prohibition denounced to the party restrained. But the resources of the law [are] not yet exhausted. Against the attack of a number of invaders, or even of a single invader, the force of a single person taken at random will often be insufficient, and as to the force of the law, the force of which the application is implied in the act of prohibition, it can seldom be applied till after the mischief has been incurred. In most cases, if not in all, it will be requisite to make provision for affording farther assistance to him whom it is meant to favour: to wit such assistance as is to be met with on the spot, and is in the way to be applied at the very time at which alone assistance can be of use. This assistance may be afforded of whichever nature the impediment is which it is requisite to overcome: whether in the first instance it arise from a person or a thing. In either case, the force of the corroboration is susceptible, as it were, of two degrees: it may apply itself in the way either of simple permission, or of positive command. The occasional powers which persons are permitted to exert in corroboration of a principal power may themselves receive a farther degree of corroboration: in the first place, by a power given to third persons to render their assistance: in the next place, by a command given to the same purpose: in the first case the power in question may be Subservient powers corroborated—1. by permission of assistance. 2. by command of assistance.

[a] On these as on other occasions, in the giving powers over persons, various precautions will be requisite: but to enter into such details suits not the present purpose.

[1] MS 'doing'.

said to be corroborated by permission of assistance: in the other case, by command of assistance.

Restraint or constraint on one part—a right to services on the other.

31. We come now to speak of right to services. In order to have given you, by means of the power of punishment, a power over my active faculties, the legislator should have permitted you of your accord to perform, in a certain contingency, certain acts of the number of those which, on account of the prejudice which it [is] in the nature of them to impart to me, he is disposed in general to prohibit. Instead of this, he reserves this power in his own hands. He causes me to perform certain acts for your benefit; that is for the sake of the benefit which such acts seem calculated to produce to you: but he leaves not the motives by which [I am][1] to be induced to perform these acts, nor the time of applying those motives, to your choice. He intends, for example, that I should plough your field for you; and that I should be caused to do it whether I like to do it or not. As a means of causing me to do it, he intends accordingly that, upon the contingency of my not doing it, I should be turned out of a field of my own or kept in confinement. But he intends not to leave me exposed to so much suffering as I should be exposed to were you permitted to judge in every case in the first instance whether I had failed or not in doing what I ought to do in the way of ploughing it, or to determine the time during which I should be kept out of the possession of my field, or the time during which, or place at which, I should be kept under confinement. He, therefore, reserves these points to the determination of such magistrates who, in cases like this, are specially commissioned to execute his will. Accordingly, he either of himself commands me at once to perform the acts in question, or shews himself to be in readiness to adopt any command issued on your part to the same effect in case of your thinking fit to issue such command: reserving in his own hands in either case the enforcement of such command. In so doing, he gives you a right to my services in the behalf in question: a right to certain *services* on my part.[2]

Rights to the use of things.

31*. In what manner and by what operations powers are created, whether over things or over persons, has been already shewn. But powers are not the only things of which property may consist. It may consist also of rights, a sort of fictitious objects which, in some cases indeed, co-incide with powers, but in other

[1] MS 'you are'.

[2] In the margin, Bentham has noted at this point: 'Wherein consists the exercise of such a right? In the demanding of the services only, or in the demanding and receiving them accordingly?'

cases are essentially distinct from them. In order to give you a power over a thing, the law permitted you to exercise certain acts having their termination in that thing; and that, at any time, without waiting for the consent of any one. To give you a right to a thing, or to the use of a thing, the law takes a different course. It does not permit you to exercise any act on it in the first instance: it, however, shews itself resolved that, upon the performance of a certain act on the part of some other person, it will thereupon immediately give you such permission: and, in the meantime, it commands that person to perform that act. As soon, then, as he performs that act, you have a power over the thing: till he performs it, you have none. Or (which is but to express the same meaning in other words), if before he has performed that act, you should take upon you to meddle with the thing, you would be liable to be punished: as soon as he has performed it, you are exempt from being punished on that score.[a] This is in effect to command him to execute in your favour an act of investitive power over that thing: which power we shall have occasion to explain more particularly a little farther on.[1] It is also giving you a right to a service on his part: to wit the service which consists in his performing in your favour the act just-mentioned: another sort of right which will be consider'd immediately after the present. But as the service to be performed is referable solely to no other object than this particular thing, and is no otherwise of importance than in virtue of it's having the effect of giving you a power over this thing, it will be convenient to consider the right in question in the class of a right to things, than in that of a right to a service: for it will be convenient to have a class of rights to things in order to contrast with the class of rights to services.

32. Now, an act, we may remember, may either be of the positive or of the negative stamp: services may accordingly be either active services or services of forbearance. When the legislator, in order to procure you a benefit, commands me to do certain acts, the services on my part to which he thereby gives you

To constraint correspond active services: to restraint, services of forbearance.

[a] I ow'd you yesterday ten guineas. I have just been paying you with ten pieces of that name. I took them out of my pocket and counted them into your hand: or I laid them down on the table, and bid you take them up. You now have a power over those pieces; you have the property of the pieces. But before I performed those acts in virtue of which I am deemed to have paid you, you had no such power: you had only a right to any such pieces of money amounting to that value, as I might think fit to give you. Had you taken the pieces in question off the table before I bid you, and gone off with them, you would have committed an offence.

[1] See para. 36, p. 303 below.

a right are of the active stamp: when, in the same view, he commands me not to do such or such an act, the services to which he thereby gives you a right are services of forbearance. He commands me to plow your field for you as before: it is thereby that he gives you a right to active services: he commands me not to cut certain trees which, though growing on my own land, are of use to you in affording shelter for your field: he thereby gives you a right to services of forbearance.

Services corporal and mental.

33. Services may be consider'd again in two other points of view: 1. according to the faculties by which they are performed; and [2.] according to the object on which they are performed. With regard to the first of these points, it is plain enough that, services being the result of the active faculty, there is no sort of service in the rendering of which the mind must not be concerned as well as the body. Although the acts in which they consist should have originated in the mind, yet these acts, before they can have been productive of any effect, beneficial or otherwise, in society, must have been communicated to the body. On the other hand, let the concern which the body has in the business be ever so considerable, the production and regulation of its motions must still have originated with the mind. For distinction's sake, however, where the share which the body has in the production of the effect appears the most considerable, they may be referred to the body; where that which the mind has, to the mind. The service, for instance, which a husbandman renders to his landlord by plowing his field for him may be referred to the head of corporal service, notwithstanding the attention which it is necessary the mind should give to the guidance of the plough: the instruction which is given by the professor to his pupil may be referred to the head of mental service, notwithstanding the part which it is necessary the lips or the hand should take in the communication of it.

Services *in personam* and *in rem*.

34. Secondly, as to the object on which the service is to be performed. As the commencement of the act whereby the service is render'd is determined by the person whose faculties are in question, so the termination is determined by the object on which the service is performed. This object must belong, of course, to the class either of persons or of things. In the first case, the service may be stiled a service *in personam*, in the other case a service *in rem*. The service render'd by a surgeon is a service *in personam*, that render'd by the husbandman, as above, a service *in rem*.[a] Each

[a] The division of services into *personal* and *prædial*, as distinguished by the Roman law, is ambiguous and unexhaustive. It does not quadrate with either of those given in the text.

of these classes again may be divided indefinitely according to the nature of the persons or things on which the acts in question are to be performed, according to the natures and tendencies of those acts which are to be performed, and according to the occasion or circumstances in which they are to be performed.

35. Power, consider'd with respect to the individual person by whom [it is][1] exercised, may be distinguished again into direct and indirect. It may be stiled direct, when the acts in which the exercise of it consists are the acts of the very person by whom the power is said to be possessed: in this case, it may be styled the power or right of occupation: it may be termed indirect, when those acts, though still taking their origin in some measure from his will, are not his acts, but those of some other person. Power (and right) direct and indirect.

36. Indirect power or right may again be divided into investitive and divestitive. It may be stiled investitive power when the will of the one person is that such or such another should perform the acts in question: divestitive, when the will of the former is that the latter, having exercised them, should exercise them no longer: in the former case, we see the acts which result from the will of the person consider'd as being in possession of the power are of the positive kind: in the other, of the negative kind. Let us see how these powers are created. Power indirect—investitive and divestitive.

37. The law shews itself resolved that, upon the event of my declaring that such is my will in this behalf, it will issue those mandates, that set of permissions, prohibitions, dispensations and commands, by the issuing of which it will have given you a power of occupation over the land in question. It is by so doing that it gives me an investitive power over the land in question. By this means, it in a manner adopts the expression of [my][2] will, and turns it into a law. Power investitive how created—upon the appearance of such a signal.

38. You are already in possession of the direct power over the land; or what comes to the same thing, you are about to possess it. The law shews itself resolved that, upon the event of my declaring that such is my will in this behalf, it will revoke or forbear to issue those mandates by the issuing of which it gave or would have given you such power of occupation. It is by so doing that it gives me a divestitive power over the land in question. Power divestitive.

39. It will be proper to observe that the exercise of either branch of the indirect power is a very different thing from the Exercise of an indirect power, what.

[1] MS 'they are'. The sentence originally began 'Power and right', but though Bentham has marked 'and right' for deletion, he has failed to amend the words 'they are'.

[2] MS 'your'. Bentham originally wrote this paragraph with the subject in the second person singular, but failed in this particular instance to change the subject to the first person singular.

exercise of the direct power. The act by which a direct power is exercised is an act which terminates in the person or thing which is the object of the power. The act by which the indirect power is exercised is any act which serves as a sign of my entertaining the desire in question.

The exercise of an investitive power is one sort of investitive event: the exercise of the divestitive power one sort of divestitive event: of these two events consider'd in a general point of view, more will be said a little farther on.[1]

Rights direct and indirect.

40. This division into direct and indirect is applicable to unconsummated rights as well as to powers.

Investitive and divestitive powers of the 1st, 2nd and 3rd &c. orders.

41. The law shews itself resolved that, upon the event of my declaring it to be my will that, upon the event of your declaring it to be your will, that a third person shall have a direct power over the land, it shall happen accordingly. In this way, it gives me a sort of indirect power which may be stiled an investitive power of the 2d order: and so with respect to the divestitive power. In the same manner, it may constitute investitive powers of the third, fourth or fifth orders, and so on.

Conditional investitive power—power of control by non-assent.

42. When the law shew'd itself resolved to give you the direct power over a thing in the event of my declaring such to be my will, such declaration of will on my part may be consider'd as a kind of signal which the law waits for, in order to invest you with such power. But, in the same manner, it might have taken the expression of the last of any number of wills or of any proportion of any such number of wills for the signal. In this case, the investitive power may be consider'd as residing in the whole number of such persons in conjunction, each of them having a joint share in it: or what comes to the same thing, a conditional investitive power may be consider'd as residing in any one of them, each one of the rest having a power of controul by non-assent.[a]

Defeasible investitive power—power of control by dissent.

43. The law shews itself resolved that, in the event of my declaring it to be my will that you should have a direct power over the thing in question, it will, at the end of a certain time after such declaration, confer on you such power, provided a third person does not within that time declare it to be his will that you should not possess such power. In this case, I may be said to have a conditional investitive power over the land in question; and such third person may be said to possess another sort of power of

[a] This is the sort of power which the members of a corporation possess over the lands and other articles that are the property of the corporation.

[1] See para. 67, p. 309 below.

controul over the investitive power: a power of controul by dissent.

Principal modifications of which the indirect powers are susceptible.

44. It appears, then, that the investitive and divestitive powers may each of them be possessed either exclusively or inexclusively: when inexclusively, each of the sharers may exercise it indiscriminately[1] or in association only, that is not but in conjunction with the rest: if in association, the share he has may either be a power of controul by non-assent, or a power of control by dissent.[2]

Other modifications of the indirect powers dismissed.

45. Moreover, the persons who share in the power in question may, on the occasion of their exercising it, be divided into groupes; which groupes may be indefinitely diversified: but the consideration of these and the other variations that may attend the constitution and operations of corporate bodies is not necessary to the present purpose.

Buying and selling, a mutual exercise of the investitive power.

46. A mutual exercise of the investitive power by two persons in favour of each other is called buying and selling. Or more fully thus. You have the investitive power over a measure of corn: I have the like power over a measure of wine. You exercise in my favour the investitive power that you have over the corn, in consideration that I exercise in your favour the investitive power I have over the [wine]:[3] doing thus, we may each of us be said to buy and to sell: you buy my wine with your corn: you sell your corn for my wine: I buy your corn with my wine: I sell my wine for your corn.

Buying and selling, where money is concerned.

47. If either of the articles consist in what is called money, or in what serves as money, the application of the words buy and sell is not thus reciprocal: he who buys the money is not said to buy, but only to sell: he who sells the money is not said to sell, but only to buy: the one of them only is accordingly stiled the buyer, the other only the seller: just as if buying and selling were two different operations. The reason of this peculiarity in language is not to the present purpose: it is sufficient to observe the fact.

Giving, what.

48. If the power in question be exercised on one side only, he who exercises it is said to *give*: and sometimes, where it is necessary to distinguish the present case from a case in which the word give has been made use of in speaking of buying and selling, he is said to give the thing *gratis*, or *for nothing*.

Conveying, what.

49. The word convey is employ'd indifferently in either case: in that of buying and selling, as in that of giving.

Different modes of buying and selling.

50. The terms buying and selling, giving and conveying, are applicable to any other direct power or right as well as to the

[1] In the margin, Bentham has indicated that a note should be inserted at this point, but the corresponding marginal comment is illegible.

[2] In the margin, Bentham has indicated that a note should be inserted at this point, but the corresponding marginal comment is illegible.

[3] MS 'corn'.

general or residuary power over a thing: buying services with things is called hiring services: rendering services in return for things, or selling a right to services for things, is called doing work for hire: buying the use of a thing for a time is called hiring it: selling the use of a thing for a time is called letting it, or letting it out to hire.

A compact or contract is to be distinguished from a conveyance.

51. A conveyance ought to be distinguished from a pact or covenant: whether it be a covenant to render services one's self, or to convey a right to services or any other property: a pact or covenant is the expression of an intention to do some act or other, for the benefit of some person or other, and, in case of the not doing, to incur certain penalties to be inflicted by the law. Let the act in question be an act of conveyance: such a sort of act whereby any thing, suppose a dwelling-house, is convey'd. If I convey to you a house of mine and then enter into it without your consent, I am punishable as for a trespass upon your house, just as I should have been, had the house never been mine: if I only covenant to convey it before such a time and have not convey'd it by that time, and the law gives it's sanction to the promise contained in my covenant, in such case, although I enter into the house without your consent, I am punishable not as for a trespass upon your house, but in another manner, as for the breach of this my covenant.[a]

Persons for whose benefit a power is designed. Power beneficial or fiduciary.

52. Thus far with respect to the nature of the powers and rights themselves in which property consists. We now come to speak of the party or parties for whose benefit they are to be exercised. For the benefit of somebody they must have been designed, so long as the legislator has acted with a view to utility, or, in short, with any view whatever. This party or parties must have been either the person himself to whom the power is given or some other: in the first case, the power may be stiled a beneficial power or simply a power; in the other case, a fiduciary power or trust.

Fiduciary private, semi-public or public.

53. In this latter case again, the beneficiary, as hath been already observed,[1] may be either 1. an assignable individual or individuals: 2. a subordinate class of persons individually unassign-

[a] What renders it the more necessary to advert to this distinction is that the word contract, which in English is used only in synonymity with covenant, is in Latin and some of the other European languages put in synonymity not only with covenant but with conveyance: at least certain particular conveyances or instruments of conveyance are called contracts.[2]

---

[1] See *An Introduction to the Principles of Morals and Legislation* (*CW*), Ch. XVI, para. 29, p. 221, and §7, pp. 314–15 below.

[2] Bentham may have had in mind, for instance, the use of the term *contrat de cession* in French law.

able, or 3. the public at large: trusts may accordingly be distinguished into private, semi-public and public trusts.

Power fiduciary how created.

54. The law permitts me to enter upon and walk over a field, of which the general property is in you: thus much it might do for my sake: in which case the power it gives me would be of the beneficial kind. But it does not stop there: it does not content itself with permission: it commands me to enter into your field in order to plough it for you: it thereby renders the power a fiduciary one. Here, then, lies the difference between a beneficial power and a fiduciary one. The legal operation by which the power is constituted is in the first case a permission alone: in the other case, it is a permission with a command super-added to it.

Power fiduciary imports right to services.

Restraint on you in favour of a third person.

55. Let us observe the several results of this operation of the law. To me it affords liberty as against restraint: but at the same time it takes away a portion of the liberty I have as against constraint: to you it affords a right to my services. If the beneficiary be a person different from him against whom the trustee is left at liberty, that is, in the present case, from the general proprietor of the land, there are three persons concerned in point of interest in the operation: and with reference to these three it produces so many different results. I have a power, for example, of taking turf out of your field in trust, that is for the use of another person. In this case, if the power I have is backed, as it will commonly be, by a prohibition of disturbance addressed to you, the metaphorical results will stand as follows: to me, in the first place, liberty as against restraint as before: in the next place, constraint, as before: to you, restraint: to the third person, a right to my services, as before.[1]

The operations of the executive magistrate are liable not to quadrate with those of the legislative.

59. Hitherto, it has been all along taken for granted that, in the establishment and maintenance of property, the legislator and the executive magistrate go hand in hand: that the prohibitions and commands whereby those several sorts of property are created are constantly enforced; and that, accordingly, the adjective commands by which the substantive commands given to the above purport are enforced, are constantly and punctually observed. But from various accidents it will every now and then happen otherwise: the course taken by the executive magistrate will be

[1] In the text, Bentham has noted at this point: 'Weakness of the invest. power alone: strength of it when coupled with the divestitive.' The gap in the numbering of the paragraphs may indicate Bentham's intention to develop this point, though there is no gap in the pagination. According to the corresponding marginal contents sheet at UC xcix. 87, the text for three marginal contents, across two pages, is missing at this point. The marginal contents read as follows: '**56.** On one part, liberty as against restraint but accompanied by constraint: on another part, restraint: on another, right to services.

'**57.** Weakness of the investitive power, where alone.

'**58.** Strength of it where coupled with the divestitive.'

unconformable to that chalked out to him by the legislator. It is this distinction that seems to be the source of certain distinctions which the whole phraseology of the law of property is continually bringing into use. These distinctions being to be explained, now then is the time for exhibiting the import of the word possession, as well as certain other words which could not till now have been conv[en]iently display'd.

Occupation, what.

60. To understand what it is to possess, we must understand what it is to occupy.

A man may be said to occupy a thing when he performs any acts having their termination in that thing. If a man occupies a thing, it will be for the sake of some benefit to be thereby derived from that thing to either himself or some other person: the nature of the thing and the nature of the benefit to be derived from it will determine the nature of the act which is termed occupation. A piece of land is made use of in one way, a house in another, a garment in another, a piece of household furniture in another, an article of food or fewel in another.

Various senses of the word possession analysed.

61. Possession must be distinguished into physical and legal: physical again into physical possession as against physical obstacles, and physical possession as against human obstacles: and legal into legal possession *de jure* and legal possession *de facto*. Possession in general, in a loose way of speaking, may be said to be the absence of obstacles opposed to occupation: or, in other words, it is the liberty of occupation. As far as this liberty results from the situation which the thing is in, setting aside the interference of law, the possession may be termed physical: as far as it results from the aspect of the law, it may be termed legal. So much for a general idea of the nature of possession: but a subject so intricate demands more particular explanations.

Physical possession as against physical obstacles.

62. You may be said to have the physical possession of a thing as against physical obstacles, when it appears that, in the event of your exerting your endeavours to use it, you will occupy it accordingly: in this sense, you are in possession of the water at the bottom of your well, if you have tackle and strength and time enough, and so forth, to draw it up: of a horse which is on a common, provided the common is near enough for you to go upon presently, and provided that, if you have got upon it, you can catch him: of the stone which is in a quarry upon the common, provided the stone does not lie too deep for you to dig it out. Now, as the strength of the endeavours that are necessary to produce the effect in question, or in other words the difficulty of producing it, will be apt to vary by insensible degrees, it will be difficult in most instances to draw the line between the case in which a man has, and that in which he has not, this species of possession: so that if two persons were disposed to dispute upon the question whether a given person were or were not in this sense in possession of a given thing, they might go on disputing without end.

63. You may be said to have the physical possession of a thing as against human obstacles at large when there is not, on the part of the will of any other person, any impediment sufficient to prevent you from occupying or making use of it. Thus you are, physically speaking, in possession of the coat which is on your back at any rate: of a coat which is in the next room to you, provided nobody hinders you from getting at it: of a coat which is at the taylor's, provided the taylor and every body else is disposed to let you have it. Physical possession as against human obstacles.

64. You may be said to be in the legal possession of a thing *de jure*, if you are in such a case that the law has issued such mandates as have the effect of prohibiting other persons from disturbing you in the physical possession, or, what comes to the same thing, in the occupation, of it: or at least of preventing its own officers from giving you such disturbance. Legal possession *de jure*.

65. You may be said to be in the legal possession of a thing *de facto*, when it appears that the executive magistrate to whom the secondary mandates of the legislator are addressed will, in case an occasion should take place, do that which he ought to do upon the supposition that the mandates above mentioned are established in your favour: or in other words will, in case of disturbance, do what is requisite to maintain you in the physical possession of it as against human obstacles. Legal possession *de facto*.

66. To have the legal possession of a thing is, in other words, to be entitled to it,[1] or to have a title to it: this title may, if the legal possession in question is the legal possession *de jure*, be termed a good, lawful or valid title: if the legal possession in question is the legal possession *de facto*, an actual or effectual title. Title may be good, lawful, valid: or actual, effectual.

67. Now, the time during which any given person is in possession of any given thing must, it is evident, have certain boundaries: if no others, those at least which limit the man's life. It must have, accordingly, on the one hand a commencement, and on the other a termination. The æra or moment of it's commencement must be marked out by one event: that of it's termination by another: the former of these may be termed an[2] investitive event with respect to this period of time: the latter, the divestitive. Investitive and divestitive event.

[1] In the margin, Bentham has noted at this point: 'i.e. a title to the possession of a power over it.'

[2] MS orig. 'the'.

The two species of legal possession and title commonly go together.

68. It appears, then, that in every case the fictitious entity called a title is constituted by some investitive event; and so many sorts as there are of investitive events, so many sorts are there of titles. From the happening at which any article in the catalogue of these investitive events takes place to the time at which any article in the catalogue of divestitive events takes place, the title subsists: upon the happening of any article in the latter catalogue, it is at an end. During this same period also, you are said to possess the thing in question, or to be in possession of it, meaning legal possession: in the legal possession *de jure*, if the aspects of the legislator are in favour of your occupying it: in the legal possession *de facto*, if the conduct or procedure of the executive magistrate be or appear likely to be in favour of your occupying it: in both together, if both the aspects of the legislator are, and the administration of the [magistrate][1] appears likely to be, in favour of it. Now, it is but by accident that the administration of the executive magistrate fails of being conformable to the mandates of the legislator: the design and expectation is that it should always be conformable to them: and so it actually is in common, even in the worst order'd governments that are. In common, then, these two species of possession go together: and so they may of course be deemed to do where nothing is said to the contrary. Wherever, then, the phrase legal possession is introduced, it may be taken for granted, if nothing is said to the contrary, that what is said of legal possession in general is meant to be applied to both these kinds of it.

Investitive event purely natural or voluntary.

[69]. The investitive event may either be voluntary or natural: it may be termed voluntary where the commencement of the title is effected by the will of some person purposely manifested in the intention of causing it to commence: as if you were expressly to declare it to be your will that I should have such or such a portion of your land: it may be termed natural where the commencement of the title is effected by an event in the production of which the will of man has ordinarily no concern: as if you were to die, whereupon, according to a rule of law established in that behalf, I were to succeed to the legal possession of your land. Now, it is in the case where the investitive event is voluntary that the person whose will is in question is said to have the investitive power over the thing in question. And the case is the same with divestitive events and divestitive power.

Investitive event may be simple or complex.

70. Hitherto, in order to avoid perplexity, we have been speaking of the investitive event as if it never consisted of any more than one single event at a time. But the truth is that it may be either simple or

[1] MS del. 'legislator'.

complex: and that to any degree of complexity. It may consist either of one single event, such as the death of a man: or of the sum of any number of events of any sort, natural or voluntary: such as the death of a man produced by the sentence of a court of justice: the performance of the ceremonies necessary to confiscation or of the ceremonies instituted for the purpose of establishing the authenticity of his testament; and so on. But as the unity of an act or other event depends solely upon the custom of language, any number of such events may, to certain purposes, be spoken of as one.

Possession is permanent—occupation instantaneous.

71. It will be proper to observe the difference between possession and occupation: between possessing a power of occupying a thing, and exercising that power. To occupy a thing, you must perform some act: an act having it's termination in the thing in question: to possess a thing, it is not necessary that you should yourself perform any act: possession is not any real, but only a fictitious, mode of action. It is not necessary so much as that any body else should perform any act: all that is necessary is that things should be so circumstanced as to make it appear that, in case such or such another person were to take such and such steps of which the tendency would be to prevent your occupying it were you so disposed, the executive magistrate would do, or at least according to law ought to do, what depended upon him for preventing or punishing such transgression. Occupation, that is the exercise of a power, therefore, is characterizable and diversified by the acts of which it may consist: possession of a power or right is characterizable by nothing but the time during which it lasts. Possession is something permanent and continual: occupation and exercise are instantaneous.

Right of possession is the same as right to a thing.

72. Along with the word possession, we hear also of the right of possession: the nature of this right will easily be apprehended from what has been said of a right to things. Right to a thing, and right to the possession of a thing, are expressions of the same meaning: and perhaps the case is, that the [latter][1] alone is the original and proper phrase of which the [former][2] is but an elliptical abridgment. To have possession of a thing is to have the power over a thing: to have a right to the possession of a thing, is to have a right to the thing.

When a man has actually the legal possession of a thing, in this case, too, it is common to speak of him as having the right of possession also: but in this case, the phrase right of possession has a different meaning from what it has in the former. To give him what is meant by the right of possession, as explained above,

[1] MS 'former'. [2] MS 'latter'.

would, in this case, be narrowing his interest in the land, instead of enlarging it. In this case, then, to say that he has the right of possession, or in other words a right to the possession along with the possession itself, means only as much as to say that the possession he has of the thing is *not* defeasible by eviction: to say that he has the possession without having the right of possession is as much as to say that the possession he has *is* defeasible by eviction. The right of possession is not to be confounded with what was spoken of just now under the appellation of the legal possession *de jure*. A man may have the former without having the latter; as in the case above exemplified. A man may have the latter without having the former; in truth, if he has the latter he can not be said to have the former as above explained: if he has already the permission to do what he pleases with the thing in question, he can not be said to be in the same condition with one who as yet has not that permission, but waits to have it conferred on him by the act of another person.[1]

[§7. *Conclusion.*]

Connection. Thus inextricably is the penal branch of the law interwoven with the civil: that with which we are here immediately concerned, with that with which here we have no such immediate concern: in order to settle and arrange the former, it became, therefore, unavoidably necessary to look through all the latter: so toilsome and so arduous when pursued with care and industry is the business of arrangement. Before we conclude it may be not amiss to gather up, in the way of recapitulation, the broken hints that have been given in the course of this chapter and thereby to give a sort of analytical sketch of the whole business of the art of legislation.

Purposes of legislation—producing good—avoiding to produce evil. The art of legislation has two general objects or purposes in view; the one direct and positive, to add to the happiness of the community: the other indirect and negative, to avoid doing any thing by which that happiness may be diminished.

[1] The following fragment at UC lxxxviii. 137, though paginated to form the continuation of the text at this point, appears to be abandoned: 'We may now, perhaps, be in a condition to ascertain what the operations are by which the law gives protection for property. For such species of property as consist in a power over things, the protection it gives in the first instance is afforded by prohibition: by the prohibition of any acts by which the possession or the exercise of such power would be disturbed: for such as consist in a right to certain services on the part of certain persons, if those services be of the negative stamp, also by prohibition: by prohibition of the acts in the abstaining from which those services consist: for such as consist in a right to certain services of the positive kind, by command: to wit by command to render such services to the person in question.'

To enable it to compass the former of these purposes, it has two great instruments or engines: 1. coercion: and 2. remuneration. Coercion is either 1. physical, or 2. moral; viz: by punishment. Physical coercion, by which a human being is treated upon the footing of an inanimate machine, it is evident enough can be made but little use of, by reason of the vast and incessant expence it would cost in point of labour and attention on the part of those whose business it must be made to apply it. Remuneration is also in comparison employ'd but little, for various reasons, one of which is the boundless expence it would require, and the absolute want of a fund from which that expence could be supplied.

Two instruments—cocrcion and reward—coercion is either physical or by punishment.

Having these instruments to work with, the way in which the law promotes the happiness of any given man, is by influencing *action*.

Method of operation—imposing obligations.

Take any individual for example. The actions which it influences must be either his *own* or those of *other* individuals. His own actions it cannot influence in any material degree by reward, on account of the expence. Whether it can be consistent with the abovementioned *collateral* purpose of legislation, in other words, whether it can be worth while, to attempt to influence them by co-ercive methods, is a matter that in most cases lies very open to dispute.

Obligations absolute × relative, barren × productive of a right.

As to the actions of other men, the way in which it may promote his happiness by influencing those actions is either by causing such as would be productive of *inconvenience* to him to be *abstained from*, or by causing such as are productive of *advantage* to him to be *performed*. In as far as by coercive methods it causes or endeavours to cause an action to be abstained from or performed, it is thereby said to impose, give birth to or create an obligation or duty. Duties, accordingly, are either duties of *abstinence*, i: e: negative duties, or duties of *performance*, i: e: positive duties.

Obligations positive × negative.

Now, the objects on which the actions in question are capable of *terminating* are either *things* or *persons*. Now, it is by causing certain actions to be abstained from on the part of other men which would lessen the advantage you are capable of reaping either for yourself or others from certain things, at the same time that you or such or such persons of your appointment are not caused to abstain from certain actions by which that happiness may be promoted, that you have *power* given you over those things. Power over things is constituted, then, by the imposing of duties of abstinence on other persons. This power, according to the amplitude of it, is termed either the *property* of, or a property or *interest* in, the thing in question. This power, then, either you are left free to exercise or not according as may contribute most to

Objects of the conduct regulated—things or persons.

Duties of performance = services. Power over things beneficial × fiduciary.

your own advantage, in which case it may be stiled a beneficial power, or it is coupled with a duty, in other words you are bound to exercise it for the sake of some other party, in which case it is called a *trust*.

Power over persons—three degrees of it.

When the acts you are left free to perform are such whereby the interest of other individuals (like yourself) is liable to be affected, you are thereby said to have a power over those individuals. In this case, in as far as you possess the power in question, you possess an exemption from the duty of *abstinence* as far as concerns the acts to the performance of which your power extends. This exemption, then, on your part may either stand single or it may be coupled with an assistant duty (subservient to the same design) on the part of other men. In the first case, it may be stiled a *naked* or *uncorroborated* power: in the other case, it may be stiled a *corroborated* power. This assistant duty will either be [1.] a duty of forbearance, viz: the duty of abstaining from all such acts as may tend to prevent you from exercising the power in question, or 2. a duty of performance, viz: the duty of performing such acts as may enable you to overcome any obstacle that may oppose itself to the exercise of that power. Power over persons may accordingly be consider'd as susceptible of three degrees of perfection. Power in the first, lowest, or least perfect degree, is where it is not made any body's duty to oppose you, in case of your going about to exercise it. Power in the second or middle degree is where not only it is not made any body's duty to oppose you in case of your going about to exercise it, but it is made every body's duty not to oppose you in case of your going about to exercise it. Power in the third, highest, or most perfect degree is where not only it is made every body's duty not to oppose you in case of your going about to exercise it, but in case of your meeting with any obstacle to the exercise of it, whether from the party over whom it is to be exercised, or any other person, or in short from any other cause, it is made the duty of such or such persons to enable you to overcome such obstacles.[a]

The beneficiary may be 1. an individual. 2. a class. 3. the public.

With regard to fiduciary power, whether it be power over things or power over persons, the party to be benefited may consist either of a single individual, or of divers individuals. When it consists of

[a] In point of fact, it is not always that, where power over persons is given, it is given in the highest degree. In that degree, however, it ought always to be given where it is given at all, since upon no other terms can a man be assured the enjoyment of it. Power and the benefits for the sake of which it is conferred are left in a very precarious state when the enjoyment of it is made to depend upon the physical strength of the person on whom it is conferred, or on the caprice of those who may happen to be about him.

divers individuals, these individuals may either be assignable or unassignable. When unassignable, the number of them may either be limitable to a multitude less than the whole multitude of individuals in the state, or it may not. First, then, where the party to be benefited consists of a single assignable individual or a number of assignable individuals, in either case the trust may be termed a private one. 2. Where it consists of an unassignable number of persons limitable to a multitude less than the multitude which compose the state,[1] it may be termed a semi-public trust. 3. Where the number of persons to be benefited is not limitable to a multitude less than that which composes the state, it may be termed a *public* trust.[2]

But power, we may remember, whether it be beneficial or fiduciary, depends upon duty. It is constituted by the prescribing duties, that is, again, by commanding acts: to wit on the part of persons other than him to whom the power is given.[3] That branch of the law which prescribes those duties to which correspond power of the beneficial kind and private trusts may be termed Private Law: that which prescribes those duties to which correspond semi-public and public trusts, Constitutional Law.

Duty, however, does not necessarily confer power. A duty which consists in the abstaining from such acts by the performance of which, or of performing such acts by the non-performance of which, a man would suffer in his person confers no power.[4]

Acts of which the tendency is mischievous in the first instance are either mischievous upon the whole, or not. Those which are not mischievous upon the whole are either simply innocent, that is indifferent, or else beneficial upon the whole. Those which are indifferent, if any such there be, are not worth taking any account of. Those which are mischievous upon the whole are so either to an assignable individual or individuals, or to individuals unassignable. Those which are so to an assignable individual are so, either to the agent himself or to some other person. Those which are so to individuals unassignable are so either to the whole state, or to a subordinate class or division of it's members. Those which are so to an assignable individual, whether it be the agent himself or another, affect him either in point of person, in point of property, in point of reputation, or in point of condition in life. As to acts which,

[1] In the margin, Bentham has noted at this point: 'included within class of persons or a number of persons determined by a natural territorial division'.

[2] The following two paragraphs have been crossed through by Bentham.

[3] The following sentence has been marked by Bentham for possible deletion.

[4] In the margin, Bentham has noted at this point: 'N.B. It confers, however, in this case an inconsummate right.'

though they may be mischievous (as well as beneficial or innocent), in the first instance are permitted, whether under the notion of their being beneficial upon the whole, or because the interests of those to whom they may be prejudicial are neglected, the performance of these acts is termed the exercise of a *power*. Power is either over persons or over things. And in both cases it is either beneficial or fiduciary.[1]

Private Law. So much, then, of the law as is occupied in prohibiting acts which are mischievous upon the whole to an individual or to a subordinate class of unassignable individuals, and in constituting private beneficiary powers and trusts, may be termed Private Law. So much as is occupied in prohibiting acts which are mischievous upon the whole to the state at large, and in constituting public and semi-public powers, may be termed Constitutional Law. Of both these divisions, so much as contains the penal clause, together with a concise designation of the particular offence, including the circumstances peculiarly belonging to that sort of offence, may be termed the penal branch of the Law: so much of it as consists of definitional or directory matter exhibiting in detail a specification of such circumstances the absence or presence of which enters into the description of a multitude of offences in common may be termed the *civil* branch of the law.[2]

Constitutional Law.

Penal branch of law.

Civil branch.

Private law: integrant parts of. Again, the civil branch of Private Law may be divided into: 1. the law of property (viz: beneficial property in things): 2. the law of services (viz: beneficial property in the services of persons): 3. the law of Private Trusts: and 4. Family-Law: exhibiting the rights, powers and obligations incident to the several modes of natural relationship.

Right—how resulting out of duty. An act is a real entity: a law is another. A duty or obligation is a fictitious entity, conceived as resulting from the union of the two former. A law commanding or forbidding an act thereby creates a duty or obligation. A right is another fictitious entity, a kind of secondary fictitious entity, resulting out of a duty. Let any given duty be proposed; either somebody is the better for it or nobody. If nobody, no such duty ought to be created: neither is there any right that corresponds to it. If somebody, this somebody is either the party bound, or some other. If it be he himself, then the duty, if such it may be called, is a duty he owes to himself: neither in this

[1] The following two paragraphs have been crossed through by Bentham.

[2] In the margin, Bentham has noted at this point: 'A particular code is carried to it's utmost pitch of simplicity when the matter of it is such that it can not be divided into any two parcels in one of which one set of persons, and in another a different set of persons, are interested in the same manner.'

case is there any *right* that corresponds to it. If it be any other party, then is it a duty owing to some other party: and then that other party has at any rate a right: a right to have this duty performed: perhaps also a *power*: a power to compel the performance of such duty.

Notion of duty a common measure.

What is it that every article of law has in common with the rest? It issues commands, and by so doing it creates *duties*: or, what is another word for the same thing, *obligations*. The idea of duty is concerned in every thing that belongs to law. It is from hence that the differences and resemblances of the various branches of law are to be traced as from their common source.

The notion of command leads to that of duty: that of duty to that of exemption, that of power and that of right:[1] that of exemption to that of privilege: power and duty together, that of trust.

Of duties, some are productive of a power; others not: those which are not may be stiled barren. Barren duties might subsist were there but one person in the world; suppose Adam. Duties constituting power require at least two persons: if the power be coupled with a trust, and the beneficiary of the trust be not the same person with the person on whom the duty is imposed, they require three.

Necessity of the above definitions.

Of all the words that occur in language, there are few that are more familiar, that is occur more frequently, than those of which I have been giving an explanation: at the same time, I think it may be observed with confidence, that there are few that are so far from being clearly understood. If it be true that our ideas are derived all of them from our senses, and that the only way of rendering any of our ideas clear and determinate is to trace it up to the sensible objects in which it originates, the only method that can be taken for explaining them to the purpose is the method I have just been taking here. This method is that of defining these and other names of fictitious entities, not *per genus et differentiam*, nor by any other of the methods which are applicable to real entities, but by a method which I have ventured to stile that of paraphrasis: a method new in itself and which, therefore, if mentioned at all, must be mentioned by a new name. Now, this method is one that most assuredly has never been taken hitherto: if, therefore, they are now properly explained, this is the first time they have ever been so. These explanations, then, dry and tedious as they are, seemed indispensable: since without them no part of what follows[2]

[1] In the margin, Bentham has noted at this point: 'Right is either naked, or armed with power.'

[2] i.e. the projected penal code.

could have been clearly and perfectly understood. No wonder that legislators should not any where have done precisely what they ought to do, when they have never hitherto had a clear understanding of what it is they themselves have actually been doing. No wonder they have so often handled their instruments improperly, when as yet they have not so much as learnt to distinguish one of them from another.

APPENDIX F[1]

Law of property.

The laws relative to property may be consider'd in various points of view. To apprehend the nature of them, the relation they bear to the rest of the system, and how they are reducible to the notion of a mandate or its opposites, we must call back to mind what was said of the offences relative to property in the preceding chapter.[2] Let us begin with that sort of property which is the most simple: the principles observed in the explanation of this case will serve with little variation for the explanation of the cases where it is the most complex. The most simple case is where the proprietary subject, as we may call it, is corporeal, determinate and single. This case I will now endeavour to explain.

First conception of the laws of property to be taken from the offence of wrongful occupation.

To understand the nature of the laws of property, it will be requisite to recur to that enumeration we had occasion to make in the last chapter of the possible offences relative to property.[3] It will also be necessary to recollect[a] that an offence, and the law whereby that offence is created, are a sort of correlatives; so that for every offence, there is a law: viz: a law of the mandative or imperative kind: and for every law of the imperative kind, there is an offence: and that accordingly, the offence being given, the law is given also, or the law being given, the offence. Now, in the list of the offences against property, the radical one seems to be that which we have stiled *wrongful occupation of property*: it is to that offence that the law, by which the most simple and elementary species of proprietary right is created, corresponds. This is the leading offence by reference to which the nature of those other offences may most commodiously be explained.

But without the idea of some particular sort of corporeal object before our eyes, it will be difficult to reason clearly. Let the proprietary subject, then, be a certain piece of land, a field, the offence which consists in the wrongful occupation of this property

Example where the proprietary subject is a particular field.

[a] supra | |.[4]

[1] For the provenance of the following material, and its relationship to §16, pp. 168–84 above, see the Editorial Introduction, p. xxxiv above.

[2] See *An Introduction to the Principles of Morals and Legislation* (*CW*), Ch. XVI, para. 35, pp. 226–32.

[3] Ibid.

[4] In the margin, Bentham has noted at this point: 'This depends upon the place where this article is inserted.' For a remark to this effect see, for instance, Appendix E, §6, para. 2, pp. 287–8 above.

will be any act[a] in virtue of which the agent may be said to meddle with this field. But the name of the offence reflects the act which is the object of the law: the offence, then, being the act of meddling with the field, the act which is the object of the law, the act commanded, is the negative act of not meddling with the [field].[1] Annexing, then, the expression of will to the act thus expressed, we have the whole substance of the law; which amounts to this, 'let no one, Rusticus excepted' (so we will call the proprietor) 'and those whom he allows, meddle with such or such a field.' Here, then, we have an example of one form in which the substance of a law of property creating property may be expressed.

This law may be resolved into two: 1. a general prohibition: and 2. a particular permission taken out of it.

But in this law we see there is an exceptive clause. Now, every law in which there is an exceptive clause may be resolved into two provisions. These provisions, where the law is, as it is here, of the negative or prohibitive kind, are 1. a primordial mandate of the prohibitive kind, the more extensive of the two: 2. a superventitious mandate of the permissive kind, which is the least extensive of the two, being revocative, but revocative *pro tanto* only, and not *pro toto*, of the former. No man shall meddle with the garment (describing it): . . . Prætextatus and such other persons as he allows may meddle with the garment.

Infinitude of the laws of property upon this plan.

Viewing the matter in this light, it is not to be wonder'd if a man should be alarmed at first at the multitude of the laws to which the head of property may give occasion. To that multitude, it must be acknowledged, there are no bounds. In the first place, we have a different law for every distinct proprietary subject: and matter is infinitely divisible. In the next place, we have a new law every time the subject changes hands: and that may happen fifty times in a day. But we are as yet got but a very little way in the enumeration of the circumstances which may give occasion to different laws relative to the same individual subject. In the example above exhibited, it is taken for granted that the subject belongs solely to one person, that it is his not only for a certainty but at present, and not only for the present but for ever, that when he chooses to make use of it, he may make what use of it he pleases, and that he may make use of one part of it as well as of another, that he may let any one whom he thinks fit make use of it, and that to warrant him in making use of it he has no

[a] Such extraordinary cases excepted in which the law may think fit to allow one man to trespass upon the property of another and which, though alluded to for the sake of exactness, may here be laid out of the question.

[1] MS 'coat'. Bentham had originally chosen to use the example of a coat, whose proprietor was Prætextatus, but on this occasion, and in the final sentence of the next paragraph, has neglected to amend the text accordingly.

need to wait for any particular event, or for the consent of any other person. But a piece of land may belong part of it to Rusticus, part of it to another person or any other number of persons: it may be his not till a year hence, or any number of years hence: nor then unless such a person have died first, or unless such a person have died without issue, or have married, and so on through any number of imaginable contingencies: it may be his for a year only or two years, or any other determinate number of years, and not for ever: or, whether certain or contingent, perpetual (if nothing prevent) or temporary, it may be liable to pass from him upon the happening of any event in his power or out of his power, such as the death of another person or his own marriage, or the failing to pay money on account of rent or taxes, or in short any other account that can be imagined: he may have a right only to feed his cattle upon it or only such and such particular cattle, or only to cut wood from it, or only to dig ore out of it, or only to build upon it, or only to pass over it: he alone may have a right to dig ore out of the bowels of it, while another man alone has the right of cultivating the surface of it: or the case may be that neither he nor any body else may have the right of making use of it without the consent of one or two or any other number of persons, as may happen where the land is vested in a corporation, the members of which, possessing the right they have in it in trust, have no right of making any use of it individually. In many of these cases, for every different modification of the right, there will require a different law; and in all of them there will require either a different law or a different clause to be added to the unconditional standard law. I have taken the example from the immoveable class of subjects: because those are the subjects which afford room for the greatest variety of modifications on the part of the proprietary right: but there are some moveable subjects likewise which perhaps give room for all these modifications; and there are none but what give room to some of them.

That infinitude may be reduced by translating the laws out of the imperative into the assertive form.

The laws, then, to which any one single proprietary subject may give occasion being infinite, how is it possible, it may be asked, to comprize the collection of the whole body of the laws relative to property within the limited compass of a code? Certainly, to draw them out at length and conceived in the imperative form is not possible. But the modes of expressing imperation, as there hath already been occasion to observe, are indefinitely numerous.[a] Of

[a] supra §. [14.][1] {Signs} 4.[2] and §. 12. {Aspect}.[3]

[1] MS '15.' For Bentham's reordering of §§ 14 and 15 see the Editorial Introduction, p. xxvi above.

[2] See § 14, para. 117, pp. 163–4 above.

[3] See § 12, para. 53 n., pp. 115–16 n. above.

these, many are indirect and have nothing of imperation upon the face of them; bearing the form not of imperative but of common assertive propositions: as if they were the words not of the lawgiver but of some one else who was giving an account of what the lawgiver had done. Now, as in the imperative form the laws relative to this head would swell to an infinite degree of expansion: so in this narrative or assertive form they may be reduced to an almost infinite degree of compression. To describe and distinguish the several contrivances by which, in different cases, this concentration may be effected would require a volume.[a]

Among the laws which create property, conveyances are included in which the imperation is

It hath been observed on a former occasion[1] that private conveyances, in as far as they are legal, that is adopted by the legislator, are so many laws or assemblages of laws. This being admitted, a body of the laws, to be compleat, must be understood as including *inter alia* the whole body of conveyances: a compleat

Expansion and condensation both throw a law out of the imperative into the assertive form.

[a] It may be observed, that where the texture of a law is dilated, or a number of laws are compacted into one,[1] it will generally happen that the greatest part of the matter will be translated out of the imperative into the assertive form. In the former case, expositions are subjoined to the words made use of in the expression of the mandate. In the case of consolidation, the first process is to reduce the multitude of mandatory phrases into one. But it will seldom happen that this general provision shall be exactly commensurate in point of amplitude to the sum of the several specific provisions which it is meant to include, and at the same time equal to them in point of precision and perspicuity. Two sorts of matter, then, will one or both of them require to be annexed to it: qualificative matter to reduce it to the proper standard in point of amplitude: expositive matter to give it the requisite degree of precision and perspicuity. But whether the matter be of the one sort or the other, it will in both cases make its appearance most naturally and advantageously in the assertive form. Thus it is that, in consolidation, every step after the first is the same as in dilatation: and in both cases the great bulk of the discourse is in the assertive form, the part which points to imperation being nothing but a sort of *punctum saliens*, as it were, a mere microscopic object, in comparison of the rest.

As to the rest, all that can be done here is to give notice to the reader: inasmuch that, being aware of the metamorphosis, he may be master of a thread which will conduct him at any time from the artificial and superinduced, to the native and primæval, form of the several provisions of the law. To exhibit in this latter form all these provisions collectively is impossible: but it is no more than what a man must be able to do with regard to each one of them taken separately, ere he can possess any accurate comprehension either of the nature and operation of such provision taken by itself, or of the relation it bears towards the other parts of the system. For a law of any kind, or any part of a law of any kind, to have any effect, a man must be punishable in case of his disobeying it: but to have an idea of a case in which a man is punishable for any act is to have the idea of an offence: and to have the idea of an offence, the signification of the will of him who makes it such being added, is to have the idea of a command.

[1] See §4, pp. 47–50 above.

[2] MS orig. 'consolidated'.

body of the laws taken at any given period will, therefore, include a compleat collection of the several conveyances which, within the dominion of the state, are in force at the instant of that period. Not that conveyances are on this account to be reckoned laws in any other sense than that in which any other commands issued in the exercise of powers are laws; those not excepted which are issued by parents, masters and other domestic power-holders for any the most trivial purposes of a private family. For the legislator, then, to take any separate notice of them is impossible. All that he can do, and all that it is requisite he should do, is to describe in general terms such as he thinks proper to adopt, and thereupon, explicitly or implicitly, such others as he thinks proper not to adopt: in other words, such as are to be deemed *good* or *valid*, and such as are to be deemed *void*. Now, those are good or valid which are made in such *form* as it is thought proper to acknowledge for good form by him who has a good title, or to speak shortly a title, to convey, in favour of him who has a good title to take or receive: those bad or void which are made in such form as it is thought proper to hold for bad, by one who has no good title, or, as the phrase is, no title, to convey, or in favour of one who has no good title or no title to take or receive.

performed by the law and the right-giver conjointly.

But a sort of an event which is allow'd to give a man a title to [a] proprietary subject of one sort may not perhaps be allow'd to give him a title to a proprietary subject of another sort: and an individual event which gives a man a title to one individual proprietary subject does not thereby give him a title to another individual proprietary subject.

Moreover, an event which is allow'd to give to a person of one sort a title to a proprietary subject of a given sort may not be allow'd to give a title as to a proprietary subject of that sort to a person of another sort.

Also, as to events that depend upon the act of man, an event which, if it resulted from the act of a person of one sort would be allow'd to give to a person of a given sort a title as to a proprietary subject of a given sort, may not be allow'd to produce that effect where it results from the act of a person of another sort, as in the case of minors, prodigals, trust-holders and the like.

Hence, the whole branch of the law relative to conveyances may be comprized in the exposition of a few such words as proprietary subject, proprietary right, proprietor or right-holder, title, form of conveyance, and the like; of which exposition every distinguishable clause, by being applied to any particular conveyance that came into controversy, might be translated into a command.

Cases in which the property is established by the law alone in the first instance.

It is thus that, by being applied to and combined in a manner with the expression of the wills of individual power-holders, that branch of the law which concerns conveyances is transformable into and carries the effect of a command. But there is another branch of the law, still referable to the offence of wrongful occupation, in which the matter of the command is furnished by the legislator solely and immediately without needing to be applied to the mandate of any private power-holder. This includes the cases where the title of him in whose favour the law is made is constituted either by an event which is altogether in his own power or by an event of any other kind in which, in as far at least as concerns the effect thus given to it, no other person's will has any participation: as is the case, for instance, with the titles derived from occupancy, improvement, natural increment and succession *ab intestato*. In this latter set of cases, the connection between the assertive matter of the law and the idea of a command as emaning from the legislator will not be quite so remote as in the former. In the one case we may have a compleat law, in the other case we can not, without descending to that degree of minuteness and particularity as to take in the mandates of individuals.

Of the expositive matter belonging to the law against wrongful occupation, a great part belongs in common to the laws correlative to the other offences against property.

Thus it is that, in one or other of these ways, a great part of the matter of the law is naturally, and in a manner necessarily, thrown into the assertive form, constituting a kind of exposition of some such word as the word *title*.[1]

This word, then, we see is a word that will be wanted to make part of the definition of the offence entitled wrongful occupation of property. But this same word, or what is equivalent to it, will be equally stood in need of for compleating the several definitions of the several other acts which are ranked under the head of offences concerning property. Thus wrongful non-investment of property is the forbearing to render a man that sort of service which consists in the conveying to him or investing him with a title to a certain proprietary subject, he having a title to such service: wrongful divestment of property, in the doing of any of those acts which are deemed by the law to divest a man of such a title, the wrongdoer having no title so to do: and so on in a manner that may be easily imagined.

The laws relative to the offence of wrongful occupation reducible to one—1. in the conditional form:

We have shewn how it is that, to the single offence of wrongful occupation, considering the matter in one point of view, there may belong an infinite multitude of laws. But such as the offence is, such is the law: therefore, if the offence is *one*, the law, consider'd in a certain point of view, must be *one* also. Consider'd in this point

[1] In the text, Bentham has noted at this point: 'Quære.'

of view, the law, when expressed in the imperative form, will run in this wise, 'Let no man perform—' or 'let no man committ wrongful occupation,' that is an act of wrongful occupation, understood of property. This law, then, as we have shewn already, will, in order to be explicit enough, stand in need of ample, and those very ample, expositions: out of which expositions and the several distinguishable clauses in them may be constructed, by a proper method of translation, as many laws as there may be occasion for to match with the several individual offences that may come under this title.

In the formulary just exhibited, the law may be consider'd as being couched in the conditional form; the epithet wrongful prefixed to the term occupation being expressive of a specificant circumstance: viz: the *wrongfulness* of the act of occupation. But a law in the conditional form may always be converted into an unconditional provision with exceptive clauses—with exceptions taken out of it.[a] This, accordingly, is the case with the law in question. Omitting in the first instance the conditionalizing or limitative epithet wrongful, the law in the unconditional form will stand thus: 'Let no man perform any act of occupation:' or to express the same meaning with less stiffness: 'let no man occupy any proprietary subject.' After that come the several exceptions, which may be all included under some such single formulary as this—except he have a title so to do: and then, in order to accommodate the general proposition to the particular case of each proprietary right-holder, will come the exposition of the word title and of the other leading terms, such as proprietary subject, proprietary right, proprietary right-holder, proprietary right-giver, proprietary right-taker, form of conveyance, and so forth, as above. 2. in the unconditional form with exceptions.

Of the several forms above-mentioned, perhaps this latter is the clearest, and that which places the station which the fundamental law of property occupies in the most satisfactory point of view. Upon this plan the leading provision is one simple mandate: a mandate which is the primordial work of the law itself[1] without needing the co-operation of individuals, which contains what there is universal in the law of property, and what must necessarily be applicable to every *corpus juris* whatsoever.[2] The last formulary the plainest.

[a] v. supra §. 12. {Aspect}.[3]

[1] In the margin, Bentham has noted at this point: 'This is most of a piece with the other laws.'

[2] In the margin, Bentham has noted at this point: 'Apparent absurdity of it while it stands without the exceptions.'

[3] See §12, para. 70, pp. 125–6 above.

INDEX OF SUBJECTS

Note. The following is a unified index which refers to the texts of the main work and the Appendices included in the volume.

References to Bentham's notes and text that appears in editorial footnotes are given by means of the page number(s) followed by the letter 'n'.

The symbol 'v' is used to indicate 'as distinct from' or 'as opposed to'.

INDEX OF NAMES

Note. The following is an index of names appearing in the Editorial Introduction, text, and footnotes. References to footnotes, whether Bentham's or the editor's, are indicated by 'n.' Bentham's other works are indicated under his name.